THE FABER BOOK OF MODERN VERSE

THE FABER BOOK OF MODERN VERSE

edited by

MICHAEL ROBERTS

THIRD EDITION

Revised, and with a new supplement of poems chosen by

DONALD HALL

FABER AND FABER
3 QUEEN SQUARE
London

First published in 1936
by Faber and Faber Limited
3 Queen Square London WC1
First published in Faber Paper Covered Editions 1960
This new edition 1965
Reprinted 1966, 1968, 1970 and 1973
Printed in Great Britain by
Jarrold and Sons Ltd, Norwich

ISBN 0 571 06348 9 (*Faber Paper Covered Editions*)

ISBN 0 571 06307 1 (*hard bound edition*)

EDITOR'S NOTE

I wish to thank those poets who have helped me in the selection and arrangement of their work. The opinions which some of them have expressed on the subject of anthologies are well known, and their collaboration in the present book does not indicate any change in that general attitude. Where the text of the poems in this book differs from that of earlier printed versions, the change has been made at the author's request.

POETS

CONTENTS

INTRODUCTION TO THE FIRST EDITION

More often than prose or mathematics, poetry is received in a hostile spirit, as if its publication were an affront to the reader; yet most of the poetry which is published probably appears because, at the time of writing, it delighted the writer and convinced him that it held some profound significance or some exact description which he hoped that others, too, might see. One might expect that any poetry depending upon a very personal experience or a relatively private use of words would be ignored; and certainly a great deal of new poetry does meet with indifference because it seems private and incomprehensible. There remains, however, a considerable body of poetry which excites an active animosity, not because it states opinions and expresses feelings which are repugnant to the ordinary man, but because the reader feels compelled to argue that it is not poetry at all: many of the poems in this book aroused that animosity on their first appearance. Much of that hostility has now vanished: it is seen that these poets were saying things which were true, and important, and which could not be said as well in any other way. In that sense, it might be claimed that this collection represents the most significant poetry of this age; but the omission of Charles Sorley, Walter de la Mare, Edmund Blunden, Edwin Muir,[1] William Plomer, Roy Campbell, all of whom seem to me to have written good poems without having been compelled to make any notable development of poetic technique, is sufficient evidence that this is not intended to be a comprehensive anthology of the best poems of our age.

The poems in the book were, with few exceptions, first printed after 1910. This date is arbitrary, and so are some of the inclusions and omissions. I have included only poems

[1] Added to this Third Edition. D.H.

which seem to me to add to the resources of poetry, to be likely to influence the future development of poetry and language, and to please me for reasons neither personal nor idiosyncratic. But the capacity to provoke controversy has been neither a necessary nor a sufficient condition for inclusion. Mr. Yeats is included, although the breadth of his appeal has always placed him beyond controversy, but it is worth noting that in his images, approximations to ordinary speech rhythms, political implications and private references, and in his strictly poetic[1] use of myth and legend, he has anticipated many of the devices of the younger men. The earlier poems of some of the older poets are omitted, and the later included, when it is in the later work that a significant development appears. A number of young poets who have written good poems are included, although the full significance of their innovations is not yet wholly clear. Perhaps the most general characteristic of the poems in this book is that they seldom record a recognized 'poetical' experience.

To most readers it will not be surprising that an anthology of modern poetry should begin with Hopkins: but I do not mean to suggest that his poetry made a complete break with the poetry of the past and marked the inauguration of a new age. In rhythm and in imagery, as well as in the thoughts and feelings which he intended to express, he differed from most of the English poets of his time, but there was no sharp discontinuity. Doughty, born only a year before Hopkins, resembled him in his inversions, his alliteration, the violence of his syntax, and above all in the emphasis which he succeeded in placing on accumulated masses of nouns, verbs, adjectives and adverbs, often unleavened by prepositions or conjunctions. Doughty's poetry is massive and uneven: a strong case could have been made out for including it; but it lacks that intensity which, in the poetry

[1] The word 'poetic' is here used to describe a special concentration of sensuous impression, idea and evocation in a word or phrase. The word 'poetical' is used to describe an attempted evocation by conventional symbols, of a state of mind sometimes called mystical.

of Hopkins, was the expression of an important moral conflict, related to an outer social and intellectual conflict.

It is not possible to compile an anthology of serious poetry without reflecting the social and moral problems of our time; but writing may be poetic without being either moral or didactic. Poetry may be intended to amuse, or to ridicule, or to persuade, or to produce an effect which we feel to be more valuable than amusement and different from instruction; but primarily poetry is an exploration of the possibilities of language. It does not aim directly at consolation or moral exhortation, nor at the expression of exquisite moments, but at an extension of significance; and it might be argued that a too self-conscious concern with 'contemporary' problems deflects the poet's effort from his true objective. The technical merit of a poem is measured by its accuracy, not by the importance of a rough approximation to what is being said, nor by the number of people to whom it is immediately intelligible. If a poet is incomprehensible to many people, but clearly intelligible to a few, as Hopkins appeared to be when his collected poems were first published, it may be because he is speaking of things not commonly experienced and is using subtleties of rhythm and imagery not used in ordinary speech, and therefore not widely understood. If it can be shown that a poet's use of language is valid for some people, we cannot dismiss his way of speaking as mere 'obscurity' and idiosyncrasy, though we may regret the necessity for such a rhetoric as we may regret the necessity for scientific jargon and mathematical notation.

The significant point about Hopkins was, however, not that he invented a style different from the current poetic style, but that, working in subterranean fashion, he moulded a style which expressed the tension and disorder that he found inside himself. Good poetry is more likely to be written about subjects which are, to the writer, important, than about unimportant subjects, because only on subjects of personal importance to himself does he feel the need for that accuracy of speech which itself lessens the tension which it describes. Deliberately to imitate a style arising from one poet's crisis would be absurd, but something similar is likely to appear when a crisis of a general kind arouses a personal conflict in many poets. The conflict may be the product of a fractured personality or a decaying society, or, like some of the 'problems' of academic philosophy, a result of the deficiencies of language. The terms of the conflict may be intellectual, when people are torn between conflicting systems of ideas. They may be theological, when people argue that they themselves should be perfect, being the children of God, but are perplexed by the recognition that they are evil. The terms may be political and aesthetic, when people cling to some features of the existing state, but see that there can be no good future until that state is overthrown. Sometimes, as in Donne, several of these terminologies are superimposed, serving as metaphors for each other, and concentrating, intensifying, and ultimately simplifying the problems by this poetic identification. For 'problems' of this kind are seldom independent; there is a relation between the personal and moral problem and the political and intellectual.

To those who have not felt some adumbration of such a crisis, the expression and resolution of conflict and disorder must appear like the strained muscles and distorted features of a strong man pretending to lift stupendous but non-existent weights. But for those who have come near to feeling the crisis themselves, the poetry is important. Words do something more than call up ideas and emotions out of a lumber-room: they call them up, but they never replace them exactly where they were. A good descriptive poem may enable us to be more articulate, to perceive more clearly, and to distinguish more readily between sensitive and sentimental observation, than before. But a poem may do more than that: even though we may not accept the poet's explicit doctrine, it may change the configuration of the mind and alter our responses to certain situations: it may harmonize conflicting emotions just as a good piece of reasoning may show the fallacy of an apparent contradiction in logic.

But the poetic use of language can cause discord as easily as it can cure it. A bad poem, a psychologically disordered poem, if it is technically effective may arouse uneasiness or nausea or anger in the reader. A sentimental poem, which deals with a situation by ignoring some of the factors, is offensive in this way; and a poem is equally confusing if it takes into account greater complexities of thought and intricacies of feeling than the reader has ever noticed. It unsettles the mind—and by the mind I mean more than the conscious mind; and the reader expends the energy he originally brought to the poem in trivial irritation with the poet.

It is very natural that this should be the first response of many readers to 'new' poetry, but in so far as the poet is a good poet, the situation will remedy itself. The problem which worried the poet will worry other people, or the new grounds which he saw for delight and hope will become apparent to them too: perhaps their recognition of the new element will be accelerated by his writing. But in either case they will welcome the way of speech which makes them articulate. Sometimes, as in the case of Hopkins, the problem which is his today is the world's tomorrow. Sometimes his writing is significant primarily for only a few of each generation, as when it is evoked by some remote place or rare experience or an intricate thought which few can follow. Sometimes it expresses only the problem of few or many people at one particular moment. But in each case, if the writer is a good poet, good in the sense of being rhetorically effective, his writing has a value over and above that of its immediate appeal: he has added to the possibilities of speech, he has discovered evocative rhythms and image-sequences unknown before. It may happen that in some future state of society there will be no people in the position of Mr. Eliot's Prufrock, and therefore no people for whom the poem is actual. But the rhetorical merit of the poem remains: it has said something which could not be said in ordinary speech, and said it exactly, and people who are interested in effective expression will read it. Pope and

Erasmus Darwin both wrote poems which were chiefly of didactic interest in their own time, but the elegance of Pope's writing keeps it alive today, whereas the poetry of Erasmus Darwin is almost forgotten. Chaucer has influenced English poetry and English language more than Langland, though Langland was, and is, the nearer to the thought and feeling of the common people.

In contrast to the previous twenty years, when the 'decadence' of the content of certain poems was continually discussed, critical discussion for the past thirty years has been concerned most often with the form, or alleged formlessness, of modern poetry. In the narrow sense, the word 'form' is used to describe special metrical and stanzaic patterns: in a wider sense it is used for the whole set of relationships involving the sensuous imagery and the auditory rhetoric of a poem. A definite 'form' in the narrower (and older) sense is not an asset unless it is an organized part of the 'form' in the wider sense, for the final value of a poem always springs from the inter-relation of form and content. In a good poet a change or development of technique always springs from a change or development of subject-matter.

If, then, we are to discuss technical innovations effectively, we must also discuss content; and here, at once, an important point appears. Roughly speaking, the poets in this book may be divided into two classes: those whose poetry is primarily a defence and vindication of existing cultural values, and those who, using the poetic qualities of the English language, try to build up poetry out of the realities implicit in the language, and which they find in their own minds rather than base it upon humanistic learning and memories of other poetry. The poets of the first kind possess what might be called a 'European' sensibility: they are aware of Baudelaire, Corbière, Rimbaud, Laforgue and the later Symbolists (it is notable that German poetry has had little influence upon them), they turn to Dante or Cavalcanti more readily than to Milton, they are more likely to be interested in a Parisian movement in poetry, such as Surrealism, than in the corresponding tendency in *Alice Through the Looking Glass* or Young's *Night Thoughts*. Most of them are Americans by birth, but their appeal is as much to the English as to the American reader. Among their English predecessors they might number Donne, Crashaw and Pope.

Poets in whose work the 'English' element predominates take the language as they find it, developing the implications of its idioms, metaphors and symbols. They are 'first order' poets: that is to say, it is not necessary to have a wide acquaintance with European literature, or even with English literature, to appreciate their work. They may be given an ancestry in Langland, Skelton, Doughty, on the one hand, and Blake, Shelley and perhaps Edward Lear, on the other, but their work does not depend upon a knowledge of literary history: it is an intensification of qualities inherent in the English language itself, and for this reason it is less easy to translate than that of the 'European' poets, in whose poems the specific properties of the language they are using is a more casual element.

These classes are not exclusive: they represent two moods of poetry rather than two kinds of poet. The poetry of W. B. Yeats, for example, must be considered under both headings: but the work of Ezra Pound and T. S. Eliot is clearly 'European' in cast. Robert Graves for a time hesitated between the two, then identified himself with that view of poetry which Laura Riding has increasingly emphasized—poetry as the final residue of significance in language, freed from extrinsic decoration, superficial contemporaneity, and didactic bias.

The 'European' poet is acutely aware of the social world in which he lives, he criticizes it, but in a satirical rather than in an indignant manner, he adjusts himself to it, he is interested in its accumulated store of music, painting, sculpture, and even in its bric-à-brac. There is something of the dandy, something of the dilettante, in his make-up, but he is aware of the futility and evanescence of all this, and of the irresponsibility of big business, conventional politics and mass education. He is witty, and acutely self-conscious. His attitude is the outcome of a genuine care for much that is valuable in the past, and it gains its strength from a desire to preserve these things: to preserve them, not by violence, but by exercise, for they are not 'things' at all, but certain attitudes and activities.

Every vital age, perhaps, sees its own time as crucial and full of perils, but the problems and difficulties of our own age necessarily appear more urgent to us than those of any other, and the need for an evaluating, clarifying poetry has never been greater than it appears to be today. Industrial changes have broken up the old culture, based on an agricultural community in which poor and wealthy were alike concerned, and on a Church which bore a vital relation to the State. Parallel with this, and related to it, there has been a decay of the old moral and religious order, and a change in the basis of education, which has become more and more strictly scientific. Religion and classical learning, which once provided myths and legends symbolizing the purposes of society and the role of the individual, have declined, and the disorder weighs heavily upon the serious poet, whether in England or America.

It is the theme of many of the poems of Mr. Pound, and of Mr. Eliot's *Waste Land*. We find the American poets, Hart Crane and Allen Tate, seeing the situation in these terms:

> 'The Parthenon in stucco, art for the sake of death'.

And the poets—Mr. Yeats among them—have attempted to clarify their own vision by expressing the disorder which they see about them, and by finding and defining those things in the older tradition which they hold to be valuable and necessary:

> Things fall apart; the centre cannot hold;
> Mere anarchy is loosed upon the world,
> The blood-dimmed tide is loosed, and everywhere

The ceremony of innocence is drowned;
The best lack all conviction, while the worst
Are full of passionate intensity.

If the poet is in the 'European' tradition, he describes the elements of civilization wherever he finds them: in Rome, in Greece, in Confucius, or in the Church of the Middle Ages; and against these he contrasts the violence and disorder of contemporary life. It is inevitable that poetry concerned with such issues should have political implications; but the poet is not arguing for one party against another: he is remodelling the basis upon which political creeds are founded, though sometimes immediate implications may appear in his poems.

Younger poets than Mr. Eliot and Mr. Pound may feel more acutely the inter-relation of culture and politics, but nevertheless they would agree with Mr. Auden that 'poetry is not concerned with telling people what to do, but with extending our knowledge of good and evil, perhaps making the necessity for action more urgent and its nature more clear, but only leading us to the point where it is possible for us to make a rational and moral choice'.

The problem, as we see on turning to Clough's *Amours de Voyage* (1849), is not wholly new. Clough had, as Bagehot says, 'an unusual difficulty in forming a creed as to the unseen world; he could not get the visible world out of his head; his strong grasp of plain facts and obvious matters was a difficulty to him. . . . He has himself given us in a poem, now first published, a very remarkable description of this curious state of mind. He has prefixed to it the characteristic motto, '*Il doutait de tout même de l'amour*'. It is the delineation of a certain love-passage in the life of a hesitating young gentleman, who was in Rome at the time of the revolution of 1848; who could not make up his mind about the revolution, who could not make up his mind whether he liked Rome, who could not make up his mind whether he liked the young lady, who let her go away without him, who went in pursuit of her and could not make out which way to look for her, who, in fine, has some sort of religion but cannot tell himself what it is. . . .'

Amours de Voyage was written in conversational hexameters, in a tone of semi-satire and half-belief,

Rome disappoints me much; I hardly as yet understand, but
Rubbishy seems the word that most exactly would suit it.
. . . .
Luther, they say, was unwise; like a half-taught German, he could not
See that old follies were passing most tranquilly out of remembrance;
Leo the Tenth was employing all efforts to clear out abuses;
Jupiter, Juno, and Venus, Fine Arts, and Fine Letters, the Poets,
Scholars, and Sculptors, and Painters, were quietly clearing away the
Martyrs, and Virgins, and Saints, or at any rate Thomas Aquinas:
He must forsooth make a fuss and distend his huge Wittenberg lungs, and
Bring back Theology once yet again in a flood upon Europe.

The resemblance to Mr. Pound's *Cantos*, in tone and intention, is obvious, and there is the same detachment, the same denial of commonly-accepted responsibility that is found in *Mauberley* and *Prufrock*:

Dulce it is, and *decorum* no doubt, for the country to fall,—to
Offer one's blood an oblation to Freedom, and die for the Cause; yet
Still, individual culture is also something. . . .

and the detachment passes easily into a kind of semi-serious raillery, which springs from a feeling that the generally-accepted code is all wrong, and yet that there is no other to take its place:

> Am I prepared to lay down my life for the British
>   female?
> Really, who knows? One has bowed and talked, till,
>   little by little,
> All the natural heat has escaped of the chivalrous
>   spirit.
> Oh, one conformed, of course; but one doesn't die
>   for good manners,
> Stab or shoot, or be shot, by way of graceful attention.
> No, if it should be at all, it should be on the
>   barricades there . . . .
> Sooner far by the side of the damned and dirty
>   plebeians.
> Ah, for a child in the street I could strike; for the
>   full-blown lady—
> Somehow, Eustace, alas! I have not felt the vocation.

There is the same introspection, the same self-mockery that is found in the poetry of Jules Laforgue, the same dissatisfaction with ready-made analysis, and the same intense conviction that there is an underlying problem which is not to be laughed away:

> I am in love, meantime, you think; no doubt you
>   would think so.
> I am in love, you say; with those letters, of course,
>   you would say so.
> I am in love, you declare. . . .
> I am in love, you say: I do not think so, exactly.

There are lines which recall the more 'metaphysical' passages of T. S. Eliot with their echoes of Chapman and Webster:

> I do not like being moved: for the will is excited; and
>   action

Is a most dangerous thing; I tremble for something
  factitious,
Some malpractice of heart and illegitimate process;
We are so prone to these things, with our terrible
  notions of duty.

and there are passages of lyrical fine writing, such as we find in *The Waste Land* and the *Cantos*:

Tibur is beautiful, too, and the orchard slopes, and
  the Anio
Falling, falling yet, to the ancient lyrical cadence;
Tibur and Anio's tide; . . .

There are obvious technical resemblances (I am not denying the obvious differences) in tempo, pitch and rhythm, but Eliot and Pound differ from Clough in their greater compression and intensity. Although Clough's poem sustains its narrative interest, his hexameters, however freely handled, become irritating, and his imagery is often diffuse and unexciting. Browning and Walt Whitman, both of whom anticipated many of the habits of the modern poets, suffer from the same long-windedness. They do not compress a situation into a single memorable image, and Clough did not feel the problem of his young man as intensely as Ezra Pound and T. S. Eliot felt it in 1912. Clough suspected that the *malaise* was due to a fault in himself, and Bagehot, a sensitive critic, agreed with him; but for Pound and Eliot the problem was external: it was society and its standards that were crumbling. A culture adapted to the older aristocratic system of landed proprietors was falling to pieces in a world governed by big business. Civilization was becoming 'a few score of broken statues, an old bitch gone in the teeth' or 'a heap of broken images'. It was necessary to sift out from the mass of habits, institutions and conventions the traditions which were worth preserving.

For the moment all that the poet could do was to concentrate upon surfaces: in a world in which moral, intellectual and aesthetic values were all uncertain, only sense impressions were certain and could be described exactly. From such minute particulars perhaps something could be built up. In 1913 a few poets, shocked at the vagueness and facility of the poetry of the day, determined:

1. To use the language of common speech, but to employ always the *exact* word, not the merely decorative word.

2. To create new rhythms—as the expression of new moods. We do not insist upon 'Free-verse' as the only method of writing poetry. . . . We do believe that the individuality of a poet may often be better expressed in free verse than in conventional forms.

3. To allow absolute freedom in the choice of subject.

4. To present an image. We are not a school of painters, but we believe that poetry should render particulars exactly and not deal with vague generalities.

5. To produce poetry that is hard and clear, never blurred or indefinite.

6. Finally, most of us believe that concentration is the very essence of poetry.

Edited by Ezra Pound, a number of 'Imagist' anthologies appeared; T. E. Hulme wrote some of the earliest Imagist poems. Amy Lowell, F. S. Flint, H.D., J. G. Fletcher, Richard Aldington, T. S. Eliot and Ezra Pound himself at one time or other were members of the group, and the later development of the movement appears in the work of Marianne Moore. T. S. Eliot had been influenced by Baudelaire, Laforgue and Rimbaud. Ezra Pound was impressed by the work of Villon and the Provençal and early Italian poets. F. S. Flint was interested in the later Symbolists—Samain, Kahn, Jammes, Rodenbach and the earlier Verhaeren—as well as more recent writers, Vildrac, Romains, Duhamel. The name 'Imagist' itself recalls 'Symbolist', and the Imagists themselves sometimes confused the image, the clear evocation of a material thing, with the symbol, the word which stirs subconscious memories. Such, indeed, was their intention: their poetry was meant to widen outwards like the ripples from a stone dropped in clear water. But the scope of 'pure' Imagist poetry was limited to clear renderings of visual experience: the poetry of H.D. shows both the possibilities and the limitations of the method.

It was natural that there should be a movement away from poeticality of subject and from the direct expression of emotion when the poets were in doubt about standards of art and morals: for the moment *any* emotion seemed sentimental to their realism. But the realism itself was often deceptive. Wallace Stevens in *The Emperor of Ice-Cream* writes a poem to insist that only the commonplace is real: let 'be' be the end of 'seem'; but the reality he describes is itself highly-coloured, and the poem contains more than a clear visual image. When he writes:

Take from the dresser of deal,
Lacking the three glass knobs, that sheet
On which she embroidered fantails once
And spread it so as to cover her face.
If her horny feet protrude, they come
To show how cold she is, and dumb—

I am fairly sure that he is writing with some vague memory of Mantegna's picture of the dead Christ and certainly that recollection makes the image more impressive.

The poetry of Wallace Stevens and Miss Sitwell still shows the Imagist concentration upon the sensuous surface of things, but even with the latitude which they allow themselves, Imagism is limited in scope; and as Mr. Pound has recorded: 'at a particular date in a particular room, two authors, neither engaged in picking the others' pocket, decided that the dilution of *vers libre*, Amygism, Lee Masterism, general floppiness had gone too far and that some counter-current must be set going. Parallel situation centuries ago in China. Remedy prescribed *Emaux et Cameés* (or the Bay State Hymn Book). Rhyme and regular strophes.

'Results: Poems in Mr. Eliot's *second* volume, not contained in his first *Prufrock* (Egoist, 1917), also *H. S. Mauberley*.'

Between 1920 and 1926, many poets were trying to write long poems which would present a unified view of the social crisis as they saw it, and imply their criticism of it. Conrad Aiken, who had been for a brief time influenced by the ideals of the Imagists, began to work for something which would lead to more profound and more highly organized poems, and turned to music. The predominant pattern of his poems is musical, whereas the more important pattern of some poems, as St. J. Perse's *Anabase* (translated by T. S. Eliot), is one of vivid visual and tactile images.

Conrad Aiken's *Senlin* (1918), T. S. Eliot's *The Waste Land* (1922), Richard Aldington's *Fool i' the Forest* (1925), and Archibald MacLeish's *Hamlet of A. MacLeish* (1928), were all poems of this kind. *The Waste Land* is the most concise, the most evocative, the widest in scope, and the most highly organized of these poems. It possesses 'imaginative order', by which I mean, that to some minds it is cogent even before its narrative and argumentative continuity is grasped. This 'imaginative order' is not something arbitrary, specific and inexplicable. If the images which are used to denote complex situations were replaced by abstractions, much of the apparent incoherence of the poem would vanish. It would become a prose description of the condition of the world, a restatement of a myth and a defence of the tragic view of life. But being a poem it does more than this; a poem expresses not merely the idea of a social or scientific fact, but also the sensation of thinking or knowing, and it does not merely defend the tragic view, it may communicate it.

The images and rhythms of *The Waste Land* are not conventionally poetical: their aura of suggestion radiates from a definite meaning relating to the ordinary world, and their full significance is not seen until the essentially tragic attitude of the poem is grasped. The omission of explanatory connecting matter when contrasting a 'modern' situation with an old or the life of one class with that of another may be puzzling at first, but given a general understanding of the poem it becomes clear. Thus one situation may be described in the terms and rhythms appropriate to another, so that both the similarities and the differences are illuminated.

It is not only the 'European' poets who are concerned with these problems, nor are they the only poets who aim at poetic concentration and whose work therefore presents initial difficulties. These spring from several sources. There is the intellectual difficulty which arises from the poet's use of some little-known fact, or some idea hard to grasp; there is the difficulty which comes from the unusual use of metaphor; and there is the difficulty which arises when the poet is making a deliberately fantastic use of words.

The obscurity which arises from the use of little-known or intricate ideas is easily removed. Some of the obscurity of Mr. Eliot's poetry and Mr. Empson's is of this kind: it needs only elucidatory notes to make it vanish, and it should be remembered that, because the ideas of science are widely known and generally believed, the poet who uses them is on safer ground than the man who makes classical allusions which, although they are accepted as poetical, are neither exactly appreciated nor fully understood.

The difficulty which arises from an unusual use of metaphor is less easy to remove: it depends far more upon the goodwill of the reader. Metaphor and simile are fundamental to civilized speech: but they have one serious disadvantage, the moment you say one thing is 'like' another, you remind the reader that the two things are, after all, different; and there may be an effect of dilution and long-windedness which is inimical to poetry. The poet, therefore, condenses his metaphor. Hart Crane in *Voyages III*, referring to the rhythm of the motion of a boat through a thickly clustered archipelago, speaks of 'adagios of islands'. Similarly, in *Faustus and Helen III* the speed and altitude of an aeroplane are suggested by the idea of 'nimble blue plateaus'. This kind of compressed metaphor is also found in the poetry of Stephen Spender:

Eye, gazelle, delicate wanderer,
Drinker of horizon's fluid line.

This condensation may demand an initial effort of understanding in the reader, but once the meaning is understood, the aptness and convenience of the phrase is obvious; it becomes part of one's habit of thought, and the understanding of these compressed analogies becomes, after a time, no more difficult than the understanding of a simile or a more prosaic and long-winded metaphor.

The condensation of metaphor involves no denial of logic: it is simply an extension of the implications of grammar, the development of a notation which, being less cumbersome, enables us to think more easily. It may be compared to the invention of a new notation, say that of Leibnitz or Hamilton, in mathematics: the new is defined in terms of the old, it is a shorthand which must be learned by patient effort, but, once learnt, it makes possible the solution of problems which were too complicated to attack before. The human head can only carry a certain amount of notation at any one moment, and poetry takes up less space than prose.

The third difficulty, that which springs from a deliberately fantastic use of words, is less than one might imagine. We accept, willingly, the fantastic sequences of nursery-rhyme and fairy-tale; and only a confusion of thought makes us demand, as we grow older, that poetry should always give us enlightenment or high moral doctrine. The poet has a right to play, and the reader to enjoy that play. The solemn attacks on the more riotously comic of Mr. Cummings' poems are themselves ridiculous. There is in all poetry an element of verbal play; and in nonsense verses, in the poetry of Mr. Cummings, in Mr. Madge's *Lusty Juventus* and in the early poetry of Miss Sitwell, this element often predominates. It is found in Miss Riding's *Tillaquils* which, because it actualizes a strange experience of a kind which the reader has been accustomed to regard as 'abstract', tends to be read, like her better-known poem, *The Quids*, as a satire upon academic metaphysics.

Verbal play is a form of fantasy, and when we relax and abandon ourselves to such poetry we find that some of it makes too deep an impression on our minds to be called 'play' at all. In the joke-poem we may give ourselves up to the casual association of words, but many readers find this abandonment difficult when something more serious appears to be involved. They are prepared to enjoy poetry which tells a story or states a moral, but they distrust the abandonment of common sense and accepted habits of language, believing, rightly, that if common sense is abandoned, then the way is open to all nonsense, incoherence and private fantasy.

'There is a mental existence within us . . . which is not less energetic than the conscious flow, an absent mind which haunts us like a ghost or a dream and is an essential part of our lives. Incidentally . . . the unconscious life of the mind bears a wonderful resemblance to the supposed feature of imagination. . . . To lay bare the automatic or unconscious action of the mind is indeed to unfold a tale which outvies the romances of giants and ginns, wizards in their palaces, and captives in the Domdaniel roots of the sea.'[1]

There are no rules to guide us, no histories to enable us to check our facts: but it is a simple experimental fact that certain people do agree that 'imaginative order' is found in certain specified poems, and not in others. In so far as those people are normal, it therefore seems that the poem, though 'subjective' in the old sense, is 'objective' in so far as it describes something which is part of the experience of a number of people. Poetry changes in its emphasis from one time to another, and just as, in recent years, there has been a decline in the writing of descriptive poetry (a decline which the Imagists attempted to check), so in the near future we may see greater emphasis placed on poetry as a means of appealing directly to the subconscious mind, and less on poetry as a conscious criticism of life.

[1] E. S. Dallas, *The Gav Science* (1866).

As we see from the quotation from Dallas, the critical theory appropriate to such poetry is not new. Hints of its method are found in the older critics, and in Shelley. 'Poetry', said Shelley, 'differs in this respect from logic, that it is not subject to the control of the active powers of the mind, and that its birth and recurrence have no necessary connexion with the consciousness or will.' Sometimes the reason for the order of the images of such poems and the cause of their effectiveness are fairly obvious. Their power and order may come from casual memory, or from the make-up of the mind, from the deep impressions of early childhood, or from the influence of the birth trauma, or from the structure of the language itself. The meaning of a word is never a simple thing, a 'standing-for' an object or relation: it is the whole complex set of grammatical habits and associations of ideas which have grown up from our first hearing of it, and the poet exploits this symbolism of words as he exploits the more directly 'psychological' symbolism or substitution value of images. It is possible, therefore, for a poem to be professedly realistic and yet to have the vigour and insistence of a dream or nightmare. Good poetry always has something of this quality, but the nightmare may be directly verbal, rather than visual. Robert Graves is, I think, a poet whose poetry is mainly verbal. That is to say, although there is often a visual picture corresponding to his poems, the effect of the poem depends upon the direct evocative effect of the words, not on the visual stimulus.

Among the poems which deliberately free themselves from logic there are not only the joke-poems, which are simply an exercise of poetic energy showing the word-sense of the poet; but also the relaxation-poems, which range from those in which words associate themselves mainly according to relations and similarities of sound (as in Miss Sitwell's *Hornpipe*), to those which are day-dream narratives. Of these, one of the more obvious types is the wandering-ego poem in which the 'I'—'On a bat's back I do fly'—paces beside the ocean, passes through caves and dismal gorges, is prisoned in miserable dungeons, rises to craggy heights and is carried upon the wind. A poem of this kind has often a tremendous self-importance which becomes inflated until the ego dominates the entire world and we arrive at the great passages in Whitman, where, Charles Madge has pointed out, the ego passes over all the earth and eventually 'dissolves in lacy jags'.

Then again, there are the poems which, like *Kubla Khan* or, to take a modern example, Dylan Thomas's '*Light breaks where no sun shines*', correspond to dream-fantasies of a sexual type. The woods, the hills, the rushing stream—all become substitutes for other things, and the reader (and perhaps the poet), unaware of what is happening in his own mind, is puzzled at the strange excitement which he finds in the succession of images.

In some poems, the dream-quality is exaggerated and the structure which is believed to characterize the fantasies of the deeper levels in sleep is deliberately made the model for the structure of the poem. The *Parade Virtues for a Dying Gladiator* of Sacheverell Sitwell is of that kind, and so, too, are the poems which the Surrealists, and their English admirer, David Gascoyne, aim at producing. Such poems, if they are the product of a normal mind, may become fascinating when we get over their initial strangeness; but the 'order' of such poems is not necessarily identical with the 'imaginative order' of myth and legend. The poem may be a good one without being socially important, or it may be fascinating without being specifically poetic. It might, for example, be more effective as a film than it is in printed words.

But although good poems may sometimes be shown to correspond to standard types of dream, good poetry is not likely to be written by working to fit a standard pattern. Even allegory, which would seem to require constant reference to a preconceived design, cannot be written in cold blood: the writer must be interested in the story itself, not merely in the underlying 'meaning', and the story must develop with the overpowering inevitability of a dream.

There are some writers who might say that if a poem has this kind of inevitability, it need not have commonsense logic or narrative sense as well. Certainly good poems of this kind have been written, though personally I prefer poems in which the compulsion of the image sequence is matched by a natural development of argument or narrative. *Kubla Khan* owes its force to its image-order, but it owes its popularity to the fact that it possesses a loose narrative order which saves the reader from the awkward fear of being taken in by nonsense. Furthermore, the two currents, the narrative and the fantastic, reinforce each other, just as the coalescence of narrative and imaginative pattern give life and force to myth and legend.

To myths, rather than to dreams, many poets still turn for the content of their poems, and the researches of Sir James Frazer and other anthropologists have provided the *motif* of a few good poems and many bad ones. Myths are more than fumbling attempts to explain historical and scientific facts: they control and organize the feeling, thought and action of a people: their function is symbolic as well as significant. But often the stories have become the conventional material of second-rate poetry, and have become perverted so that the symbolism has been lost, and we are left with the mere husk of a story, a story easily discredited by scientific and historical research. When Mr. Yeats turned to the myth as a means of giving shape and significance to his vision of the world, he was returning to the essential purpose of the myth and setting an example which Mr. Eliot, among others, has followed. But the modern reader cannot be expected to be influenced by a myth whose plain narrative sense is counter to his everyday beliefs. Either the poet must break away from any such direct narrative, or he must attempt, as I think Mr. Day Lewis has attempted in his *Flight* poem, to present a story credible in the ordinary everyday sense. If the poet turns to an existing myth or legend, however shop-soiled, and sees in it a profound significance, he will see the legend itself exemplified and symbolized in the world about him.

'So', says Hart Crane, in an unpublished manuscript, 'I found "Helen" sitting in a street car; the Dionysian revels of her court and her seduction were transferred to a Metropolitan roof garden with a jazz orchestra: and the *katharsis* of the fall of Troy I saw approximated in the recent world war. . . .

'It is a terrific problem that faces the poet today—a world that is so in transition from a decayed culture toward a reorganization of human evaluations that there are few common terms, general denominators of speech, that are solid enough or that ring with any vibration or spiritual conviction. The great mythologies of the past (including the Church) are deprived of enough façade even to launch good raillery against. Yet much of their traditions are operative still—in millions of chance combinations of related and unrelated detail, psychological reference, figures of speech, precepts, etc. These are all part of our common experience and the terms, at least partially, of that very experience when it defines or extends itself.

'The deliberate program, then, of a "break" with the past or tradition seems to me to be a sentimental fallacy. . . . The poet has a right to draw on whatever practical resources he finds in books or otherwise about him. He must tax his sensibility and his touchstone of experience for the proper selections of these themes and details, however,—and that is where he either stands, or falls into useless archaeology.

'I put no particular value on the simple objective of "modernity". . . . It seems to me that a poet will accidentally define his time well enough simply by reacting honestly and to the full extent of his sensibilities to the states of passion, experience and rumination that fate forces on him, first hand. He must, of course, have a sufficiently universal basis of experience to make his imagination selective and valuable. . . .

'I am concerned with the future of America . . . because I feel persuaded that here are destined to be discovered certain as yet undefined spiritual quantities, perhaps a new hierarchy of faith not to be developed so completely elsewhere. And in this process I like to feel myself as a potential factor; certainly I must speak in its terms. . . .

'But to fool one's self that definitions are being reached by merely referring frequently to skyscrapers, radio antennae, steam whistles, or other surface phenomena of our time is merely to paint a photograph. I think that what is interesting and significant will emerge only under the conditions of our submission to, and examination and assimilation of the organic effects on us of these and other fundamental factors of our experience. It can certainly not be an organic expression otherwise. And the expression of such values may often be as well accomplished with the vocabulary and blank verse of the Elizabethans as with the calligraphic tricks and slang used so brilliantly at times by an impressionist like Cummings.'

If a poet is to give new life to a legend, if indeed he is to write good poetry at all, he must charge each word to its maximum poetic value. It must appeal concurrently to all the various levels of evocation and interpretation: experiments in new rhythms and new images, if they are not used in this specifically poetic way, are of no more than technical interest. In discussing new technical devices a distinction must be drawn between those which produce an effect upon the reader even before he has noticed them, and those which, like some of the devices of Mr. Cummings, attract the reader's attention and lead him to infer, by ordinary reasoning, what effect the poet intended to produce. There are, I think, many examples of the first kind in this book, and of the many auditory devices of this kind, none, perhaps, are more effective, or have had greater effect upon later poets, than those of Wilfred Owen.

In Owen's poetry, the use of half-rhymes is not merely the result of an attempt to escape from the over-obviousness of rhyme-led poetry, though Owen probably discovered its possibilities in that way. His innovations are important because his sound-effects directly reinforce the general effect which he is trying to produce. In Owen's war poetry, the half-rhymes almost invariably fall from a vowel of high pitch to one of low pitch, producing an effect of frustration, disappointment, hopelessness. In other poets, rising half-rhymes are used, which produce the opposite effect, without reaching out to the full heartiness of rhyme. Full end-rhyme itself is felt by many modern poets to be too arbitrary and too noisy for serious poetry, unless modified, as Hopkins modifies it, by taking some of the stress off the last syllable of the line either by stressing earlier syllables, or by placing the emphasis of meaning, as distinct from metre, elsewhere. If they use end-rhymes at all, it is often for satiric purposes, or in a modified form, rhyming stressed with unstressed syllables, as Sacheverell Sitwell has done, and thus producing an uncertain, tentative, hesitating effect in keeping with the poet's purpose.

Nevertheless rhyme, like meaning and metre, is one of the possible elements in a verbal pattern, and few poets abandon it entirely. The sense of order in complication is part of the fascination of poetry, and often, as in the poetry of C. Day Lewis, internal rhymes, carefully but not obviously placed, are used to produce a pattern running counter to sense and rhythm and to add that intricacy and richness which marks the difference between part-song and unison.

Even when the poet writes, apparently, in a regular metre, he may use effects ignored in the formal rules of prosody and grammar. Thus Owen, in the second stanza of *Futility*, retards the movement of the first four lines by punctuation and intricacy of syntax, so that the fifth line, unimpeded, comes out with a terrific force, continued, though less vigorously and a little more slowly, as though one added a conclusive afterthought, in the final couplet. Similarly, in William Empson's *Note on Local Flora* the first seven lines form a single intricate sentence, retarding the pace, so that the eighth line, again an unimpeded sentence, is stamped with the emphasis of conviction, and the concluding couplet comes strongly, but comparatively quietly, as a conclusive deduction might do.

Often an effect of logic in a poem which, when examined, proves illogical, is due to auditory rhetoric[1] rather than to fantasy. The poetry of Edith and Sacheverell Sitwell shows, for example, not only an unusually vivid use of sensuous impressions, and of image-patterns based, like nursery rhymes, on the compelling force of dreams, but also an effective use of sound-patterns having this convincing facility of speech. The poetry of Edith Sitwell, like the poetry of Vachel Lindsay and E. E. Cummings, needs to be read aloud, with careful changes of rhythm, volume, pitch and tempo. A practised reader will be able to determine these variations for himself: in a good poem they are usually implied, but the pointing of the Psalms is an example of the use of typography to help the reader. Similarly, Hopkins, in his effort to extract the utmost poetic value from the varied stress of words, resorts to a system of accents and markings; and Mr. Cummings takes a great deal of trouble to show, by typographical devices, how his poems should be read. More conventional poets are less violent in their fluctuations, and less helpful in their methods. To read poetry as it should be read requires considerable practice. Most people tend to over-emphasize any regular metrical pattern which may be the background to the rhythm of the poem, and at the same time they raise the voice to a deliberately 'poetical' key and make use of fluctuations of pitch which bring their reading nearer to singing than to talking. It is characteristic of modern poets in general that they fight as hard as they can against this tendency, which seems to them not to increase the significance of the poetry, but to diminish it by asserting an arbitrary music at the expense of meaning, and to read their poems as songs, and necessarily bad songs, is to misread them completely.

When in pre-war days a few poets began to write, not in regular metres, but in cadences, as Whitman and the

[1] I use the word 'rhetoric' here, as elsewhere, in the technical, not the popular sense. There is good rhetoric and bad rhetoric, and there is rhetoric used in a good cause and in a bad, but rhetoric itself is not necessarily bad.

translators of the Bible had done, it was objected that this practice would destroy the art of verse entirely. It is true that a more delicate sensibility and a more careful training are necessary if we are to appreciate cadenced verse, and it is true that the existence of cadenced verse blurs the distinction between prose and poetry; but the critical vocabulary must be revised to fit the facts: to deny the facts and close your ears to the rhythms is to behave like the Inquisitor who refused to look through Galileo's telescope. Every discovery creates disorder: it is not the duty of the critic to prevent discovery or to deny it, but to create new order to replace the older. Today, the quarrel over cadenced verse has died down, and it is very hard to draw a sharp line, or to see any purpose in trying to draw a sharp line, between 'free' verse and *varied* regular verse. One or two points may be noted, however. There is verse which is intended to be 'free': that is to say, whose rhythm is composed to please the ear alone; there is verse which is quantitative, depending on a recurrent pattern of long and short syllables; there is verse which is accentual, depending on a recurrent pattern of accented and unaccented syllables; and there is syllabic verse. In the latter (some of the poems of Marianne Moore and Herbert Read are examples) the lines are evaluated by the number of syllables they contain, and the pattern will be something like this—11:11:11:6. It is not very difficult to train the ear to recognize and enjoy syllabic patterns, and if it is objected that this training is 'unnatural' it must be pointed out that all training is 'unnatural' and yet inevitable. Even the writer of 'free' verse has been trained to enjoy and detect certain patterns, and his 'free' verse often shows the skeleton of a 'regular' pattern underneath.

These effects are not felt by every reader: to some, the devices are merely evidence of technical incompetence. It is, however, demonstrable that some people respond to them without having them pointed out; the only possible conclusion is that these people are more sensitive to language than the others. The only objection to such devices is that it would never be possible to teach everyone to respond to them, therefore they tend to cut off one section of the community from another. But the same objection could be brought against the theory of tensors, and it is as necessary that some members of the community should explore the possibilities of language and use it to control and clarify emotional, spiritual and sensuous experience, as it is that others should use their mathematical notation to codify and organize our scientific knowledge.

Modern poets have been decreasingly concerned with sound-effects as independent entities, and today the auditory rhetoric of poetry is dictated, not by its own rules, but by the central impulse of the poem. Perhaps for this reason, no adequate study of auditory rhetoric exists. Prosody is little more than an enumeration and naming of all the possible combinations of stressed and unstressed syllables. It takes no account of the variety of stresses, or of the quantitative patterns interwoven with accentual patterns, and it ignores the 'laws' of consonant and vowel sequences. It becomes useless if it loses sight of its original purpose and erects itself into a system of unchanging orthodoxy. In criticism all general rules and classifications are elucidatory: and new discoveries or the introduction of matters previously thought to be irrelevant may compel us to amend them or admit their limitations.

The critic tries to make distinctions and to discover rules valid for the widest possible variety of purpose; but for different purposes different classifications may be necessary, and this is true not only of the classifications which we use in discussing the technique of poetry, but also of those which we use when speaking of the poets. Where, as in the criticism of poetry, we are dealing with something as complex as personalities, any division must be arbitrary. An historical or categorical label never prescribes the ultimate achievements of the poet, it merely tells us where to look for them; and from time to time, if we are to recognize the poet as a mobile force, new categories are needed.

Often the new dividing line between the categories may

not be far removed from the old; and it may be objected that the classification which results from a distinction between the 'English' sensibility and 'European' sensibility does not differ very much from the distinction between 'romantic' and 'classic' writers, or between 'pure' poetry and 'didactic and descriptive' poetry. There is, however, a difference in the points on which it focuses our attention. Any distinction in terms of schools and tendencies is misleading if we use it for any purpose beyond concentrating our attention for a moment on one aspect of the work of one or two selected writers; and if for the moment I have classified poets, it is merely as a shop-window arrangement, a tactful use of contrasts to focus attention on certain qualities, and to lessen some of the difficulty which readers find when they approach modern poetry for the first time.

New poetry is never popular unless it accepts the prejudices of the immediate past, and, giving an aura of heroism to actions which are already inevitable, stifles those misgivings out of which the real decisions of the present are to grow. Often in reading poems for this anthology, I have come upon one which, though its beginning seemed to show an apprehension beyond the commonplace, lapsed at the end into a false simplicity: a statement in familiar terms which had been given no new significance and depth. I have found Mr. Aldington's poems, in spite of their innovations, disappointing in that way; the earlier poems of Mr. Monro, and many of the poems of Mr. Cummings affect me similarly. The poet has seen something, and almost seen it clearly; and then at the end, unable to say it, he has been content to say some lesser thing, and the true poem remains unwritten.

For a time, the false poem may be more popular than the true one could have been. 'The poet', Johnson said, 'must divest himself of the prejudice of his age and country; he must consider right and wrong in their abstracted and invariable state; he must disregard present laws and opinions, and rise to general and transcendental truths, which will always be the same. He must, therefore, content himself with the slow progress of his name, contemn the praise of his own time, and commit his claims to the justice of posterity.'

Sometimes it is argued that readers, too, must leave the judgment of contemporary literature to posterity; but the judgment of posterity is only another name for the accumulated judgments of those who read most carefully and with least prejudice and preconception. To read merely to concur in the judgments of our ancestors is to inhibit all spontaneous response and to miss the pleasure of that reading which moulds the opinions, tastes and actions of our time. The first important thing about contemporary literature is that it *is* contemporary: it is speaking to us and for us, here, now. Judgment can only follow an act of sympathy and understanding, and to let our appreciation grow outwards from that which immediately appeals to us is both wiser and more enjoyable than to echo the judgments of others or to restrict and sour our appreciation by hastily attacking anything which at first seems difficult or irritating.

MICHAEL ROBERTS, 1936

INTRODUCTION TO THE THIRD EDITION

When Michael Roberts first published this book twenty-eight years ago, it introduced a generation of English readers to modern poetry. Roberts died in 1948 before making a projected second edition, but he left notes which Anne Ridler used in preparing the edition of 1951. Two poets were added and two omitted by Roberts' wishes, and a few selections were altered. Mrs. Ridler made other changes and added a supplement of sixty-eight pages of new English poets. When I took on this new revision, I was asked to start from the Roberts text rather than the Ridler. I had sixty-eight pages in which to account for twenty-eight years of English and American poetry. Also, I wanted to repair certain omissions from the original book, notably the poems of Hugh MacDiarmid and William Carlos Williams. Since it was obvious that sixty-eight pages would not do, I chose to omit several of the original poets, and thin out the number of pages given to some others. In 1936, it was agreeable that Wallace Stevens' poems should occupy three pages, while Sacheverell Sitwell's took ten; in 1964, it seemed something to change. With the approval of Janet Adam-Smith, who is Michael Roberts' widow, a number of pages were saved for newer poems.

In revising the contents of the selections made by Michael Roberts, I have followed what we came grandly to call the 'principle of availability'. I would like to have printed Wallace Stevens' *Sunday Morning*, but of course it was available to Roberts, and not chosen by him, and so if I used it I would be revising his opinions. Instead, I have added later (and I think excellent) poems by the same poet. I have not tampered with the original selections except to omit or to substitute poems written after 1936.

It is more difficult to be sure that one has not tampered

with the spirit of the anthology, as expressed in the introduction. I feel less certain about the word 'modern' than I would have felt in 1936. Should I omit Philip Larkin because he is not 'modern'? I see no useful sense of the word in which he *is*, yet the anthology is unthinkable without him. On the other hand, I have omitted at least one poet I admire because his best work is ballads which call to mind their ancient originals; it would seem *too* absurd to pretend they are 'modern'. Doubtless I have also used my idea of modernity to excuse my omission of several other poets whom I do not really like anyway.

The English came late to modern art, in painting and sculpture and music and poetry. 1936 is late for a book which introduces people to Hopkins and Yeats and Eliot. Sometimes I wonder if England ever came to modern art at all. While Stravinsky and Picasso and Henry Moore—to mention one Englishman at least—were inventing forms and techniques, W. H. Auden was 'experimenting' with sonnets and off-rhyme and Anglo-Saxon metres. Of course I am unfair to Auden, but I do not think I am inaccurate to the history of modern poetry in English. In the sense that Spain and Latin America and France and Germany had modernist poets—new forms, and new experiences of the spirit—perhaps England and America are only beginning.

D.H.

POETRY

GERARD MANLEY HOPKINS

THE WRECK OF THE DEUTSCHLAND

To the
happy memory of five Franciscan Nuns
exiles by the Falk Laws
drowned between midnight and morning of
Dec. 7th 1875

PART THE FIRST

1

Thou mastering me
God! giver of breath and bread;
World's strand, sway of the sea;
Lord of living and dead;
Thou hast bound bones and veins in me, fastened me flesh,
And after it almost unmade, what with dread,
Thy doing: and dost thou touch me afresh?
Over again I feel thy finger and find thee.

2

I did say yes
O at lightning and lashed rod;
Thou heardst me truer than tongue confess
Thy terror, O Christ, O God;
Thou knowest the walls, altar and hour and night:
The swoon of a heart that the sweep and the hurl of thee trod
Hard down with a horror of height:
And the midriff astrain with leaning of, laced with fire of stress.

3

The frown of his face
Before me, the hurtle of hell
Behind, where, where was a, where was a place?
I whirled out wings that spell
And fled with a fling of the heart to the heart of the
Host.
My heart, but you were dovewinged, I can tell,
Carrier-witted, I am bold to boast,
To flash from the flame to the flame then, tower from
the grace to the grace.

4

I am soft sift
In an hourglass—at the wall
Fast, but mined with a motion, a drift,
And it crowds and it combs to the fall;
I steady as a water in a well, to a poise, to a pane,
But roped with, always, all the way down from the tall
Fells or flanks of the voel, a vein
Of the gospel proffer, a pressure, a principle, Christ's
gift.

5

I kiss my hand
To the stars, lovely-asunder
Starlight, wafting him out of it; and
Glow, glory in thunder;
Kiss my hand to the dappled-with-damson west:
Since, tho' he is under the world's splendour and
wonder,
His mystery must be instressed, stressed;
For I greet him the days I meet him, and bless when I
understand.

6

Not out of his bliss
Springs the stress felt

Nor first from heaven (and few know this)
Swings the stroke dealt—
Stroke and a stress that stars and storms deliver,
That guilt is hushed by, hearts are flushed by and melt—
But it rides time like riding a river
(And here the faithful waver, the faithless fable and miss).

7

It dates from day
Of his going in Galilee;
Warm-laid grave of a womb-life grey;
Manger, maiden's knee;
The dense and the driven Passion, and frightful sweat;
Thence the discharge of it, there its swelling to be,
Though felt before, though in high flood yet—
What none would have known of it, only the heart, being hard at bay.

8

Is out with it! Oh,
We lash with the best or worst
Word last! How a lush-kept plush-capped sloe
Will, mouthed to flesh-burst,
Gush!—flush the man, the being with it, sour or sweet,
Brim, in a flash, full!—Hither then, last or first,
To hero of Calvary, Christ's feet—
Never ask if meaning it, wanting it, warned of it—men go.

9

Be adored among men,
God, three-numberèd form;
Wring thy rebel, dogged in den,
Man's malice, with wrecking and storm.
Beyond saying sweet, past telling of tongue,
Thou art lightning and love, I found it, a winter and warm;

Father and fondler of heart thou hast wrung:
Hast thy dark descending and most art merciful then.

10

With an anvil-ding
And with fire in him forge thy will
Or rather, rather then, stealing as Spring
Through him, melt him but master him still:
Whether at once, as once at a crash Paul,
Or as Austin, a lingering-out sweet skill,
Make mercy in all of us, out of us all
Mastery, but be adored, but be adored King.

PART THE SECOND

11

'Some find me a sword; some
The flange and the rail; flame,
Fang, or flood' goes Death on drum,
And storms bugle his fame.
But wé dream we are rooted in earth—Dust!
Flesh falls within sight of us, we, though our flower the same,
Wave with the meadow, forget that there must
The sour scythe cringe, and the blear share come.

12

On Saturday sailed from Bremen,
American-outward-bound,
Take settler and seamen, tell men with women,
Two hundred souls in the round—
O Father, not under thy feathers nor ever as guessing
The goal was a shoal, of a fourth the doom to be drowned;
Yet did the dark side of the bay of thy blessing
Not vault them, the millions of rounds of thy mercy not reeve even them in?

13

Into the snows she sweeps,
Hurling the haven behind,
The Deutschland, on Sunday; and so the sky keeps,
For the infinite air is unkind,
And the sea flint-flake, black-backed in the regular blow,
Sitting Eastnortheast, in cursed quarter, the wind;
Wiry and white-fiery and whirlwind-swivellèd snow
Spins to the widow-making unchilding unfathering deeps.

14

She drove in the dark to leeward,
She struck—not a reef or a rock
But the combs of a smother of sand: night drew her
Dead to the Kentish Knock;
And she beat the bank down with her bows and the
ride of her keel:
The breakers rolled on her beam with ruinous shock;
And canvas and compass, the whorl and the wheel
Idle for ever to waft her or wind her with, these she
endured.

15

Hope had grown grey hairs,
Hope had mourning on,
Trenched with tears, carved with cares,
Hope was twelve hours gone;
And frightful a nightfall folded rueful a day
Nor rescue, only rocket and lightship, shone,
And lives at last were washing away:
To the shrouds they took,—they shook in the hurling and
horrible airs.

16

One stirred from the rigging to save
The wild woman-kind below,
With a rope's end round the man, handy and
brave—

He was pitched to his death at a blow,
For all his dreadnought breast and braids of thew:
They could tell him for hours, dandled the to and fro
Through the cobbled foam-fleece, what could he do
With the burl of the fountains of air, buck and the flood
of the wave?

17

They fought with God's cold—
And they could not and fell to the deck
(Crushed them) or water (and drowned them) or
rolled
With the sea-romp over the wreck.
Night roared, with the heart-break hearing a heart-
broke rabble,
The woman's wailing, the crying of child without
check—
Till a lioness arose breasting the babble,
A prophetess towered in the tumult, a virginal tongue
told.

18

Ah, touched in your bower of bone
Are you! turned for an exquisite smart,
Have you! make words break from me here all alone,
Do you!—mother of being in me, heart.
O unteachably after evil, but uttering truth,
Why, tears! is it? tears; such a melting, a madrigal
start!
Never-eldering revel and river of youth,
What can it be, this glee? the good you have there of
your own?

19

Sister, a sister calling
A master, her master and mine!—
And the inboard seas run swirling and hawling;
The rash smart sloggering brine

Blinds her; but she that weather sees one thing, one;
Has one fetch in her: she rears herself to divine
Ears, and the call of the tall nun
To the men in the tops and the tackle rode over the storm's brawling.

20

She was first of a five and came
Of a coifèd sisterhood.
(O Deutschland, double a desperate name!
O world wide of its good!
But Gertrude, lily, and Luther, are two of a town,
Christ's lily and beast of the waste wood:
From life's dawn it is drawn down,
Abel is Cain's brother and breasts they have sucked the same.)

21

Loathed for a love men knew in them,
Banned by the land of their birth,
Rhine refused them. Thames would ruin them;
Surf, snow, river and earth
Gnashed: but thou art above, thou Orion of light;
Thy unchancelling poising palms were weighing the worth,
Thou martyr-master: in thy sight
Storm flakes were scroll-leaved flowers, lily showers—sweet heaven was astrew in them.

22

Five! the finding and sake
And cipher of suffering Christ.
Mark, the mark is of man's make
And the word of it Sacrificed.
But he scores it in scarlet himself on his own bespoken,
Before-time-taken, dearest prizèd and priced—
Stigma, signal, cinquefoil token

For lettering of the lamb's fleece, ruddying of the-rose
flake.

23

Joy fall to thee, father Francis,
Drawn to the Life that died;
With the gnarls of the nails in thee, niche of the
lance, his
Lovescape crucified
And seal of his seraph-arrival! and these thy daughters
and five-livèd and leavèd favour and pride,
Are sisterly sealed in wild waters,
To bathe in his fall-gold mercies, to breathe in his all-fire
glances.

24

Away in the lovable west,
On a pastoral forehead of Wales,
I was under a roof here, I was at rest,
And they the prey of the gales;
She to the black-about air, to the breaker, the thickly
Falling flakes, to the throng that catches and quails
Was calling 'O Christ, Christ, come quickly':
The cross to her she calls Christ to her, christens her
wild-worst Best.

25

The majesty! what did she mean?
Breathe, arch and original Breath.
Is it love in her of the being as her lover had been?
Breathe, body of lovely Death.
They were else-minded then, altogether, the men
Woke thee with a *we are perishing* in the weather of
Gennesareth.
Or is it that she cried for the crown then,
The keener to come at the comfort for feeling the
combating keen?

26

For how to the heart's cheering
The down-dugged ground-hugged grey
Hovers off, the jay-blue heavens appearing
Of pied and peeled May!
Blue-beating and hoary-glow height; or night, still higher,
With belled fire and the moth-soft Milky Way,
What by your measure is the heaven of desire,
The treasure never eyesight got, nor was ever guessed what for the hearing?

27

No, but it was not these.
The jading and jar of the cart,
Time's tasking, it is fathers that asking for ease
Of the sodden-with-its-sorrowing heart,
Not danger, electrical horror; then further it finds
The appealing of the Passion is tenderer in prayer apart:
Other, I gather, in measure her mind's
Burden, in wind's burly and beat of endragonèd seas.

28

But how shall I . . . make me room there:
Reach me a . . . Fancy, come faster—
Strike you the sight of it? look at it loom there,
Thing that she . . . there then! the Master,
Ipse the only one, Christ, King, Head:
He was to cure the extremity where he had cast her;
Do, deal, lord it with living and dead;
Let him ride, her pride, in his triumph, despatch and have done with his doom there

29

Ah! there was a heart right!
There was single eye!

Read the unshapeable shock night
And knew the who and the why;
Wording it how but by him that present and past,
Heaven and earth are word of, worded by?—
The Simon Peter of a soul! to the blast
Tarpeian-fast, but a blown beacon of light.

30

Jesu, heart's light,
Jesu, maid's son,
What was the feast followed the night
Thou hadst glory of this nun?—
Feast of the one woman without stain.
For so conceivèd, so to conceive thee is done;
But here was heart-throe, birth of a brain,
Word, that heard and kept thee and uttered thee outright.

31

Well, she has thee for the pain, for the
Patience; but pity of the rest of them!
Heart, go and bleed at a bitterer vein for the
Comfortless unconfessed of them—
No not uncomforted: lovely-felicitous Providence
Finger of a tender of, O of a feathery delicacy, the
breast of the
Maiden could obey so, be a bell to, ring of it, and
Startle the poor sheep back! is the shipwrack then a
harvest, does tempest carry the grain
for thee?

32

I admire thee, master of the tides,
Of the Yore-flood, of the year's fall;
The recurb and the recovery of the gulf's sides,
The girth of it and the wharf of it and the wall;
Stanching, quenching ocean of a motionable mind;
Ground of being, and granite of it: past all

Grasp God, throned behind
Death with a sovereignty that heeds but hides, bodes
but abides;

33

With a mercy that outrides
The all of water, an ark
For the listener; for the lingerer with a love glides
Lower than death and the dark;
A vein for the visiting of the past-prayer, pent in
prison,
The-last-breath penitent spirits—the uttermost mark
Our passion plungèd giant risen,
The Christ of the Father compassionate, fetched in the
storm of his strides.

34

Now burn, new born to the world,
Double-naturèd name,
The heaven-flung, heart-fleshed, maiden-furled
Miracle-in-Mary-of-flame,
Mid-numbered He in three of the thunder-throne!
Not a dooms-day dazzle in his coming nor dark as he
came;
Kind, but royally reclaiming his own;
A released shower, let flash to the shire, not a lightning
of fire hard-hurled.

35

Dame, at our door
Drowned, and among our shoals,
Remember us in the roads, the heaven-haven of the
Reward:
Our King back, oh, upon English souls!
Let him easter in us, be a dayspring to the dimness
of us, be a crimson-cresseted east,

More brightening her, rare-dear Britain, as his reign rolls,
Pride, rose, prince, hero of us, high-priest,
Our hearts' charity's hearth's fire, our thoughts' chivalry's throng's Lord.

FELIX RANDAL

Felix Randal the farrier, O he is dead then? my duty all ended,
Who have watched his mould of man, big-boned and hardy-handsome
Pining, pining, till time when reason rambled in it and some
Fatal four disorders, fleshed there, all contended?

Sickness broke him. Impatient he cursed at first, but mended
Being anointed and all; though a heavenlier heart began some
Months earlier, since I had our sweet reprieve and ransom
Tendered to him. Ah well, God rest him all road ever he offended!

This seeing the sick endears them to us, us too it endears.
My tongue had taught thee comfort, touch had quenched thy tears,
Thy tears that touched my heart, child, Felix, poor Felix Randal;

How far from then forethought of, all thy more boisterous years,
When thou at the random grim forge, powerful amidst peers,
Didst fettle for the great grey drayhorse his bright and battering sandal!

PIED BEAUTY

Glory be to God for dappled things—
For skies of couple-colour as a brinded cow;
For rose-moles all in stipple upon trout that swim;
Fresh-firecoal chestnut-falls; finches' wings;
Landscape plotted and pieced—fold, fallow, and plough;
And áll trádes, their gear and tackle and trim.

All things counter, original, spare, strange;
Whatever is fickle, freckled (who knows how?)
With swift, slow; sweet, sour; adazzle, dim;
He fathers-forth whose beauty is past change:
Praise him.

ANDROMEDA

Now Time's Andromeda on this rock rude,
With not her either beauty's equal or
Her injury's, looks off by both horns of shore,
Her flower, her piece of being, doomed dragon's food.
Time past she has been attempted and pursued
By many blows and banes; but now hears roar
A wilder beast from West than all were, more
Rife in her wrongs, more lawless, and more lewd.

Her Perseus linger and leave her tó her extremes?—
Pillowy air he treads a time and hangs
His thoughts on her, forsaken that she seems,
All while her patience, morselled into pangs,
Mounts; then to alight disarming, no one dreams,
With Gorgon's gear and barebill, thongs and fangs.

THE CANDLE INDOORS

Some candle clear burns somewhere I come by.
I muse at how its being puts blissful back
With yellowy moisture mild night's blear-all black,
Or to-fro tender trambeams truckle at the eye.
By that window what task what fingers ply,
I plod wondering, a-wanting, just for lack
Of answer the eagerer a-wanting Jessy or Jack
There—God to aggrándise, God to glorify.—

Come you indoors, come home; your fading fire
Mend first and vital candle in close heart's vault:
You there are master, do your own desire;
What hinders? Are you beam-blind, yet to a fault
In a neighbour deft-handed? are you that liar
And, cast by conscience out, spendsavour salt?

INVERSNAID

This darksome burn, horseback brown,
His rollrock highroad roaring down,
In coop and in comb the fleece of his foam
Flutes and low to the lake falls home.

A windpuff-bonnet of fáwn-fróth
Turns and twindles over the broth
Of a pool so pitchblack, féll-frówning,
It rounds and rounds Despair to drowning.

Degged with dew, dappled with dew
Are the groins of the braes that the brook treads through,
Wiry heathpacks, flitches of fern,
And the beadbonny ash that sits over the burn.

What would the world be, once bereft
Of wet and of wilderness? Let them be left,
O let them be left, wildness and wet;
Long live the weeds and the wilderness yet.

THE WINDHOVER

To Christ our Lord

I caught this morning morning's minion, king-
dom of daylight's dauphin, dapple-dawn-drawn
Falcon, in his riding
Of the rolling level underneath him steady air, and
striding
High there, how he rung upon the rein of a wimpling
wing
In his ecstasy! then off, off forth on swing,
As a skate's heel sweeps smooth on a bow-bend: the
hurl and gliding
Rebuffed the big wind. My heart in hiding
Stirred for a bird,—the achieve of, the mastery of the
thing!

Brute beauty and valour and act, oh, air, pride, plume,
here
Buckle! AND the fire that breaks from thee then, a
billion
Times told lovelier, more dangerous, O my chevalier!

No wonder of it: shéer plód makes plough down
sillion
Shine, and blue-bleak embers, ah my dear,
Fall, gall themselves, and gash gold-vermilion.

'AS KINGFISHERS CATCH FIRE, DRAGONFLIES DRAW FLAME'

As kingfishers catch fire, dragonflies dráw fláme;
As tumbled over rim in roundy wells
Stones ring; like each tucked string tells, each hung bell's
Bow swung finds tongue to fling out broad its name;
Each mortal thing does one thing and the same:
Deals out that being indoors each one dwells;
Selves—goes itself; *myself* it speaks and spells,
Crying *Whát I do is me: for that I came.*

I say móre: the just man justices;
Kéeps gráce: thát keeps all his goings graces;
Acts in God's eye what in God's eye he is—
Chríst—for Christ plays in ten thousand places,
Lovely in limbs, and lovely in eyes not his
To the Father through the features of men's faces.

HARRY PLOUGHMAN

Hard as hurdle arms, with a broth of goldish flue
Breathed round; the rack of ribs; the scooped flank; lank
Rope-over thigh; knee-nave; and barrelled shank—
    Head and foot, shoulder and shank—
By a grey eye's heed steered well, one crew, fall to;
Stand at stress. Each limb's barrowy brawn, his thew
That onewhere curded, onewhere sucked or sank—
        Soared or sank—,
Though as a beechbole firm, finds his, as at a roll-call, rank
And features, in flesh, what deed he each must do—
    His sinew-service where do.
He leans to it, Harry bends, look. Back, elbow, and liquid waist

In him, all quail to the wallowing o' the plough:
    's cheek crimsons; curls
Wag or crossbridle, in a wind lifted, windlaced—
        See his wind- lilylocks-laced;
Churlsgrace, too, child of Amansstrength, how it hangs
    or hurls
Them—broad in bluff hide his frowning feet lashed!
    raced
With, along them, cragiron under and cold furls—
        With-a-fountain's shining-shot furls.

'NO WORST, THERE IS NONE. PITCHED PAST PITCH OF GRIEF'

No worst, there is none. Pitched past pitch of grief,
More pangs will, schooled at forepangs, wilder wring.
Comforter, where, where is your comforting?
Mary, mother of us, where is your relief?
My cries heave, herds-long; huddle in a main, a chief
Woe, world-sorrow; on an age-old anvil wince and sing—
Then lull, then leave off. Fury had shrieked 'No lingering!
Let me be fell: force I must be brief'.

O the mind, mind has mountains; cliffs of fall
Frightful, sheer, no-man-fathomed. Hold them cheap
May who ne'er hung there. Nor does long our small
Durance deal with that steep or deep. Here! creep,
Wretch, under a comfort serves in a whirlwind: all
Life death does end and each day dies with sleep.

SPELT FROM SIBYL'S LEAVES

Earnest, earthless, equal, attuneable, | vaulty, vol-
    uminous, . . . stupendous
Evening strains to be tíme's vást, | womb-of-all, home-
    of-all, hearse-of-all night.

Her fond yellow hornlight wound to the west, | her wild
hollow hoarlight hung to the height
Waste; her earliest stars, earl-stars, | stárs principal,
overbend us,
Fíre-féaturing heaven. For earth | her being has un-
bound, her dapple is at an end, as-
tray or aswarm, all throughther, in throngs; | self ín
self steepèd and páshed—quíte
Disremembering, dísmémbering | áll now. Heart, you
round me right
With: Óur évening is over us; óur night | whélms,
whélms, ánd will end us.
Only the beak-leaved boughs dragonish | damask the
tool-smooth bleak light; black,
Ever so black on it. Óur tale, O óur oracle! | Lét life,
wáned, ah lét life wind
Off hér once skéined stained véined varíety | upon, áll on
twó spools; párt, pen, páck
Now her áll in twó flocks, twó folds—black, white:|
right, wrong; reckon but, reck but, mind
But thése two; wáre of a wórld where bút these | twó
Tell, each off the óther; of a rack
Where, selfwrung, selfstrung, sheathe- and shelterless, |
thóughts agaínst thoughts ín groans grínd.

'MY OWN HEART LET ME MORE HAVE PITY ON; LET'

My own heart let me more have pity on; let
Me live to my sad self hereafter kind,
Charitable; not live this tormented mind
With this tormented mind tormenting yet.
I cast for comfort I can no more get
By groping round my comfortless, than blind
Eyes in their dark can day or thirst can find
Thirst's all-in-all in all a world of wet.

Soul, self; come, poor Jackself, I do advise
You, jaded, let be; call off thoughts awhile
Elsewhere; leave comfort root-room; let joy size
At God knows when to God knows what; whose smile
's not wrung, see you; unforeseen times rather—as
    skies
Betweenpie mountains—lights a lovely mile.

THAT NATURE IS A HERACLITEAN FIRE AND OF THE COMFORT OF THE RESURRECTION

Cloud-puffball, torn tufts, tossed pillows |
    flaunt forth, then chevy on an air-
built thoroughfare: heaven-roysterers, in gay-gangs |
    they throng: they glitter in marches.
Down roughcast, down dazzling whitewash, | wher-
    ever an elm arches,
Shivelights and shadowtackle in long | lashes lace, lance,
    and pair.
Delightfully the bright wind boisterous | ropes,
    wrestles, beats earth bare
Of yestertempest's creases; in pool and rut peel parches
Squandering ooze to squeezed | dough, crust, dust;
    stanches, starches
Squadroned masks and manmarks | treadmire toil there
Footfretted in it. Million-fuelèd, | nature's bonfire
    burns on.
But quench her bonniest, dearest | to her, her clearest-
    selvèd spark
Man, how fast his firedint, | his mark on mind, is gone!
Both are in an unfathomable, all is in an enormous dark
Drowned. O pity and indig | nation! Manshape, that
    shone
Sheer off, disseveral, a star, | death blots black out;
    nor mark
        Is any of him at all so stark

But vastness blurs and time | beats level. Enough! the
Resurrection,
A heart's-clarion! Away grief's gasping, | joyless days,
dejection.
Across my foundering deck shone
A beacon, an eternal beam. | Flesh fade, and mortal trash
Fall to the residuary worm; | world's wildfire, leave but
ash:
In a flash, at a trumpet crash,
I am all at once what Christ is, | since he was what I am,
and
This Jack, joke, poor potsherd, | patch, matchwood,
immortal diamond,
Is immortal diamond.

W. B. YEATS

AN IRISH AIRMAN FORESEES HIS DEATH

I know that I shall meet my fate
Somewhere among the clouds above;
Those that I fight I do not hate,
Those that I guard I do not love;
My country is Kiltartan Cross,
My countrymen Kiltartan's poor,
No likely end could bring them loss
Or leave them happier than before.
Nor law, nor duty bade me fight,
Nor public men, nor cheering crowds,
A lonely impulse of delight
Drove to this tumult in the clouds;
I balanced all, brought all to mind,
The years to come seemed waste of breath,
A waste of breath the years behind
In balance with this life, this death.

EASTER, 1916

I have met them at close of day
Coming with vivid faces
From counter or desk among grey
Eighteenth-century houses.
I have passed with a nod of the head
Or polite meaningless words,
Or have lingered awhile and said
Polite meaningless words,
And thought before I had done
Of a mocking tale or a gibe
To please a companion

Around the fire at the club,
Being certain that they and I
But lived where motley is worn:
All changed, changed utterly:
A terrible beauty is born.

That woman's days were spent
In ignorant good-will,
Her nights in argument
Until her voice grew shrill.
What voice more sweet than hers
When, young and beautiful,
She rode to harriers?
This man had kept a school
And rode our wingèd horse;
This other his helper and friend
Was coming into his force;
He might have won fame in the end,
So sensitive his nature seemed,
So daring and sweet his thought.
This other man I had dreamed
A drunken, vainglorious lout.
He had done most bitter wrong
To some who are near my heart,
Yet I number him in the song;
He, too, has resigned his part
In the casual comedy;
He, too, has been changed in his turn,
Transformed utterly:
A terrible beauty is born.

Hearts with one purpose alone
Through summer and winter seem
Enchanted to a stone
To trouble the living stream.
The horse that comes from the road,
The rider, the birds that range
From cloud to tumbling cloud,

Minute by minute they change;
A shadow of cloud on the stream
Changes minute by minute;
A horse-hoof slides on the brim,
And a horse plashes within it;
The long-legged moor-hens dive,
And hens to moor-cocks call;
Minute by minute they live:
The stone's in the midst of all.

Too long a sacrifice
Can make a stone of the heart.
O when may it suffice?
That is Heaven's part, our part
To murmur name upon name,
As a mother names her child
When sleep at last has come
On limbs that had run wild.
What is it but nightfall?
No, no, not night but death;
Was it needless death after all?
For England may keep faith
For all that is done and said.
We know their dream; enough
To know they dreamed and are dead;
And what if excess of love
Bewildered them till they died?
I write it out in a verse—
MacDonagh and MacBride
And Connolly and Pearse
Now and in time to be,
Wherever green is worn,
Are changed, changed utterly:
A terrible beauty is born.

September 25, 1916

THE SECOND COMING

Turning and turning in the widening gyre
The falcon cannot hear the falconer;
Things fall apart; the centre cannot hold;
Mere anarchy is loosed upon the world,
The blood-dimmed tide is loosed, and everywhere
The ceremony of innocence is drowned;
The best lack all conviction, while the worst
Are full of passionate intensity.

Surely some revelation is at hand;
Surely the Second Coming is at hand.
The Second Coming! Hardly are those words out
When a vast image out of *Spiritus Mundi*
Troubles my sight: somewhere in sands of the desert
A shape with lion body and the head of a man,
A gaze blank and pitiless as the sun,
Is moving its slow thighs, while all about it
Reel shadows of the indignant desert birds.
The darkness drops again; but now I know
That twenty centuries of stony sleep
Were vexed to nightmare by a rocking cradle,
And what rough beast, its hour come round at last,
Slouches towards Bethlehem to be born?

A DIALOGUE OF SELF AND SOUL

I

MY SOUL. I summon to the winding ancient stair;
Set all your mind upon the steep ascent,
Upon the broken, crumbling battlement,
Upon the breathless starlit air,
Upon the star that marks the hidden pole;
Fix every wandering thought upon

That quarter where all thought is done:
Who can distinguish darkness from the soul?

MY SELF. The consecrated blade upon my knees
Is Sato's ancient blade, still as it was,
Still razor-keen, still like a looking-glass
Unspotted by the centuries;
That flowering, silken, old embroidery, torn
From some court-lady's dress and round
The wooden scabbard bound and wound,
Can, tattered, still protect, faded adorn.

MY SOUL. Why should the imagination of a man
Long past his prime remember things that are
Emblematical of love and war?
Think of ancestral night that can,
If but imagination scorn the earth
And intellect its wandering
To this and that and t'other thing,
Deliver from the crime of death and birth.

MY SELF. Montashigi, third of his family, fashioned it
Five hundred years ago, about it lie
Flowers from I know not what embroidery—
Heart's purple—and all these I set
For emblems of the day against the tower
Emblematical of the night,
And claim as by a soldier's right
A charter to commit the crime once more.

MY SOUL. Such fullness in that quarter overflows
And falls into the basin of the mind
That man is stricken deaf and dumb and blind,
For intellect no longer knows
Is from the *Ought*, or *Knower* from the *Known*—
That is to say, ascends to Heaven;
Only the dead can be forgiven;
But when I think of that my tongue's a stone.

II

MY SELF. A living man is blind and drinks his drop.
What matter if the ditches are impure?
What matter if I live it all once more?
Endure that toil of growing up;
The ignominy of boyhood; the distress
Of boyhood changing into man;
The unfinished man and his pain
Brought face to face with his own clumsiness;

The finished man among his enemies?—
How in the name of Heaven can he escape
That defiling and disfigured shape
The mirror of malicious eyes
Casts upon his eyes until at last
He thinks that shape must be his shape?
And what's the good of an escape
If honour find him in the wintry blast?

I am content to live it all again
And yet again, if it be life to pitch
Into the frog-spawn of a blind man's ditch,
A blind man battering blind men;
Or into that most fecund ditch of all,
The folly that man does
Or must suffer, if he woos
A proud woman not kindred of his soul.

I am content to follow to its source,
Every event in action or in thought;
Measure the lot; forgive myself the lot!
When such as I cast out remorse
So great a sweetness flows into the breast
We must laugh and we must sing,
We are blest by everything,
Everything we look upon is blest.

FOR ANNE GREGORY

'Never shall a young man,
Thrown into despair
By those great honey-coloured
Ramparts at your ear,
Love you for yourself alone
And not your yellow hair.'

'But I can get a hair-dye
And set such colour there,
Brown, or black, or carrot,
That young men in despair
May love me for myself alone
And not my yellow hair.'

'I heard an old religious man
But yesternight declare
That he had found a text to prove
That only God, my dear,
Could love you for yourself alone
And not your yellow hair.'

BYZANTIUM

The unpurged images of day recede;
The Emperor's drunken soldiery are abed;
Night resonance recedes, night-walker's song
After great cathedral gong;
A starlit or a moonlit dome disdains
All that man is,
All mere complexities,
The fury and the mire of human veins.

Before me floats an image, man or shade,
Shade more than man, more image than a shade;
For Hades' bobbin bound in mummy-cloth
May unwind the winding path;
A mouth that has no moisture and no breath
Breathless mouths may summon;
I hail the superhuman;
I call it death-in-life and life-in-death.

Miracle, bird or golden handiwork,
More miracle than bird or handiwork,
Planted on the star-lit golden bough,
Can like the cocks of Hades crow,
Or, by the moon embittered, scorn aloud
In glory of changeless metal
Common bird or petal
And all complexities of mire and blood.

At midnight on the Emperor's pavement flit
Flames that no faggot feeds, nor steel has lit,
Nor storm disturbs, flames begotten of flame,
Where blood-begotten spirits come
And all complexities of fury leave,
Dying into a dance,
An agony of trance,
An agony of flame that cannot singe a sleeve.

Astraddle on the dolphin's mire and blood,
Spirit after spirit! The smithies break the flood,
The golden smithies of the Emperor!
Marbles of the dancing floor
Break bitter furies of complexity,
Those images that yet
Fresh images beget,
That dolphin-torn, that gong-tormented sea.

1930

MERU

Civilisation is hooped together, brought
Under a rule, under the semblance of peace
By manifold illusion; but man's life is thought,
And he, despite his terror, cannot cease
Ravening through century after century,
Ravening, raging, and uprooting that he may come
Into the desolation of reality:
Egypt and Greece, good-bye, and good-bye, Rome!

Hermits upon Mount Meru or Everest,
Caverned in night under the drifted snow,
Or where that snow and winter's dreadful blast
Beat down upon their naked bodies, know
That day brings round the night, that before dawn
His glory and his monuments are gone.

LAPIS LAZULI

(*For Harry Clifton*)

I have heard that hysterical women say
They are sick of the palette and fiddle-bow,
Of poets that are always gay,
For everybody knows or else should know
That if nothing drastic is done
Aeroplane and Zeppelin will come out,
Pitch like King Billy bomb-balls in
Until the town lie beaten flat.

All perform their tragic play,
There struts Hamlet, there is Lear,
That's Ophelia, that Cordelia;
Yet they, should the last scene be there,

The great stage curtain about to drop,
If worthy their prominent part in the play,
Do not break up their lines to weep.
They know that Hamlet and Lear are gay;
Gaiety transfiguring all that dread.
All men have aimed at, found and lost;
Black out; Heaven blazing into the head:
Tragedy wrought to its uttermost.
Though Hamlet rambles and Lear rages,
And all the drop-scenes drop at once
Upon a hundred thousand stages,
It cannot grow by an inch or an ounce.

On their own feet they came, or on shipboard,
Camel-back, horse-back, ass-back, mule-back,
Old civilisations put to the sword.
Then they and their wisdom went to rack:
No handiwork of Callimachus,
Who handled marble as if it were bronze,
Made draperies that seemed to rise
When sea-wind swept the corner, stands;
His long lamp-chimney shaped like the stem
Of a slender palm, stood but a day;
All things fall and are built again,
And those that build them again are gay.

Two Chinamen, behind them a third,
Are carved in lapis lazuli,
Over them flies a long-legged bird,
A symbol of longevity;
The third, doubtless a serving-man,
Carries a musical instrument.

Every discoloration of the stone,
Every accidental crack or dent,
Seems a water-course or an avalanche,
Or lofty slope where it still snows
Though doubtless plum or cherry-branch

Sweetens the little half-way house
Those Chinamen climb towards, and I
Delight to imagine them seated there;
There, on the mountain and the sky,
On all the tragic scene they stare.
One asks for mournful melodies;
Accomplished fingers begin to play.
Their eyes mid many wrinkles, their eyes,
Their ancient, glittering eyes, are gay.

THE STATUES

Pythagoras planned it. Why did the people stare?
His numbers, though they moved or seemed to move
In marble or in bronze, lacked character.
But boys and girls, pale from the imagined love
Of solitary beds, knew what they were,
That passion could bring character enough,
And pressed at midnight in some public place
Live lips upon a plummet-measured face.

No! Greater than Pythagoras, for the men
That with a mallet or a chisel modelled these
Calculations that look but casual flesh, put down
All Asiatic vague immensities,
And not the banks of oars that swam upon
The many-headed foam at Salamis.
Europe put off that foam when Phidias
Gave women dreams and dreams their looking-glass.

One image crossed the many-headed, sat
Under the tropic shade, grew round and slow,
No Hamlet thin from eating flies, a fat
Dreamer of the Middle Ages. Empty eyeballs knew
That knowledge increases unreality, that
Mirror on mirror mirrored is all the show.

When gong and conch declare the hour to bless
Grimalkin crawls to Buddha's emptiness.

When Pearse summoned Cuchulain to his side,
What stalked through the Post Office? What intellect.
What calculation, number, measurement, replied?
We Irish, born into that ancient sect
But thrown upon this filthy modern tide
And by its formless spawning fury wrecked,
Climb to our proper dark, that we may trace
The lineaments of a plummet-measured face.

April 9, 1938.

LONG-LEGGED FLY

That civilisation may not sink,
Its great battle lost,
Quiet the dog, tether the pony
To a distant post;
Our master Caesar is in the tent
Where the maps are spread,
His eyes fixed upon nothing,
A hand under his head.
Like a long-legged fly upon the stream
His mind moves upon silence.

That the topless towers be burnt
And men recall that face,
Move most gently if move you must
In this lonely place.
She thinks, part woman, three parts a child,
That nobody looks; her feet
Practise a tinker shuffle
Picked up on a street.
Like a long-legged fly upon the stream
Her mind moves upon silence.

That girls at puberty may find
The first Adam in their thought,
Shut the door of the Pope's chapel,
Keep those children out.
There on that scaffolding reclines
Michael Angelo.
With no more sound than the mice make
His hand moves to and fro.
Like a long-legged fly upon the stream
His mind moves upon silence.

A BRONZE HEAD

Here at right of the entrance this bronze head,
Human, superhuman, a bird's round eye,
Everything else withered and mummy-dead.
What great tomb-haunter sweeps the distant sky
(Something may linger there though all else die;)
And finds there nothing to make its terror less
Hysterica passio of its own emptiness?

No dark tomb-haunter once; her form all full
As though with magnanimity of light,
Yet a most gentle woman; who can tell
Which of her forms has shown her substance right?
Or maybe substance can be composite,
Profound McTaggart thought so, and in a breath
A mouthful held the extreme of life and death.

But even at the starting-post, all sleek and new,
I saw the wildness in her and I thought
A vision of terror that it must live through
Had shattered her soul. Propinquity had brought
Imagination to that pitch where it casts out
All that is not itself: I had grown wild
And wandered murmuring everywhere, 'My child, my
child!'

Or else I thought her supernatural;
As though a sterner eye looked through her eye
On this foul world in its decline and fall;
On gangling stocks grown great, great stocks run dry,
Ancestral pearls all pitched into a sty,
Heroic reverie mocked by clown and knave,
And wondered what was left for massacre to save.

THE CIRCUS ANIMALS' DESERTION

I

I sought a theme and sought for it in vain,
I sought it daily for six weeks or so.
Maybe at last, being but a broken man,
I must be satisfied with my heart, although
Winter and summer till old age began
My circus animals were all on show,
Those stilted boys, that burnished chariot,
Lion and woman and the Lord knows what.

II

What can I but enumerate old themes?
First that sea-rider Oisin led by the nose
Through three enchanted islands, allegorical dreams,
Vain gaiety, vain battle, vain repose,
Themes of the embittered heart, or so it seems,
That might adorn old songs or courtly shows;
But what cared I that set him on to ride,
I, starved for the bosom of his faery bride?

And then a counter-truth filled out its play,
The Countess Cathleen was the name I gave it;
She, pity-crazed, had given her soul away,
But masterful Heaven had intervened to save it.

I thought my dear must her own soul destroy,
So did fanaticism and hate enslave it,
And this brought forth a dream and soon enough
This dream itself had all my thought and love.

And when the Fool and Blind Man stole the bread
Cuchulain fought the ungovernable sea;
Heart-mysteries there, and yet when all is said
It was the dream itself enchanted me:
Character isolated by a deed
To engross the present and dominate memory.
Players and painted stage took all my love,
And not those things that they were emblems of.

III

Those masterful images because complete
Grew in pure mind but out of what began?
A mound of refuse or the sweepings of a street,
Old kettles, old bottles, and a broken can,
Old iron, old bones, old rags, that raving slut
Who keeps the till. Now that my ladder's gone,
I must lie down where all the ladders start,
In the foul rag-and-bone shop of the heart.

T. E. HULME

AUTUMN

A touch of cold in the Autumn night—
I walked abroad,
And saw the ruddy moon lean over a hedge
Like a red-faced farmer.
I did not stop to speak, but nodded,
And round about were the wistful stars
With white faces like town children.

MANA ABODA

Beauty is the marking-time, the stationary vibration, the feigned ecstasy of an arrested impulse unable to reach its natural end.

Mana Aboda, whose bent form
The sky in archèd circle is,
Seems ever for an unknown grief to mourn.
Yet on a day I heard her cry:
'I weary of the roses and the singing poets—
Josephs all, not tall enough to try'.

ABOVE THE DOCK

Above the quiet dock in midnight,
Tangled in the tall mast's corded height,
Hangs the moon. What seemed so far away
Is but a child's balloon, forgotten after play.

THE EMBANKMENT

(The fantasia of a fallen gentleman on a cold, bitter night.)

Once, in finesse of fiddles found I ecstasy,
In a flash of gold heels on the hard pavement.
Now see I
That warmth's the very stuff of poesy.
Oh, God, make small
The old star-eaten blanket of the sky,
That I may fold it round me and in comfort lie.

CONVERSION

Light-hearted I walked into the valley wood
In the time of hyacinths,
Till beauty like a scented cloth
Cast over, stifled me. I was bound
Motionless and faint of breath
By loveliness that is her own eunuch.

Now pass I to the final river
Ignominiously, in a sack, without sound,
As any peeping Turk to the Bosphorus.

EZRA POUND

NEAR PERIGORD

A Perigord, pres del muralh
Tan que i puosch' om gitar ab malh.

You'd have men's hearts up from the dust
And tell their secrets, Messire Cino,
Right enough? Then read between the lines of Uc St.
    Circ,
Solve me the riddle, for you know the tale.

Bertrans, En Bertrans, left a fine canzone:
'Maent, I love you, you have turned me out.
The voice at Montfort, Lady Agnes' hair,
Bel Miral's stature, the viscountess' throat,
Set all together, are not worthy of you . . .'
And all the while you sing out that canzone,
Think you that Maent lived at Montaignac,
One at Chalais, another at Malemort
Hard over Brive—for every lady a castle,
Each place strong.

        Oh, *is* it easy enough?
Tairiran held hall in Montaignac,
His brother-in-law was all there was of power
In Perigord, and this good union
Gobbled all the land, and held it later for some hundred
    years.
And our En Bertrans was in Altafort,
Hub of the wheel, the stirrer-up of strife,
As caught by Dante in the last wallow of hell—
The headless trunk 'that made its head a lamp',
For separation wrought out separation,
And he who set the strife between brother and brother
And had his way with the old English king,

Viced in such torture for the 'counterpass'.
How would you live, with neighbours set about you—
Poictiers and Brive, untaken Rochecouart,
Spread like the finger-tips of one frail hand;
And you on that great mountain of a palm—
Not a neat ledge, not Foix between its streams,
But one huge back half-covered up with pine,
Worked for and snatched from the string-purse of
    Born—
The four round towers, four brothers—mostly fools:
What could he do but play the desperate chess,
And stir old grudges?
        'Pawn your castles, lords!
Let the Jews pay.'
        And the great scene—
(That, maybe, never happened!)
        Beaten at last,
Before the hard old king:
        'Your son, ah, since he died
My wit and worth are cobwebs brushed aside
In the full flare of grief. Do what you will.'

Take the whole man, and ravel out the story.
He loved this lady in castle Montaignac?
The castle flanked him—he had need of it.
You read to-day, how long the overlords of Perigord,
The Talleyrands, have held the place; it was no transient
    fiction.
And Maent failed him? Or saw through the scheme?

And all his net-like thought of new alliance?
Chalais is high, a-level with the poplars.
Its lowest stones just meet the valley tips
Where the low Dronne is filled with water-lilies.
And Rochecouart can match it, stronger yet,
The very spur's end, built on sheerest cliff,
And Malemort keeps its close hold on Brive,
While Born, his own close purse, his rabbit warren,

His subterranean chamber with a dozen doors,
A-bristle with antennae to feel roads,
To sniff the traffic into Perigord.
And that hard phalanx, that unbroken line,
The ten good miles from there to Maent's castle,
All of his flank—how could he do without her?
And all the road to Cahors, to Toulouse?
What would he do without her?

'Papiol,
Go forthright singing—Anhes, Cembelins.
There is a throat; ah, there are two white hands;
There is a trellis full of early roses,
And all my heart is bound about with love.
Where am I come with compound flatteries—
What doors are open to fine compliment?'
And every one half jealous of Maent?
He wrote the catch to pit their jealousies
Against her; give her pride in them?

Take his own speech, make what you will of it—
And still the knot, the first knot, of Maent?

Is it a love poem? Did he sing of war?
Is it an intrigue to run subtly out,
Born of a jongleur's tongue, freely to pass
Up and about and in and out the land,
Mark him a craftsman and a strategist?
(St. Leider had done as much at Polhonac,
Singing a different stave, as closely hidden.)
Oh, there is precedent, legal tradition,
To sing one thing when your song means another,
'*Et albirar ab lor bordon—*'
Foix' count knew that. What is Sir Bertrans' singing?
Maent, Maent, and yet again Maent,
Or war and broken heaumes and politics?

II

End fact. Try fiction. Let us say we see
En Bertrans, a tower-room at Hautefort,
Sunset, the ribbon-like road lies, in red cross-light,
Southward toward Montaignac, and he bends at a table
Scribbling, swearing between his teeth; by his left hand
Lie little strips of parchment covered over,
Scratched and erased with *al* and *ochaisos*.
Testing his list of rhymes, a lean man? Bilious?
With a red straggling beard?
And the green cat's-eye lifts toward Montaignac.

Or take his 'magnet' singer setting out,
Dodging his way past Aubeterre, singing at Chalais
In the vaulted hall,
Or, by a lichened tree at Rochecouart
Aimlessly watching a hawk above the valleys,
Waiting his turn in the midsummer evening,
Thinking of Aelis, whom he loved heart and soul . . .
To find her half alone, Montfort away,
And a brown, placid, hated woman visiting her,
Spoiling his visit, with a year before the next one.
Little enough?
Or carry him forward. 'Go through all the courts,
My Magnet,' Bertrans had said.

We came to Ventadour
In the mid love court, he sings out the canzon,
No one hears save Arrimon Luc D'Esparo—
No one hears aught save the gracious sound of compliments.
Sir Arrimon counts on his fingers, Montfort,
Rochecouart, Chalais, the rest, the tactic,
Malemort, guesses beneath, sends word to Cœur-de-Lion:
The compact, de Born smoked out, trees felled
About his castle, cattle driven out!
Or no one sees it, and En Bertrans prospered?

And ten years after, or twenty, as you will,
Arnaut and Richard lodge beneath Chalus:
The dull round towers encroaching on the field,
The tents tight drawn, horses at tether
Farther and out of reach, the purple night,
The crackling of small fires, the bannerets,
The lazy leopards on the largest banner,
Stray gleams on hanging mail, an armourer's torch-flare
Melting on steel.

And in the quietest space
They probe old scandals, say de Born is dead;
And we've the gossip (skipped six hundred years).
Richard shall die to-morrow—leave him there
Talking of *trobar clus* with Daniel.
And the 'best craftsman' sings out his friend's song,
Envies its vigour . . . and deplores the technique,
Dispraises his own skill?—That's as you will.
And they discuss the dead man,
Plantagenet puts the riddle: 'Did he love her?'
And Arnaut parries: 'Did he love your sister?
True, he has praised her, but in some opinion
He wrote that praise only to show he had
The favour of your party; had been well received.'
'You knew the man.'
'*You* knew the man.'
'I am an artist, you have tried both métiers.'
'You were born near him.'
'Do we know our friends?'
'Say that he saw the castles, say that he loved Maent!'
'Say that he loved her, does it solve the riddle?'
End the discussion, Richard goes out next day
And gets a quarrel-bolt shot through his vizard,
Pardons the bowman, dies,

Ends our discussion. Arnaut ends
'In sacred odour'—(that's apocryphal!)
And we can leave the talk till Dante writes:

Surely I saw, and still before my eyes
Goes on that headless trunk, that bears for light
Its own head swinging, gripped by the dead hair,
And like a swinging lamp that says, 'Ah me!
I severed men, my head and heart
Ye see here severed, my life's counterpart.'

Or take En Bertrans?

III

Ed eran due in uno, ed uno in due;
Inferno, XXVIII, 125

Bewildering spring, and by the Auvezere
Poppies and day's eyes in the green émail
Rose over us; and we knew all that stream,
And our two horses had traced out the valleys;
Knew the low flooded lands squared out with poplars,
In the young days when the deep sky befriended.
  And great wings beat above us in the twilight,
And the great wheels in heaven
Bore us together . . . surging . . . and apart . . .
Believing we should meet with lips and hands,
  High, high and sure . . . and then the counter-thrust:
'Why do you love me? Will you always love me?
But I am like the grass, I cannot love you.'
Or, 'Love, and I love and love you,
And hate your mind, not *you*, your soul, your hands.'

So to this last estrangement, Tairiran!

There shut up in his castle, Tairiran's,
She who had nor ears nor tongue save in her hands,
Gone—ah, gone—untouched, unreachable!
She who could never live save through one person,
She who could never speak save to one person,
And all the rest of her a shifting change,
A broken bundle of mirrors . . . !

EXILE'S LETTER

To So-Kin of Rakuyo, ancient friend, Chancellor of Gen.
Now I remember that you built me a special tavern
By the south side of the bridge at Ten-Shin.
With yellow gold and white jewels, we paid for songs and
 laughter
And we were drunk for month on month, forgetting the
 kings and princes.
Intelligent men came drifting in from the sea and from
 the west border,
And with them, and with you especially
There was nothing at cross purpose,
And they made nothing of sea-crossing or of mountain-
 crossing,
If only they could be of that fellowship,
And we all spoke out our hearts and minds, and without
 regret.
And then I was sent off to South Wei,
  smothered in laurel groves,
And you to the north of Raku-hoku
Till we had nothing but thoughts and memories in
 common.

And then, when separation had come to its worst,
We met, and travelled into Sen-Go
Through all the thirty-six folds of the turning and
 twisting waters,
Into a valley of the thousand bright flowers,
That was the first valley;
And into ten thousand valleys full of voices and pine-
 winds.
And with silver harness and reins of gold,
Out came the East of Kan foreman and his company.
And there came also the 'True man' of Shi-yo to meet
 me,
Playing on a jewelled mouth-organ.

In the storied houses of San-Ko they gave us more
Sennin music,
Many instruments, like the sound of young phoenix
broods.
The foreman of Kan Chu, drunk, danced
because his long sleeves wouldn't keep still
With that music playing,
And I, wrapped in brocade, went to sleep with my head
on his lap,
And my spirit so high it was all over the heavens,
And before the end of the day we were scattered like
stars, or rain.
I had to be off to So, far away over the waters,
You back to your river-bridge.

And your father, who was brave as a leopard,
Was governor in Hei Shu, and put down the barbarian
rabble.
And one May he had you send for me,
despite the long distance.
And what with broken wheels and so on, I won't say it
wasn't hard going,
Over roads twisted like sheep's guts.
And I was still going, late in the year,
in the cutting wind from the North,
And thinking how little you cared for the cost,
and you caring enough to pay it.
And what a reception:
Red jade cups, food well set on a blue jewelled table,
And I was drunk, and had no thought of returning.
And you would walk out with me to the western corner
of the castle,
To the dynastic temple, with water about it clear as blue
jade,
With boats floating, and the sound of mouth-organs and
drums,
With ripples like dragon-scales, going grass-green on the
water,

Pleasure lasting, with courtesans, going and coming
without hindrance,
With the willow flakes falling like snow,
And the vermilioned girls getting drunk about sunset,
And the water, a hundred feet deep, reflecting green
eyebrows
—Eyebrows painted green are a fine sight in young
moonlight,
Gracefully painted—
And the girls singing back at each other,
Dancing in transparent brocade,
And the wind lifting the song, and interrupting it,
Tossing it up under the clouds.
And all this comes to an end.
And is not again to be met with.
I went up to the court for examination,
Tried Layu's luck, offered the Choyo song,
And got no promotion,
and went back to the East Mountains
White-headed.

And once again, later, we met at the South bridge-head.
And then the crowd broke up, you went north to San
palace,
And if you ask how I regret that parting:
It is like the flowers falling at Spring's end
Confused, whirled in a tangle.
What is the use of talking, and there is no end of talking,
There is no end of things in the heart.
I call in the boy,
Have him sit on his knees here
To seal this,
And send it a thousand miles, thinking.

By Rihaku

POUR L'ELECTION DE SON SEPULCHRE

I

For three years, out of key with his time,
He strove to resuscitate the dead art
Of poetry; to maintain 'the sublime'
In the old sense. Wrong from the start—

No, hardly, but seeing he had been born
In a half-savage country, out of date;
Bent resolutely on wringing lilies from the acorn;
Capaneus; trout for factitious bait;

"*Ἴδμεν γάρ τοι πάνθ', ὅσ' ἐνὶ Τροίῃ*
Caught in the unstopped ear;
Giving the rocks small lee-way
The chopped seas held him, therefore, that year.

His true Penelope was Flaubert,
He fished by obstinate isles;
Observed the elegance of Circe's hair
Rather than the mottoes on sundials.

Unaffected by 'the march of events',
He passed from men's memory in *l' an trentiesme,*
De son eage; the case presents
No adjunct to the Muses' diadem.

II

The age demanded an image
Of its accelerated grimace,
Something for the modern stage,
Not, at any rate, an Attic grace;

Not, not certainly, the obscure reveries
Of the inward gaze;
Better mendacities
Than the classics in paraphrase!

The 'age demanded' chiefly a mould in plaster,
Made with no loss of time,
A prose kinema, not, not assuredly, alabaster
Or the 'sculpture' of rhyme.

III

The tea-rose tea-gown, etc.
Supplants the mousseline of Cos,
The pianola 'replaces'
Sappho's barbitos.

Christ follows Dionysus,
Phallic and ambrosial
Made way for macerations;
Caliban casts out Ariel.

All things are a flowing,
Sage Heracleitus says;
But a tawdry cheapness
Shall outlast our days.

Even the Christian beauty
Defects—after Samothrace;
We see *τὸ καλὸν*
Decreed in the market-place.

Faun's flesh is not to us,
Nor the saint's vision.
We have the Press for wafer;
Franchise for circumcision.

All men, in law, are equals.
Free of Pisistratus,
We choose a knave or an eunuch
To rule over us.

O bright Apollo,
τίν' ἄνδρα, τίν' ἥρωα, τίνα θεὸν
What god, man, or hero
Shall I place a tin wreath upon!

IV

These fought in any case,
and some believing,
pro domo, in any case . . .

Some quick to arm,
some for adventure,
some from fear of weakness,
some from fear of censure,
some for love of slaughter, in imagination,
learning later . . .
some in fear, learning love of slaughter;

Died some, pro patria,
non 'dulce' non 'et decor' . . .
walked eye-deep in hell
believing in old men's lies, then unbelieving
came home, home to a lie,
home to many deceits,
home to old lies and new infamy;
usury age-old and age-thick
and liars in public places.

Daring as never before, wastage as never before.
Young blood and high blood,
fair cheeks and fine bodies;

fortitude as never before

frankness as never before,
disillusions as never told in the old days,
hysterias, trench confessions,
laughter out of dead bellies.

V

There died a myriad,
And of the best, among them,
For an old bitch gone in the teeth,
For a botched civilization,

Charm, smiling at the good mouth,
Quick eyes gone under earth's lid,

For two gross of broken statues,
For a few thousand battered books.

HOMAGE TO SEXTUS PROPERTIUS: XII

Who, who will be the next man to entrust his girl to a
friend?
Love interferes with fidelities;
The gods have brought shame on their relatives;
Each man wants the pomegranate for himself;
Amiable and harmonious people are pushed incontinent
into duels,
A Trojan and adulterous person came to Menelaus under
the rites of hospitium,
And there was a case in Colchis, Jason and that woman
in Colchis;
And besides, Lynceus,
you were drunk.

Could you endure such promiscuity?
She was not renowned for fidelity;
But to jab a knife in my vitals, to have passed on a swig
of poison,
Preferable, my dear boy, my dear Lynceus,
Comrade, comrade of my life, of my purse, of my
person;
But in one bed, in one bed alone, my dear Lynceus,
I deprecate your attendance;
I would ask a like boon of Jove.

And you write of Acheloüs, who contended with
Hercules,
You write of Adrastus' horses and the funeral rites of
Achenor,

And you will not leave off imitating Aeschylus.
Though you make a hash of Antimachus,
You think you are going to do Homer.
And still a girl scorns the gods,
Of all these young women
not one has enquired the cause of the world,
Nor the modus of lunar eclipses
Nor whether there be any patch left of us
After we cross the infernal ripples,
nor if the thunder fall from predestination;
Nor anything else of importance.

Upon the Actian marshes Virgil is Phoebus' chief of police,
He can tabulate Caesar's great ships.
He thrills to Ilian arms,
He shakes the Trojan weapons of Aeneas,
And casts stores on Lavinian beaches.
Make way, ye Roman authors,
clear the street O ye Greeks,
For a much larger Iliad is in the course of construction
(and to Imperial order)
Clear the streets O ye Greeks!
And you also follow him 'neath Phrygian pine shade':
Thyrsis and Daphnis upon whittled reeds,
And how ten sins can corrupt young maidens;
Kids for a bribe and pressed udders,
Happy selling poor loves for cheap apples.

Tityrus might have sung the same vixen;
Corydon tempted Alexis,
Head farmers do likewise, and lying weary amid their oats
They get praise from tolerant Hamadryads.

Go on, to Ascraeus' prescription, the ancient,
respected, Wordsworthian:
A flat field for rushes, grapes grow on the slope.'

And behold me, a small fortune left in my house.
Me, who had no general for a grandfather!
I shall triumph among young ladies of indeterminate character,
My talent acclaimed in their banquets,
I shall be honoured with yesterday's wreaths.

And the god strikes to the marrow.

Like a trained and performing tortoise,
I would make verse in your fashion, if she should command it,
With her husband asking a remission of sentence,
And even this infamy would not attract numerous readers
Were there an erudite or violent passion,
For the nobleness of the populace brooks nothing below its own altitude.
One must have resonance, resonance and sonority . . .
like a goose.

Varro sang Jason's expedition,
Varro, of his great passion Leucadia,
There is song in the parchment; Catullus the highly indecorous,
Of Lesbia, known above Helen;
And in the dyed pages of Calvus,
Calvus mourning Quintilia,
And but now Gallus had sung of Lycoris.
Fair, fairest Lycoris—
The waters of Styx poured over the wound:
And now Propertius of Cynthia, taking his stand among these.

CANTO XIII

Kung walked
by the dynastic temple
and into the cedar grove,
and then out by the lower river,

And with him Khieu Tchi
          and Tian the low speaking
And 'we are unknown', said Kung,
You will take up charioteering?
          'Then you will become known,
'Or perhaps I should take up charioteering, or archery?
'Or the practice of public speaking?'
And Tseu-lou said, 'I would put the defences in order,'
And Khieu said, 'If I were lord of a province
I would put it in better order than this is.'
And Tchi said, 'I should prefer a small mountain temple,
'With order in the observances,
          with a suitable performance of the ritual,'
And Tian said, with his hand on the strings of his lute
The low sounds continuing
          after his hand left the strings,
And the sound went up like smoke, under the leaves,
And he looked after the sound:
          'The old swimming hole,
'And the boys flopping off the planks,
'Or sitting in the underbrush playing mandolins.'
          And Kung smiled upon all of them equally.
And Thseng-sie desired to know:
          'Which had answered correctly?'
And Kung said, 'They have all answered correctly,
'That is to say, each in his nature.'
And Kung raised his cane against Yuan Jang,
          Yuan Jang being his elder,
For Yuan Jang sat by the roadside pretending to
          be receiving wisdom.
And Kung said
          'You old fool, come out of it,
'Get up and do something useful.'
          And Kung said
'Respect a child's faculties
'From the moment it inhales the clear air,
'But a man of fifty who knows nothing
          'Is worthy of no respect.'

And 'When the prince has gathered about him
'All the savants and artists, his riches will be fully
employed.'
And Kung said, and wrote on the bo leaves:
'If a man have not order within him
'He cannot spread order about him;
'And if a man have not order within him
'His family will not act with due order;
'And if the prince have not order within him
'He cannot put order in his dominions.'
And Kung gave the words 'order'
and 'brotherly deference'
And said nothing of the 'life after death'.
And he said
'Anyone can run to excesses,
'It is easy to shoot past the mark,
'It is hard to stand firm in the middle.'

And they said: 'If a man commit murder
'Should his father protect him, and hide him?'
And Kung said:
'He should hide him.'

And Kung gave his daughter to Kong-Tchang
Although Kong-Tchang was in prison.
And he gave his niece to Nan-Young
although Nan-Young was out of office.
And Kung said 'Wang ruled with moderation,
'In his day the State was well kept,
'And even I can remember
'A day when the historians left blanks in their writings,
'I mean for things they didn't know,
'But that time seems to be passing.'
And Kung said, 'Without character you will
be unable to play on that instrument
'Or to execute the music fit for the Odes.
'The blossoms of the apricot
blow from the east to the west,
'And I have tried to keep them from falling.'

From CANTO CXV

The scientists are in terror
and the European mind stops
Wyndham Lewis taking blindness
rather than have his mind stop

night under wind mid garofani
the petals are almost still.

Mozart, Linnaeus, Sulmona,

When one's friends hate each other
how can there be peace in the world
Their asperities diverted me in my green time.

A blown husk that is finished
but the light sings eternal
a pale flare over marshes
Where the salt hay whispers to tide's change

Time, space,
neither life nor death is the answer.

and of men seeking good,
doing evil.

in meine Heimat
where the dead walked
and the living were made of cardboard

T. S. ELIOT

SWEENEY AMONG THE NIGHTINGALES

ὤμοι, πέπληγμαι καιρίαν πληγὴν ἔσω

Apeneck Sweeney spreads his knees
Letting his arms hang down to laugh,
The zebra stripes along his jaw
Swelling to maculate giraffe.

The circles of the stormy moon
Slide westward toward the River Plate,
Death and the Raven drift above
And Sweeney guards the horned gate.

Gloomy Orion and the Dog
Are veiled; and hushed the shrunken seas;
The person in the Spanish cape
Tries to sit on Sweeney's knees

Slips and pulls the table cloth
Overturns a coffee-cup,
Reorganised upon the floor
She yawns and draws a stocking up;

The silent man in mocha brown
Sprawls at the window-sill and gapes;
The waiter brings in oranges
Bananas figs and hothouse grapes;

The silent vertebrate in brown
Contracts and concentrates, withdraws;
Rachel *née* Rabinovitch
Tears at the grapes with murderous paws;

She and the lady in the cape
Are suspect, thought to be in league;
Therefore the man with heavy eyes
Declines the gambit, shows fatigue,

Leaves the room and reappears
Outside the window, leaning in,
Branches of wistaria
Circumscribe a golden grin;

The host with someone indistinct
Converses at the door apart,
The nightingales are singing near
The Convent of the Sacred Heart,

And sang within the bloody wood
When Agamemnon cried aloud,
And let their liquid siftings fall
To stain the stiff dishonoured shroud.

THE WASTE LAND

'NAM Sibyllam quidem Cumis ego ipse oculis meis vidi in ampulla pendere, et cum illi pueri dicerent: Σιβυλλα τί θέλεις; *respondebat illa:* ἀποθανεῖν θέλω.'

For Ezra Pound
il miglior fabbro

I. THE BURIAL OF THE DEAD

April is the cruellest month, breeding
Lilacs out of the dead land, mixing
Memory and desire, stirring
Dull roots with spring rain.
Winter kept us warm, covering

Earth in forgetful snow, feeding
A little life with dried tubers.
Summer surprised us, coming over the Starnbergersee
With a shower of rain; we stopped in the colonnade,
And went on in sunlight, into the Hofgarten,
And drank coffee, and talked for an hour.
Bin gar keine Russin, stamm' aus Litauen, echt deutsch.
And when we were children, staying at the archduke's,
My cousin's, he took me out on a sled,
And I was frightened. He said, Marie,
Marie, hold on tight. And down we went.
In the mountains, there you feel free.
I read, much of the night, and go south in the winter.

What are the roots that clutch, what branches grow
Out of this stony rubbish? Son of man,
You cannot say, or guess, for you know only
A heap of broken images, where the sun beats,
And the dead tree gives no shelter, the cricket no relief,
And the dry stone no sound of water. Only
There is shadow under this red rock,
(Come in under the shadow of this red rock),
And I will show you something different from either
Your shadow at morning striding behind you
Or your shadow at evening rising to meet you;
I will show you fear in a handful of dust.

Frisch weht der Wind
Der Heimat zu,
Mein Irisch Kind,
Wo weilest du?

'You gave me hyacinths first a year ago;
'They called me the hyacinth girl.'
—Yet when we came back, late, from the Hyacinth
garden,
Your arms full, and your hair wet, I could not
Speak, and my eyes failed, I was neither

Living nor dead, and I knew nothing,
Looking into the heart of light, the silence.
Od' und leer das Meer.

Madame Sosostris, famous clairvoyante,
Had a bad cold, nevertheless
Is known to be the wisest woman in Europe,
With a wicked pack of cards. Here, said she,
Is your card, the drowned Phoenician Sailor,
(Those are pearls that were his eyes. Look!)
Here is Belladonna, the Lady of the Rocks,
The lady of situations.
Here is the man with three staves, and here the Wheel,
And here is the one-eyed merchant, and this card,
Which is blank, is something he carries on his back,
Which I am forbidden to see. I do not find
The Hanged Man. Fear death by water.
I see crowds of people, walking round in a ring.
Thank you. If you see dear Mrs. Equitone,
Tell her I bring the horoscope myself:
One must be so careful these days.

Unreal City,
Under the brown fog of a winter dawn,
A crowd flowed over London Bridge, so many,
I had not thought death had undone so many.
Sighs, short and infrequent, were exhaled,
And each man fixed his eyes before his feet.
Flowed up the hill and down King William Street,
To where Saint Mary Woolnoth kept the hours
With a dead sound on the final stroke of nine.
There I saw one I knew, and stopped him, crying:
    'Stetson!
'You who were with me in the ships at Mylae!
'That corpse you planted last year in your garden,
'Has it begun to sprout? Will it bloom this year?
'Or has the sudden frost disturbed its bed?
'Oh keep the Dog far hence, that's friend to men,

'Or with his nails he'll dig it up again!
'You! hypocrite lecteur!—mon semblable,—mon frère!'

II. A GAME OF CHESS

The Chair she sat in, like a burnished throne,
Glowed on the marble, where the glass
Held up by standards wrought with fruited vines
From which a golden Cupidon peeped out
(Another hid his eyes behind his wing)
Doubled the flames of sevenbranched candelabra
Reflecting light upon the table as
The glitter of her jewels rose to meet it,
From satin cases poured in rich profusion;
In vials of ivory and coloured glass
Unstoppered, lurked her strange synthetic perfumes,
Unguent, powdered, or liquid—troubled, confused
And drowned the sense in odours; stirred by the air
That freshened from the window, these ascended
In fattening the prolonged candle-flames,
Flung their smoke into the laquearia,
Stirring the pattern on the coffered ceiling.
Huge sea-wood fed with copper
Burned green and orange, framed by the coloured stone,
In which sad light a carvèd dolphin swam.
Above the antique mantel was displayed
As though a window gave upon the sylvan scene
The change of Philomel, by the barbarous king
So rudely forced; yet there the nightingale
Filled all the desert with inviolable voice
And still she cried, and still the world pursues,
'Jug Jug' to dirty ears.
And other withered stumps of time
Were told upon the walls; staring forms
Leaned out, leaning, hushing the room enclosed.
Footsteps shuffled on the stair.
Under the firelight, under the brush, her hair
Spread out in fiery points
Glowed into words, then would be savagely still.

'My nerves are bad to-night. Yes, bad. Stay with me.
'Speak to me. Why do you never speak. Speak.
'What are you thinking of? What thinking? What?
'I never know what you are thinking. Think.'

I think we are in rats' alley
Where the dead men lost their bones.

'What is that noise?'
The wind under the door.
'What is that noise now? What is the wind doing?'
Nothing again Nothing.
'Do
'You know nothing? Do you see nothing? Do you remember
'Nothing?'
I remember
Those are pearls that were his eyes.
'Are you alive, or not? Is there nothing in your head?'
But

O O O O that Shakespeherian Rag—
It's so elegant
So intelligent
'What shall I do now? What shall I do?'
'I shall rush out as I am, and walk the street
'With my hair down, so. What shall we do tomorrow?
'What shall we ever do?'
The hot water at ten.
And if it rains, a closed car at four.
And we shall play a game of chess,
Pressing lidless eyes and waiting for a knock upon the door.

When Lil's husband got demobbed, I said—
I didn't mince my words, I said to her myself,
HURRY UP PLEASE ITS TIME
Now Albert's coming back, make yourself a bit smart.
He'll want to know what you done with that money he gave you

To get yourself some teeth. He did, I was there.
You have them all out, Lil, and get a nice set,
He said, I swear, I can't bear to look at you.
And no more can't I, I said, and think of poor Albert,
He's been in the army four years, he wants a good time,
And if you don't give it him, there's others will, I said.
Oh is there, she said. Something o' that, I said.
Then I'll know who to thank, she said, and give me a
straight look.
HURRY UP PLEASE ITS TIME
If you don't like it you can get on with it, I said,
Others can pick and choose if you can't.
But if Albert makes off, it won't be for lack of telling.
You ought to be ashamed, I said, to look so antique.
(And her only thirty-one.)
I can't help it, she said, pulling a long face,
It's them pills I took, to bring it off, she said.
(She's had five already, and nearly died of young George.)
The chemist said it would be all right, but I've never
been the same.
You *are* a proper fool, I said.
Well, if Albert won't leave you alone, there it is, I said,
What you get married for if you don't want children?
HURRY UP PLEASE ITS TIME
Well, that Sunday Albert was home, they had a hot
gammon,
And they asked me in to dinner, to get the beauty of it
hot—
HURRY UP PLEASE ITS TIME
HURRY UP PLEASE ITS TIME
Goonight Bill. Goonight Lou. Goonight May. Goonight.
Ta ta. Goonight. Goonight.
Good night, ladies, good night, sweet ladies, good night,
good night.

III. THE FIRE SERMON

The river's tent is broken: the last fingers of leaf
Clutch and sink into the wet bank. The wind

Crosses the brown land, unheard. The nymphs are
departed.
Sweet Thames, run softly, till I end my song.
The river bears no empty bottles, sandwich papers,
Silk handkerchiefs, cardboard boxes, cigarette ends
Or other testimony of summer nights. The nymphs are
departed.
And their friends, the loitering heirs of City directors;
Departed, have left no addresses.
By the waters of Leman I sat down and wept . . .
Sweet Thames, run softly till I end my song,
Sweet Thames, run softly, for I speak not loud or long.
But at my back in a cold blast I hear
The rattle of the bones, and chuckle spread from ear to
ear.
A rat crept softly through the vegetation
Dragging its slimy belly on the bank
While I was fishing in the dull canal
On a winter evening round behind the gashouse
Musing upon the king my brother's wreck
And on the king my father's death before him.
White bodies naked on the low damp ground
And bones cast in a little low dry garret,
Rattled by the rat's foot only, year to year.
But at my back from time to time I hear
The sound of horns and motors, which shall bring
Sweeney to Mrs. Porter in the spring.
O the moon shone bright on Mrs. Porter
And on her daughter
They wash their feet in soda water
Et O ces voix d'enfants, chantant dans la coupole!

Twit twit twit
Jug jug jug jug jug jug
So rudely forc'd.
Tereu
Unreal City
Under the brown fog of a winter noon

Mr. Eugenides, the Smyrna merchant
Unshaven, with a pocket full of currants
C.i.f. London: documents at sight,
Asked me in demotic French
To luncheon at the Cannon Street Hotel
Followed by a weekend at the Metropole.

At the violet hour, when the eyes and back
Turn upward from the desk, when the human engine waits
Like a taxi throbbing waiting,
I Tiresias, though blind, throbbing between two lives,
Old man with wrinkled female breasts, can see
At the violet hour, the evening hour that strives
Homeward, and brings the sailor home from sea,
The typist home at teatime, clears her breakfast, lights
Her stove, and lays out food in tins.
Out of the window perilously spread
Her drying combinations touched by the sun's last rays,
On the divan are piled (at night her bed)
Stockings, slippers, camisoles, and stays.
I Tiresias, old man with wrinkled dugs
Perceived the scene, and foretold the rest—
I too awaited the expected guest.
He, the young man carbuncular, arrives,
A small house agent's clerk, with one bold stare,
One of the low on whom assurance sits
As a silk hat on a Bradford millionaire.
The time is now propitious, as he guesses,
The meal is ended, she is bored and tired,
Endeavours to engage her in caresses
Which still are unreproved, if undesired.
Flushed and decided, he assaults at once;
Exploring hands encounter no defence;
His vanity requires no response,
And makes a welcome of indifference.
(And I Tiresias have foresuffered all
Enacted on this same divan or bed;

I who have sat by Thebes below the wall
And walked among the lowest of the dead.)
Bestows one final patronising kiss,
And gropes his way, finding the stairs unlit . . .

She turns and looks a moment in the glass,
Hardly aware of her departed lover;
Her brain allows one half-formed thought to pass;
'Well now that's done: and I'm glad it's over.'
When lovely woman stoops to folly and
Paces about her room again, alone,
She smooths her hair with automatic hand,
And puts a record on the gramophone.

'This music crept by me upon the waters'
And along the Strand, up Queen Victoria Street.
O City city, I can sometimes hear
Beside a public bar in Lower Thames Street,
The pleasant whining of a mandoline
And a clatter and a chatter from within
Where fishmen lounge at noon: where the walls
Of Magnus Martyr hold
Inexplicable splendour of Ionian white and gold.

The river sweats
Oil and tar
The barges drift
With the turning tide
Red sails
Wide
To leeward, swing on the heavy spar.
The barges wash
Drifting logs
Down Greenwich reach
Past the Isle of Dogs.
Weialala leia
Wallala leialala
Elizabeth and Leicester
Beating oars

The stern was formed
A gilded shell
Red and gold
The brisk swell
Rippled both shores
Southwest wind
Carried down stream
The peal of bells
White towers

Weialala leia
Wallala leialala

'Trams and dusty trees.
Highbury bore me. Richmond and Kew
Undid me. By Richmond I raised my knees
Supine on the floor of a narrow canoe.'

'My feet are at Moorgate, and my heart
Under my feet. After the event
He wept. He promised "a new start."
I made no comment. What should I resent?'

'On Margate Sands.
I can connect
Nothing with nothing.
The broken fingernails of dirty hands.
My people humble people who expect
Nothing.'

la la

To Carthage then I came

Burning burning burning burning
O Lord Thou pluckest me out
O Lord Thou pluckest

burning

IV. DEATH BY WATER

Phlebas the Phoenician, a fortnight dead,
Forgot the cry of gulls, and the deep sea swell
And the profit and loss.
                                        A current under sea
Picked his bones in whispers. As he rose and fell
He passed the stages of his age and youth
Entering the whirlpool.
                                        Gentile or Jew
O you who turn the wheel and look to windward,
Consider Phlebas, who was once handsome and tall as
    you.

V. WHAT THE THUNDER SAID

After the torchlight red on sweaty faces
After the frosty silence in the gardens
After the agony in stony places
The shouting and the crying
Prison and palace and reverberation
Of thunder of spring over distant mountains
He who was living is now dead
We who were living are now dying
With a little patience

Here is no water but only rock
Rock and no water and the sandy road
The road winding above among the mountains
Which are mountains of rock without water
If there were water we should stop and drink
Amongst the rock one cannot stop or think
Sweat is dry and feet are in the sand
If there were only water amongst the rock
Dead mountain mouth of carious teeth that cannot spit
Here one can neither stand nor lie nor sit
There is not even silence in the mountains
But dry sterile thunder without rain

There is not even solitude in the mountains
But red sullen faces sneer and snarl
From doors of mudcracked houses
                                                    If there were water
  And no rock
  If there were rock
  And also water
  And water
  A spring
  A pool among the rock
  If there were the sound of water only
  Not the cicada
  And dry grass singing
  But sound of water over a rock
  Where the hermit-thrush sings in the pine trees
  Drip drop drip drop drop drop drop
  But there is no water

Who is the third who walks always beside you?
When I count, there are only you and I together
But when I look ahead up the white road
There is always another one walking beside you
Gliding wrapt in a brown mantle, hooded
I do not know whether a man or a woman
—But who is that on the other side of you?

What is that sound high in the air
Murmur of maternal lamentation
Who are those hooded hordes swarming
Over endless plains, stumbling in cracked earth
Ringed by the flat horizon only
What is the city over the mountains
Cracks and reforms and bursts in the violet air
Falling towers
Jerusalem Athens Alexandria
Vienna London
Unreal

A woman drew her long black hair out tight
And fiddled whisper music on those strings
And bats with baby faces in the violet light
Whistled, and beat their wings
And crawled head downward down a blackened wall
And upside down in air were towers
Tolling reminiscent bells, that kept the hours
And voices singing out of empty cisterns and exhausted
wells.

In this decayed hole among the mountains
In the faint moonlight, the grass is singing
Over the tumbled graves, about the chapel
There is the empty chapel, only the wind's home.
It has no windows, and the door swings,
Dry bones can harm no one.
Only a cock stood on the rooftree
Co co rico co co rico
In a flash of lightning. Then a damp gust
Bringing rain

Ganga was sunken, and the limp leaves
Waited for rain, while the black clouds
Gathered far distant, over Himavant.
The jungle crouched, humped in silence.
Then spoke the thunder
DA
Datta: what have we given?
My friend, blood shaking my heart
The awful daring of a moment's surrender
Which an age of prudence can never retract
By this, and this only, we have existed
Which is not to be found in our obituaries
Or in memories draped by the beneficent spider
Or under seals broken by the lean solicitor
In our empty rooms
DA
Dayadhvam: I have heard the key

Turn in the door once and turn once only
We think of the key, each in his prison
Thinking of the key, each confirms a prison
Only at nightfall, aethereal rumours
Revive for a moment a broken Coriolanus
DA
Damyata: The boat responded
Gaily, to the hand expert with sail and oar
The sea was calm, your heart would have responded
Gaily, when invited, beating obedient
To controlling hands

I sat upon the shore
Fishing, with the arid plain behind me
Shall I at least set my lands in order?
London Bridge is falling down falling down falling down
Poi s'ascose nel foco che gli affina
Quando fiam ceu chelidon—O swallow swallow
Le Prince d'Aquitaine à la tour abolie
These fragments I have shored against my ruins
Why then Ile fit you. Hieronymo's mad againe.
Datta. Dayadhvam. Damyata.
Shantih shantih shantih

JOURNEY OF THE MAGI

'A cold coming we had of it,
Just the worst time of the year
For a journey, and such a long journey:
The ways deep and the weather sharp,
The very dead of winter.'
And the camels galled, sore-footed, refractory,
Lying down in the melting snow.
There were times we regretted
The summer palaces on slopes, the terraces,
And the silken girls bringing sherbet.

Then the camel men cursing and grumbling
And running away, and wanting their liquor and women,
And the night-fires going out, and the lack of shelters,
And the cities hostile and the towns unfriendly
And the villages dirty and charging high prices:
A hard time we had of it.
At the end we preferred to travel all night,
Sleeping in snatches,
With the voices singing in our ears, saying
That this was all folly.

Then at dawn we came down to a temperate valley,
Wet, below the snow line, smelling of vegetation;
With a running stream and a water-mill beating the
    darkness,
And three trees on the low sky,
And an old white horse galloped away in the meadow.
Then we came to a tavern with vine-leaves over the lintel,
Six hands at an open door dicing for pieces of silver,
And feet kicking the empty wine-skins.
But there was no information, and so we continued
And arrived at evening, not a moment too soon
Finding the place; it was (you may say) satisfactory.

All this was a long time ago, I remember,
And I would do it again, but set down
This set down
This: were we led all that way for
Birth or Death? There was a Birth, certainly,
We had evidence and no doubt. I had seen birth and
    death,
But had thought they were different; this Birth was
Hard and bitter agony for us, like Death, our death.
We returned to our places, these Kingdoms,
But no longer at ease here, in the old dispensation,
With an alien people clutching their gods.
should be glad of another death.

MARINA

Quis hic locus, quae regio, quae mundi plaga?

What seas what shores what grey rocks and what islands
What water lapping the bow
And scent of pine and the woodthrush singing through the fog
What images return
O my daughter.

Those who sharpen the tooth of the dog, meaning
Death
Those who glitter with the glory of the humming bird, meaning
Death
Those who sit in the stye of contentment, meaning
Death
Those who suffer the ecstasy of the animals, meaning
Death

Are become unsubstantial, reduced by a wind,
A breath of pine, and the woodsong fog
By this grace dissolved in place

What is this face less clear and clearer
The pulse in the arm, less strong and stronger—
Given or lent? more distant than stars and nearer than the eye
Whispers and small laughter between leaves and hurrying feet
Under sleep, where all the waters meet.

Bowsprit cracked with ice and paint cracked with heat.
I made this, I have forgotten
And remember.

The rigging weak and the canvas rotten
Between one June and another September.
Made this unknowing, half conscious, unknown, my own.
The garboard strake leaks, the seams need caulking.
This form, this face, this life
Living to live in a world of time beyond me; let me
Resign my life for this life, my speech for that unspoken,
The awakened, lips parted, the hope, the new ships.

What seas what shores what granite islands towards my
 timbers
And woodthrush calling through the fog
My daughter.

LITTLE GIDDING

I

Midwinter spring is its own season
Sempiternal though sodden towards sundown,
Suspended in time, between pole and tropic.
When the short day is brightest, with frost and fire,
The brief sun flames the ice, on pond and ditches,
In windless cold that is the heart's heat,
Reflecting in a watery mirror
A glare that is blindness in the early afternoon.
And glow more intense than blaze of branch, or brazier,
Stirs the dumb spirit: no wind, but pentecostal fire
In the dark time of the year. Between melting and freezing
The soul's sap quivers. There is no earth smell
Or smell of living thing. This is the spring time
But not in time's covenant. Now the hedgerow
Is blanched for an hour with transitory blossom
Of snow, a bloom more sudden
Than that of summer, neither budding nor fading,
Not in the scheme of generation.

Where is the summer, the unimaginable
Zero summer?

If you came this way,
Taking the route you would be likely to take
From the place where you would be likely to come from,
If you came this way in may time, you would find the hedges
White again, in May, with voluptuary sweetness.
It would be the same at the end of the journey,
If you came at night like a broken king,
If you came by day not knowing what you came for,
It would be the same, when you leave the rough road
And turn behind the pig-sty to the dull facade
And the tombstone. And what you thought you came for
Is only a shell, a husk of meaning
From which the purpose breaks only when it is fulfilled
If at all. Either you had no purpose
Or the purpose is beyond the end you figured
And is altered in fulfilment. There are other places
Which also are the world's end, some at the sea jaws,
Or over a dark lake, in a desert or a city—
But this is the nearest, in place and time,
Now and in England.

If you came this way,
Taking any route, starting from anywhere,
At any time or at any season,
It would always be the same: you would have to put off
Sense and notion. You are not here to verify,
Instruct yourself, or inform curiosity
Or carry report. You are here to kneel
Where prayer has been valid. And prayer is more
Than an order of words, the conscious occupation
Of the praying mind, or the sound of the voice praying.
And what the dead had no speech for, when living,
They can tell you, being dead: the communication
Of the dead is tongued with fire beyond the language of
the living.

Here, the intersection of the timeless moment
Is England and nowhere. Never and always.

2

Ash on an old man's sleeve
Is all the ash the burnt roses leave.
Dust in the air suspended
Marks the place where a story ended.
Dust inbreathed was a house—
The wall, the wainscot and the mouse.
The death of hope and despair,
        This is the death of air.

    There are flood and drouth
Over the eyes and in the mouth,
Dead water and dead sand
Contending for the upper hand.
The parched eviscerate soil
Gapes at the vanity of toil,
Laughs without mirth.
        This is the death of earth.

    Water and fire succeed
The town, the pasture and the weed.
Water and fire deride
The sacrifice that we denied.
Water and fire shall rot
The marred foundations we forgot,
Of sanctuary and choir.
        This is the death of water and fire.

    In the uncertain hour before the morning
        Near the ending of interminable night
        At the recurrent end of the unending
After the dark dove with the flickering tongue
    Had passed below the horizon of his homing
    While the dead leaves still rattled on like tin

Over the asphalt where no other sound was
    Between three districts whence the smoke arose
    I met one walking, loitering and hurried
As if blown towards me like the metal leaves
    Before the urban dawn wind unresisting.
    And as I fixed upon the down-turned face
That pointed scrutiny with which we challenge
    The first-met stranger in the waning dusk
    I caught the sudden look of some dead master
Whom I had known, forgotten, half recalled
    Both one and many; in the brown baked features
    The eyes of a familiar compound ghost
Both intimate and unidentifiable.
    So I assumed a double part, and cried
    And heard another's voice cry: 'What! are *you* here?'
Although we were not. I was still the same,
    Knowing myself yet being someone other—
    And he a face still forming; yet the words sufficed
To compel the recognition they preceded.
    And so, compliant to the common wind,
    Too strange to each other for misunderstanding,
In concord at this intersection time
    Of meeting nowhere, no before and after,
    We trod the pavement in a dead patrol.
I said: 'The wonder that I feel is easy,
    Yet ease is cause of wonder. Therefore speak:
    I may not comprehend, may not remember.'
And he: 'I am not eager to rehearse
    My thought and theory which you have forgotten.
    These things have served their purpose: let them be.
So with your own, and pray they be forgiven
    By others, as I pray you to forgive
    Both bad and good. Last season's fruit is eaten
And the fullfed beast shall kick the empty pail.
    For last year's words belong to last year's language
    And next year's words await another voice.
But, as the passage now presents no hindrance
    To the spirit unappeased and peregrine

Between two worlds become much like each other,
So I find words I never thought to speak
In streets I never thought I should revisit
When I left my body on a distant shore.
Since our concern was speech, and speech impelled us
To purify the dialect of the tribe
And urge the mind to aftersight and foresight,
Let me disclose the gifts reserved for age
To set a crown upon your lifetime's effort.
First, the cold friction of expiring sense
Without enchantment, offering no promise
But bitter tastelessness of shadow fruit
As body and soul begin to fall asunder.
Second, the conscious impotence of rage
At human folly, and the laceration
Of laughter at what ceases to amuse.
And last, the rending pain of re-enactment
Of all that you have done, and been; the shame
Of motives late revealed, and the awareness
Of things ill done and done to others' harm
Which once you took for exercise of virtue.
Then fools' approval stings, and honour stains.
From wrong to wrong the exasperated spirit
Proceeds, unless restored by that refining fire
Where you must move in measure, like a dancer.'
The day was breaking. In the disfigured street
He left me, with a kind of valediction,
And faded on the blowing of the horn.

3

There are three conditions which often look alike
Yet differ completely, flourish in the same hedgerow:
Attachment to self and to things and to persons,
detachment
From self and from things and from persons; and,
growing between them, indifference
Which resembles the others as death resembles life,

Being between two lives—unflowering, between
The live and the dead nettle. This is the use of memory:
For liberation—not less of love but expanding
Of love beyond desire, and so liberation
From the future as well as the past. Thus, love of a
country
Begins as attachment to our own field of action
And comes to find that action of little importance
Though never indifferent. History may be servitude,
History may be freedom. See, now they vanish,
The faces and places, with the self which, as it could,
loved them,
To become renewed, transfigured, in another pattern.

Sin is Behovely, but
All shall be well, and
All manner of thing shall be well.
If I think, again, of this place,
And of people, not wholly commendable,
Of no immediate kin or kindness,
But some of peculiar genius,
All touched by a common genius,
United in the strife which divided them;
If I think of a king at nightfall,
Of three men, and more, on the scaffold
And a few who died forgotten
In other places, here and abroad,
And of one who died blind and quiet,
Why should we celebrate
These dead men more than the dying?
It is not to ring the bell backward
Nor is it an incantation
To summon the spectre of a Rose.
We cannot revive old factions
We cannot restore old policies
Or follow an antique drum.
These men, and those who opposed them
And those whom they opposed

Accept the constitution of silence
And are folded in a single party.
Whatever we inherit from the fortunate
We have taken from the defeated
What they had to leave us—a symbol:
A symbol perfected in death.
And all shall be well and
All manner of thing shall be well
By the purification of the motive
In the ground of our beseeching.

4

The dove descending breaks the air
With flame of incandescent terror
Of which the tongues declare
The one discharge from sin and error.
The only hope, or else despair
    Lies in the choice of pyre or pyre—
    To be redeemed from fire by fire.

    Who then devised the torment? Love.
Love is the unfamiliar Name
Behind the hands that wove
The intolerable shirt of flame
Which human power cannot remove.
    We only live, only suspire
    Consumed by either fire or fire.

5

What we call the beginning is often the end
And to make an end is to make a beginning.
The end is where we start from. And every phrase
And sentence that is right (where every word is at home,
Taking its place to support the others,
The word neither diffident nor ostentatious,

An easy commerce of the old and the new,
The common word exact without vulgarity,
The formal work precise but not pedantic,
The complete consort dancing together)
Every phrase and every sentence is an end and a
    beginning,
Every poem an epitaph. And any action
Is a step to the block, to the fire, down the sea's throat
Or to an illegible stone: and that is where we start.
We die with the dying:
See, they depart, and we go with them.
We are born with the dead:
See, they return, and bring us with them.
The moment of the rose and the moment of the yew-tree
Are of equal duration. A people without history
Is not redeemed from time, for history is a pattern
Of timeless moments. So, while the light fails
On a winter's afternoon, in a secluded chapel
History is now and England.
With the drawing of this Love and the voice of this Calling

We shall not cease from exploration
And the end of all our exploring
Will be to arrive where we started
And know the place for the first time.
Through the unknown, remembered gate
When the last of earth left to discover
Is that which was the beginning;
At the source of the longest river
The voice of the hidden waterfall
And the children in the apple-tree
Not known, because not looked for
But heard, half-heard, in the stillness
Between two waves of the sea.
Quick now, here, now, always—
A condition of complete simplicity
(Costing not less than everything)

And all shall be well and
All manner of thing shall be well
When the tongues of flame are in-folded
Into the crowned knot of fire
And the fire and the rose are one.

HAROLD MONRO

BITTER SANCTUARY

I

She lives in the porter's room; the plush is nicotined.
Clients have left their photos there to perish.
She watches through green shutters those who press
To reach unconsciousness.
She licks her varnished thin magenta lips,
She picks her foretooth with her finger nail,
She pokes her head out to greet new clients, or
To leave them (to what torture) waiting at the door.

II

Heat has locked the heavy earth,
Given strength to every sound.
He, where his life still holds him to the ground,
In anaesthesia, groaning for re-birth,
Leans at the door.
From out the house there comes the dullest flutter;
A lackey; and thin giggling from behind that shutter.

III

His lost eyes lean to find the number.
Follows his knuckled rap, and hesitating curse.
He cannot wake himself; he may not slumber;
While on the long white wall across the road
Drives the thin outline of a dwindling hearse.

IV

Now the door opens wide.

HE: 'Is there room inside?'
SHE: 'Are you past the bounds of pain?'

HE: 'May my body lie in vain
Among the dreams I cannot keep!'
SHE: 'Let him drink the cup of sleep.'

V

Thin arms and ghostly hands; faint sky-blue eyes;
Long drooping lashes, lids like full-blown moons,
Clinging to any brink of floating skies:
What hope is there? What fear?—Unless to wake and see
Lingering flesh, or cold eternity.

O yet some face, half living, brings
Far gaze to him and croons—
SHE: 'You're white. You are alone.
Can you not approach my sphere?'
HE: 'I'm changing into stone.'
SHE: 'Would I were! Would *I* were!'
Then the white attendants fill the cup.

VI

In the morning through the world,
Watch the flunkeys bring the coffee;
Watch the shepherds on the downs,
Lords and ladies at their toilet,
Farmers, merchants, frothing towns.

But look how he, unfortunate, now fumbles
Through unknown chambers, and unheedful stumbles.
Can he evade the overshadowing night?
Are there not somewhere chinks of braided light?

VII

How do they leave who once are in those rooms?
Some may be found, they say, deeply asleep
In ruined tombs.
Some in white beds, with faces round them. Some
Wander the world, and never find a home.

CONRAD AIKEN

PRELUDE XIV

—You went to the verge, you say, and come back safely?
Some have not been so fortunate,—some have fallen.
Children go lightly there, from crag to crag,
And coign to coign,—where even the goat is wary,—
And make a sport of it. . . . They fling down pebbles,
Following, with eyes undizzied, the long curve,
The long slow outward curve, into the abyss,
As far as eye can follow; and they themselves
Turn back, unworried, to the here and now . . . .
But you have been there, too?—

—I saw at length
The space-defying pine, that on the last
Outjutting rock has cramped its powerful roots.
There stood I too: under that tree I stood:
My hand against its resinous bark: my face
Turned out and downward to the fourfold kingdom.
The wind roared from all quarters. The waterfall
Came down, it seemed, from Heaven. The mighty sound
Of pouring elements,—earth, air, and water,—
The cry of eagles, chatter of falling stones,—
These were the frightful language of that place.
I understood it ill, but understood.—

—You understood it? Tell me, then, its meaning.
It was an all, a nothing, or a something?
Chaos, or divine love, or emptiness?
Water and earth and air and the sun's fire?
Or else, a question, simply?—

—Water and fire were there,
And air and earth; there too was emptiness;

All, and nothing, and something too, and love.
But these poor words, these squeaks of ours, in which
We strive to mimic, with strained throats and tongues,
The spawning and outrageous elements—
Alas, how paltry are they! For I saw—

—What did you see?

—I saw myself and God.
I saw the ruin in which godhead lives:
Shapeless and vast: the strewn wreck of the world:
Sadness unplumbed: misery without bound.
Wailing I heard, but also I heard joy.
Wreckage I saw, but also I saw flowers.
Hatred I saw, but also I saw love. . . .
And thus, I saw myself.

—And this alone?

—And this alone awaits you, when you dare
To that sheer verge where horror hangs, and tremble
Against the falling rock; and, looking down,
Search the dark kingdom. It is to self you come,—
And that is God. It is the seed of seeds:
Seed for disastrous and immortal worlds.

It is the answer that no question asked.

PRELUDE XXIX

What shall we do—what shall we think—what shall we
say—?
Why, as the crocus does, on a March morning,
With just such shape and brightness; such fragility;
Such white and gold, and out of just such earth.
Or as the cloud does on the northeast wind—

Fluent and formless; or as the tree that withers.
What are we made of, strumpet, but of these?
Nothing. We are the sum of all these accidents—
Compounded all our days of idiot trifles,—
The this, the that, the other, and the next;
What x or y said, or old uncle thought;
Whether it rained or not, and at what hour;
Whether the pudding had two eggs or three,
And those we loved were ladies. . . . Were they ladies?
And did they read the proper books, and simper
With proper persons, at the proper teas?
O Christ and God and all deciduous things—
Let us void out this nonsense and be healed.

There is no doubt that we shall do, as always,
Just what the crocus does. There is no doubt
Your Helen of Troy is all that she has seen,—
All filth, all beauty, all honor and deceit.
The spider's web will hang in her bright mind,—
The dead fly die there doubly; and the rat
Find sewers to his liking. She will walk
In such a world as this alone could give—
This of the moment, this mad world of mirrors
And of corrosive memory. She will know
The lecheries of the cockroach and the worm,
The chemistry of the sunset, the foul seeds
Laid by the intellect in the simple heart. . . .
And knowing all these things, she will be she.

She will be also the sunrise on the grassblade—
But pay no need to that. She will be also
The infinite tenderness of the voice of morning—
But pay no heed to that. She will be also
The grain of elmwood, and the ply of water,
Whirlings in sand and smoke, wind in the ferns,
The fixed bright eyes of dolls. . . . And this is all.

PRELUDE LVI

Rimbaud and Verlaine, precious pair of poets,
Genius in both (but what is genius?) playing
Chess on a marble table at an inn
With chestnut blossom falling in blond beer
And on their hair and between knight and bishop—
Sunlight squared between them on the chess-board
Cirrus in heaven, and a squeal of music
Blown from the leathern door of St. Sulpice—

Discussing, between moves, iamb and spondee
Anacoluthon and the open vowel
God the great peacock with his angel peacocks
And his dependent peacocks the bright stars:
Disputing too of fate as Plato loved it,
Or Sophocles, who hated and admired,
Or Socrates, who loved and was amused:

Verlaine puts down his pawn upon a leaf
And closes his long eyes, which are dishonest,
And says 'Rimbaud, there is one thing to do:
We must take rhetoric, and wring its neck! . . .'

Rimbaud considers gravely, moves his Queen;
And then removes himself to Timbuctoo.

And Verlaine dead,—with all his jades and mauves;
And Rimbaud dead in Marseilles with a vision,
His leg cut off, as once before his heart;
And all reported by a later lackey,
Whose virtue is his tardiness in time.

Let us describe the evening as it is:—
The stars disposed in heaven as they are:
Verlaine and Shakspere rotting, where they rot,
Rimbaud remembered, and too soon forgot;

Order in all things, logic in the dark;
Arrangement in the atom and the spark;
Time in the heart and sequence in the brain—

Such as destroyed Rimbaud and fooled Verlaine.
And let us then take godhead by the neck—

And strangle it, and with it, rhetoric.

H. D.

EVENING

The light passes
from ridge to ridge,
from flower to flower—
the hypaticas, wide-spread
under the light
grow faint—
the petals reach inward,
the blue tips bend
toward the bluer heart
and the flowers are lost.

The cornel-buds are still white,
but shadows dart
from the cornel-roots—
black creeps from root to root
each leaf
cuts another leaf on the grass,
shadow seeks shadow,
then both leaf
and leaf-shadow are lost.

SEA ROSE

Rose, harsh rose,
marred and with stint of petals,
meagre flower, thin,
sparse of leaf,
More precious
than a wet rose
single on a stem—
you are caught in the drift.

Stunted, with small leaf,
you are flung on the sand,
you are lifted
in the crisp sand
that drives in the wind.

Can the spice-rose
drip such acrid fragrance
hardened in a leaf?

CHOROS FROM MORPHEUS

'Dream—dark-winged'

I

Give me your poppies,
poppies, one by one,
red poppies,
white ones,
red ones set by white;
I'm through with protestation;
my delight
knows nothing of the mind
or argument;
let me be done
with brain's intricacies;
your insight
has driven deeper
than the lordliest tome
of Attic thought
or Cyrenian logic;
O strange, dark Morpheus,
covering me with wings,
you give the subtle fruit
Odysseus scorned
that left his townsmen fainting on the sands,

you bring the siren note,
the lotus-land;
O let me rest
at last,
at last,
at last;
your touch is sweeter
than the touch of Death;
O I am tired of measures
like deft oars;
the beat and ringing
of majestic song;
give me your poppies;
I would lie along
hot rocks, listening;
still my ambition
that would rear and chafe
like chariot horses
waiting for the race;
let me forget
the spears of Marathon.

MARIANNE MOORE

THE STEEPLE-JACK

Dürer would have seen a reason for living
in a town like this, with eight stranded whales
to look at; with the sweet sea air coming into your house
on a fine day, from water etched
with waves as formal as the scales
on a fish.

One by one, in two's, in three's, the seagulls keep
flying back and forth over the town clock,
or sailing around the lighthouse without moving the
wings—
rising steadily with a slight
quiver of the body—or flock
mewing where

a sea the purple of the peacock's neck is
paled to greenish azure as Dürer changed
the pine green of the Tyrol to peacock blue and guinea
grey. You can see a twenty-five-
pound lobster; and fishnets arranged
to dry. The

whirlwind fife-and-drum of the storm bends the salt
marsh grass, disturbs stars in the sky and the
star on the steeple; it is a privilege to see so
much confusion. Disguised by what
might seem austerity, the sea-
side flowers and

trees are favoured by the fog so that you have
the tropics at first hand: the trumpet-vine,
fox-glove, giant snap-dragon, a salpiglossis that has

spots and stripes; morning-glories, gourds,
or moon-vines trained on fishing-twine
at the back

door. There are no banyans, frangipani, nor
jack-fruit trees; nor an exotic serpent
life. Ring lizard and snake-skin for the foot, or
crocodile;
but here they've cats, not cobras, to
keep down the rats. The diffident
little newt

with white pin-dots on black horizontal spaced
out bands lives here; yet there is nothing that
ambition can buy or take away. The college student
named Ambrose sits on the hill-side
with his not-native books and hat
and sees boats

at sea progress white and rigid as if in
a groove. Liking an elegance of which
the source is not bravado, he knows by heart the antique
sugar-bowl-shaped summer-house of
interlacing slats, and the pitch
of the church

spire, not true, from which a man in scarlet lets
down a rope as a spider spins a thread;
he might be part of a novel, but on the sidewalk a
sign says C. J. Poole, Steeple Jack,
in black and white; and one in red
and white says

Danger. The church portico has four fluted
Columns, each a single piece of stone, made
modester by white-wash. This would be a fit haven for
waifs, children, animals, prisoners,
and presidents who have repaid
sin-driven

senators by not thinking about them. There
  are a school-house, a post-office in a
store, fish-houses, hen-houses, a three-masted
    schooner on
the stocks. The hero, the student,
  the steeple-jack, each in his way,
is at home.

It could not be dangerous to be living
  in a town like this, of simple people,
who have a steeple-jack placing danger signs by the
    church
while he is gilding the solid-
  pointed star, which on a steeple
stands for hope.

BLACK EARTH

Openly, yes,
with the naturalness
  of the hippopotamus or the alligator
  when it climbs out on the bank to experience the

sun, I do these
things which I do, which please
  no one but myself. Now I breathe and now I am sub-
  merged; the blemishes stand up and shout when the
    object

in view was a
renaissance; shall I say
  the contrary? The sediment of the river which
  encrusts my joints, makes me very gray but I am used

to it, it may
remain there; do away
  with it and I am myself done away with, for the
  patina of circumstance can but enrich what was

there to begin
with. This elephant-skin
  which I inhabit, fibred over like the shell of
  the cocoanut, this piece of black grass through which
    no light

can filter—cut
into checkers by rut
  upon rut of unpreventable experience—
  it is a manual for the peanut-tongued and the

hairy-toed. Black
but beautiful, my back
  is full of the history of power. Of power? What
  is powerful and what is not? My soul shall never

be cut into
by a wooden spear; through-
  out childhood to the present time, the unity of
  life and death has been expressed by the circumference

described by my
trunk; nevertheless I
  perceive feats of strength to be inexplicable after
  all; and I am on my guard; external poise, it

has its centre
well nurtured—we know
  where—in pride; but spiritual poise, it has its centre
    where?
  My ears are sensitized to more than the sound of

the wind. I see
and I hear, unlike the
  wandlike body of which one hears so much, which
    was made
  to see and not to see; to hear and not to hear;

that tree-trunk without
roots, accustomed to shout
its own thoughts to itself like a shell, maintained intact
by who knows what strange pressure of the atmos-
phere; that

spiritual
brother to the coral-
plant, absorbed into which, the equable sapphire light
becomes a nebulous green. The I of each is to

the I of each
a kind of fretful speech
which sets a limit on itself; the elephant is
black earth preceded by a tendril? Compared with those

phenomena
which vacillate like a
translucence of the atmosphere, the elephant is
that on which darts cannot strike decisively the first

time, a substance
needful as an instance
of the indestructibility of matter; it
has looked at the electricity and at the earth-

quake and is still
here; the name means thick. Will
depth be depth, thick skin be thick, to one who can
see no
Beautiful element of unreason under it?

TO A STEAM ROLLER

The illustration
is nothing to you without the application.
You lack half wit. You crush all the particles down
into close conformity, and then walk back and
forth on them.

Sparkling chips of rock
are crushed down to the level of the parent block.
Were not 'impersonal judgment in aesthetic
matters, a metaphysical impossibility', you

might fairly achieve
it. As for butterflies, I can hardly conceive
of one's attending upon you, but to question
the congruence of the complement is fain, if it
exists.

TO A SNAIL

If 'compression is the first grace of style',
you have it. Contractility is a virtue
as modesty is a virtue.
It is not the acquisition of any one thing
that is able to adorn,
or the incidental quality that occurs
as a concomitant of something well said,
that we value in style,
but the principle that is hid:
in the absence of feet, 'a method of conclusions';
'a knowledge of principles',
in the curious phenomenon of your occipital horn.

SILENCE

My father used to say,
'Superior people never make long visits,
have to be shown Longfellow's grave
or the glass flowers at Harvard.
Self-reliant like the cat—
that takes its prey to privacy,

the mouse's limp tail hanging like a shoelace from its
    mouth—
they sometimes enjoy solitude,
and can be robbed of speech
by speech which has delighted them.
The deepest feeling always shows itself in silence;
not in silence, but restraint'.
Nor was he insincere in saying, 'Make my house your
    inn'.
Inns are not residences.

WALLACE STEVENS

TEA AT THE PALAZ OF HOON

Not less because in purple I descended
The western day through what you called
The loneliest air, not less was I myself.

What was the ointment sprinkled on my beard?
What were the hymns that buzzed beside my ears?
What was the sea whose tide swept through me there?

Out of my mind the golden ointment rained,
And my ears made the blowing hymns they heard.
I was myself the compass of that sea:

I was the world in which I walked, and what I saw
Or heard or felt came not but from myself;
And there I found myself more truly and more strange.

THE EMPEROR OF ICE-CREAM

Call the roller of big cigars,
The muscular one, and bid him whip
In kitchen cups concupiscent curds.
Let the wenches dawdle in such dress
As they are used to wear, and let the boys
Bring flowers in last month's newspapers.
Let be be finale of seem.
The only emperor is the emperor of ice-cream.

Take from the dresser of deal,
Lacking the three glass knobs, that sheet
On which she embroidered fantails once
And spread it so as to cover her face.

If her horny feet protrude, they come
To show how cold she is, and dumb.
Let the lamp affix its beam.
The only emperor is the emperor of ice-cream.

THE ROCK

I. SEVENTY YEARS LATER

It is an illusion that we were ever alive,
Lived in the houses of mothers, arranged ourselves
By our own motions in a freedom of air.

Regard the freedom of seventy years ago.
It is no longer air. The houses still stand,
Though they are rigid in rigid emptiness.

Even our shadows, their shadows, no longer remain.
The lives these lived in the mind are at an end.
They never were . . . The sounds of the guitar

Were not and are not. Absurd. The words spoken
Were not and are not. It is not to be believed.
The meeting at noon at the edge of the field seems like

An invention, an embrace between one desperate clod
And another in a fantastic consciousness,
In a queer assertion of humanity:

A theorem proposed between the two—
Two figures in a nature of the sun,
In the sun's design of its own happiness,

As if nothingness contained a métier,
A vital assumption, an impermanence
In its permanent cold, an illusion so desired

That the green leaves came and covered the high rock,
That the lilacs came and bloomed, like a blindness cleaned,
Exclaiming bright sight, as it was satisfied,

In a birth of sight. The blooming and the musk
Were being alive, an incessant being alive,
A particular of being, that gross universe.

II. THE POEM AS ICON

It is not enough to cover the rock with leaves.
We must be cured of it by a cure of the ground
Or a cure of ourselves, that is equal to a cure

Of the ground, a cure beyond forgetfulness.
And yet the leaves, if they broke into bud,
If they broke into bloom, if they bore fruit,

And if we ate the incipient colorings
Of their fresh culls might be a cure of the ground.
The fiction of the leaves is the icon

Of the poem, the figuration of blessedness,
And the icon is the man. The pearled chaplet of spring,
The magnum wreath of summer, time's autumn snood,

Its copy of the sun, these cover the rock.
These leaves are the poem, the icon and the man.
These are a cure of the ground and of ourselves,

In the predicate that there is nothing else.
They bud and bloom and bear their fruit without change.
They are more than leaves that cover the barren rock

They bud the whitest eye, the pallidest sprout,
New senses in the engenderings of sense,
The desire to be at the end of distances,

The body quickened and the mind in root.
They bloom as a man loves, as he lives in love.
They bear their fruit so that the year is known,

As if its understanding was brown skin,
The honey in its pulp, the final found,
The plenty of the year and of the world.

In this plenty, the poem makes meanings of the rock,
Of such mixed motion and such imagery
That its barrenness becomes a thousand things

And so exists no more. This is the cure
Of leaves and of the ground and of ourselves.
His words are both the icon and the man.

III. FORMS OF THE ROCK IN A NIGHT-HYMN

The rock is the gray particular of man's life,
The stone from which he rises, up—and—ho,
The step to the bleaker depths of his descents . . .

The rock is the stern particular of the air,
The mirror of the planets, one by one,
But through man's eye, their silent rhapsodist,

Turquoise the rock, at odious evening bright
With redness that sticks fast to evil dreams;
The difficult rightness of half-risen day.

The rock is the habitation of the whole,
Its strength and measure, that which is near, point A
In a perspective that begins again

At B: the origin of the mango's rind.
It is the rock where tranquil must adduce
Its tranquil self, the main of things, the mind,

The starting point of the human and the end,
That in which space itself is contained, the gate
To the enclosure, day, the things illumined

By day, night and that which night illumines,
Night and its midnight—minting fragrances,
Night's hymn of the rock, as in a vivid sleep.

NOT IDEAS ABOUT THE THING BUT THE THING ITSELF

At the earliest ending of winter,
In March, a scrawny cry from outside
Seemed like a sound in his mind.

He knew that he heard it,
A bird's cry, at daylight or before,
In the early March wind.

The sun was rising at six,
No longer a battered panache above snow . . .
It would have been outside.

It was not from the vast ventriloquism
Of sleep's faded papier-mâché . . .
The sun was coming from outside.

That scrawny cry—it was
A chorister whose c preceded the choir.
It was part of the colossal sun,

Surrounded by its choral rings,
Still far away. It was like
A new knowledge of reality.

THE WORLD AS MEDITATION

J'ai passé trop de temps à travailler mon violon,
à voyager. Mais l'exercice essentiel du compositeur
—la méditation—rien ne l'a jamais suspendu en
moi . . . Je vis un rêve permanent, qui ne s'arrête
ni nuit ni jour.

Georges Enesco

Is it Ulysses that approaches from the east,
The interminable adventurer? The trees are mended.
That winter is washed away. Someone is moving

On the horizon and lifting himself up above it.
A form of fire approaches the cretonnes of Penelope,
Whose mere savage presence awakens the world in which
she dwells.

She has composed, so long, a self with which to welcome
him,
Companion to his self for her, which she imagined,
Two in a deep-founded sheltering, friend and dear friend.

The trees had been mended, as an essential exercise
In an inhuman meditation, larger than her own.
No winds like dogs watched over her at night.

She wanted nothing he could not bring her by coming
alone.
She wanted no fetchings. His arms would be her necklace
And her belt, the final fortune of their desire.

But was it Ulysses? Or was it only the warmth of the sun
On her pillow? The thought kept beating in her like her
heart.
The two kept beating together. It was only day.

It was Ulysses and it was not. Yet they had met,
Friend and dear friend and a planet's encouragement.
The barbarous strength within her would never fail.

She would talk a little to herself as she combed her hair.
Repeating his name with its patient syllables,
Never forgetting him that kept coming constantly so near.

THE COURSE OF A PARTICULAR

Today the leaves cry, hanging on branches swept by wind,
Yet the nothingness of winter becomes a little less.
It is still full of icy shades and shapen snow.

The leaves cry . . . One holds off and merely hears the
cry.
It is a busy cry, concerning someone else.
And though one says that one is part of everything,

There is a conflict, there is a resistance involved;
And being part is an exertion that declines:
One feels the life of that which gives life as it is.

The leaves cry. It is not a cry of divine attention,
Nor the smoke-drift of puffed-out heroes, nor human cry.
It is the cry of leaves that do not transcend themselves,

In the absence of fantasia, without meaning more
Than they are in the final finding of the air, in the thing
Itself, until, at last, the cry concerns no one at all.

OF MERE BEING

The palm at the end of the mind,
Beyond the last thought, rises
In the bronze distance,

A gold-feathered bird
Sings in the palm, without human meaning,
Without human feeling, a foreign song.

You know then that it is not the reason
That makes us happy or unhappy.
The bird sings. Its feathers shine.

The palm stands on the edge of space.
The wind moves slowly in the branches.
The bird's fire-fangled feathers dangle down.

D. H. LAWRENCE

END OF ANOTHER HOME HOLIDAY

When shall I see the half-moon sink again
Behind the black sycamore at the end of the garden?
When will the scent of the dim white phlox
Creep up the wall to me, and in at my open window?

Why is it, the long, slow stroke of the midnight bell
  (Will it never finish the twelve?)
Falls again and again on my heart with a heavy reproach?

The moon-mist is over the village, out of the mist
    speaks the bell,
And all the little roofs of the village bow low, pitiful,
    beseeching, resigned.
—Speak, you my home! What is it I don't do well?

Ah home, suddenly I love you
As I hear the sharp clean trot of a pony down the road,
Succeeding sharp little sounds dropping into silence
Clear upon the long-drawn hoarseness of a train across
    the valley.

. . . .

The light has gone out, from under my mother's door.
      That she should love me so!—
      She, so lonely, greying now!
      And I leaving her,
      Bent on my pursuits!

        Love is the great Asker.
        The sun and the rain do not ask the secret
        Of the time when the grain struggles down in
            the dark.

The moon walks her lonely way without
anguish,
Because no-one grieves over her departure.

Forever, ever by my shoulder pitiful love will linger,
Crouching as little houses crouch under the mist when
I turn.
Forever, out of the mist, the church lifts up a reproachful
finger,
Pointing my eyes in wretched defiance where love hides
her face to mourn.

Oh! but the rain creeps down to wet the grain
That struggles alone in the dark,
And asking nothing, patiently steals back again!
The moon sets forth o' nights
To walk the lonely, dusky heights
Serenely, with steps unswerving;
Pursued by no sigh of bereavement,
No tears of love unnerving
Her constant tread:
While ever at my side,
Frail and sad, with grey, bowed head,
The beggar-woman, the yearning-eyed
Inexorable love goes lagging.

The wild young heifer, glancing distraught,
With a strange new knocking of life at her side
Runs seeking a loneliness.
The little grain draws down the earth, to hide.
Nay, even the slumberous egg, as it labours under
the shell
Patiently to divide and self-divide,
Asks to be hidden, and wishes nothing to tell.

But when I draw the scanty cloak of silence over my eyes
Piteous love comes peering under the hood;
Touches the clasp with trembling fingers, and tries

To put her ear to the painful sob of my blood;
While her tears soak through to my breast,
  Where they burn and cauterise.

. . . .

The moon lies back and reddens.
In the valley a corncrake calls
  Monotonously,
With a plaintive, unalterable voice, that deadens
  My confident activity;
With a hoarse, insistent request that falls
  Unweariedly, unweariedly,
  Asking something more of me,
    Yet more of me.

SONG OF A MAN WHO HAS COME THROUGH

Not I, not I, but the wind that blows through me!
A fine wind is blowing the new direction of Time.
If only I let it bear me, carry me, if only it carry me!
If only I am sensitive, subtle, oh, delicate, a winged gift!
If only, most lovely of all, I yield myself and am borrowed
By the fine, fine wind that takes its course through the
  chaos of the world
Like a fine, an exquisite chisel, a wedge-blade inserted;
If only I am keen and hard like the sheer tip of a wedge
Driven by invisible blows,
The rock will split, and we shall come at the wonder, we
  shall find the Hesperides.

Oh, for the wonder that bubbles into my soul,
I would be a good fountain, a good well-head,
Would blur no whisper, spoil no expression.

What is the knocking?
What is the knocking at the door in the night?
It is somebody wants to do us harm.

No, no, it is the three strange angels.
Admit them, admit them.

SNAKE

A snake came to my water-trough
On a hot, hot day, and I in pyjamas for the heat,
To drink there.

In the deep, strange-scented shade of the great dark
carob-tree
I came down the steps with my pitcher
And must wait, must stand and wait, for there he was at
the trough before me.

He reached down from a fissure in the earth-wall in the
gloom
And trailed his yellow-brown slackness soft-bellied down,
over the edge of the stone trough
And rested his throat upon the stone bottom,
And where the water had dripped from the tap, in a
small clearness,
He sipped with his straight mouth,
Softly drank through his straight gums, into his slack
long body,
Silently.

Someone was before me at my water-trough,
And I, like a second comer, waiting.

He lifted his head from his drinking, as cattle do,
And looked at me vaguely, as drinking cattle do,

And flickered his two-forked tongue from his lips, and
mused a moment,
And stooped and drank a little more,
Being earth-brown, earth-golden from the burning
bowels of the earth
On the day of Sicilian July, with Etna smoking.

The voice of my education said to me
He must be killed,
For in Sicily the black, black snakes are innocent, the
gold are venomous.

And voices in me said, If you were a man
You would take a stick and break him now, and finish
him off.

But must I confess how I liked him,
How glad I was he had come like a guest in quiet, to
drink at my water-trough
And depart peaceful, pacified, and thankless,
Into the burning bowels of this earth?

Was it cowardice, that I dared not kill him?
Was it perversity, that I longed to talk to him?
Was it humility, to feel so honoured?
I felt so honoured.

And yet those voices:
If you were not afraid, you would kill him!

And truly I was afraid, I was most afraid,
But even so, honoured still more
That he should seek my hospitality
From out the dark door of the secret earth.

He drank enough
And lifted his head, dreamily, as one who has drunken,
And flickered his tongue like a forked night on the air, so
black,

Seeming to lick his lips,
And looked around like a god, unseeing, into the air,
And slowly turned his head,
And slowly, very slowly, as if thrice adream,
Proceeded to draw his slow length curving round
And climb again the broken bank of my wall-face.

And as he put his head into that dreadful hole,
And as he slowly drew up, snake-easing his shoulders,
 and entered farther,
A sort of horror, a sort of protest against his withdrawing
 into that horrid black hole,
Deliberately going into the blackness, and slowly drawing
 himself after,
Overcame me now his back was turned.

I looked round, I put down my pitcher,
I picked up a clumsy log
And threw it at the water-trough with a clatter.

I think it did not hit him,
But suddenly that part of him that was left behind
 convulsed in undignified haste,
Writhed like lightning, and was gone
Into the black hole, the earth-lipped fissure in the
 wall-front,
At which, in the intense still noon, I stared with
 fascination.

And immediately I regretted it.
I thought how paltry, how vulgar, what a mean act!
I despised myself and the voices of my accursed human
 education.

And I thought of the albatross,
And I wished he would come back, my snake.

For he seemed to me again like a king,
Like a king in exile, uncrowned in the underworld,
Now due to be crowned again.

And so, I missed my chance with one of the lords
Of life.
And I have something to expiate;
A pettiness.

Taormina

BAVARIAN GENTIANS

Not every man has gentians in his house
in Soft September, at slow, Sad Michaelmas.

Bavarian gentians, big and dark, only dark
darkening the day-time torch-like with the smoking
 blueness of Pluto's gloom,
ribbed and torch-like, with their blaze of darkness
 spread blue
down flattening into points, flattened under the sweep
 of white day
torch-flower of the blue-smoking darkness, Pluto's
 dark-blue daze,
black lamps from the halls of Dio, burning dark blue,
giving off darkness, blue darkness, as Demeter's pale
 lamps give off light,
lead me then, lead me the way.

Reach me a gentian, give me a torch
let me guide myself with the blue, forked torch of this
 flower
down the darker and darker stairs, where blue is
 darkened on blueness.
even where Persephone goes, just now, from the
 frosted September
to the sightless realm where darkness is awake upon the
 dark
and Persephone herself is but a voice

or a darkness invisible enfolded in the deeper dark
of the arms Plutonic, and pierced with the passion of
    dense gloom,
among the splendour of torches of darkness, shedding
    darkness on the lost bride and her groom.

ISAAC ROSENBERG

RETURNING, WE HEAR THE LARKS

Sombre the night is:
And, though we have our lives, we know
What sinister threat lurks there.

Dragging these anguished limbs, we only know
This poison-blasted track opens on our camp—
On a little safe sleep.

But hark! Joy—joy—strange joy.
Lo! Heights of night ringing with unseen larks:
Music showering on our upturned listening faces.

Death could drop from the dark
As easily as song—
But song only dropped,
Like a blind man's dreams on the sand
By dangerous tides;
Like a girl's dark hair, for she dreams no ruin lies there,
Or her kisses where a serpent hides.

THE BURNING OF THE TEMPLE

Fierce wrath of Solomon,
Where sleepest thou? O see,
The fabric which thou won
Earth and ocean to give thee—
O look at the red skies.

Or hath the sun plunged down?
What is this molten gold—
These thundering fires blown

Through heaven, where the smoke rolled?
Again the great king dies.

His dreams go out in smoke.
His days he let not pass
And sculptured here are broke,
Are charred as the burnt grass,
Gone as his mouth's last sighs.

DEAD MAN'S DUMP

The plunging limbers over the shattered track
Racketed with their rusty freight,
Stuck out like many crowns of thorns,
And the rusty stakes like sceptres old
To stay the flood of brutish men
Upon our brothers dear.

The wheels lurched over sprawled dead
But pained them not, though their bones crunched;
Their shut mouths made no moan.
They lie there huddled, friend and foeman,
Man born of man, and born of woman;
And shells go crying over them
From night till night and now.

Earth has waited for them,
All the time of their growth
Fretting for their decay:
Now she has them at last!
In the strength of their strength
Suspended—stopped and held.

What fierce imaginings their dark souls lit?
Earth! Have they gone into you?
Somewhere they must have gone,

And flung on your hard back
Is their souls' sack,
Emptied of God-ancestralled essences.
Who hurled them out? Who hurled?

None saw their spirits' shadow shake the grass,
Or stood aside for the half used life to pass
Out of those doomed nostrils and the doomed mouth,
When the swift iron burning bee
Drained the wild honey of their youth.

What of us who, flung on the shrieking pyre,
Walk, our usual thoughts untouched,
Our lucky limbs as on ichor fed,
Immortal seeming ever?
Perhaps when the flames beat loud on us,
A fear may choke in our veins
And the startled blood may stop.

The air is loud with death,
The dark air spurts with fire,
The explosions ceaseless are.
Timelessly now, some minutes past,
These dead strode time with vigorous life,
Till the shrapnel called 'An end!'
But not to all. In bleeding pangs
Some borne on stretchers dreamed of home,
Dear things, war-blotted from their hearts.

A man's brains splattered on
A stretcher-bearer's face;
His shook shoulders slipped their load,
But when they bent to look again
The drowning soul was sunk too deep
For human tenderness.

They left this dead with the older dead,
Stretched at the cross roads.

Burnt black by strange decay
Their sinister faces lie,
The lid over each eye;
The grass and coloured clay
More motion have than they,
Joined to the great sunk silences.

Here is one not long dead.
His dark hearing caught our far wheels,
And the choked soul stretched weak hands
To reach the living word the far wheels said;
The blood-dazed intelligence beating for light,
Crying through the suspense of the far torturing wheels
Swift for the end to break
Or the wheels to break,
Cried as the tide of the world broke over his sight,
'Will they come? Will they ever come?'
Even as the mixed hoofs of the mules,
The quivering-bellied mules,
And the rushing wheels all mixed
With his tortured upturned sight.

So we crashed round the bend,
We heard his weak scream,
We heard his very last sound,
And our wheels grazed his dead face.

BREAK OF DAY IN THE TRENCHES

The darkness crumbles away—
It is the same old druid Time as ever.
Only a live thing leaps my hand—
A queer sardonic rat—
As I pull the parapet's poppy
To stick behind my ear.
Droll rat, they would shoot you if they knew

Your cosmopolitan sympathies
(And God knows what antipathies).
Now you have touched this English hand
You will do the same to a German—
Soon, no doubt, if it be your pleasure
To cross the sleeping green between.
It seems you inwardly grin as you pass
Strong eyes, fine limbs, haughty athletes
Less chanced than you for life,
Bonds to the whims of murder,
Sprawled in the bowels of the earth,
The torn fields of France.
What do you see in our eyes
At the shrieking iron and flame
Hurled through still heavens?
What quaver—what heart aghast?
Poppies whose roots are in man's veins
Drop, and are ever dropping;
But mine in my ear is safe,
Just a little white with the dust.

From MOSES: A PLAY

The Young Hebrew speaks:

Yesterday as I lay nigh dead with toil
Underneath the hurtling crane oiled with our blood,
Thinking to end all and let the crane crush me,
He came by and bore me into the shade:
O, what a furnace roaring in his blood
Thawed my congealed sinews and tingled my own
Raging through me like a strong cordial.
He spoke! Since yesterday
Am I not larger grown?
I've seen men hugely shapen in soul,
Of such unhuman shaggy male turbulence
They tower in foam miles from our neck-strained sight,

And to their shop only heroes come;
But all were cripples to this speed
Constrained to the stables of flesh.
I say there is a famine in ripe harvest
When hungry giants come as guests:
Come knead the hills and ocean into food,
There is none for him.
The streaming vigours of his blood erupting
From his halt tongue are like an anger thrust
Out of a madman's piteous craving for
A monstrous balked perfection.

WILFRED OWEN

FROM MY DIARY, JULY 1914

Leaves
  Murmuring by myriads in the shimmering trees.
Lives
  Wakening with wonder in the Pyrenees.
Birds
  Cheerily chirping in the early day.
Bards
  Singing of summer scything thro' the hay.
Bees
  Shaking the heavy dews from bloom and frond.
Boys
  Bursting the surface of the ebony pond.
Flashes
  Of swimmers carving thro' the sparkling cold.
Fleshes
  Gleaming with wetness to the morning gold.
A mead
  Bordered about with warbling water brooks.
A maid
  Laughing the love-laugh with me; proud of looks.
The heat
  Throbbing between the upland and the peak.
Her heart
  Quivering with passion to my pressed cheek.
Braiding
  Of floating flames across the mountain brow.
Brooding
  Of stillness; and a sighing of the bough.
Stirs
  Of leaflets in the gloom; soft petal-showers;
Stars
  Expanding with the starr'd nocturnal flowers.

EXPOSURE

Our brains ache, in the merciless iced east winds that
knive us . . .
Wearied we keep awake because the night is silent . . .
Low, drooping flares confuse our memory of the
salient . . .
Worried by silence, sentries whisper, curious, nervous,
But nothing happens.

Watching, we hear the mad gusts tugging on the wire,
Like twitching agonies of men among its brambles.
Northward, incessantly, the flickering gunnery rumbles,
Far off, like a dull rumour of some other war.
What are we doing here?

The poignant misery of dawn begins to grow . . .
We only know war lasts, rain soaks, and clouds sag
stormy.
Dawn massing in the east her melancholy army
Attacks once more in ranks on shivering ranks of gray,
But nothing happens.

Sudden successive flights of bullets streak the silence.
Less deadly than the air that shudders black with snow,
With sidelong flowing flakes that flock, pause, and renew,
We watch them wandering up and down the wind's
nonchalance,
But nothing happens.

Pale flakes with fingering stealth come feeling for our
faces—
We cringe in holes, back on forgotten dreams, and stare,
snow-dazed,
Deep into grassier ditches. So we drowse, sun-dozed,
Littered with blossoms trickling where the blackbird
fusses.
Is it that we are dying?

Slowly our ghosts drag home: glimpsing the sunk fires, glozed
With crusted dark-red jewels; crickets jingle there;
For hours the innocent mice rejoice: the house is theirs;
Shutters and doors, all closed: on us the doors are closed,—
We turn back to our dying.

Since we believe not otherwise can kind fires burn;
Nor ever suns smile true on child, or field, or fruit.
For God's invincible spring our love is made afraid;
Therefore, not loath, we lie out here; therefore were born,
For love of God seems dying.

To-night, His frost will fasten on this mud and us,
Shrivelling many hands, puckering foreheads crisp.
The burying-party, picks and shovels in their shaking grasp,
Pause over half-known faces. All their eyes are ice,
But nothing happens.

GREATER LOVE

Red lips are not so red
As the stained stones kissed by the English dead.
Kindness of wooed and wooer
Seems shame to their love pure.
O Love, your eyes lose lure
When I behold eyes blinded in my stead!

Your slender attitude
Trembles not exquisite like limbs knife-skewed,
Rolling and rolling there
Where God seems not to care;
Till the fierce Love they bear
Cramps them in death's extreme decrepitude.

Your voice sings not so soft,—
  Though even as wind murmuring through raftered loft,—
Your dear voice is not dear,
Gentle, and evening clear,
As theirs whom none now hear,
  Now earth has stopped their piteous mouths that coughed.

Heart, you were never hot,
  Nor large, nor full like hearts made great with shot;
And though your hand be pale,
Paler are all which trail
Your cross through flame and hail:
  Weep, you may weep, for you may touch them not.

MENTAL CASES

Who are these? Why sit they here in twilight?
Wherefore rock they, purgatorial shadows,
Drooping tongues from jaws that slob their relish,
Baring teeth that leer like skulls' teeth wicked?
Stroke on stroke of pain,—but what slow panic,
Gouged these chasms round their fretted sockets?
Ever from their hair and through their hands' palms
Misery swelters. Surely we have perished
Sleeping, and walk hell; but who these hellish?

—These are men whose minds the Dead have ravished.
Memory fingers in their hair of murders,
Multitudinous murders they once witnessed.
Wading sloughs of flesh these helpless wander,
Treading blood from lungs that had loved laughter.
Always they must see these things and hear them,
Batter of guns and shatter of flying muscles,
Carnage incomparable, and human squander,
Rucked too thick for these men's extrication.

Therefore still their eyeballs shrink tormented
Back into their brains, because on their sense
Sunlight seems a blood-smear; night comes blood-black;
Dawn breaks open like a wound that bleeds afresh
—Thus their heads wear this hilarious, hideous,
Awful falseness of set-smiling corpses.
—Thus their hands are plucking at each other;
Picking at the rope-knouts of their scourging;
Snatching after us who smote them, brother,
Pawing us who dealt them war and madness.

FUTILITY

Move him into the sun—
Gently its touch awoke him once,
At home, whispering of fields unsown.
Always it woke him, even in France,
Until this morning and this snow.
If anything might rouse him now
The kind old sun will know.

Think how it wakes the seeds,—
Woke, once, the clays of a cold star.
Are limbs, so dear-achieved, are sides,
Full-nerved—still warm—too hard to stir?
Was it for this the clay grew tall?
—O what made fatuous sunbeams toil
To break earth's sleep at all?

ANTHEM FOR DOOMED YOUTH

What passing-bells for these who die as cattle?
Only the monstrous anger of the guns.
Only the stuttering rifles' rapid rattle
Can patter out their hasty orisons.

No mockeries for them from prayers or bells,
   Nor any voice of mourning save the choirs,—
The shrill, demented choirs of wailing shells;
   And bugles calling for them from sad shires.

What candles may be held to speed them all?
   Not in the hands of boys, but in their eyes
Shall shine the holy glimmers of good-byes.
   The pallor of girls' brows shall be their pall;
Their flowers the tenderness of silent minds,
And each slow dusk a drawing-down of blinds.

STRANGE MEETING

It seemed that out of battle I escaped
Down some profound dull tunnel, long since scooped
Through granites which titanic wars had groined.
Yet also there encumbered sleepers groaned,
Too fast in thought or death to be bestirred.
Then, as I probed them, one sprang up, and stared
With piteous recognition in fixed eyes,
Lifting distressful hands as if to bless.
And by his smile, I knew that sullen hall,
By his dead smile I knew we stood in Hell.
With a thousand pains that vision's face was grained;
Yet no blood reached there from the upper ground,
And no guns thumped, or down the flues made moan.
'Strange friend', I said, 'here is no cause to mourn.'
'None', said the other, 'save the undone years,
The hopelessness. Whatever hope is yours,
Was my life also; I went hunting wild
After the wildest beauty in the world,
Which lies not calm in eyes, or braided hair,
But mocks the steady running of the hour,
And if it grieves, grieves richlier than here.
For by my glee might many men have laughed,

And of my weeping something had been left,
Which must die now. I mean the truth untold,
The pity of war, the pity war distilled.
Now men will go content with what we spoiled.
Or, discontent, boil bloody, and be spilled.
They will be swift with swiftness of the tigress,
None will break ranks, though nations trek from progress.
Courage was mine, and I had mystery,
Wisdom was mine, and I had mastery;
To miss the march of this retreating world
Into vain citadels that are not walled.
Then, when much blood had clogged their chariot-wheels
I would go up and wash them from sweet wells,
Even with truths that lie too deep for taint.
I would have poured my spirit without stint
But not through wounds; not on the cess of war.
Foreheads of men have bled where no wounds were.
I am the enemy you killed, my friend.
I knew you in this dark; for so you frowned
Yesterday through me as you jabbed and killed.
I parried; but my hands were loath and cold.
Let us sleep now. . . .'

HERBERT READ

MY COMPANY

Foule! Ton âme entière est debout
dans mon corps.

JULES ROMAINS

I

You became
In many acts and quiet observances
A body and a soul, entire.

I cannot tell
What time your life became mine:
Perhaps when one summer night
We halted on the roadside
In the starlight only,
And you sang your sad home-songs,
Dirges which I standing outside you
Coldly condemned.

Perhaps, one night, descending cold
When rum was mighty acceptable,
And my doling gave birth to sensual gratitude.

And then our fights: we've fought together
Compact, unanimous;
And I have felt the pride of leadership.

In many acts and quiet observances
You absorbed me:
Until one day I stood eminent
And saw you gathered round me,
Uplooking,
And about you a radiance that seemed to beat
With variant glow and to give
Grace to our unity.

But, God! I know that I'll stand
Someday in the loneliest wilderness,
Someday my heart will cry
For the soul that has been, but that now
Is scattered with the winds,
Deceased and devoid.

I know that I'll wander with a cry:
'O beautiful men, O men I loved,
O whither are you gone, my company?'

2

My men go wearily
With their monstrous burdens.

They bear wooden planks
And iron sheeting
Through the area of death.

When a flare curves through the sky
They rest immobile.

Then on again,
Sweating and blaspheming—
'Oh, bloody Christ!'

My men, my modern Christs,
Your bloody agony confronts the world.

3

A man of mine
 lies on the wire.
It is death to fetch his soulless corpse.

A man of mine
 lies on the wire;
And he will rot
And first his lips
The worms will eat.

It is not thus I would have him kissed,
But with the warm passionate lips
Of his comrade here

4

I can assume
A giant attitude and godlike mood,
And then detachedly regard
All riots, conflicts and collisions.

The men I've lived with
Lurch suddenly into a far perspective;
They distantly gather like a dark cloud of birds.
In the autumn sky.

Urged by some unanimous
Volition or fate,
Clouds clash in opposition;
The sky quivers, the dead descend;
Earth yawns.

They are all of one species.

From my giant attitude,
In godlike mood,
I laugh till space is filled
With hellish merriment.

Then again I assume
My human docility,
Bow my head
And share their doom.

BEATA L'ALMA

Beata l'alma, ove non corre tempo.
MICHELANGELO

I

Time ends when vision sees its lapse in
liberty. The seven
sleepers quit their den and wild
lament-
ations fill our voiceless bodies. Echoes only are.

You will never understand the mind's
misanthropy, nor see
that all is foul and fit to
screech in.
It is an eye's anarchy: men are ghoulish stumps

and the air a river of opaque
filth. God! I cannot see
to design these stark reaches, these
bulging
contours pressed against me in the maddening dark.

A blindman's buff and no distilling
of song for the woeful
scenes of agony. Never
will rest
the mind an instant in its birdlike flutterings.

Could I impress my voice on the plas-
tic darkness, or lift an
inviolate lanthorn from
a ship
in the storm I might have ease. But why? No fellows

would answer my hullallo, and my
lanthorn would lurch on the
mast till it dipped under the
wet waves
and the hissing darkness healed the wide wound of light.

A cynic race—to bleak ecstasies
we are driven by our
sombre destiny. Men's shouts
are not
glad enough to echo in our groined hearts. We know

war and its dead, and famine's bleached bones;
black rot overreaching
the silent pressure of life
in fronds
of green ferns and in the fragile shell of white flesh.

2

New children must be born of gods in
a deathless land, where the
uneroded rocks bound clear
from cool
glassy tarns, and no flaw is in mind or flesh.

Sense and image they must refashion—
they will not recreate
love: love ends in hate; they will
not use
words: words lie. The structure of events alone is

comprehensible and to single
perceptions communic-
ation is not essential.
Art ends;
the individual world alone is valid

and that gives ease. The water is still;
    the rocks are hard and veined,
  metalliferous, yielding
      an ore
of high worth. In the sky the unsullied sun lake.

CRANACH

But once upon a time
the oakleaves and the wild boars
Antonio Antonio
the old wound is bleeding.

We are in Silvertown
we have come here with a modest ambition
to know a little bit about the river
eating cheese and pickled onions on a terrace by the
    Thames.

Sweet Thames! the ferry glides across your bosom
like Leda's swan.
The factories ah slender graces
sly naked damsels nodding their downy plumes.

JOHN CROWE RANSOM

VISION BY SWEETWATER

Go and ask Robin to bring the girls over
To Sweetwater, said my Aunt; and that was why
It was like a dream of ladies sweeping by
The willows, clouds, deep meadowgrass, and the river.

Robin's sisters and my Aunt's lily daughter
Laughed and talked, and tinkled light as wrens
If there were a little colony all hens
To go walking by the steep turn of Sweetwater.

Let them alone, dear Aunt, just for one minute
Till I go fishing in the dark of my mind:
Where have I seen before, against the wind,
These bright virgins, robed and bare of bonnet,

Flowing with music of their strange quick tongue
And adventuring with delicate paces by the stream,—
Myself a child, old suddenly at the scream
From one of the white throats which it hid among?

CAPTAIN CARPENTER

Captain Carpenter rose up in his prime
Put on his pistols and went riding out
But had got well-nigh nowhere at that time
Till he fell in with ladies in a rout.

It was a pretty lady and all her train
That played with him so sweetly but before
An hour she'd taken a sword with all her main
And twined him of his nose for evermore.

Captain Carpenter mounted up one day
And rode straightway into a stranger rogue
That looked unchristian but be that as may
The Captain did not wait upon prologue.

But drew upon him out of his great heart
The other swung against him with a club
And cracked his two legs at the shinny part
And let him roll and stick like any tub.

Captain Carpenter rode many a time
From male and female took he sundry harms
He met the wife of Satan crying 'I'm
The she-wolf bids you shall bear no more arms'.

Their strokes and counters whistled in the wind
I wish he had delivered half his blows
But where she should have made off like a hind
The bitch bit off his arms at the elbows.

And Captain Carpenter parted with his ears
To a black devil that used him in this wise
O Jesus ere his threescore and ten years
Another had plucked out his sweet blue eyes.

Captain Carpenter got up on his roan
And sallied from the gate in hell's despite
I heard him asking in the grimmest tone
If any enemy yet there was to fight?

'To any adversary it is fame
If he risk to be wounded by my tongue
Or burnt in two beneath my red heart's flame
Such are the perils he is cast among.

'But if he can he has a pretty choice
From an anatomy with little to lose
Whether he cut my tongue and take my voice
Or whether it be my round red heart he choose.'

It was the neatest knave that ever was seen
Stepping in perfume from his lady's bower
Who at this word put in his merry mien
And fell on Captain Carpenter like a tower.

I would not knock old fellows in the dust
But there lay Captain Carpenter on his back
His weapons were the old heart in his bust
And a blade shook between rotten teeth alack.

The rogue in scarlet and gray soon knew his mind
He wished to get his trophy and depart
With gentle apology and touch refined
He pierced him and produced the Captain's heart.

God's mercy rest on Captain Carpenter now
I thought him Sirs an honest gentleman
Citizen husband soldier and scholar enow
Let jangling kites eat of him if they can.

But God's deep curses follow after those
That shore him of his goodly nose and ears
His legs and strong arms at the two elbows
And eyes that had not watered seventy years.

The curse of hell upon the sleek upstart
Who got the Captain finally on his back
And took the red red vitals of his heart
And made the kites to whet their beaks clack clack.

DEAD BOY

The little cousin is dead, by foul subtraction,
A green bough from Virginia's aged tree,
And neither the county kin love the transaction
Nor some of the world of outer dark, like me.

He was not a beautiful boy, nor good, nor clever,
A black cloud full of storms too hot for keeping,
A sword beneath his mother's heart,—yet never
Woman bewept her babe as this is weeping.

A pig with a pasty face, I had always said.
Squealing for cookies, kinned by pure pretence
With a noble house. But the little man quite dead,
I can see the forebears' antique lineaments.

The elder men have strode by the box of death
To the wide flag porch, and muttering low send round
The bruit of the day. O friendly waste of breath!
Their hearts are hurt with a deep dynastic wound.

He was pale and little, the foolish neighbors say;
The first-fruits, saith the preacher, the Lord hath taken;
But this was the old tree's late branch wrenched away,
Aggrieving the sapless limbs, the shorn and shaken.

JUDITH OF BETHULIA

Beautiful as the flying legend of some leopard,
She had not yet chosen her great captain or prince
Depositary to her flesh, and our defence;
And a wandering beauty is a blade out of its scabbard.
You know how dangerous, gentlemen of three-score?
May you know it yet ten more.

Nor by process of veiling she grew the less fabulous.
Gray or blue veils, we were desperate to study
The invincible emanations of her white body,
And the winds at her ordered raiment were ominous.
Might she walk in the market, sit in the council of
soldiers?
Only of the extreme elders.

But a rare chance was the girl's then, when the Invader
Trumpeted from the south, and rumbled from the north,
Beleaguered the city from four quarters of the earth,
Our soldiery too craven and sick to aid her—
Where were the arms could countervail his horde?
Her beauty was the sword.

She sat with the elders, and proved on their blear visage
How bright was the weapon unrusted in her keeping,
While he lay surfeiting on their harvest heaping,
Wasting the husbandry of their rarest vintage—
And dreaming of the broad-breasted dames for concubine?
These floated on his wine.

He was lapped with bay-leaves, and grass and fumiter
    weed,
And from under the wine-film encountered his mortal
    vision.
For even within his tent she accomplished his derision;
She loosed one veil and another, standing unafraid;
And he perished. Nor brushed her with even so much as
    a daisy?
She found his destruction easy.

The heathen are all perished. The victory was furnished,
We smote them hiding in our vineyards, barns, annexes,
And now their white bones clutter the holes of foxes,
And the chieftain's head, with grinning sockets, and
    varnished—
Is it hung on the sky with a hideous epitaphy?
No, the woman keeps the trophy.

May God send unto the virtuous lady her prince.
It is stated she went reluctant to that orgy,
Yet a madness fevers our young men, and not the clergy
Nor the elders have turned them unto modesty since.
Inflamed by the thought of her naked beauty with desire?
Yes, and chilled with fear and despair.

ALLEN TATE

HORATIAN EPODE
TO THE DUCHESS OF MALFI

DUCHESS: *'Who am I?'*
BOSOLA: *'Thou art a box of worm-seed, at best but a salvatory of green mummy.'*

The stage is about to be swept of corpses.
You have no more chance than an infusorian
Lodged in a hollow molar or an eohippus.
Come, now, no prattle of remergence with the
ὄντως ὄν.

. . . .

As (the form requires the myth)
A Greek girl stood once in the prytaneum
Of Carneades, hearing mouthings of Probability,
Then mindful of love dashed her brain on a megalith,

So you, O nameless Duchess who die young,
Meet death somewhat lovingly
And I am filled with a pity of beholding skulls.
There was no pride like yours.

Now considerations of the Void coming after,
Not changed by the strict gesture of your death,
Split the straight line of pessimism
Into two infinities.

It is moot whether there be divinities
As I finish this play by Webster:
The street cars are still running however
And the katharsis fades in the warm water of a yawn.
1922

IDIOT

The idiot greens the meadow with his eyes,
The meadow creeps, implacable and still;
A dog barks; the hammock swings; he lies.
One, two, three, the cows bulge on the hill.

Motion, which is not time, erects snowdrifts
While sister's hand sieves waterfalls of lace.
With a palm fan closer than death, he lifts
The Ozarks and tilted seas across his face.

In the long sunset where impatient sound
Strips niggers to a multiple of backs,
Flies yield their heat, magnolias drench the ground
With Appomattox! The shadows lie in stacks.

The julep glass weaves echoes in Jim's kinks
While ashy Jim puts murmurs in the day:
Now in the idiot's heart a chamber stinks
Of dead asters—as the potter's field, of May.

All evening the marsh is a slick pool
Where dream wild hares, witch hazel, pretty girls.
'Up from the important picnic of a fool
Those rotted asters!' Eddy on eddy swirls

The innocent mansion of a panther's heart!
It crumbles; tick-tick, time drags it in;
And now his arteries lag and now they start
Reverence with the frigid gusts of sin.

The stillness pelts the eye, assaults the hair;
A beech sticks out a branch to warn the stars;
A lightning-bug jerks angles in the air,
Diving. 'I am the captain of new wars!'

The dusk runs down the lane, driven like hail;
Far-off a precise whistle is escheat
To the dark; and then the towering weak and pale
Covers his eyes with memory like a sheet.

1926

THE MEDITERRANEAN

Quem das finem, rex magne, dolorum?

Where we went in the boat was a long bay
A slingshot wide walled in by towering stone,
Peaked margin of antiquity's delay—
And we went there out of time's monotone:

Where we went in the black hull no light moved
But a gull white-winged along the feckless wave;
The breeze, unseen but fierce as a body loved,
That boat drove onward like a willing slave;

Where we went in the small ship the seaweed
Parted and gave to us the murmuring shore
And we made feast and in our secret need
Devoured the very plates Aeneas bore:

Where derelict you see through the low twilight
The green coast that you thunder-tossed would win
Drop sail, and hastening to drink all night
Eat dish and bowl—to take the sweet land in!

Where we feasted and caroused on the sandless
Pebbles, affecting our day of piracy,
What prophecy of eaten plates could landless
Wanderers fulfil by the ancient sea?

We for that time might taste the famous age
Eternal here yet hidden from our eyes

When lust of power undid its stuffless rage;
They, in a wineskin, bore earth's paradise.

—Let us lie down once more by the breathing side
Of ocean, where our live forefathers sleep
As if the Known Sea still were a month wide—
Atlantis howls but is no longer steep!

What country shall we conquer, what fair land
Unman our conquest and locate our blood?
We've cracked the hemispheres with careless hand:
Now, from the Gates of Hercules we flood

Westward, westward till the barbarous brine
Whelms us to the tired world where tasseling corn,
Fat beans, grapes sweeter than muscadine
Rot on the vine: in that land were we born.

1932

THE OATH

It was near evening, the room was cold,
Half-dark; Uncle Ben's brass bullet-mould
And powder horn, and Major Bogan's face
Above the fire, in the half-light, plainly said
There's naught to kill but the animated dead;
Horn nor mould nor Major follows the chase.
Being cold I urged Lytle to the fire
In the blank twilight, with not much left untold
By two old friends when neither's a great liar;
We sat down evenly in the smoky chill.
There's precious little to say betwixt day and dark,
Perhaps a few words on the implacable will
Of time sailing like a magic barque
Or something as fine for the amenities,
Till the dusk seals the window, the fire grows bright

And the wind saws the hill with a swarm of bees.
Now meditating a little on the firelight
We heard the darkness grapple with the night
And give an old man's valedictory wheeze
From his westward breast between his polar jaws;
So Lytle asked: Who are the dead?
Who are the living and the dead? . . .
And nothing more was said;
But I leaving Lytle to that dream
Decided what it is in time that gnaws
The ageing fury of a mountain stream,
When suddenly as an ignorant mind will do
I thought I heard the dark pounding its head
On a rock, crying *Who are the dead?*
Lytle turned with an oath—By God, it's true!
1930

ODE TO THE CONFEDERATE DEAD

Row after row with strict impunity
The headstones yield their names to the element,
The wind whirrs without recollection;
In the riven troughs the splayed leaves
Pile up, of nature the casual sacrament
To the seasonal eternity of death,
Then driven by the fierce scrutiny
Of heaven to their business in the vast breath
They sough the rumour of mortality.

Autumn is desolation in the plot
Of a thousand acres, where these memories grow
From the inexhaustible bodies that are not
Dead, but feed the grass row after rich row:
Remember now the autumns that have gone—
Ambitious November with the humors of the year,
With a particular zeal for every slab,

Staining the uncomfortable angels that rot
On the slabs, a wing chipped here, an arm there:
The brute curiosity of an angel's stare
Turns you like them to stone,
Transforms the heaving air,
Till plunged to a heavier world below
You shift your sea-space blindly,
Heaving, turning like the blind crab.

Dazed by the wind, only the wind
The leaves flying, plunge

You know who have waited by the wall
The twilit certainty of an animal;
Those midnight restitutions of the blood
You know—the immitigable pines, the smoky frieze
Of the sky, the sudden call; you know the rage—
The cold pool left by the mounting flood—
The rage of Zeno and Parmenides.
You who have waited for the angry resolution
Of those desires that should be yours tomorrow,
You know the unimportant shrift of death
And praise the vision
And praise the arrogant circumstance
Of those who fall
Rank upon rank, hurried beyond decision—
Here by the sagging gate, stopped by the wall.

Seeing, seeing only the leaves
Flying, plunge and expire

Turn your eyes to the immoderate past
Turn to the inscrutable infantry rising
Demons out of the earth—they will not last.
Stonewall, Stonewall—and the sunken fields of hemp
Shiloh, Antietam, Malvern Hill, Bull Run.

Lost in that orient of the thick and fast
You will curse the setting sun.

Cursing only the leaves crying
Like an old man in a storm

You hear the shout—the crazy hemlocks point
With troubled fingers to the silence which
Smothers you, a mummy, in time. The hound bitch
Toothless and dying, in a musty cellar
Hears the wind only.
Now that the salt of their blood
Stiffens the saltier oblivion of the sea,
Seals the malignant purity of the flood,
What shall we, who count our days and bow
Our heads with a commemorial woe,
In the ribboned coats of grim felicity,
What shall we say of the bones, unclean—
Their verdurous anonymity will grow—
The ragged arms, the ragged heads and eyes
Lost in these acres of the insane green?
The grey lean spiders come; they come and go;
In a tangle of willows without light
The singular screech-owl's bright
Invisible lyric seeds the mind
With the furious murmur of their chivalry.

We shall say only, the leaves
Flying, plunge and expire

We shall say only, the leaves whispering
In the improbable mist of nightfall
That flies on multiple wing:
Night is the beginning and the end,
And in between the ends of distraction
Waits mute speculation, the patient curse
That stones the eyes, or like the jaguar leaps
For his own image in a jungle pool, his victim.

What shall we say who have knowledge
Carried to the heart? Shall we take the act
To the grave? Shall we, more hopeful, set up the grave
In the house? The ravenous grave?

Leave now
The turnstile and the old stone wall:
The gentle serpent, green in the mulberry bush,
Riots with his tongue through the hush—
Sentinel of the grave who counts us all!
1926-1930

HART CRANE

NORTH LABRADOR

A land of leaning ice
Hugged by plaster-grey arches of sky,
Flings itself silently
Into eternity.

'Has no one come here to win you,
Or left you with the faintest blush
Upon your glittering breasts?
Have you no memories, O Darkly Bright?'

Cold-hushed, there is only the shifting of moments
That journeyed toward no Spring—
No birth, no death, no time nor sun
In answer.

RECITATIVE

Regard the capture here, O Janus-faced,
As double as the hands that twist this glass.
Such eyes at search or rest you cannot see;
Reciting pain or glee, how can you bear!

Twin shadowed halves: the breaking second holds
In each the skin alone, and so it is
I crust a plate of vibrant mercury
Borne cleft to you, and brother in the half.

Inquire this much-exacting fragment smile,
Its drums and darkest blowing leaves ignore,—
Defer though, revocation of the tears
That yield attendance to one crucial sign.

Look steadily—how the wind feasts and spins
The brain's disk shivered against lust. Then watch
While darkness, like an ape's face, falls away,
And gradually white buildings answer day.

Let the same nameless gulf beleaguer us—
Alike suspend us from atrocious sums
Built floor by floor on shafts of steel that grant
The plummet heart, like Absalom, no stream.

The highest tower,—let her ribs palisade
Wrenched gold of Nineveh;—yet leave the tower.
The bridge swings over salvage, beyond wharves;
A wind abides the ensign of your will . . .

In alternating bells have you not heard
All hours clapped dense into a single stride?
Forgive me for an echo of these things,
And let us walk through time with equal pride.

FOR THE MARRIAGE OF FAUSTUS AND HELEN

III

Capped arbiter of beauty in this street
That narrows darkly into motor dawn,—
You, here beside me, delicate ambassador
Of intricate slain numbers that arise
In whispers, naked of steel;
religious gunman!
Who faithfully, yourself, will fall too soon,
And in other ways than as the wind settles
On the sixteen thrifty bridges of the city:
Let us unbind our throats of fear and pity.

We even,

Who drove speediest destruction
In corymbulous formations of mechanics,—
Who hurried the hill breezes, spouting malice
Plangent over meadows, and looked down
On rifts of torn and empty houses
Like old women with teeth unjubilant
That waited faintly, briefly and in vain:

We know, eternal gunman, our flesh remembers
The tensile boughs, the nimble blue plateaus,
The mounted, yielding cities of the air!
That saddled sky that shook down vertical
Repeated play of fire—no hypogeum
Of wave or rock was good against one hour.
We did not ask for that, but have survived,
And will persist to speak again before
All stubble streets that have not curved
To memory, or known the ominous lifted arm
That lowers down the arc of Helen's brow
To saturate with blessing and dismay.

A goose, tobacco and cologne—
Three winged and gold-shod prophecies of heaven,
The lavish heart shall always have to leaven
And spread with bells and voices, and atone
The abating shadows of our conscript dust.

Anchises' navel, dripping of the sea,—
The hands Erasmus dipped in gleaming tides,
Gathered the voltage of blown blood and vine;
Delve upward for the new and scattered wine,

O brother-thief of time, that we recall.
Laugh out the meagre penance of their days
Who dare not share with us the breath released,
The substance drilled and spent beyond repair

For golden, or the shadow of gold hair.
Distinctly praise the years, whose volatile
Blamed bleeding hands extend and thresh the height
The imagination spans beyond despair,
Outpacing bargain, vocable and prayer.

CUTTY SARK

O, the navies old and oaken
O, the Temeraire no more!

MELVILLE

I met a man in South Street, tall—
a nervous shark tooth swung on his chain.
His eyes pressed through green grass
—green glasses, or bar lights made them
so—
shine—
GREEN—
eyes—
stepped out—forgot to look at you
or left you several blocks away—

in the nickel-in-the-slot piano jogged
'Stamboul Nights'—weaving somebody's nickel—
sang—

O Stamboul Rose—dreams weave the rose!

Murmurs of Leviathan he spoke,
and rum was Plato in our heads . . .

'It's S.S. *Ala*—Antwerp—now remember kid
to put me out at three she sails on time.
I'm not much good at time any more keep
weakeyed watches sometimes snooze—' his bony hands

got to beating time . . . 'A whaler once—
I ought to keep time and get over it—I'm a
Democrat—I know what time it is—No
I don't want to know what time it is—that
damned white Arctic killed my time . . .'

O Stamboul Rose—drums weave—

'I ran a donkey engine down there on the Canal
in Panama—got tired of that—
then Yucatan selling kitchenware—beads—
have you seen Popocatepetl—birdless mouth
with ashes sifting down—?
and then the coast again . . .'

Rose of Stamboul O coral Queen—
teased remnants of the skeletons of cities—
and galleries, galleries of watergutted lava
snarling stone—green—drums—drown—

Sing!
'—that spiracle!' he shot a finger out the door . . .
'O life's a geyser—beautiful—my lungs—
No—I can't live on land—!'

I saw the frontiers gleaming of his mind;
or are there frontiers—running sands sometimes
running sands—somewhere—sands running . . .
Or they may start some white machine that sings.
Then you may laugh and dance the axletree—
steel—silver—kick the traces—and know—

ATLANTIS ROSE drums wreathe the rose,
the star floats burning in a gulf of tears
and sleep another thousand—
interminably

long since somebody's nickel—stopped—
playing—

A wind worried those wicker-neat lapels, the
swinging summer entrances to cooler hells . . .

Outside a wharf truck nearly ran him down
—he lunged up Bowery way while the dawn
was putting the Statue of Liberty out—that
torch of hers you know—

I started walking home across the Bridge . . .

. . . .

Blithe Yankee vanities, turreted sprites, winged
British repartees, skil-
ful savage sea-girls
that bloomed in the spring—Heave, weave
those bright designs the trade winds drive . . .

Sweet opium and tea, Yo-ho!
Pennies for porpoises that bank the keel!
Fins whip the breeze around Japan!

Bright skysails ticketing the Line, wink round the
Horn
to Frisco, Melbourne . . .
Pennants, parabolas—
clipper dreams indelible and ranging,
baronial white on lucky blue!

Perennial-*Cutty*-trophied-*Sark*!
Thermopylæ, Black Prince, Flying Cloud through Sunda
—scarfed of foam, their bellies veered green esplanades,
locked in wind-humors, ran their eastings down;

at Java Head freshened the nip
(*sweet opium and tea!*)
and turned and left us on the lee . . .

Buntlines tusselling (91 days, 20 hours and anchored!)
Rainbow, Leander
(last trip a tragedy)—where can you be
Nimbus? and you rivals two—

a long tack keeping—

Taeping?
Ariel?

E. E. CUMMINGS

ONE X

death is more than
certain a hundred these
sounds crowds odours it
is in a hurry
beyond that any this
taxi smile or angle we do

not sell and buy
things so necessary as
is death and unlike shirts
neckties trousers
we cannot wear it out

no sir which is why
granted who discovered
America ether the movies
may claim general importance

to me to you nothing is
what particularly
matters hence in a

little sunlight and less
moonlight ourselves against the worms

hate laugh shimmy

TWO X

16 heures
l'Etoile

the communists have fine Eyes

some are young some old none
look alike the flics rush
batter the crowd sprawls collapses
singing knocked down trampled the kicked by
flics rush (the

Flics, tidiyum, are
very tidiyum reassuringly similar,
they all have very tidiyum
mustaches, and very
tidiyum chins, and just above
their very tidiyum ears their
very tidiyum necks begin)
                                        let us add

that there are 50 (fifty) flics for every
one (1) communist and
all the flics are very organically
arranged
and their nucleus (composed
of captains in freshly-creased
-uniforms with only-just-
shined buttons
tidiyum
before and behind) has a nucleolus:

the Prefect of Police

(a dapper derbied
creature, swaggers daintily
twiddling
his tiny cane
and mazurkas about tweak-
ing his wing collar pecking at his im

-peccable cravat directing being
shooting his cuffs

saluted everywhere saluting
reviewing processions of minions
tappingpeopleontheback

'allezcirculez')

—my   he's brave . . .
the
communists pick
up themselves friends
& their hats legs &

arms brush dirt coats
smile looking hands
spit blood teeth

the Communists have (very) fine eyes
(which stroll hither and thither through the
evening in bruised narrow questioning faces)

FOUR III

here's a little mouse) and
what does he think about, i
wonder as over this
floor (quietly with

bright eyes) drifts (nobody
can tell because
Nobody knows, or why
jerks Here &, here,
gr(oo)ving the room's Silence) this like
a littlest
poem a
(with wee ears and see?

tail frisks)
                (gonE)
'mouse',
            We are not the same you and

i, since here's a little he
or is
it It
? (or was something we saw in the mirror)?

therefore we'll kiss; for maybe
what was Disappeared
into ourselves
who (look). ,startled

LAURA RIDING

THE TILLAQUILS

Dancing lamely on a lacquered plain,
Never a Tillaquil murmurs for legs.
Embrace rustles a windy wistfulness,
But feels for no hands.
Scant stir of being, yet rather they
Unfulfilled unborn than failing alive,
Escaping the public shame of history.

Once only two Tillaquils nearly a man and a woman
Violated a hopeless code with hope,
Slept a single dream seeming in time.
'Come,' he cried, coaxing her,
'Stairs stream upward not for rest at every step
But to reach the top always before Death.'
'Softly,' she whispered,
'Or two Tillaquils will wake.'

Death they passed always over and over,
Life grew always sooner and sooner.
But love like a grimace
Too real on Life's face
Smiled two terrified dreams of Tillaquils
Tremblingly down the falling flights;
Who saved themselves in waking
The waste of being something.
And danced traditionally
To nothingness and never;
With only a lost memory
Punishing this foolish pair
That nearly lived and loved
In one nightmare.

LUCRECE AND NARA

Astonished stood Lucrece and Nara,
Face flat to face, one sense and smoothness.
'Love, is this face or flesh,
Love, is this you?'
One breath drew the dear lips close and whispered,
'Nara, is there a miracle can last?'
'Lucrece, is there a simple thing can stay?'

Unnoticed as a single raindrop
Broke each dawn until
Blindness as the same day fell.
'How is the opalescence of my white hand, Nara?
Is it still pearly cool?'
'How is the faintness of my neck, Lucrece?
Is it blood shy with warmth, as always?'

Ghostly they clung and questioned
A thousand years, not yet eternal,
True to their fading,
Through their long watch defying
Time to make them whole, to part them.

A gentle clasp and fragrance played and hung
A thousand years and more
Around earth closely.
'Earth will be long enough,
Love has no elsewhere.'

And when earth ended, was devoured
One shivering midsummer
At the dissolving border,
A sound of light was felt.
'Nara, is it you, the dark?'
'Lucrece, it is you, the quiet?'

THE WIND, THE CLOCK, THE WE

The wind has at last got into the clock—
Every minute for itself.
There's no more sixty,
There's no more twelve,
It's as late as it's early.

The rain has washed out the numbers.
The trees don't care what happens.
Time has become a landscape
Of suicidal leaves and stoic branches—
Unpainted as fast as painted.
Or perhaps that's too much to say,
With the clock swimming in itself
And the minutes given leave to die.

The sea's no picture at all.
To sea, then: that's time now,
And every mortal heart's a sailor
Sworn to vengeance on the wind,
To hurl life back into the thin teeth
Out of which first it whistled,
An idiotic defiance of it knew not what
Screeching round the studying clock.

Now there's neither ticking nor blowing.
The ship has gone down with its men,
The sea with the ship, the wind with the sea.
The wind at last got into the clock,
The clock at last got into the wind,
The world at last got out of itself.
At last we can make sense, you and I,
You lone survivor on paper,
The wind's boldness and the clock's care
Become a voiceless language,
And I the story hushed in it—

Is more to say of me?
Do I say more than self-choked hesitation
Can repeat word for word after me,
The script not altered by a breath
Of perhaps meaning otherwise?

THE FLOWERING URN

And every prodigal greatness
Must creep back into strange home,
Must fill the empty matrix of
The never-begotten perfect son
Who never can be born.

And every quavering littleness
Must pale more tinily than it knows
Into the giant hush whose sound
Reverberates within itself
As tenderest numbers cannot improve.

And from this jealous secrecy
Will rise itself, will flower up
The likeness kept against false seed:
When death-whole is the seed
And no new harvest will fraction sowing.

Will rise the same peace that held
Before fertility's lie awoke
The virgin sleep of Mother All:
The same but for the way in flowering
It speaks of fruits that could not be.

NOR IS IT WRITTEN

Nor is it written that you may not grieve.
There is no rule of joy, long may you dwell
Not smiling yet in that last pain,

On that last supper of the heart's palate.
It is not written that you must take joy
In that not thus again shall you sit down
To spread that mingled banquet
Which the deep larder of illusion spilled
Like ancient riches in time grown not astonishing.
Lean to the cloth awhile, and yet awhile,
And even may your eyes caress
Proudly the used abundance.
It is not written in what heart
You may not pass from ancient plenty
Into the straitened nowadays.
To each is given secrecy of heart,
To make himself what heart he please
In stirring up from that fond table
To sit him down at this sharp meal.
It shall not here be asked of him
'What thinks your heart?'
Long may you sorely to yourself accuse
This single bread and truth,
This disenchanted understanding.
It is not counted what loud passions
Your heart in ancient private keeps alive.
To each is given what defeat he will.

AUSPICE OF JEWELS

They have connived at those jewelled fascinations
That to our hands and arms and ears
And heads and necks and feet
And all the winding stalk
Extended the mute spell of the face.

They have endowed the whole of us
With such a solemn gleaming
As in the dark of flesh-love
But the face at first did have.

We are studded with wide brilliance
As the world with towns and cities—
The travelling look builds capitals
Where the evasive eye may rest
Safe from the too immediate lodgement.

Obscure and bright these forms
Which as the women of their lingering thought
In slow translucence we have worn.
And the silent given glitter locks us
In a not false unplainness:
Have we ourselves been sure
What steady countenance to turn them?

Until now—when this passionate neglect
Of theirs, and our twinkling reluctance,
Are like the reader and the book
Whose fingers and whose pages have confided
But whose sight and sense
Meet in a chilly time of strangeness;

And it is once more early, anxious,
And so late, it is intolerably the same
Not speaking coruscation
That both we and they made endless, dream-long,
Lest be cruel to so much love
The closer shine of waking,
And what be said sound colder
Than the ghastly love-lisp.

Until now—when to go jewelled
We must despoil the drowsy masquerade
Where gloom of silk and gold
And glossy dazed adornments
Kept safe from flagrant realness
The forgeries of ourselves we were—
When to be alive as love feigned us
We must steal death and its wan splendours
From the women of their sighs we were.

For we are now otherwise luminous.
The light which was spent in jewels
Has performed upon the face
A gradual eclipse of rccognition.
We have passed from plaintivc visibility
Into total rareness,
And from this reunion of ourselves and them
Under the snuffed lantern of time
Comes an astonished flash like truth
Or the unseen-unheard entrance of someone
Whom eyes and ears in their dotage
Have forgotten for dead or lost.

(And hurrying toward distracted glory,
Gemmed lady-pageants, bells on their hearts,
By restless knights attended
Whose maudlin plumes and pommels
Urge the adventure past return.)

ROBERT GRAVES

QUAYSIDE

And glad to find, on again looking at it,
It was not nearly so good as I had thought—
You know the ship is moving when you see
The boxes on the quayside sliding away
And growing smaller—and having real delight
When the port's cleared and the coast out of sight,
And ships are few, each on its proper course,
With no occasion for approach or discourse.

O LOVE IN ME

O love, be fed with apples while you may,
And feel the sun and go in royal array,
A smiling innocent on the heavenly causeway.

Though in what listening horror for the cry
That soars in outer blackness dismally,
The dumb blind beast, the paranoiac fury,

Be warm, enjoy the season, lift your head,
Exquisite in the pulse of tainted blood,
That shivering glory not to be despised.

Take your delight in momentariness,
Walk between dark and dark, a shining space
With the grave's narrowness, though not its peace.

LOST ACRES

These acres, always again lost
  By every new Ordnance-survey

And searched for at exhausting cost
  Of time and thought, are still away.

They have their paper-substitute—
  Intercalation of an inch
At the so many thousandth foot:
  And no one parish feels the pinch.

But lost they are, despite all care,
  So perhaps likeliest to be bound
Together in a piece somewhere,
  A plot of undiscovered ground.

Invisible, they have the spite
  To swerve the tautest measuring chain
And the exact theodolite
  Perched every side of them in vain.

Yet there's no scientific need
  To plot these acres of the mind
With prehistoric fern and reed
  And monsters such as heroes find.

They have, no doubt, their flowers, their birds,
  Their trees behind the phantom fence,
But of the substance of mere words:
  To walk there would be loss of sense.

THE BARDS

Their cheeks are blotched for shame, their running verse
Stumbles, with marrow-bones the drunken diners
Pelt them as they delay:
It is a something fearful in the song
Plagues them, an unknown grief that like a churl
Goes commonplace in cowskin

And bursts unheralded, crowing and coughing,
An unpilled holly-club twirled in his hand,
Into their many-shielded, samite-curtained
Jewel-bright hall where twelve kings sit at chess
Over the white-bronze pieces and the gold,
And by a gross enchantment
Flails down the rafters and leads off the queens—
The wild-swan-breasted, the rose-ruddy-cheeked
Raven-haired daughters of their admiration—
To stir his black pots and to bed on straw.

FLYING CROOKED

The butterfly, the cabbage-white,
(His honest idiocy of flight)
Will never now, it is too late,
Master the art of flying straight,
Yet has—who knows so well as I?—
A just sense of how not to fly:
He lurches here and here by guess
And God and hope and hopelessness.
Even the aerobatic swift
Has not his flying-crooked gift.

OGRES AND PYGMIES

Those famous men of old, the Ogres—
They had long beards and stinking arm-pits.
They were wide-mouthed, long-yarded and great-bellied
Yet of not taller stature, Sirs, than you.
They lived on Ogre-Strand, which was no place
But the churl's terror of their proud extent,
Where every foot was three-and-thirty inches
And every penny bought a whole sheep.

Now of their company none survive, not one,
The times being, thank God, unfavourable
To all but nightmare memory of them.
Their images stand howling in the waste,
(The winds enforced against their wide mouths)
Whose granite haunches king and priest must yearly
Buss, and their cold knobbed knees.
So many feats they did to admiration:
With their enormous lips they sang louder
Than ten cathedral choirs, with their grand yards
Stormed the most rare and obstinate maidenheads,
With their strong-gutted and capacious bellies
Digested stones and glass like ostriches.
They dug great pits and heaped great cairns,
Deflected rivers, slew whole armies,
And hammered judgements for posterity—
For the sweet-cupid-lipped and tassel-yarded
Delicate-stomached dwellers
In Pygmy Alley, where with brooding on them
A foot is shrunk to seven inches
And twelve-pence will not buy a spare rib.
And who would choose between Ogres and Pygmies—
The thundering text, the snivelling commentary—
Reading between such covers he will likely
Prove his own disproportion and not laugh.

ON DWELLING

Courtesies of good-morning and good-evening
From rustic lips fail as the town encroaches:
Soon nothing passes but the cold quick stare
Of eyes that see ghosts, yet too many for fear.

Here I too walk, silent myself, in wonder
At a town not mine though plainly coextensive
With mine, even in days coincident:
In mine I dwell, in theirs like them I haunt.

And the green country, should I turn again there?
My bumpkin neighbours loom even ghostlier:
Like trees they murmur or like blackbirds sing
Courtesies of good-morning and good-evening.

ON PORTENTS

If strange things happen where she is,
So that men say that graves open
And the dead walk, or that futurity
Becomes a womb and the unborn are shed,
Such portents are not to be wondered at,
Being tourbillions in Time made
By the strong pulling of her bladed mind
Through that ever-reluctant element.

TO BRING THE DEAD TO LIFE

To bring the dead to life
Is no great magic.
Few are wholly dead:
Blow on a dead man's embers
And a live flame will start.

Let his forgotten griefs be now,
And now his withered hopes;
Subject your pen to his handwriting
Until it prove as natural
To sign his name as yours.

Limp as he limped,
Swear by the oaths he swore;
If he wore black, affect the same;
If he had gouty fingers,
Be yours gouty too.

Assemble tokens intimate of him—
A ring, a purse, a chair:
Around these elements then build
A home familiar to
The greedy revenant.

So grant him life, but reckon
That the grave which housed him
May not be empty now:
You in his spotted garments
Must yourself lie wrapped.

TO JUAN AT THE WINTER SOLSTICE

There is one story and one story only
That will prove worth your telling,
Whether as a learned bard or gifted child;
To it all lines or lesser gauds belong
That startle with their shining
Such common stories as they stray into.

Is it of trees you tell, their months and virtues,
Or strange beasts that beset you,
Of birds that croak at you the Triple will?
Or of the Zodiac and how slow it turns
Below the Boreal Crown,
Prison of all true kings that ever reigned?

Water to water, ark again to ark,
From woman back to woman:
So each new victim treads unfalteringly
The never altered circuit of his fate,
Bringing twelve peers as witness
Both to his starry rise and starry fall.

Or is it of the Virgin's silver beauty,
All fish below the thighs?
She in her left hand bears a leafy quince;
When with her right she crooks a finger, smiling,
How may the King hold back?
Royally then he barters life for love.

Or of the undying snake from the chaos hatched,
Whose coils contain the ocean,
Into whose chops with naked sword he springs,
Then in black water, tangled by the reeds,
Battles three days and nights,
To be spewed up beside her scalloped shore?

Much snow is falling, winds roar hollowly,
The owl hoots from the elder,
Fear in your heart cries to the loving-cup:
Sorrow to sorrow as the sparks fly upward.
The log groans and confesses:
There is one story and one story only.

Dwell on her graciousness, dwell on her smiling,
Do not forget what flowers
The great boar trampled down in ivy time.
Her brow was creamy as the crested wave,
Her sea-blue eyes were wild
But nothing promised that is not performed.

IN BROKEN IMAGES

He is quick, thinking in clear images;
I am slow, thinking in broken images.

He becomes dull, trusting to his clear images;
I become sharp, mistrusting my broken images.

Trusting his images, he assumes their relevance;
Mistrusting my images, I question their relevance.

Assuming their relevance, he assumes the fact;
Questioning their relevance, I question the fact.

When the fact fails him, he questions his senses;
When the fact fails me, I approve my senses.

He continues quick and dull in his clear images;
I continue slow and sharp in my broken images.

He in a new confusion of his understanding;
I in a new understanding of my confusion.

THE WHITE GODDESS

All saints revile her, and all sober men
Ruled by the God Apollo's golden mean—
In scorn of which we sailed to find her
In distant regions likeliest to hold her
Whom we desired above all things to know,
Sister of the mirage and echo.

It was a virtue not to stay,
To go our headstrong and heroic way
Seeking her out at the volcano's head,
Among pack ice, or where the track had faded
Beyond the cavern of the seven sleepers:
Whose broad high brow was white as any leper's,
Whose eyes were blue, with rowan-berry lips,
With hair curled honey-coloured to white hips.

Green sap of Spring in the young wood a-stir
Will celebrate the Mountain Mother,
And every song-bird shout awhile for her;
But we are gifted, even in November

Rawest of seasons, with so huge a sense
Of her nakedly worn magnificence
We forget cruelty and past betrayal,
Heedless of where the next bright bolt may fall.

EDITH SITWELL

THE KING OF CHINA'S DAUGHTER

The King of China's daughter,
She never would love me
Though I hung my cap and bells upon
Her nutmeg tree.
For oranges and lemons,
The stars in bright blue air,
(I stole them long ago, my dear)
Were dangling there.
The Moon did give me silver pence,
The Sun did give me gold,
And both together softly blew
And made my porridge cold;
But the King of China's daughter
Pretended not to see
When I hung my cap and bells upon
Her nutmeg tree.

HORNPIPE

Sailors come
To the drum
Out of Babylon;
  Hobby-horses
Foam, the dumb
Sky rhinoceros-glum

Watched the courses of the breakers' rocking-horses and
  with Glaucis,
Lady Venus on the settee of the horsehair sea!
Where Lord Tennyson in laurels wrote a gloria free

In a borealic iceberg came Victoria; she
Knew Prince Albert's tall memorial took the colours of
the floreal
And the borealic iceberg; floating on they see
New-arisen Madam Venus for whose sake from far
Came the fat and zebra'd emperor from Zanzibar
Where like golden bouquets lay far Asia, Africa, Cathay,
All laid before that shady lady by the fibroid Shah.
Captain Fracasse stout as any water-butt came, stood
With Sir Bacchus both a-drinking the black tarr'd grapes'
blood
Plucked among the tartan leafage
By the furry wind whose grief age
Could not wither—like a squirrel with a gold star-nut.
Queen Victoria sitting shocked upon the rocking-horse
Of a wave said to the Laureate, 'This minx of course
Is as sharp as any lynx and blacker-deeper than the
drinks and quite as
Hot as any hottentot, without remorse!

'For the minx,'
Said she,
'And the drinks,
You can see

Are hot as any hottentot and not the goods for me!'

WHEN SIR BEELZEBUB

When
Sir
Beelzebub called for his syllabub in the hotel in Hell

Where Proserpine first fell,

Blue as the gendarmerie were the waves of the sea,

(Rocking and shocking the bar-maid).

Nobody comes to give him his rum but the
Rim of the sky hippopotamus-glum
Enhances the chances to bless with a benison
Alfred Lord Tennyson crossing the bar laid
With cold vegetation from pale deputations
Of temperance workers (all signed In Memoriam)
Hoping with glory to trip up the Laureate's feet,

(Moving in classical metres) . . .

Like Balaclava, the lava came down from the
Roof, and the sea's blue wooden gendarmerie
Took them in charge while Beelzebub roared for his rum.
. . . None of them come!

THE BAT

Castellated, tall
From battlements fall
Shades on heroic
Lonely grass,
Where the moonlight's echoes die and pass.
Near the rustic boorish,
Fustian Moorish,
Castle wall of the ultimate Shade,
With his cloak castellated as that wall, afraid,
The mountebank doctor,
The old stage quack,
Where decoy duck dust
Began to clack,
Watched Heliogabalusene the Bat
In his furred cloak hang head down from the flat
Wall, cling to what is convenient,
Lenient.
'If you hang upside down with squeaking shrill,
You will see dust, lust, and the will to kill,

And life is a matter of which way falls
Your tufted turreted Shade near these walls.
For muttering guttering shadow will plan
If you're ruined wall, or pygmy man,'
Said Heliogabalusene, 'or a pig,
Or the empty Cæsar in tall periwig.'
And the mountebank doctor,
The old stage quack,
Spread out a black membraned wing of his cloak
And his shuffling footsteps seem to choke,
Near the Castle wall of the ultimate Shade
Where decoy duck dust
Quacks, clacks, afraid.

RICHARD EBERHART

THE GROUNDHOG

In June, amid the golden fields,
I saw a groundhog lying dead.
Dead lay he; my senses shook,
And mind outshot our naked frailty.
There lowly in the vigorous summer
His form began its senseless change,
And made my senses waver dim
Seeing nature ferocious in him.
Inspecting close his maggot's might
And seething cauldron of his being,
Half with loathing, half with a strange love,
I poked him with an angry stick.
The fever arose, became a frame
And Vigour circumscribed the skies,
Immense energy in the sun,
And through my frame a sunless trembling.
My stick had done nor good nor harm.
Then stood I silent in the day
Watching the object, as before;
And kept my reverence for knowledge
Trying for control, to be still,
To quell the passion of the blood;
Until I had bent down on my knees
Praying for joy in the sight of decay.
And so I left; and I returned
In Autumn strict of eye, to see
The sap gone out of the groundhog,
But the bony sodden hulk remained.
But the year had lost its meaning,
And in intellectual chains
I lost both love and loathing,
Mured up in the wall of wisdom.

Another summer took the fields again
Massive and burning, full of life,
But when I chanced upon the spot
There was only a little hair left,
And bones bleaching in the sunlight
Beautiful as architecture;
I watched them like a geometer,
And cut a walking stick from a birch.
It has been three years, now.
There is no sign of the groundhog.
I stood there in the whirling summer,
My hand capped a withered heart,
And thought of China and of Greece,
Of Alexander in his tent;
Of Montaigne in his tower,
Of Saint Theresa in her wild lament.

THE FURY OF AERIAL BOMBARDMENT

You would think the fury of aerial bombardment
Would rouse God to relent; the infinite spaces
Are still silent. He looks on shock-pried faces.
History, even, does not know what is meant.

You would feel that after so many centuries
God would give man to repent; yet he can kill
As Cain could, but with multitudinous will,
No farther advanced than in his ancient furies.

Was man made stupid to see his own stupidity?
Is God by definition indifferent, beyond us all?
Is the eternal truth man's fighting soul
Wherein the Beast ravens in its own avidity?

Of Van Wettering I speak, and Averill,
Names on a list, whose faces I do not recall
But they are gone to early death, who late in school
Distinguished the belt feed lever from the belt holding pawl.

WILLIAM EMPSOM

INVITATION TO JUNO

Lucretius could not credit centaurs;
Such bicycle he deemed asynchronous.
'Man superannuates the horse;
Horse pulses will not gear with ours.'

Johnson could see no bicycle would go;
'You bear yourself, and the machine as well.'
Gennets for germans sprang not from Othello,
And Ixion rides upon a single wheel.

Courage. Weren't strips of heart culture seen
Of late mating two periodicities?
Could not Professor Charles Darwin
Graft annual upon perennial trees?

CAMPING OUT

And now she cleans her teeth into the lake:
Gives it (God's grace) for her own bounty's sake
What morning's pale and the crisp mist debars:
Its glass of the divine (that Will could break)
Restores, beyond Nature: or lets Heaven take
(Itself being dimmed) her pattern, who half awake
Milks between rocks a straddled sky of stars.

Soap tension the star pattern magnifies.
Smoothly Madonna through-assumes the skies
Whose vaults are opened to achieve the Lord.
No, it is we soaring explore galaxies,
Our bullet boat light's speed by thousands flies.
Who moves so among stars their frame unties;
See where they blur, and die, and are outsoared.

LEGAL FICTION

Law makes long spokes of the short stakes of men.
Your well fenced out real estate of mind
No high flat of the nomad citizen
Looks over, or train leaves behind.

Your rights extend under and above your claim
Without bound; you own land in Heaven and Hell;
Your part of earth's surface and mass the same,
Of all cosmos' volume, and all stars as well.

Your rights reach down where all owners meet, in Hell's
Pointed exclusive conclave, at earth's centre
(Your spun farm's root still on that axis dwells);
And up, through galaxies, a growing sector.

You are nomad yet; the lighthouse beam you own
Flashes, like Lucifer, through the firmament.
Earth's axis varies; your dark central cone
Wavers, a candle's shadow, at the end.

THIS LAST PAIN

This last pain for the damned the Fathers found:
'They knew the bliss with which they were not crowned.'
  Such, but on earth, let me foretell,
  Is all, of heaven or of hell.

Man, as the prying housemaid of the soul,
May know her happiness by eye to hole:
  He's safe; the key is lost; he knows
  Door will not open, nor hole close.

'What is conceivable can happen too,'
Said Wittgenstein, who had not dreamt of you;
  But wisely; if we worked it long
  We should forget where it was wrong:

Those thorns are crowns which, woven into knots,
Crackle under and soon boil fools' pots;
  And no man's watching, wise and long,
  Would ever stare them into song.

Thorns burn to a consistent ash, like man;
A splendid cleanser for the frying-pan:
  And those who leap from pan to fire
  Should this brave opposite admire.

All those large dreams by which men long live well
Are magic-lanterned on the smoke of hell;
  This then is real, I have implied,
  A painted, small, transparent slide.

These the inventive can hand-paint at leisure,
Or most emporia would stock our measure;
  And feasting in their dappled shade
  We should forget how they were made.

Feign then what's by a decent tact believed
And act that state is only so conceived,
  And build an edifice of form
  For house where phantoms may keep warm.

Imagine, then, by miracle, with me,
(Ambiguous gifts, as what gods give must be)
  What could not possibly be there,
  And learn a style from a despair.

HOMAGE TO THE BRITISH MUSEUM

There is a supreme God in the ethnological section;
A hollow toad shape, faced with a blank shield.
He needs his belly to include the Pantheon,
Which is inserted through a hole behind.

At the navel, at the points formally stressed, at the organs
of sense,
Lice glue themselves, dolls, local deities,
His smooth wood creeps with all the creeds of the world.

Attending there let us absorb the cultures of nations
And dissolve into our judgement all their codes.
Then, being clogged with a natural hesitation
(People are continually asking one the way out),
Let us stand here and admit that we have no road.
Being everything, let us admit that is to be something,
Or give ourselves the benefit of the doubt;
Let us offer our pinch of dust all to this God,
And grant his reign over the entire building.

NOTE ON LOCAL FLORA

There is a tree native in Turkestan,
Or further east towards the Tree of Heaven,
Whose hard cold cones, not being wards to time,
Will leave their mother only for good cause;
Will ripen only in a forest fire;
Wait, to be fathered as was Bacchus once,
Through men's long lives, that image of time's end.
I knew the Phœnix was a vegetable.
So Semele desired her deity
As this in Kew thirsts for the Red Dawn.

MISSING DATES

Slowly the poison the whole blood stream fills.
It is not the effort nor the failure tires.
The waste remains, the waste remains and kills.

It is not your system or clear sight that mills
Down small to the consequence a life requires;
Slowly the poison the whole blood stream fills.

They bled an old dog dry yet the exchange rills
Of young dog blood gave but a month's desires;
The waste remains, the waste remains and kills.

It is the Chinese tombs and the slag hills
Usurp the soil, and not the soil retires.
Slowly the poison the whole blood stream fills.

Not to have fire is to be a skin that shrills.
The complete fire is death. From partial fires
The waste remains, the waste remains and kills.

It is the poems you have lost, the ills
From missing dates, at which the heart expires.
Slowly the poison the whole blood stream fills.
The waste remains, the waste remains and kills.

C. DAY LEWIS

'AS ONE WHO WANDERS INTO OLD WORKINGS'

As one who wanders into old workings
Dazed by the noonday, desiring coolness,
Has found retreat barred by fall of rockface;
Gropes through galleries where granite bruises
Taut palm and panic patters close at heel;
Must move forward as tide to the moon's nod,
As mouth to breast in blindness is beckoned.
Nightmare nags at his elbow and narrows
Horizon to pinpoint, hope to hand's breadth.
Slow drip the seconds, time is stalactite,
For nothing intrudes here to tell the time,
Sun marches not, nor moon with muffled step.
He wants an opening,—only to break out,
To see the dark glass cut by day's diamond,
To relax again in the lap of light.

But we seek a new world through old workings,
Whose hope lies like seed in the loins of earth,
Whose dawn draws gold from the roots of darkness.
Not shy of light nor shrinking from shadow
Like Jesuits in jungle we journey
Deliberately bearing to brutish tribes
Christ's assurance, arts of agriculture.
As a train that travels underground track
Feels current flashed from far-off dynamos,
Our whirling with impetus elsewhere
Generated we run, are ruled by rails.
Train shall spring from tunnel to terminus,
Out on to plain shall the pioneer plunge,
Earth reveal what veins fed, what hill covered.
Lovely the leap, explosion into light.

'YOU THAT LOVE ENGLAND'

You that love England, who have an ear for her music,
The slow movement of clouds in benediction,
Clear arias of light thrilling over her uplands,
Over the chords of summer sustained peacefully;
Ceaseless the leaves' counterpoint in a west wind lively,
Blossom and river rippling loveliest allegro,
And the storms of wood strings brass at year's finale:
Listen. Can you not hear the entrance of a new theme?

You who go out alone, on tandem or on pillion,
Down arterial roads riding in April,
Or sad beside lakes where hill-slopes are reflected
Making fires of leaves, your high hopes fallen:
Cyclists and hikers in company, day excursionists,
Refugees from cursed towns and devastated areas;
Know you seek a new world, a saviour to establish
Long-lost kinship and restore the blood's fulfilment.

You who like peace, good sticks, happy in a small way
Watching birds or playing cricket with schoolboys,
Who pay for drinks all round, whom disaster chose not;
Yet passing derelict mills and barns roof-rent
Where despair has burnt itself out—hearts at a standstill,
Who suffer loss, aware of lowered vitality;
We can tell you a secret, offer a tonic; only
Submit to the visiting angel, the strange new healer.

You above all who have come to the far end, victims
Of a run-down machine, who can bear it no longer;
Whether in easy chairs chafing at impotence
Or against hunger, bullies and spies preserving
The nerve for action, the spark of indignation—
Need fight in the dark no more, you know your enemies.
You shall be leaders when zero hour is signalled,
Wielders of power and welders of a new world.

'SUPPOSE THAT WE'

Suppose that we, to-morrow or the next day,
Came to an end—in storm the shafting broken,
Or a mistaken signal, the flange lifting—
Would that be premature, a text for sorrow?

Say what endurance gives or death denies us.
Love's proved in its creation, not eternity:
Like leaf or linnet the true heart's affection
Is born, dies later, asks no reassurance.

Over dark wood rises one dawn felicitous,
Bright through awakened shadows fall her crystal
Cadenzas, and once for all the wood is quickened.
So our joys visit us, and it suffices.

Nor fear we now to live who in the valley
Of the shadow of life have found a causeway;
For love restores the nerve and love is under
Our feet resilient. Shall we be weary?

Some say we walk out of Time altogether
This way into a region where the primrose
Shows an immortal dew, sun at meridian
Stands up for ever and in scent the lime tree.

This is a land which later we may tell of.
Here-now we know, what death cannot diminish
Needs no replenishing; yet certain are, though
Dying were well enough, to live is better.

Passion has grown full man by his first birthday.
Running across the bean-fields in a south wind,
Fording the river mouth to feel the tide-race—
Child's play that was, though proof of our possessions.

Now our research is done, measured the shadow,
The plains mapped out, the hills a natural bound'ry.
Such and such is our country. There remains to
Plough up the meadowland, reclaim the marshes.

THE CONFLICT

I sang as one
Who on a tilting deck sings
To keep their courage up, though the wave hangs
That shall cut off their sun.

As storm-cocks sing,
Flinging their natural answer in the wind's teeth,
And care not if it is waste of breath
Or birth-carol of spring.

As ocean-flyer clings
To height, to the last drop of spirit driving on
While yet ahead is land to be won
And work for wings.

Singing I was at peace,
Above the clouds, outside the ring:
For sorrow finds a swift release in song
And pride its poise.

Yet living here,
As one between two massing powers I live
Whom neutrality cannot save
Nor occupation cheer.

None such shall be left alive:
The innocent wing is soon shot down,
And private stars fade in the blood-red dawn
Where two worlds strive.

The red advance of life
Contracts pride, calls out the common blood,
Beats song into a single blade,
Makes a depth-charge of grief.

Move then with new desires,
For where we used to build and love
Is no man's land, and only ghosts can live
Between two fires.

A TIME TO DANCE

For those who had the power
  of the forest fires that burn
Leaving their source in ashes
  to flush the sky with fire:
Those whom a famous urn
  could not contain, whose passion
Brimmed over the deep grave
  and dazzled epitaphs:
For all that have won us wings
  to clear the tops of grief,
My friend who within me laughs
  bids you dance and sing.

Some set out to explore
  earth's limit, and little they recked if
Never their feet came near it
  outgrowing the need for glory:
Some aimed at a small objective
  but the fierce updraught of their spirit
Forced them to the stars.
  Are honoured in public who built
The dam that tamed a river;
  or holding the salient for hours
Against odds, cut off and killed,
  are remembered by one survivor.

All these. But most for those
  whom accident made great,
As a radiant chance encounter
  of cloud and sunlight grows
Immortal on the heart:
  whose gift was the sudden bounty
Of a passing moment, enriches
  the fulfilled eye for ever.
Their spirits float serene
  above time's roughest reaches,
But their seed is in us and over
  our lives they are evergreen.

MAPLE AND SUMACH

Maple and sumach down this autumn ride—
Look, in what scarlet character they speak!
For this their russet and rejoicing week
Trees spend a year of sunsets on their pride.
You leaves drenched with the lifeblood of the year—
What flamingo dawns have wavered from the east,
What eves have crimsoned to their toppling crest
To give the fame and transience that you wear!
Leaf-low he shall lie soon: but no such blaze
Briefly can cheer man's ashen, harsh decline;
His fall is short of pride, he bleeds within
And paler creeps to the dead end of his days.
O light's abandon and the fire-crest sky
Speak in me now for all who are to die!

IN THE HEART OF CONTEMPLATION

In the heart of contemplation—
Admiring, say, the frost-flowers of the white lilac,
Or lark's song busily sifting like sand-crystals
Through the pleased hourglass an afternoon of summer,

Or your beauty, dearer to me than these—
Discreetly a whisper in the ear,
The glance of one passing my window recall me
From lark, lilac, you, grown suddenly strangers.

In the plump and pastoral valley
Of a leisure time, among the trees like seabirds
Asleep on a glass calm, one shadow moves—
The sly reminder of the forgotten appointment.
All the shining pleasures, born to be innocent,
Grow dark with a truant's guilt:
The day's high heart falls flat, the oaks tremble,
And the shadow sliding over your face divides us.

In the act of decision only,
In the hearts cleared for action like lovers naked
For love, this shadow vanishes: there alone
There is nothing between our lives for it to thrive on.
You and I with lilac, lark and oak-leafed
Valley are bound together
As in the astounded clarity before death.
Nothing is innocent now but to act for life's sake.

THE SITTING

(*for Laurence Gowing*)

So like a god I sit here,
One of those stone dreamers quarried from solitude,
A genius—if ever there was one—of the place:
The mountain's only child, lips aloof as a snow line,
Forearms impassive along the cloud-base of aeons,
Eyes heavy on distance—
Graven eyes that flinch not, flash not, if eagles
Clap their wings in my face.

With hieratic gestures
He the suppliant, priest, interpreter, subtly
Wooing my virtue, officiates by the throne.
I know the curious hands are shaping, reshaping the
image
Of what is only an image of things impalpable.
I feel how the eyes strain
To catch a truth behind the oracular presence—
Eyes that augur through stone.

And the god asks, 'What have I for you
But the lichenous shadow of thought veiling my temple,
The runnels a million time-drops have chased on my
cheek?'
And the man replies, 'I will show you the creed of your
bone, I'll draw you
The shape of solitude to which you were born.'
And the god cries, 'I am meek,
Brushed by an eagle's wing; and a voice bids me
Speak. But I cannot speak.'

The god thinks, Let him project, if
He must, his passionate shapings on my stone heart,
Wrestle over my body with his sprite,
Through these blind eyes imagine a skin-deep world in
perspective:
Let him make, if he will, the crypt of my holy mountain
His own: let even the light
That bathes my temple become as it were an active
Property of his sight.

O man, O innocent artist
Who paint me with green of your fields, with amber or
yellow
Of love's hair, red of the heart's blood, eyebright blue,
Conjuring forms and rainbows out of an empty mist—

Your hand is upon me, as even now you follow
Up the immortal clue
Threading my veins of emerald, topaz, amethyst,
And know not it ends in you.

ALL GONE

The sea drained off, my poverty's uncovered—
Sand, sand, a rusted anchor, broken glass,
The listless sediment of sparkling days
When through a paradise of weed joy wavered.

The sea rolled up like a blind, oh pitiless light
Revealing, shrivelling all! Lacklustre weeds
My hours, my truth a salt-lick. Love recedes
From rippled flesh bared without appetite.

A stranded time, neap and annihilation
Of spirit. Gasping on the inglorious rock,
I pray the sea return, even though its calm
Be treachery, its virtue a delusion.

Put forth upon my sands, whether to mock,
Revive or drown, a liberating arm!

W. H. AUDEN

PROLOGUE

O love, the interest itself in thoughtless Heaven
Make simpler daily the beating of man's heart; within
There in the ring where name and image meet

Inspire them with such a longing as will make his thought
Alive like patterns a murmuration of starlings
Rising in joy over wolds unwittingly weave;

Here too on our little reef display your power,
This fortress perched on the edge of the Atlantic scarp
The mole between all Europe and the exile-crowded sea;

And make us as Newton was who in his garden watching
The apple falling towards England became aware
Between himself and her of an eternal tie.

For now that dream which so long has contented our will,
I mean, of uniting the dead into a splendid empire,
Under whose fertilising flood the Lancashire moss

Sprouted up chimneys and Glamorgan hid a life
Grim as a tidal rock-pool's in its glove-shaped valleys,
Is already retreating into her maternal shadow;

Leaving the furnaces gasping in the impossible air
The flotsam at which Dumbarton gapes and hungers,
While upon wind-loved Rowley no hammer shakes

The cluster of mounds like a midget golf course, graves
Of some who created these intelligible dangerous marvels;
Affectionate people, but crude their sense of glory.

Far-sighted as falcons, they looked down another future.
For the seed in their loins were hostile, though afraid of
their pride,
And tall with a shadow now, inertly wait

In bar, in netted chicken-farm, in lighthouse,
Standing on these impoverished constricting acres,
The ladies and gentlemen apart, too much alone.

Consider the years of the measured world begun,
The barren spiritual marriage of stone and water.
Yet, O, at this very moment of our hopeless sigh

When inland they are thinking their thoughts but are
watching these islands
As children in Chester look to Moel Fammau to decide
On picnics by the clearness or withdrawal of her treeless
crown,

Some dream, say yes, long coiled in the ammonite's
slumber
Is uncurling, prepared to lay on our talk and kindness
Its military silence, its surgeon's idea of pain.

And called out of tideless peace by a living sun
As when Merlin, tamer of horses, and his lords to whom
Stonehenge was still a thought, the Pillars passed

And into the undared ocean swung north their prow,
Drives through the night and star-concealing dawn
For the virgin roadsteads of our hearts an unwavering
keel.

'WATCH ANY DAY'

Watch any day his nonchalant pauses, see
His dextrous handling of a wrap as he
Steps after into cars, the beggar's envy.

'There is a free one' many say, but err.
He is not that returning conqueror,
Nor ever the poles' circumnavigator.

But poised between shocking falls on razor-edge
Has taught himself this balancing subterfuge
Of the accosting profile, the erect carriage.

The song, the varied action of the blood
Would drown the warning from the iron wood
Would cancel the inertia of the buried:

Travelling by daylight on from house to house
The longest way to the intrinsic peace,
With love's fidelity and with love's weakness.

'TALLER TO-DAY, WE REMEMBER'

Taller to-day, we remember similar evenings,
Walking together in the windless orchard
Where the brook runs over the gravel, far from the
    glacier.

Again in the room with the sofa hiding the grate,
Look down to the river when the rain is over,
See him turn to the window, hearing our last
Of Captain Ferguson.

It is seen how excellent hands have turned to
    commonness.
One staring too long, went blind in a tower,
One sold all his manors to fight, broke through, and
    faltered.

Nights come bringing the snow, and the dead howl
Under the headlands in their windy dwelling
Because the Adversary put too easy questions
On lonely roads.

But happy now, though no nearer each other,
We see the farms lighted all along the valley;
Down at the mill-shed the hammering stops
And men go home.

Noises at dawn will bring
Freedom for some, but not this peace
No bird can contradict: passing, but is sufficient now
For something fulfilled this hour, loved or endured.

'CONSIDER THIS AND IN OUR TIME'

Consider this and in our time
As the hawk sees it or the helmeted airman:
The clouds rift suddenly—look there
At cigarette-end smouldering on a border
At the first garden party of the year.
Pass on, admire the view of the massif
Through plate-glass windows of the Sport Hotel;
Join there the insufficient units
Dangerous, easy, in furs, in uniform
And constellated at reserved tables
Supplied with feelings by an efficient band
Relayed elsewhere to farmers and their dogs
Sitting in kitchens in the stormy fens.

Long ago, supreme Antagonist,
More powerful than the great northern whale
Ancient and sorry at life's limiting defect,
In Cornwall, Mendip, or the Pennine moor
Your comments on the highborn mining captains,
Found they no answer, made them wish to die
—Lie since in barrows out of harm.
You talk to your admirers every day
By silted harbours, derelict works,

In strangled orchards, and the silent comb
Where dogs have worried or a bird was shot.
Order the ill that they attack at once:
Visit the ports and, interrupting
The leisurely conversation in the bar
Within a stone's throw of the sunlit water,
Beckon your chosen out. Summon
Those handsome and diseased youngsters, those women
Your solitary agents in the country parishes;
And mobilize the powerful forces latent
In soils that make the farmer brutal
In the infected sinus, and the eyes of stoats.
Then, ready, start your rumour, soft
But horrifying in its capacity to disgust
Which, spreading magnified, shall come to be
A polar peril, a prodigious alarm,
Scattering the people, as torn-up paper
Rags and utensils in a sudden gust,
Seized with immeasurable neurotic dread.

Financier, leaving your little room
Where the money is made but not spent,
You'll need your typist and your boy no more;
The game is up for you and for the others,
Who, thinking, pace in slippers on the lawns
Of College Quad or Cathedral Close,
Who are born nurses, who live in shorts
Sleeping with people and playing fives.
Seekers after happiness, all who follow
The convolutions of your simple wish,
It is later than you think; nearer that day
Far other than that distant afternoon
Amid rustle of frocks and stamping feet
They gave the prizes to the ruined boys.
You cannot be away, then, no
Not though you pack to leave within an hour,
Escaping humming down arterial roads:
The date was yours; the prey to fugues,

Irregular breathing and alternate ascendancies
After some haunted migratory years
To disintegrate on an instant in the explosion of mania
Or lapse for ever into a classic fatigue.

'SIR, NO MAN'S ENEMY'

Sir, no man's enemy, forgiving all
But will his negative inversion, be prodigal:
Send to us power and light, a sovereign touch
Curing the intolerable neural itch,
The exhaustion of weaning, the liar's quinsy,
And the distortions of ingrown virginity.
Prohibit sharply the rehearsed response
And gradually correct the coward's stance;
Cover in time with beams those in retreat
That, spotted, they turn though the reverse were great;
Publish each healer that in city lives
Or country houses at the end of drives;
Harrow the house of the dead; look shining at
New styles of architecture, a change of heart.

'OUR HUNTING FATHERS'

Our hunting fathers told the story
  Of the sadness of the creatures,
Pitied the limits and the lack
  Set in their finished features;
Saw in the lion's intolerant look,
Behind the quarry's dying glare
Love raging for the personal glory
  That reason's gift would add,
The liberal appetite and power,
  The rightness of a god.

Who nurtured in that fine tradition
  Predicted the result,
Guessed Love by nature suited to
  The intricate ways of guilt;
That human company could so
His southern gestures modify
And make it his mature ambition
  To think no thought but ours,
To hunger, work illegally,
  And be anonymous?

A BRIDE IN THE '30'S

(For Madame Mangeot)

Easily, my dear, you move, easily your head
And easily as through leaves of a photograph album I'm
    led
Through the night's delights and the day's impressions
Past the tall tenements and the trees in the wood
Though sombre the sixteen skies of Europe
        And the Danube flood.

Looking and loving our behaviours pass
The stones the steels and the polished glass;
Lucky to love the new pansy railway
The sterile farms where his looks are fed,
And in the policed unlucky city
        Lucky his bed.

He from these lands of terrifying mottoes
Makes worlds as innocent as Beatrix Potter's;
Through bankrupt countries where they mend the roads
Along the endless plains his will is
Intent as a collector to pursue
        His greens and lilies.

Easy for him to find in your face
The pool of silence and the tower of grace
To conjure a camera into a wishing rose
Simple to excite in the air from a glance
The horses, the fountains, the sidedrum, the trombone
And the dance, the dance.

Summoned by such a music from our time
Such images to audience come
As vanity cannot dispel nor bless:
Hunger and love in their variations
Grouped invalids watching the flight of the birds
And single assassins.

Ten thousand of the desperate marching by
Five feet, six feet, seven feet high:
Hitler and Mussolini in their wooing poses
Churchill acknowledging the voter's greeting
Roosevelt at the microphone, Van Lubbe laughing
And our first meeting.

But love except at our proposal
Will do no trick at his disposal;
Without opinions of his own performs
The programme that we think of merit,
And through our private stuff must work
His public spirit.

Certain it became while we were still incomplete
There were certain prizes for which we would never
compete;
A choice was killed by every childish illness,
The boiling tears among the hothouse plants,
The rigid promise fractured in the garden,
And the long aunts.

And every day there bolted from the field
Desires to which we could not yield;
Fewer and clearer grew the plans,

Schemes for a life and sketches for a hatred,
And early among my interesting scrawls
Appeared your portrait.

You stand now before me, flesh and bone
These ghosts would like to make their own.
Are they your choices? O, be deaf
To hatred proffering immediate pleasure
Glory to swap her fascinating rubbish
For your one treasure.

Be deaf too standing uncertain now,
A pine tree shadow across your brow,
To what I hear and wish I did not,
The voice of love saying lightly, brightly
'Be Lubbe, Be Hitler, but be my good
Daily, nightly'.

The power which corrupts, that power to excess
Thc beautiful quite naturally possess:
To them the fathers and the children turn
And all who long for their destruction
The arrogant and self-insulted wait
The looked instruction.

Shall idleness ring then your eyes like the pest?
O will you unnoticed and mildly like the rest,
Will you join the lost in their sneering circles,
Forfeit the beautiful interest and fall
Where the engaging face is the face of the betrayer
And the pang is all?

Wind shakes the tree; the mountains darken:
And the heart repeats though we would not hearken;
'Yours the choice to whom the gods awarded
The language of learning and the language of love
Crooked to move as a moneybug or a cancer
Or straight as a dove'.

EPILOGUE FROM 'THE ORATORS'

'O where are you going?' said reader to rider,
'That valley is fatal when furnaces burn,
Yonder's the midden whose odours will madden,
That gap is the grave where the tall return.'

'O do you imagine', said fearer to farer,
'That dusk will delay on your path to the pass,
Your diligent looking discover the lacking
Your footsteps feel from granite to grass?'

'O what was that bird', said horror to hearer,
'Did you see that shape in the twisted trees?
Behind you swiftly the figure comes softly,
The spot on your skin is a shocking disease?'

'Out of this house'—said rider to reader
'Yours never will'—said farer to fearer
'They're looking for you'—said hearer to horror
As he left them there, as he left them there.

IN MEMORY OF W. B. YEATS

(*d.* Jan. 1939)

I

He disappeared in the dead of winter:
The brooks were frozen, the airports almost deserted,
And snow disfigured the public statues;
The mercury sank in the mouth of the dying day.
O all the instruments agree
The day of his death was a dark cold day.

Far from his illness
The wolves ran on through the evergreen forests,
The peasant river was untempted by the fashionable
quays;
By mourning tongues
The death of the poet was kept from his poems.

But for him it was his last afternoon as himself,
An afternoon of nurses and rumors;
The provinces of his body revolted,
The squares of his mind were empty,
Silence invaded the suburbs,
The current of his feeling failed: he became his admirers.

Now he is scattered among a hundred cities
And wholly given over to unfamiliar affections;
To find his happiness in another kind of wood
And be punished under a foreign code of conscience.
The words of a dead man
Are modified in the guts of the living.

But in the importance and noise of tomorrow
When the brokers are roaring like beasts on the floor of
the Bourse,
And the poor have the sufferings to which they are fairly
accustomed,
And each in his cell of himself is almost convinced of his
freedom;
A few thousand will think of this day
As one thinks of a day when one did something slightly
unusual.
O all the instruments agree
The day of his death was a dark cold day.

2

You were silly like us: your gift survived it all;
The parish of rich women, physical decay,
Yourself; mad Ireland hurt you into poetry.

Now Ireland has her madness and her weather still,
For poetry makes nothing happen: it survives
In the valley of its saying where executives
Would never want to tamper; it flows south
From ranches of isolation and the busy griefs,
Raw towns that we believe and die in; it survives,
A way of happening, a mouth.

3

Earth, receive an honored guest;
William Yeats is laid to rest:
Let the Irish vessel lie
Emptied of its poetry.

Time that is intolerant
Of the brave and innocent,
And indifferent in a week
To a beautiful physique,

Worships language and forgives
Everyone by whom it lives;
Pardons cowardice, conceit,
Lays its honors at their feet.

Time that with this strange excuse
Pardoned Kipling and his views,
And will pardon Paul Claudel,
Pardons him for writing well.

In the nightmare of the dark
All the dogs of Europe bark,
And the living nations wait,
Each sequestered in its hate;

Intellectual disgrace
Stares from every human face,
And the seas of pity lie
Locked and frozen in each eye.

Follow, poet, follow right
To the bottom of the night,
With your unconstraining voice
Still persuade us to rejoice;

With the farming of a verse
Make a vineyard of the curse,
Sing of human unsuccess
In a rapture of distress;

In the deserts of the heart
Let the healing fountain start,
In the prison of his days
Teach the free man how to praise.

IN PRAISE OF LIMESTONE

If it form the one landscape that we the inconstant ones
  Are consistently homesick for, this is chiefly
Because it dissolves in water. Mark these rounded slopes
  With their surface fragrance of thyme and beneath
A secret system of caves and conduits; hear these springs
  That spurt out everywhere with a chuckle
Each filling a private pool for its fish and carving
  Its own little ravine whose cliffs entertain
The butterfly and the lizard; examine this region
  Of short distances and definite places:
What could be more like Mother or a fitter background
  For her son, for the nude young male who lounges
Against a rock displaying his dildo, never doubting
  That for all his faults he is loved, whose works are but
Extensions of his power to charm? From his weathered
    outcrop
  To hill-top temple, from appearing waters to
Conspicuous fountains, from a wild to a formal vineyard,
  Are ingenious but short steps that a child's wish

To receive more attention than his brothers, whether
By pleasing or teasing, can easily take.

Watch, then, the band of rivals as they climb up and down
Their steep stone gennels in twos and threes, sometimes
Arm in arm, but never, thank God, in step; or engaged
On the shady side of a square at midday in
Voluble discourse, knowing each other too well to think
There are any important secrets, unable
To conceive a god whose temper-tantrums are moral
And not to be pacified by a clever line
Or a good lay: for, accustomed to a stone that responds,
They have never had to veil their faces in awe
Of a crater whose blazing fury could not be fixed;
Adjusted to the local needs of valleys
Where everything can be touched or reached by walking,
Their eyes have never looked into infinite space
Through the lattice-work of a nomad's comb; born lucky,
Their legs have never encountered the fungi
And insects of the jungle, the monstrous forms and lives
With which we have nothing, we like to hope, in common.
So, when one of them goes to the bad, the way his mind works
Remains comprehensible: to become a pimp
Or deal in fake jewelry or ruin a fine tenor voice
For effects that bring down the house could happen to all
But the best and the worst of us . . .
That is why, I suppose,
The best and worst never stayed here long but sought
Immoderate soils where the beauty was not so external,
The light less public and the meaning of life
Something more than a mad camp. 'Come!' cried the granite wastes,
'How evasive is your humor, how accidental

Your kindest kiss, how permanent is death.' (Saints-to-be
Slipped away sighing.) 'Come!' purred the clays and gravels.
'On our plains there is room for armies to drill; rivers
Wait to be tamed and slaves to construct you a tomb
In the grand manner: soft as the earth is mankind and both
Need to be altered.' (Intendant Caesars rose and
Left, slamming the door.) But the really reckless were fetched
By an older colder voice, the oceanic whisper:
'I am the solitude that asks and promises nothing;
That is how I shall set you free. There is no love;
There are only the various envies, all of them sad.'
They were right, my dear, all those voices were right
And still are; this land is not the sweet home that it looks,
Nor its peace the historical calm of a site
Where something was settled once and for all: A backward
And dilapidated province, connected
To the big busy world by a tunnel, with a certain
Seedy appeal, is that all it is now? Not quite:
It has a worldly duty which in spite of itself
It does not neglect, but calls into question
All the Great Powers assume; it disturbs our rights. The poet,
Admired for his earnest habit of calling
The sun the sun, his mind Puzzle, is made uneasy
By these solid statues which so obviously doubt
His antimythological myth; and these gamins,
Pursuing the scientist down the tiled colonnade
With such lively offers, rebuke his concern for Nature's
Remotest aspects: I, too, am reproached, for what
And how much you know. Not to lose time, not to get caught,
Not to be left behind, not, please! to resemble
The beasts who repeat themselves, or a thing like water
Or stone whose conduct can be predicted, these

Are our Common Prayer, whose greatest comfort is music
   Which can be made anywhere, is invisible,
And does not smell. In so far as we have to look forward
   To death as a fact, nor doubt we are right: But if
Sins can be forgiven, if bodies rise from the dead,
   These modifications of matter into
Innocent athletes and gesticulating fountains,
   Made solely for pleasure, make a further point:
The blessed will not care what angle they are regarded
      from,
   Having nothing to hide. Dear, I know nothing of
Either, but when I try to imagine a faultless love
   Or the life to come, what I hear is the murmur
Of underground streams, what I see is a limestone
      landscape.

LOUIS MACNEICE

AN ECLOGUE FOR CHRISTMAS

A. I meet you in an evil time.

B. The evil bells
Put out of our heads, I think, the thought of everything else.

A. The jaded calendar revolves,
Its nuts need oil, carbon chokes the valves,
The excess sugar of a diabetic culture
Rotting the nerve of life and literature;
Therefore when we bring out the old tinsel and frills
To announce that Christ is born among the barbarous hills
I turn to you whom a morose routine
Saves from the mad vertigo of being what has been.

B. Analogue of me, you are wrong to turn to me,
My country will not yield you any sanctuary,
There is no pinpoint in any of the ordnance maps
To save you when your towns and town-bred thoughts collapse,
It is better to die *in situ* as I shall,
One place is as bad as another. Go back where your instincts call
And listen to the crying of the town-cats and the taxis again,
Or wind your gramophone and eavesdrop on great men.

A. Jazz-weary of years of drums and Hawaiian guitar,
Pivoting on the parquet I seem to have moved far
From bombs and mud and gas, have stuttered on my feet

Clinched to the streamlined and butter-smooth
trulls of the élite,
The lights irritating and gyrating and rotating in
gauze—
Pomade-dazzle, a slick beauty of gewgaws—
I who was Harlequin in the childhood of the century,
Posed by Picasso beside an endless opaque sea,
Have seen myself sifted and splintered in broken
facets,
Tentative pencillings, endless liabilities, no assets,
Abstractions scalpelled with a palette-knife
Without reference to this particular life,
And so it has gone on; I have not been allowed to be
Myself in flesh or face, but abstracting and dissecting
me
They have made of me pure form, a symbol or a
pastiche,
Stylised profile, anything but soul and flesh:
And that is why I turn this jaded music on
To forswear thought and become an automaton.

B. There are in the country also of whom I am afraid—
Men who put beer into a belly that is dead,
Women in the forties with terrier and setter who
whistle and swank
Over down and plough and Roman road and daisied
bank,
Half-conscious that these barriers over which they
stride
Are nothing to the barbed wire that has grown round
their pride.

A. And two there are, as I drive in the city, who
suddenly perturb—
The one sirening me to draw up by the kerb
The other, as I lean back, my right leg stretched
creating speed,
Making me catch and stamp, the brakes shrieking,
pull up dead:

She wears silk stockings taunting the winter wind,
He carries a white stick to mark that he is blind.

B. In the country they are still hunting, in the heavy shires
Greyness is on the fields and sunset like a line of pyres
Of barbarous heroes smoulders through the ancient air
Hazed with factory dust and, orange opposite, the moon's glare,
Goggling yokel-stubborn through the iron trees,
Jeers at the end of us, our bland ancestral ease;
We shall go down like palaeolithic man
Before some new Ice Age or Genghiz Khan.

A. It is time for some new coinage, people have got so old,
Hacked and handled and shiny from pocketing they have made bold
To think that each is himself through these accidents, being blind
To the fact that they are merely the counters of an unknown Mind.

B. A Mind that does not think, if such a thing can be,
Mechanical Reason, capricious Identity.
That I could be able to face this domination nor flinch—

A. The tin toys of the hawker move on the pavement inch by inch
Not knowing that they are wound up; it is better to be so
Than to be, like us, wound up and while running down to know—

B. But everywhere the pretence of individuality recurs—

A. Old faces frosted with powder and choked in furs.

B. The jutlipped farmer gazing over the humpbacked
wall.

A. The commercial traveller joking in the urinal.

B. I think things draw to an end, the soil is stale.

A. And over-elaboration will nothing now avail,
The street is up again, gas, electricity or drains,
Ever-changing conveniences, nothing comfortable
remains
Un-improved, as flagging Rome improved villa and
sewer
(A sound-proof library and a stable temperature).
Our street is up, red lights sullenly mark
The long trench of pipes, iron guts in the dark,
And not till the Goths again come swarming down the
hill
Will cease the clangour of the electric drill.
But yet there is beauty narcotic and deciduous
In this vast organism grown out of us:
On all the traffic islands stand white globes like
moons,
The city's haze is clouded amber that purrs and
croons,
And tilting by the noble curve bus after tall bus
comes
With an osculation of yellow light, with a glory like
chrysanthemums.

B. The country gentry cannot change, they will die in
their shoes
From angry circumstance and moral self-abuse,
Dying with a paltry fizzle they will prove their lives
to be
An ever-diluted drug, a spiritual tautology.

They cannot live once their idols are turned out,
None of them can endure, for how could they,
possibly, without
The flotsam of private property, pekingese and
polyanthus,
The good things which in the end turn to poison
and pus,
Without the bandy chairs and the sugar in the silver
tongs
And the inter-ripple and resonance of years of
dinner-gongs?
Or if they could find no more that cumulative proof
In the rain dripping off the conservatory roof?
What will happen when the only sanction the
country-dweller has—

A. What will happen to us, planked and panelled with
jazz?
Who go to the theatre where a black man dances like
an eel,
Where pink thighs flash like the spokes of a wheel,
where we feel
That we know in advance all the jogtrot and the cake-
walk jokes,
All the bumfun and the gags of the comedians in
boaters and toques,
All the tricks of the virtuosos who invert the usual—

B. What will happen to us when the State takes down
the manor wall,
When there is no more private shooting or fishing,
when the trees are all cut down,
When faces are all dials and cannot smile or frown—

A. What will happen when the sniggering machine-guns
in the hands of the young men
Are trained on every flat and club and beauty parlour
and Father's den?

What will happen when our civilisation like a long
pent balloon—

B. What will happen will happen; the whore and the
buffoon
Will come off best; no dreamers, they cannot lose
their dream
And are at least likely to be reinstated in the new
régime.
But one thing is not likely—

A. Do not gloat over yourself
Do not be your own vulture, high on some mountain
shelf
Huddle the pitiless abstractions bald about the neck
Who will descend when you crumple in the plains a
wreck.
Over the randy of the theatre and cinema I hear songs
Unlike anything—

B. The lady of the house poises the silver tongs
And picks a lump of sugar, 'ne plus ultra' she says
'I cannot do otherwise, even to prolong my days'—

A. I cannot do otherwise either, tonight I will book
my seat—

B. I will walk about the farm-yard which is replete
As with the smell of dung so with memories—

A. I will gorge myself to satiety with the oddities
Of every artiste, official or amateur,
Who has pleased me in my rôle of hero-worshipper
Who has pleased me in my rôle of individual man—

B. Let us lie once more, say 'What we think, we can'
The old idealist lie—

A. And for me before I die
Let me go the round of the garish glare—

B. And on the bare and high
Places of England, the Wiltshire Downs and the
Long Mynd
Let the balls of my feet bounce on the turf, my face
burn in the wind
My eyelashes stinging in the wind, and the sheep like
grey stones
Humble my human pretensions—

A. Let the saxophones and the xylophones
And the cult of every technical excellence, the miles of
canvas in the galleries
And the canvas of the rich man's yacht snapping and
tacking on the seas
And the perfection of a grilled steak—

B. Let all these so ephemeral things
Be somehow permanent like the swallow's tangent
wings:
Goodbye to you, this day remember is Christmas,
this morn
They say, interpret it your own way, Christ is born.

PERSEUS

Borrowed wings on his ankles,
Carrying a stone death,
The hero entered the hall,
All in the hall looked up,
Their breath frozen on them,
And there was no more shuffle or clatter in the hall at all.

So a friend of a man comes in
And leaves a book he is lending or flowers
And goes again, alive but as good as dead,
And you are left alive, no better than dead,
And you dare not turn the leaden pages of the book or
touch the flowers, the hooded and arrested hours.

Shut your eyes,
There are suns beneath your lids,
Or look in the looking-glass in the end room—
You will find it full of eyes,
The ancient smiles of men cut out with scissors and kept
in mirrors.

Ever to meet me comes, in sun or dull,
The gay hero swinging the Gorgon's head
And I am left, with the dull drumming of the sun,
suspended and dead,
Or the dumb grey-brown of the day is a leper's cloth,
And one feels the earth going round and round the globe
of the blackening mantle, a mad moth.

SNOW

The room was suddenly rich and the great bay-window
was
Spawning snow and pink roses against it
Soundlessly collateral and incompatible:
World is suddener than we fancy it.

World is crazier and more of it than we think,
Incorrigibly plural. I peel and portion
A tangerine and spit the pips and feel
The drunkenness of things being various.

And the fire flames with a bubbling sound for world
Is more spiteful and gay than one supposes—
On the tongue on the eyes on the ears in the palms of
    one's hands—
There is more than glass between the snow and the huge
    roses.

CONVERSATION

Ordinary people are peculiar too:
Watch the vagrant in their eyes
Who sneaks away while they are talking with you
Into some black wood behind the skull,
Following un-, or other, realities,
Fishing for shadows in a pool.

But sometimes the vagrant comes the other way
Out of their eyes and into yours
Having mistaken you perhaps for yesterday
Or for tomorrow night, a wood in which
He may pick up among the pine-needles and burrs
The lost purse, the dropped stitch.

Vagrancy however is forbidden; ordinary men
Soon come back to normal, look you straight
In the eyes as if to say 'It will not happen again',
Put up a barrage of common sense to baulk
Intimacy but by mistake interpolate
Swear-words like roses in their talk.

THE TRUISMS

His father gave him a box of truisms
Shaped like a coffin, then his father died;
The truisms remained on the mantelpiece
As wooden as the playbox they had been packed in
Or that other his father skulked inside.

Then he left home, left the truisms behind him
Still on the mantelpiece, met love, met war,
Sordor, disappointment, defeat, betrayal,
Till through disbeliefs he arrived at a house
He could not remember seeing before.

And he walked straight in; it was where he had come from
And something told him the way to behave.
He raised his hand and blessed his home;
The truisms flew and perched on his shoulders
And a tall tree sprouted from his father's grave.

STEPHEN SPENDER

THE PRISONERS

Far far the least of all, in want,
Are these,
The prisoners
Turned massive with their vaults and dark with dark.

They raise no hands, which rest upon their knees,
But lean their solid eyes against the night,
Dimly they feel
Only the furniture they use in cells.

Their Time is almost Death. The silted flow
Of years on years
Is marked by dawns
As faint as cracks on mud-flats of despair.

My pity moves amongst them like a breeze
On walls of stone
Fretting for summer leaves, or like a tune
On ears of stone.

Then, when I raise my hands to strike,
It is too late,
There are no chains that fall
Nor visionary liquid door
Melted with anger.

When have their lives been free from walls and dark
And airs that choke?
And where less prisoner to let my anger
Like a sun strike?

If I could follow them from room to womb
To plant some hope
Through the black silk of the big-bellied gown
There would I win.

No, no, no,
It is too late for anger,
Nothing prevails
But pity for the grief they cannot feel.

'IN RAILWAY HALLS'

In railway halls, on pavements near the traffic,
They beg, their eyes made big by empty staring
And only measuring Time, like the blank clock.

No, I shall weave no tracery of pen-ornament
To make them birds upon my singing-tree:
Time merely drives these lives which do not live
As tides push rotten stuff along the shore.

—There is no consolation, no, none
In the curving beauty of that line
Traced on our graphs through history, where the
 oppressor
Starves and deprives the poor.

Paint here no draped despairs, no saddening clouds
Where the soul rests, proclaims eternity.
But let the wrong cry out as raw as wounds
This Time forgets and never heals, far less transcends.

'NOT PALACES, AN ERA'S CROWN'

Not palaces, an era's crown
Where the mind dwells, intrigues, rests;
The architectural gold-leaved flower
From people ordered like a single mind,
I build. This only what I tell:
It is too late for rare accumulation
For family pride, for beauty's filtered dusts;
I say, stamping the words with emphasis,
Drink from here energy and only energy,
As from the electric charge of a battery,
To will this Time's change.
Eye, gazelle, delicate wanderer,
Drinker of horizon's fluid line;
Ear that suspends on a chord
The spirit drinking timelessness;
Touch, love, all senses;
Leave your gardens, your singing feasts,
Your dreams of suns circling before our sun,
Of heaven after our world.
Instead, watch images of flashing brass
That strike the outward sense, the polished will
Flag of our purpose which the wind engraves.
No spirit seek here rest. But this: No man
Shall hunger: Man shall spend equally.
Our goal which we compel: Man shall be man.

That programme of the antique Satan
Bristling with guns on the indented page
With battleship towering from hilly waves:
For what? Drive of a ruining purpose
Destroying all but its age-long exploiters.
Our programme like this, yet opposite,
Death to the killers, bringing light to life.

'AFTER THEY HAVE TIRED'

After they have tired of the brilliance of cities
And of striving for office where at last they may languish
Hung round with easy chains until
Death and Jerusalem glorify also the crossing-sweeper:
Then those streets the rich built and their easy love
Fade like old cloths, and it is death stalks through life
Grinning white through all faces
Clean and equal like the shine from snow.

In this time when grief pours freezing over us,
When the hard light of pain gleams at every street
corner,
When those who were pillars of that day's gold roof
Shrink in their clothes; surely from hunger
We may strike fire, like fire from flint?
And our strength is now the strength of our bones
Clean and equal like the shine from snow
And the strength of famine and of our enforced idleness,
And it is the strength of our love for each other.

Readers of this strange language,
We have come at last to a country
Where light equal, like the shine from snow, strikes all
faces,
Here you may wonder
How it was that works, money, interest, building, could
ever hide
The palpable and obvious love of man for man.

Oh comrades, let not those who follow after
—The beautiful generation that shall spring from our
sides—
Let not them wonder how after the failure of banks
The failure of cathedrals and the declared insanity of our
rulers,

We lacked the Spring-like resources of the tiger
Or of plants who strike out new roots to gushing waters.
But through torn-down portions of old fabric let their
 eyes
Watch the admiring dawn explode like a shell
Around us, dazing us with light like snow.

THE NORTH

Our single purpose was to walk through snow
With faces swung to their prodigious North
Like compass iron. As clerks in whited Banks
With bird-claw pens column virgin paper
To snow we added footprints.
Extensive whiteness drowned
All sense of space. We tramped through
Static, glaring days, Time's suspended blank.
That was in Spring and Autumn. Then Summer struck
Water over rocks, and half the world
Became a ship with a deep keel, the booming floes
And icebergs with their little birds.
Twittering Snow Bunting, Greenland Wheatear
Red throated Divers; imagine butterflies
Sulphurous cloudy yellow; glory of bees
That suck from saxifrage; crowberry,
Bilberry, cranberry, *Pyrola uniflora*.
There followed winter in a frozen hut
Warm enough at the kernel, but dare to sleep
With head against the wall—ice gummed my hair.
Hate Culver's loud breathing, despise Freeman's
Fidget for washing; love only the dogs
That whine for scraps and scratch. Notice
How they run better (on short journeys) with a bitch.
In that, different from us.

Return, return, you warn. We do. There is
A network of railways, money, words, words, words.

Meals, papers, exchanges, debates,
Cinema, wireless; the worst is Marriage.
We cannot sleep. At night we watch
A speaking clearness through cloudy paranoia.
These questions are white rifts. Was
Ice our anger transformed? The raw, the motionless
Skies, were these the spirit's hunger?
The continual and hypnotized march through snow
The dropping nights of precious extinction, were these
Only the wide invention of the will,
The frozen will's evasion? If this exists
In us as madness here, as coldness
In these summer, civilized sheets: is the North
Over there, a tangible real madness
A glittering simpleton, one without towns
Only with bears and fish, a staring eye,
A new and singular sex?

AN ELEMENTARY SCHOOL CLASSROOM

Far far from gusty waves, these children's faces
Like rootless weeds the torn hair round their paleness;
The tall girl with her weighed-down head; the paper-
seeming boy with rat's eyes; the stunted unlucky heir
Of twisted bones, reciting a father's gnarled disease,
His lesson from his desk. At back of the dim class
One unnoted, mild and young: his eyes live in a dream
Of squirrel's game, in tree room, other than this.

On sour cream walls, donations; Shakespeare's head
Cloudless at dawn, civilized dome riding all cities;
Belled, flowery, Tyrolese valley; open-handed map
Awarding the explicit world, of every name but here.
To few, too few, these are real windows: world and
    words and waving

Leaves, to heal. For these young lives, guilty and
dangerous
Is fantasy of travel. Surely, Shakespeare is wicked

To lives that wryly turn, under the structural Lie,
Toward smiles or hate? Amongst their heap, these
children
Wear skins peeped through by bones, and spectacles of
steel
With mended glass, like bottle bits in slag.
Tyrol is wicked; map's promising a fable:
All of their time and space are foggy slum,
So blot their maps with slums as big as doom.

Unless, dowager, governor, these pictures, in a room
Columned above childishness, like our day's future drift
Of smoke concealing war, are voices shouting
O that beauty has words and works which break
Through coloured walls and towers. The children stand
As in a climbing mountain train. This lesson illustrates
The world green in their many valleys beneath:
The total summer heavy with their flowers.

ICE

(*To M——*)

She came in from the snowing air
Where icicle-hung architecture
Strung white fleece round the Baroque square.
I saw her face freeze in her fur,
Then my lips ran to her with fire
From the chimney corner of the room,
Where I had waited in my chair.
I kissed their heat against her skin
And watched the red make the white bloom,

While, at my care, her smiling eyes
Shone with the brilliance of the ice
Outside, whose dazzling they brought in.
That day, until this, I forgot.
How is it now I so remember
Who, when she came indoors, saw not
The passion of her white December?

CHARLES MADGE

BLOCKING THE PASS

With an effort Grant swung the great block,
The swivel operated and five or six men
Crouched under the lee of the straight rock.

They waited in silence, or counting ten,
They thrust their fingers in their wet hair,
The steel sweated in their hands. And then

The clouds hurried across a sky quite bare,
The sounds of the station, three miles off, ceased,
The dusty birds hopped keeping watch. And there

Arose to what seemed as high as the sky at least,
Arose a giant and began to die,
Arose such a shape as the night in the East.

The stones sobbed, the trees gave a cry,
A tremulous wonder shook animal and plant,
And a decapitating anger stirred the sky

And alone, on a tall stone, stood Grant.

FORTUNE

The natural silence of a tree,
The motion of a mast upon the fresh-tossing sea,
Now foam-inclined, now to the sun with dignity,

Or the stone brow of a mountain
Regarded from a town, or the curvet-fountain,
Or one street-stopped in wonder at the fountain,

Or a great cloud entering the room of the sky,
Napoleon of his century,
Heard come to knowing music consciously,

Such, not us, reflect and have their day,
We are but vapour of today
Unless love's chance fall on us and call us away

As the wind takes what it can
And blowing on the fortunate face, reveals the man.

LOSS

Like the dark germs across the filter clean
So in the clear day of a thousand years
This dusty cloud is creeping to our eyes,

Here, as we grow, and are as we have been
Or living give for life some morning tears
The flowering hour bent and unconscious lies.

As in Vienna now, the wounded walls
Silently speak, as deep in Austria
The battered shape of man is without shade

So, time in metaphor, tomorrow falls
On Europe, Asia and America,
And houses vanish, even as they were made,

For yesterday is always sad, its nature
Darker than love would wish in every feature.

SOLAR CREATION

The sun, of whose terrain we creatures are,
Is the director of all human love,
Unit of time, and circle round the earth,

And we are the commotion born of love
And slanted rays of that illustrious star,
Peregrine of the crowded fields of birth,

The crowded lane, the market and the tower.
Like sight in pictures, real at remove,
Such is our motion on dimensional earth.

Down by the river, where the ragged are,
Continuous the cries and noise of birth,
While to the muddy edge dark fishes move,

And over all, like death, or sloping hill,
Is nature, which is larger and more still.

AT WAR

Fire rides calmly in the air
That blows across the fields of water
That laps the papped curve of the outspread earth.

Earth is bone and builds the house
Water the blood that softly runs inside
Air is the breath by which the fire is fed.

Earth's mouth is open and will suck you down
Water climbs over earth to reach you
The assassin air is at your throat
And fire will presently split the air.

IN CONJUNCTION

Now in the circulating torrent of the stars
Certain events are drawn correct and clear
That wear expressions of anguish and delight

Signs unmistakeable of the heavenly progress
The flying planet leaves the night-house
The twined figures fill the highest hemisphere

From which we conclude peace, and grateful offerings
While the bird of war, thunderless on leaden roof
No shadow shows on the galactic brilliance of the
 streaming breast

And beyond the fated, tragic, foursquare, immovable
 house
Evenings under the trees of calm, descending evenings
 of rest
Relenting over battlefields, evenings upholding us
Among alarms, rust and the dead, waiting to be blest.

LUSTY JUVENTUS

The sea is an acre of dull glass, the land is a table
My eyes jump down from the table and go running
 down as far as they are able
While one is still young and still able to employ
Nerves muscles sinews eyes mouth teeth head
A giant that threw a stone at Cærodunum
Transforming England into a salty pancake
Lichen-alive governed in gametosporous colonies
Crescented with calciform corollæ, a great stone marsh
With the dragons of dead Hercules debating
There is no end there is no end to the labours of Hercules
While one is still young and still able to employ
Feet fist eyes in the head a spade a spanner
Down down we go down the emblematic abyss
Adorned with the kisses of the gentry, come out on
 primrose day
To greet the Young Bolshevik Bolus rolling up with
 banners

Across the passes of snake and ladder country
Idly I flung down pieces, but the fit is ended
When one was wery young and able to employ
The empty salads of English advent and the formulæ of
seajoy.

A MONUMENT

All moves within the visual frame
All walks upon the ground or stands
Casting a shadow,

All grass, day's eye, the folded man
Suffer or wither up in stone
And stare there.

They call upon the end of the world
And the last waters overwhelming
To wash the unborn things

Bedded on time's distracted coast
Bald stones and smiling silences,
Severed, they shrink.

The hovering certainty of death
Unites the water and the sky,
Their small choice

Of evils on the watching shore.

GEORGE BARKER

SUMMER IDYLL

Sometimes in summer months, the gestate earth
Loaded to gold, the boughs arching downward
Burdened, the shallow and glucose streams
Teeming, flowers out, all gold camouflage
Of the collusive summer; but under the streams
Winter lies coldly, and coldly embedded in
The corn hunger lies germinally, want under
The abundance, poverty pulling down
The tautened boughs, and need is the seed.

Robe them in superb summer, at angles
Their bones penetrate, or with a principality
Of Spring possess them, under the breast
Space of a vacancy spreads like a foul
Ghost flower, want; and the pressure upon
The eyeballs of their spirits, upon the organs
Of their spare bodies, the pressure upon
Their movement and their merriment, loving and
Living, the pressure upon their lives like deep
Seas, becomes insufferable, to be suffered.

Sometimes the summer lessens a moment the pressure.
Large as the summer rose some rise
Bathing in rivers or at evening harrying rabbits,
Indulging in games in meadows—and some are idle,
strewn
Over the parks like soiled paper like summer
Insects, bathed in sweat or at evening harried
By watchmen, park-keepers, policemen—indulge in games
Dreaming as I dream of rest and cleanliness and cash.

And the gardens exhibit the regalia of the season
Like debutante queans, between which they wander

Blown with vague odours, seduced by the pure
Beauty, like drowned men floating in bright coral.
Summer, denuding young women, also denudes
Them, removes jackets, exposing backs—
Summer moves many up the river in boats

Trailing their fingers in the shadowed water; they
Too move by the river, and in the water shadows
Trail a hand, which need not find a bank,
Face downward like bad fruit. Cathedrals and Building
Societies, as they appear, disappear; and Beethoven
Is played more loudly to deafen the Welsh echoes,
And Summer, blowing over the Mediterranean
Like swans, like perfect swans.

TO MY MOTHER

Most near, most dear, most loved and most far,
Under the window where I often found her
Sitting as huge as Asia, seismic with laughter,
Gin and chicken helpless in her Irish hand,
Irresistible as Rabelais, but most tender for
The lame dogs and hurt birds that surround her,—
She is a procession no one can follow after
But be like a little dog following a brass band.

She will not glance up at the bomber, or condescend
To drop her gin and scuttle to a cellar,
But lean on the mahogany table like a mountain
Whom only faith can move, and so I send
O all my faith, and all my love to tell her
That she will move from mourning into morning.

GALWAY BAY

With the gulls' hysteria above me
I walked near these breakneck seas
This morning of mists, and saw them,

Tall the mysterious queens
Waltzing in on the broad
Ballroom of the Atlantic.

All veils and waterfalls and
Wailings of the distraught,
These effigies of grief moved
Like refugees over the water;
The icy empresses of the Atlantic
Rising to bring me omen.

These women woven of ocean
And sorrows, these far sea figures,
With the fish and skull in their
Vapour of faces, the icicles
Salting down from their eyelashes,
As I walked by the foreshore

Moved towards me, ululating:
O dragnet of the sweet heart
Bind us no longer! The cage
Bursts with passions and bones,
And every highspirited fish
Lives off our scuttled love!

I stood on a stone, the gulls
Crossed my vision with wings
And my hearing with caterwauling;
The hurdling wave, backbroken,
Died at my feet. Taller
Than the towering hour above me

The homing empresses of the sea
Came among me. And, shivering,
I felt death nuzzling in the nest
Of the diurnally shipwrecked
Drowned nocturnally breast.

SONNET OF FISHES

Bright drips the morning from its trophied nets
Looped along a sky flickering fish and wing,
Cobbles like salmon crowd up waterfalling
Streets where life dies thrashing as the sea forgets,
True widow, what she has lost; and, ravished, lets
The knuckledustered sun shake bullying
A fist of glory over her. Every thing,
Even the sly night, gives up its lunar secrets.

And I with pilchards cold in my pocket make
Red-eyed a way to bed. But in my blood
Crying I hear, still, the leap of the silver diver
Caught in four cords after his fatal strake:
And then, the immense imminence not understood,
Death, in a dark, in a deep, in a dream, for ever.

ELEGY IV

I

Evolving under the architrave of their love
The lovers, intertwining like doves on a doorknocker,
Sometimes have joined. And, meeting above,
Like the springing swords at a military wedding,
The kiss is consummation. From an ark of isolation
The beasts of love emerge in pairs and bring
Hymenaeals here. Antitheses meet and look deep
Into each other's eyes at Love's dictation.
And on their happy bed in a summer evening
The Lovers answer Lucretius in their sleep.

II

But who at the kiss, who has not seen, over
The waterfalling hair at the shoulder of Life,

Death from his own face staring out of a glass?
Some shall be most alone with a lover, never
Letting the sweating hand unlock that closet of
The coffined I. O sometimes, nevertheless,
The labourer at his instrument or tractor,
Bending into a state of merge with objects,
Finds the same love that, from a machine of sex,
Steps down as Venus to her invoker.

III

Labouring, the lover shall become that Apollo
Who in a Spanish square stared at a dog
Till it gave up the ghost and ran off empty.
Not alone then, the poet shall know temporary
Wedding with all things: in divine divorce less
Suffer the alienations of that loneliness
When, for an instant, awakened in the dark,
The marital poem, with bouquet and catalogue,
Tenders her gifts on his bed of the oligarch.
He shall be joined for an hour with a dog.

IV

Thanatos, thanatos! The labourer, dropping his lever,
Hides a black letter close to his heart and goes,
Thanatos, thanatos, home for the day and for ever.
Crying, from the conch of Venus the emergent Eros
Breaks free, bursts from the heart of the lover,
And, at last liberated from the individual,
The solitary confinement of an evil lease,
Returns to the perfect. Azrael, Azrael,
Enters with papers of pardon releasing
The idiot poet from a biological cell.

EPISTLE I

Meeting a monster of mourning wherever I go
Who crosses me at morning and evening also,

For whom are you miserable I ask and he murmurs
I am miserable for innumerable man: for him
Who wanders through Woolworth's gazing at tin stars;
I mourn the maternal future tense, Time's mother,
Who has him in her lap, and I mourn also her,
Time whose dial face flashes with scars.

I gave the ghost my money and he smiled and said,
Keep it for the eyeballs of the dead instead.
Why here, I asked, why is it here you come
Breaking into the evening line going to another,
Edging your axe between my pencil fingers,
Twisting my word from a comedy to a crime?
I am the face once seen never forgotten,
Whose human look your dirty page will smother.

I know what it was, he said, that you were beginning;
The rigmarole of private life's belongings.
Birth, boyhood, and the adolescent baloney. So I say
Good go ahead, and see what happens then.
I promise you horror shall stand in your shoes,
And when your register of youth is through
What will it be but about the horror of man?
Try telling about birth and observe the issue.

Epping forest where the deer and girls
Mope like lost ones looking for Love's gaols—
Among the dilapidated glades my mother wandered
With me as a kid, and sadly we saw
The deer in the rain near the trees, the leaf-hidden shit,
The Sunday papers, and the foliage's falling world;
I not knowing nothing was our possession,
Not knowing Poverty my position.

Epping Forest glutted with the green tree
Grew up again like a sweet wood inside me.
I had the deer browsing on my heart,
This was my mother; and I had the dirt.

Inside was well with the green well of love,
Outside privation, poverty, all dearth.
Thus like the pearl I came from hurt,
Like the prize pig I came from love.

Now I know what was wanting in my youth,
It was not water or a loving mouth.
It was what makes the apple-tree grow big,
The mountain fail, and the minnow die.
It was hard cash I needed at my root.
I now know that how I grew was due
To echoing guts and the empty bag—
My song was out of tune for a few notes.

Oh, my ghost cried, the charming chimes of coincidence!
I was born also there where distress collects the rents.
Guttersnipe gutless, I was planted in your guts there,
The tear of time my sperm. I rose from
The woe-womb of the want-raped mine,
Empty hunger cracked with stomach's thunder.
Remember the rags that flattered your frame
Froze hard and formed this flesh my rind.

So close over the chapter of my birth,
Blessed by distress, baptized by dearth.
How I swung myself from the tree's bough
Demonstrating death in my gay play:
How the germ of the sperm of this ghost like a worm
I caught from the cold comfort of never enough.
How by being miserable for myself I began,
And now am miserable for the mass of man.

DYLAN THOMAS

'THE FORCE THAT THROUGH THE GREEN FUSE DRIVES THE FLOWER'

The force that through the green fuse drives the flower
Drives my green age; that blasts the roots of trees
Is my destroyer.
And I am dumb to tell the crooked rose
My youth is bent by the same wintry fever.

The force that drives the water through the rocks
Drives my red blood; that dries the mouthing streams
Turns mine to wax.
And I am dumb to mouth unto my veins
How at the mountain spring the same mouth sucks.

The hand that whirls the water in the pool
Stirs the quicksand; that ropes the blowing wind
Hauls my shroud sail.
And I am dumb to tell the hanging man
How of my clay is made the hangman's lime.

The lips of time leech to the fountain head;
Love drips and gathers, but the fallen blood
Shall calm her sores.
And I am dumb to tell a weather's wind
How time has ticked a heaven round the stars.

And I am dumb to tell the lover's tomb
How at my sheet goes the same crooked worm.

'LIGHT BREAKS WHERE NO SUN SHINES'

Light breaks where no sun shines;
Where no sea runs, the waters of the heart
Push in their tides;

And, broken ghosts with glowworms in their heads,
The things of light
File through the flesh where no flesh decks the bones.

A candle in the thighs
Warms youth and seed and burns the seeds of age;
Where no seed stirs,
The fruit of man unwrinkles in the stars,
Bright as a fig;
Where no wax is, the candle shows its hairs.

Dawn breaks behind the eyes;
From poles of skull and toe the windy blood
Slides like a sea;
Nor fenced, nor staked, the gushers of the sky
Spout to the rod
Divining in a smile the oil of tears.

Night in the sockets rounds,
Like some pitch moon, the limit of the globes;
Day lights the bone;
Where no cold is, the skinning gales unpin
The winter's robes;
The film of spring is hanging from the lids.

Light breaks on secret lots,
On tips of thought where thoughts smell in the rain;
When logics die,
The secret of the soil grows through the eye,
And blood jumps in the sun;
Above the waste allotments the dawn halts.

AFTER THE FUNERAL

(*In memory of Ann Jones*)

After the funeral, mule praises, brays,
Windshake of sailshaped ears, muffle-toed tap
Tap happily of one peg in the thick

Grave's foot, blinds down the lids, the teeth in black,
The spittled eyes, the salt ponds in the sleeves,
Morning smack of the spade that wakes up sleep,
Shakes a desolate boy who slits his throat
In the dark of the coffin and sheds dry leaves,
That breaks one bone to light with a judgement clout,
After the feast of tear-stuffed time and thistles
In a room with a stuffed fox and a stale fern,
I stand, for this memorial's sake, alone
In the snivelling hours with dead, humped Ann
Whose hooded, fountain heart once fell in puddles
Round the parched worlds of Wales and drowned each
sun
(Though this for her is a monstrous image blindly
Magnified out of praise; her death was a still drop;
She would not have me sinking in the holy
Flood of her heart's fame; she would lie dumb and deep
And need no druid of her broken body).
But I, Ann's bard on a raised hearth, call all
The seas to service that her wood-tongued virtue
Babble like a bellbuoy over the hymning heads,
Bow down the walls of the ferned and foxy woods
That her love sing and swing through a brown chapel,
Bless her bent spirit with four, crossing birds.
Her flesh was meek as milk, but this skyward statue
With the wild breast and blessed and giant skull
Is carved from her in a room with a wet window
In a fiercely mourning house in a crooked year.
I know her scrubbed and sour humble hands
Lie with religion in their cramp, her threadbare
Whisper in a damp word, her wits drilled hollow,
Her fist of a face died clenched on a round pain;
And sculptured Ann is seventy years of stone.
These cloud-sopped, marble hands, this monumental
Argument of the hewn voice, gesture and psalm,
Storm me forever over her grave until
The stuffed lung of the fox twitch and cry Love
And the strutting fern lay seeds on the black sill.

A REFUSAL TO MOURN THE DEATH, BY FIRE, OF A CHILD IN LONDON

Never until the mankind making
Bird beast and flower
Fathering and all humbling darkness
Tells with silence the last light breaking
And the still hour
Is come of the sea tumbling in harness

And I must enter again the round
Zion of the water bead
And the synagogue of the ear of corn
Shall I let pray the shadow of a sound
Or sow my salt seed
In the least valley of sackcloth to mourn

The majesty and burning of the child's death.
I shall not murder
The mankind of her going with a grave truth
Nor blaspheme down the stations of the breath
With any further
Elegy of innocence and youth.

Deep with the first dead lies London's daughter,
Robed in the long friends,
The grains beyond age, the dark veins of her mother,
Secret by the unmourning water
Of the riding Thames.
After the first death, there is no other.

POEM IN OCTOBER

It was my thirtieth year to heaven
Woke to my hearing from harbour and neighbour wood
And the mussel pooled and the heron
Priested shore

The morning beckon
With water praying and call of seagull and rook
And the knock of sailing boats on the net webbed wall
Myself to set foot
That second
In the still sleeping town and set forth.

My birthday began with the water—
Birds and the birds of the winged trees flying my name
Above the farms and the white horses
And I rose
In rainy autumn
And walked abroad in a shower of all my days.
High tide and the heron dived when I took the road
Over the border
And the gates
Of the town closed as the town awoke.

A springful of larks in a rolling
Cloud and the roadside bushes brimming with whistling
Blackbirds and the sun of October
Summery
On the hill's shoulder,
Here were fond climates and sweet singers suddenly
Come in the morning where I wandered and listened
To the rain wringing
Wind blow cold
In the wood faraway under me.

Pale rain over the dwindling harbour
And over the sea wet church the size of a snail
With its horns through mist and the castle
Brown as owls
But all the gardens
Of spring and summer were blooming in the tall tales
Beyond the border and under the lark full cloud.
There could I marvel
My birthday
Away but the weather turned around.

It turned away from the blithe country
And down the other air and the blue altered sky
Streamed again a wonder of summer
With apples
Pears and red currants
And I saw in the turning so clearly a child's
Forgotten mornings when he walked with his mother
Through the parables
Of sun light
And the legends of the green chapels

And the twice told fields of infancy
That his tears burned my cheeks and his heart moved in mine.
These were the woods the river and sea
Where a boy
In the listening
Summertime of the dead whispered the truth of his joy
To the trees and the stones and the fish in the tide.
And the mystery
Sang alive
Still in the water and singingbirds

And there could I marvel my birthday
Away but the weather turned around. And the true
Joy of the long dead child sang burning
In the sun.
It was my thirtieth
Year to heaven stood there then in the summer noon
Though the town below lay leaved with October blood.
O may my heart's truth
Still be sung
On this high hill in a year's turning.

DAVID GASCOYNE

LANDSCAPE

Across the correct perspective to the painted sky
Scores of reflected bridges merging
One into the other pass, and crowds with flags
Rush over them, and clouds like acrobats
Swing on an invisible trapeze.

The light like a sharpened pencil
Writes histories of darkness on the wall,
While walls fall inwards, septic wounds
Burst open like sewn mouths, and rain
Eternally descends through planetary space.

We ask: Whence comes this light?
Whence comes the rain, the planetary
Silences, these aqueous monograms
Of our unique and isolated selves?
Only a dusty statue lifts and drops its hand.

IN DEFENCE OF HUMANISM

To M. Salvador Dali

The face of the precipice is black with lovers;
The sun above them is a bag of nails; the spring's
First rivers hide among their hair.
Goliath plunges his hand into the poisoned well
And bows his head and feels my feet walk through his
    brain.
The children chasing butterflies turn round and see him
    there,

With his hand in the well and my body growing from his
head,
And are afraid. They drop their nets and walk into the
wall like smoke.

The smooth plain with its rivers listens to the cliff
Like a basilisk eating flowers.
And the children, lost in the shadows of the catacombs,
Call to the mirrors for help:
'Strong-bow of salt, cutlass of memory,
Write on my map the name of every river.'

A flock of banners fight their way through the telescoped
forest
And fly away like birds towards the sound of roasting
meat.
Sand falls into the boiling rivers through the telescopes'
mouths
And forms clear drops of acid with petals of whirling
flame.
Heraldic animals wade through the asphyxia of planets,
Butterflies burst from their skins and grow long tongues
like plants,
The plants play games with a suit of mail like a cloud.

Mirrors write Goliath's name upon my forehead,
While the children are killed in the smoke of the
catacombs
And lovers float down from the cliff like rain.

SUPPLEMENT

WILLIAM CARLOS WILLIAMS

PORTRAIT OF A LADY

Your thighs are appletrees
whose blossoms touch the sky.
Which sky? The sky
where Watteau hung a lady's
slipper. Your knees
are a southern breeze—or
a gust of snow. Agh! what
sort of man was Fragonard?
—as if that answered
anything. Ah, yes—below
the knees, since the tune
drops that way, it is
one of those white summer days,
the tall grass of your ankles
flickers upon the shore—
Which shore?—
the sand clings to my lips—
Which shore?
Agh, petals maybe. How
should I know?
Which shore? Which shore?
I said petals from an appletree.

TO WAKEN AN OLD LADY

Old age is
a flight of small
cheeping birds
skimming
bare trees

above a snow glaze.
Gaining and failing
they are buffeted
by a dark wind—
But what?
On harsh weedstalks
the flock has rested,
the snow
is covered with broken
seedhusks
and the wind tempered
by a shrill
piping of plenty.

THE WIDOW'S LAMENT IN SPRINGTIME

Sorrow is my own yard
where the new grass
flames as it has flamed
often before but not
with the cold fire
that closes round me this year.
Thirty-five years
I lived with my husband.
The plumtree is white today
with masses of flowers.
Masses of flowers
loaded the cherry branches
and color some bushes
yellow and some red
but the grief in my heart
is stronger than they
for though they were my joy
formerly, today I noticed them
and turned away forgetting.
Today my son told me

that in the meadows,
at the edge of the heavy woods
in the distance, he saw
trees of white flowers.
I feel that I would like
to go there
and fall into those flowers
and sink into the marsh near them.

SPRING AND ALL

By the road to the contagious hospital
under the surge of the blue
mottled clouds driven from the
northeast—a cold wind. Beyond, the
waste of broad, muddy fields
brown with dried weeds, standing and fallen

patches of standing water
the scattering of tall trees

All along the road the reddish
purplish, forked, upstanding, twiggy
stuff of bushes and small trees
with dead, brown leaves under them
leafless vines—

Lifeless in appearance, sluggish
dazed spring approaches—

They enter the new world naked,
cold, uncertain of all
save that they enter. All about them
the cold, familiar wind—

Now the grass, tomorrow
the stiff curl of wildcarrot leaf

One by one objects are defined—
It quickens: clarity, outline of leaf

But now the stark dignity of
entrance—Still, the profound change
has come upon them: rooted they
grip down and begin to awaken.

THIS IS JUST TO SAY

I have eaten
the plums
that were in
the icebox

and which
you were probably
saving
for breakfast

Forgive me
they were delicious
so sweet
and so cold

A SORT OF A SONG

Let the snake wait under
his weed
and the writing
be of words, slow and quick, sharp
to strike, quiet to wait,
sleepless.

—through metaphor to reconcile
the people and the stones.
Compose. (No ideas
but in things) Invent!
Saxifrage is my flower that splits
the rocks.

A NEGRO WOMAN

carrying a bunch of marigolds
wrapped
in an old newspaper:
She carries them upright,
bare-headed,
the bulk
of her thighs
causing her to waddle
as she walks
looking into
the store window which she passes
on her way.
What is she
but an ambassador
from another world
a world of pretty marigolds
of two shades
which she announces
not knowing what she does
other
than walk the streets
holding the flowers upright
as a torch
so early in the morning.

A UNISON

The grass is very green, my friend,
and tousled, like the head of—
your grandson, yes? And the mountain,
the mountain we climbed
twenty years since for the last
time (I write this thinking
of you) is saw-horned as then
upon the sky's edge—an old barn
is peaked there also, fatefully,
against the sky. And there it is
and we can't shift it or change
it or parse it or alter it
in any way. Listen! Do you not hear
them? the singing? There it is and
we'd better acknowledge it and
write it down that way, not otherwise.
Not twist the words to mean
what we should have said but to mean
—what cannot be escaped: the
mountain riding the afternoon as
it does, the grass matted green,
green underfoot and the air—
rotten wood. Hear! Hear them!
the Undying. The hill slopes away,
then rises in the middleground,
you remember, with a grove of gnarled
maples centering the bare pasture,
sacred, surely—for what reason?
I cannot say. Idyllic!
a shrine cinctured there by
the trees, a certainty of music!
a unison and a dance, joined
at this death's festival: Something
of a shed snake's skin, the beginning
goldenrod. Or, best, a white stone,

you have seen it: *Mathilda Maria*
Fox—and near the ground's lip,
all but undecipherable, *Aet Suae,*
Anno 9—still there, the grass
dripping of last night's rain—and
welcome! The thin air, the near,
clear brook water!—and could not,
and died, unable; to escape
what the air and the wet grass—
through which, tomorrow, bejeweled,
the great sun will rise—the
unchanging mountains, forced on them—
and they received, willingly!
Stones, stones of a difference
joining the others at pace. Hear!
Hear the unison of their voices. . . .

EDWIN MUIR

THE THREE MIRRORS

I looked in the first glass
And saw the fenceless field
And like broken stones in grass
The sad towns glint and shine.
The slowly twisting vine
Scribbled with wrath the stone,
The mountain summits were sealed
In incomprehensible wrath.
The hunting roads ran on
To round the flying hill
And bring the quarry home.
But the obstinate roots ran wrong,
The lumbering fate fell wrong,
The walls were askew with ill,
Askew went every path,
The dead lay askew in the tomb.

I looked in the second glass
And saw through the twisted scroll
In virtue undefiled
And new in eternity
Father and mother and child,
The house with its single tree,
Bed and board and cross,
And the dead asleep in the knoll.
But the little blade and leaf
By an angry law were bent
To shapes of terror and grief,
By a law the field was rent,
The crack ran over the floor,
The child at peace in his play
Changed as he passed through the door,

Changed were the house and the tree,
Changed the dead in the knoll,
For locked in love and grief
Good with evil lay.

If I looked in the third glass
I should see evil and good
Standing side by side
In the ever standing wood,
The wise king safe on his throne,
The rebel raising the rout,
And each so deeply grown
Into his own place
He'd be past desire or doubt.
If I could look I should see
The world's house open wide,
The million million rooms
And the quick god everywhere
Glowing at work and at rest,
Tranquillity in the air,
Peace of the humming looms
Weaving from east to west,
And you and myself there.

THE LABYRINTH

Since I emerged that day from the labyrinth,
Dazed with the tall and echoing passages,
The swift recoils, so many I almost feared
I'd meet myself returning at some smooth corner,
Myself or my ghost, for all there was unreal
After the straw ceased rustling and the bull
Lay dead upon the straw and I remained,
Blood-splashed, if dead or alive I could not tell
In the twilight nothingness (I might have been
A spirit seeking his body through the roads

Of intricate Hades)—ever since I came out
To the world, the still fields swift with flowers, the trees
All bright with blossom, the little green hills, the sea,
The sky and all movement under it,
Shepherds and flocks and birds and the young and old,
(I stared in wonder at the young and old,
For in the maze time had not been with me;
I had strayed, it seemed, past sun and season and change,
Past rest and motion, for I could not tell
At last if I moved or stayed; the maze itself
Revolved around me on its hidden axis
And swept me smoothly to its enemy,
The lovely world)—since I came out that day,
There have been times when I have heard my footsteps
Still echoing in the maze, and all the roads
That run through the noisy world, deceiving streets
That meet and part and meet, and rooms that open
Into each other—and never a final room—
Stairways and corridors and antechambers
That vacantly wait for some great audience,
The smooth sea-tracks that open and close again,
Tracks undiscoverable, indecipherable,
Paths on the earth and tunnels underground,
And bird-tracks in the air—all seemed a part
Of the great labyrinth. And then I'd stumble
In sudden blindness, hasten, almost run,
As if the maze itself were after me
And soon must catch me up. But taking thought,
I'd tell myself, 'You need not hurry. This
Is the firm good earth. All Roads lie free before you.'
But my bad spirit would sneer, 'No, do not hurry.
No need to hurry. Haste and delay are equal
In this one world, for there's no exit, none,
No place to come to, and you'll end where you are,
Deep in the centre of the endless maze.'
I could not live if this were not illusion.
It is a world, perhaps; but there's another.
For once in a dream or trance I saw the gods

Each sitting on the top of his mountain-isle,
While down below the little ships sailed by,
Toy multitudes swarmed in the harbours, shepherds drove
Their tiny flocks to the pastures, marriage feasts
Went on below, small birthdays and holidays,
Ploughing and harvesting and life and death,
And all permissible, all acceptable,
Clear and secure as in a limpid dream.
But they, the gods, as large and bright as clouds,
Conversed across the sounds in tranquil voices
High in the sky above the untroubled sea,
And their eternal dialogue was peace
Where all these things were woven, and this our life
Was as a chord deep in that dialogue,
As easy utterance of harmonious words,
Spontaneous syllables bodying forth a world.

That was the real world; I have touched it once,
And now shall know it always. But the lie,
The maze, the wild-wood waste of falsehood, roads
That run and run and never reach an end,
Embowered in error—I'd be prisoned there
But that my soul has birdwings to fly free.

Oh these deceits are strong almost as life.
Last night I dreamt I was in the labyrinth,
And woke far on. I did not know the place.

THE HORSES

Barely a twelvemonth after
The seven days' war that put the world to sleep,
Late in the evening the strange horses came.
By then we had made our covenant with silence,
But in the first few days it was so still

We listened to our breathing and were afraid.
On the second day
The radios failed; we turned the knobs; no answer.
On the third day a warship passed us, heading north,
Dead bodies piled on the deck. On the sixth day
A plane plunged over us into the sea. Thereafter
Nothing. The radios dumb;
And still they stand in corners of our kitchens,
And stand, perhaps, turned on, in a million rooms
All over the world. But now if they should speak,
If on a sudden they should speak again,
If on the stroke of noon a voice should speak,
We would not listen, we would not let it bring
That old bad world that swallowed its children quick
At one great gulp. We would not have it again.
Sometimes we think of the nations lying asleep,
Curled blindly in impenetrable sorrow,
And then the thought confounds us with its strangeness.
The tractors lie about our fields; at evening
They look like dank sea-monsters couched and waiting.
We leave them where they are and let them rust:
'They'll moulder away and be like other loam.'
We make our oxen drag our rusty ploughs,
Long laid aside. We have gone back
Far past our fathers' land.
                                        And then, that evening
Late in the summer the strange horses came.
We heard a distant tapping on the road,
A deepening drumming; it stopped, went on again
And at the corner changed to hollow thunder.
We saw the heads
Like a wild wave charging and were afraid.
We had sold our horses in our fathers' time
To buy new tractors. Now they were strange to us
As fabulous steeds set on an ancient shield
Or illustrations in a book of knights.
We did not dare go near them. Yet they waited,
Stubborn and shy, as if they had been sent

By an old command to find our whereabouts
And that long-lost archaic companionship.
In the first moment we had never a thought
That they were creatures to be owned and used.
Among them were some half-a-dozen colts
Dropped in some wilderness of the broken world,
Yet new as if they had come from their own Eden.
Since then they have pulled our ploughs and borne our
loads
But that free servitude still can pierce our hearts.
Our life is changed; their coming our beginning.

THE ISLAND

Your arms will clasp the gathered grain
For your good time, and wield the flail
In merry fire and summer hail.
There stand the golden hills of corn
Which all the heroic clans have borne,
And bear the herdsmen of the plain,
The horseman in the mountain pass,
The archaic goat with silver horn,
Man, dog and flock and fruitful hearth.
Harvests of men to men give birth.
These the ancestral faces bred
And show as though a golden glass
Dances and temples of the dead.
Here speak through the transmuted tongue
The full grape bursting in the press,
The barley seething in the vat,
Which earth and man as one confess,
Babbling of what both would be at
In garrulous story and drunken song.
Though come a different destiny,
Though fall a universal wrong
More stern than simple savagery,

Men are made of what is made,
The meat, the drink, the life, the corn,
Laid up by them, in them reborn.
And self-begotten cycles close
About our way; indigenous art
And simple spells make unafraid
The haunted labyrinths of the heart,
And with our wild succession braid
The resurrection of the rose. (*Sicily*)

HUGH MACDIARMID

THE WATERGAW

Ae weet forenicht i' the yow-trummle
I saw yon antrin thing,
A watergaw wi' its chitterin' licht
Ayont the on-ding;
An' I thocht o' the last wild look ye gied
Afore ye deed!

There was nae reek i' the laverock's hoose
That nicht—an' nane i' mine;
But I hae thocht o' that foolish licht
Ever sin' syne;
An' I think that mebbe at last I ken
What your look meant then.

LOVE

A luvin' womman is a licht
That shows a man his waefu' plicht,
Bleezin' steady on ilka bane,
Wrigglin' sinnen an' twinin' vein,
Or fleerin' quick an' gane again,
And the mair scunnersome the sicht
The mair for love and licht he's fain
Till clear and chitterin' and nesh
Move a' the miseries o' his flesh. . . .

O WHA'S THE BRIDE?

O wha's the bride that cairries the bunch
O' thistles blinterin' white?
Her cuckold bridegroom little dreids
What he sall ken this nicht.

For closer than gudeman can come
And closer to'r than hersel',
Wha didna need her maidenheid
Has wrocht his purpose fell.

O wha's been here afore me, lass,
And hoo did he get in?
—A man that deed or was I born
This evil thing has din.

And left, as it were on a corpse,
Your maidenheid to me?
—Nae lass, gudeman, sin' Time began
'S hed ony mair to gi'e.

But I can gi'e ye kindness, lad,
And a pair o' willin' hands,
And you sall ha'e my breists like stars,
My limbs like willow wands.

And on my lips ye'll heed nae mair,
And in my hair forget,
The seed o' a' the men that in
My virgin womb ha'e met. . . .

AT MY FATHER'S GRAVE

The sunlicht still on me, you row'd in clood,
We look upon each ither noo like hills
Across a valley. I'm nae mair your son.
It is my mind, nae son o' yours, that looks,
And the great darkness o' your death comes up
And equals it across the way.
A livin' man upon a deid man thinks
And ony sma'er thocht's impossible.

THE FAIRMER'S LASS

The fairmer's lass has kilted her coats
An's muckin' oot the byre,
Her hair is a' aboot her een
An' her braid face is fire.

*'The worms ha'e a' come oot o' the earth
An' streek their lengths a' airts.
Their reid nebs eisen i' the sun
But wae's me for oor herts!*

*'The aidle-pool is a glory o' gowd
—My hert is black inside.
The worms may streek to their herts' content
But they ha'e nocht to hide.'*

THE SKELETON OF THE FUTURE

Red granite and black diorite, with the blue
Of the labradorite crystals gleaming like precious stones
In the light reflected from the snow; and behind them
The eternal lightning of Lenin's bones.

ON THE OCEAN FLOOR

Now more and more on my concern with the lifted waves
 of genius gaining
I am aware of the lightless depths that beneath them lie;
And as one who hears their tiny shells incessantly raining
On the ocean floor as the foraminifera die.

PERFECT

ON THE WESTERN SEABOARD OF SOUTH UIST

Los muertos abren los ojos a los que viven

I found a pigeon's skull on the machair,
All the bones pure white and dry, and chalky,
But perfect,
Without a crack or a flaw anywhere.

At the back, rising out of the beak,
Were domes like bubbles of thin bone,
Almost transparent, where the brain had been
That fixed the tilt of the wings.

With the exception of the first line, the words of 'Perfect' were taken from 'Porth-y-Rhyd', a short story in a collection by Glyn Jones entitled *The Blue Bed*, published by Jonathan Cape in 1937.

DAVID JONES

Two Passages from IN PARENTHESIS

I

You can hear the silence of it:
you can hear the rat of no-man's-land
rut-out intricacies,
weasel-out his patient workings,
scrut, scrut, sscrut,
harrow out-earthly, trowel his cunning paw;
redeem the time of our uncharity, to sap his own
amphibious paradise.

You can hear his carrying-parties rustle our corruptions through the night-weeds—contest the choicest morsels in his tiny conduits, bead-eyed feast on us; by a rule of his nature, at night-feast on the broken of us.

Those broad-pinioned;
blue burnished, or brinded-back;
whose proud eyes watched
the broken emblems
droop and drag dust,
suffer with us this metamorphosis.

These too have shed their fine feathers; these too have slimed their dark-bright coats; these too have condescended to dig in.

The white-tailed eagle at the battle ebb,
where the sea wars against the river
the speckled kite of Maldon
and the crow
have naturally selected to be un-winged;
to go on the belly, to
sap sap sap
with festered spines, arched under the moon; furrit with
whiskered snouts the secret parts of us.

When it's all quiet you can hear them:
scrut scrut scrut
when it's as quiet as this is.
It's so very still.
Your body fits the crevice of the bay in the most comfortable fashion imaginable.
It's cushy enough.

2

And the place of their waiting a long burrow,
in the chalk a cutting, and steep clift—
but all but too shallow against his violence.
Like in long-ship, where you flattened face to kelson for the shock-breaking on brittle pavissed free-board, and the gunnel stove, and no care to jettison the dead.

No one to care there for Aneirin Lewis spilled there
who worshipped his ancestors like a Chink
who sleeps in Arthur's lap
who saw Olwen-trefoils some moonlighted night
on precarious slats at Festubert,
on narrow foothold on le Plantin marsh—
more shaved he is to the bare bone than
Yspaddadan Penkawr.
Properly organised chemists can let make more riving power than ever Twrch Trwyth;
more blistered he is than painted Troy Towers
and unwholer, limb from limb, than any of them fallen at Catraeth
or on the seaboard-down, by Salisbury,
and no maker to contrive his funerary song.
And the little Jew lies next him
cries out for Deborah his bride
and offers for stretcher-bearers
gifts for their pains
and walnut suites in his delirium
from Grays Inn Road.

But they already look at their watches and it is zero minus seven minutes.
Seven minutes to go . . . and seventy times seven times to the minute
this drumming of the diaphragm.
From deeply inward thumping all through you beating no peace to be still in
and no one is there not anyone to stop
can't anyone—someone turn off the tap
or won't any one before it snaps.
Racked out to another turn of the screw
the acceleration heightens;
the sensibility of these instruments to register,
fails;
needle dithers disorientate.
The responsive mercury plays laggard to such fevers—
you simply can't take any more in.
And the surfeit of fear steadies to dumb incognition, so that when they give the order to move upward to align with 'A',
hugged already just under the lip of the acclivity inches below where his traversing machine-guns perforate to powder
white—
white creature of chalk pounded
and the world crumbled away
and get ready to advance
you have not capacity for added fear only the limbs are leaden to negotiate the slope and rifles all out of balance,
clumsied with long auxiliary steel
seem five times the regulation weight—
it bitches the aim as well;
and we ourselves as those small cherubs, who trail awkwardly the weapons of the God in Fine Art works.

The returning sun climbed over the hill, to lessen the shadows of small and great things; and registered the

minutes to zero hour. Their saucer hats made dial for his passage: long thin line of them, virid domes of them.
cut elliptical with light
as cupola on Byzantine wall,
stout turrets to take the shock
and helmets of salvation.
Long side by side lie like friends lie
on daisy-down on warm days
cuddled close down kindly close with the mole
in down and silky rodent,
and if you look more imtimately all manner of small
    creatures,
created-dear things creep about quite comfortably
Yet who travail until now
beneath your tin-hat shade.

                He bawls at ear-hole:
Two minutes to go.
                Minutes to excuse me to make excuse.
Responde mihi?
                for surely I must needs try them
so many, much undone
and lose on roundabouts as well and vari-coloured
polygram
to love and know
                and we have a little sister
whose breasts will be as towers
and the gilly flowers will blow next month
below the pound
with Fred Karno billed for *The Holloway*.

He's getting it now more accurately and each salvo brackets more narrowly and a couple right in, just as 'D' and 'C' are forming for the second wave.

Wastebottom married a wife on his Draft-leave but the whinnying splinter razored diagonal and mess-tin fragments drove inward and toxined underwear.

He maintained correct alignment with the others, face down, and you never would have guessed.

Perhaps they'll cancel it.
O blow fall out the officers cantcher, like a wet afternoon or the King's Birthday.
Or you read it again many times to see if it will come different:
you can't believe the Cup won't pass from
or they won't make a better show
in the Garden.
Won't someone forbid the banns
or God himself will stay their hands.
It just can't happen in our family
even though a thousand
and ten thousand at thy right hand.

Talacryn doesn't take it like Wastebottom, he leaps up & says he's dead, a-slither down the pale face—his limbs a-girandole at the bottom of the nullah,
but the mechanism slackens, unfed
and he is quite still
which leaves five paces between you and the next live one to the left.
Sidle over a bit toward where '45 Williams, and use all your lungs:
Get ready me china-plate—but he's got it before he can hear you, but it's a cushy one and he relaxes to the morning sun and smilingly, to wait for the bearers.

CHARLES OLSON

MAXIMUS, TO GLOUCESTER, SUNDAY, JULY 19

I

and they stopped before that bad sculpture
of a fisherman

—'as if one were to talk to a man's house,
knowing not what gods or heroes are'—

not knowing what a fisherman is
instead of going straight to the Bridge
and doing no more than—saying no more
than—
in the Charybdises of the
Cut waters the flowers tear off
the wreathes

the flowers
turn
the character of the sea   The sea jumps
the fate of the flower   The drowned men are
undrowned
in the eddies

of the eyes
of the flowers
opening
the sea's eyes

The disaster
is undone
What was received as alien
—the flower
on the water, that a man drowns

that he dies in water as he dies on earth, the impossible
                    that this gross fact can return to us
                                        in this upset

on a summer day
of a particular tide

that the sensation is true,
that the transformations of fire are, first of all, sea—
                    'as gold for wares wares for gold'

                    Let them be told who stopped first
                    by a bronze idol

                    A fisherman is not a successful man
                    he is not a famous man he is not a man
                    of power, these are the damned by God

II

whose surface bubbles
with these gimlets
which screw-in like

potholes, caustic
caked earth of painted
pools, Yellowstone

Park of holes
is death the diseased
presence on us, the spilling lesion

of the brilliance
it is to be alive: to walk onto it,
as Jim Bridger the first into it,

it is more true a scabious
field than it is a pretty
meadow

When a man's coffin is the sea
the whole of creation shall come to his
funeral,

it turns out; the globe
is below, all lapis

and its blue surface golded
by what happened

this afternoon: there are eyes
in this water

the flowers
from the shore,

awakened
the sea

Men are so sure they know very many things,
they don't even know night and day are one

A fisherman works without reference to
that difference. It is possible he also

by lying there when he does lie, jowl
to the sea, has another advantage: it is said,

'You rectify what can be rectified,' and when a man's
heart
cannot see this, the door of his divine intelligence is shut

let you who paraded to the Cut today
to hold memorial services to all fishermen
who have been lost at sea in a year
when for the first time not one life was lost

radar sonar radio telephone
    good engines
bed-check seaplanes goodness
    over and under us

no difference
when men come back

THEODORE ROETHKE

CUTTINGS

(Later)

This urge, wrestle, resurrection of dry sticks,
Cut stems struggling to put down feet,
What saint strained so much,
Rose on such lopped limbs to a new life?

I can hear, underground, that sucking and sobbing,
In my veins, in my bones I feel it,—
The small waters seeping upward,
The tight grains parting at last.
When sprouts break out,
Slippery as fish,
I quail, lean to beginnings, sheath-wet.

MY PAPA'S WALTZ

The whiskey on your breath
Could make a small boy dizzy;
But I hung on like death:
Such waltzing was not easy.

We romped until the pans
Slid from the kitchen shelf;
My mother's countenance
Could not unfrown itself.

The hand that held my wrist
Was battered on one knuckle;
At every step you missed
My right ear scraped a buckle.

You beat time on my head
With a palm caked hard by dirt,
Then waltzed me off to bed
Still clinging to your shirt.

THE LOST SON

I. THE FLIGHT

At Woodlawn I heard the dead cry:
I was lulled by the slamming of iron,
A slow drip over stones,
Toads brooding in wells.
All the leaves stuck out their tongues;
I shook the softening chalk of my bones,
Saying,
Snail, snail, glister me forward,
Bird, soft-sigh me home.
Worm, be with me.
This is my hard time.

Fished in an old wound,
The soft pond of repose;
Nothing nibbled my line,
Not even the minnows came.

Sat in an empty house
Watching shadows crawl,
Scratching,
There was one fly.

Voice, come out of the silence.
Say something.
Appear in the form of a spider
Or a moth beating the curtain.

Tell me:
Which is the way I take;
Out of what door do I go,
Where and to whom?

  Dark hollows said, lee to the wind,
  The moon said, back of an eel,
  The salt said, look by the sea,
  Your tears are not enough praise,
  You will find no comfort here,
  In the kingdom of bang and blab.

Running lightly over spongy ground,
Past the pasture of flat stones,
The three elms,
The sheep strewn on a field,
Over a rickety bridge
Toward the quick-water, wrinkling and rippling.

Hunting along the river,
Down among the rubbish, the bug-riddled foliage,
By the muddy pond-edge, by the bog-holes,
By the shrunken lake, hunting, in the heat of summer.

The shape of a rat?
  It's bigger than that.
  It's less than a leg
  And more than a nose,
  Just under the water
  It usually goes.

Is it soft like a mouse?
Can it wrinkle its nose?
Could it come in the house
On the tips of its toes?

  Take the skin of a cat
  And the back of an eel,

Then roll them in grease,—
That's the way it would feel.

It's sleek as an otter
With wide webby toes
Just under the water
It usually goes.

2. THE PIT

Where do the roots go?
Look down under the leaves.
Who put the moss there?
These stones have been here too long.
Who stunned the dirt into noise?
Ask the mole, he knows.
I feel the slime of a wet nest.
Beware Mother Mildew.
Nibble again, fish nerves.

3. THE GIBBER

At the wood's mouth,
By the cave's door,
I listened to something
I had heard before.

Dogs of the groin
Barked and howled,
The sun was against me,
The moon would not have me.

The weeds whined,
The snakes cried,
The cows and briars
Said to me: Die.

What a small song. What slow clouds. What dark water.
Hath the rain a father? All the caves are ice. Only the
snow's here.

I'm cold. I'm cold all over. Rub me in father and
mother.
Fear was my father, Father Fear.
His look drained the stones.

What gliding shape
Beckoning through halls,
Stood poised on the stair,
Fell dreamily down?

From the mouths of jugs
Perched on many shelves,
I saw substance flowing
That cold morning.

Like a slither of eels
That watery cheek
As my own tongue kissed
My lips awake.

Is this the storm's heart? The ground is unstilling itself.
My veins are running nowhere. Do the bones cast out their
fire?
Is the seed leaving the old bed? These buds are live as
birds.
Where, where are the tears of the world?
Let the kisses resound, flat like a butcher's palm;
Let the gestures freeze; our doom is already decided.
All the windows are burning! What's left of my life?
I want the old rage, the lash of primordial milk!
Good-bye, good-bye, old stones, the time-order is going,
I have married my hands to perpetual agitation,
I run, I run to the whistle of money.

Money money money
Water water water

How cool the grass is.
Has the bird left?
The stalk still sways.
Has the worm a shadow?
What do the clouds say?

These sweeps of light undo me.
Look, look, the ditch is running white!
I've more veins than a tree!
Kiss me, ashes, I'm falling through a dark swirl.

4. THE RETURN

The way to the boiler was dark,
Dark all the way,
Over slippery cinders
Through the long greenhouse.

The roses kept breathing in the dark.
They had many mouths to breathe with.
My knees made little winds underneath
Where the weeds slept.

There was always a single light
Swinging by the fire-pit,
Where the fireman pulled out roses,
The big roses, the big bloody clinkers.

Once I stayed all night.
The light in the morning came slowly over the white
Snow.
There were many kinds of cool
Air.
Then came steam.

Pipe-knock.

Scurry of warm over small plants.
Ordnung! Ordnung!
Papa is coming!

A fine haze moved off the leaves;
Frost melted on far panes;
The rose, the chrysanthemum turned toward the light.
Even the hushed forms, the bent yellowy weeds
Moved in a slow up-sway.

5

It was beginning winter,
An in-between time,
The landscape still partly brown:
The bones of weeds kept swinging in the wind,
Above the blue snow.

It was beginning winter.
The light moved slowly over the frozen field,
Over the dry seed-crowns,
The beautiful surviving bones
Swinging in the wind.

Light travelled over the field;
Stayed.
The weeds stopped swinging.
The mind moved, not alone,
Through the clear air, in the silence.

Was it light?
Was it light within?
Was it light within light?
Stillness becoming alive,
Yet still?

A lively understandable spirit
Once entertained you.
It will come again.
Be still.
Wait.

I KNEW A WOMAN

I knew a woman, lovely in her bones,
When small birds sighed, she would sigh back at them;
Ah, when she moved, she moved more ways than one;
The shapes a bright container can contain!
Of her choice virtues only gods should speak,
Or English poets who grew up on Greek
(I'd have them sing in chorus, cheek to cheek).

How well her wishes went! She stroked my chin,
She taught me Turn, and Counter-turn, and Stand;
She taught me Touch, that undulant white skin;
I nibbled meekly from her proffered hand;
She was the sickle; I, poor I, the rake,
Coming behind her for her pretty sake
(But what prodigious mowing we did make).

Love likes a gander, and adores a goose:
Her full lips pursed, the errant note to seize;
She played it quick, she played it light and loose;
My eyes, they dazzled at her flowing knees;
Her several parts could keep a pure repose,
Or one hip quiver with a mobile nose
(She moved in circles, and those circles moved).

Let seed be grass, and grass turn into hay:
I'm martyr to a motion not my own;
What's freedom for? To know eternity.
I swear she cast a shadow white as stone.
But who would count eternity in days?
These old bones live to learn her wanton ways:
(I measure time by how a body sways).

F. T. PRINCE

IN THE WOOD

The afternoon fills the grey wood
With a faint milk of mists.
As we walk some cloud suggests
A pink soft sheaf. And I would
Suddenly I were dead
So that all were out of your mind
That love is in hope to find
And so we seek: that freed
Of all but being, you stood
With a vacant glance
Or might in the grey air dance
With cheeks that match the cloud:
That within the cold wood
Like a vast eye at gaze,
A miraculous life that strays
Through votive solitude
You loitered: that fever over,
To which my passion lit
Dry sticks of unlucky wit
And the silence were your lover.

FALSE BAY

She I love leaves me and I leave my friends
In the dusky capital where I spent two years
In the cultivation of divinity.
Sitting beside my window above the sea
In this unvisited land I feel once more
How little ingenious I am. The winter ends,
The seaward slopes are covered to the shore
With a press of lilies that have silver ears.

And although I am perplexed and sad I say
'Now indulge in no dateless lamentations:
Watch only across the water the lapsed nations
And the fisherman twitch a boat across the bay.'

THE TOKEN

More beautiful than any gift you gave
You were, a child so beautiful as to seem
To promise ruin what no child can have
Or woman give. And so a Roman gem
I choose to be your token: here a laurel
Springs to its young height, hangs a broken limb
And here a group of women wanly quarrel
At a sale of Cupids. A hawk looks at them.

THE WIND IN THE TREE

She has decided that she no longer loves me.
There is nothing to be done. I long ago
As a child thought the tree sighed 'Do I know
Whether my motion makes the wind that moves me?'

R. S. THOMAS

SONG FOR GWYDION

When I was a child and the soft flesh was forming
Quietly as snow on the bare boughs of bone,
My father brought me trout from the green river
From whose chill lips the water song had flown.

Dull grew their eyes, the beautiful, blithe garland
Of stipples faded, as light shocked the brain;
They were the first sweet sacrifice I tasted,
A young god, ignorant of the blood's stain.

DEATH OF A PEASANT

You remember Davies? He died, you know,
With his face to the wall, as the manner is
Of the poor peasant in his stone croft
On the Welsh hills. I recall the room
Under the slates, and the smirched snow
Of the wide bed in which he lay,
Lonely as an ewe that is sick to lamb
In the hard weather of mid-March.
I remember also the trapped wind
Tearing the curtains, and the wild light's
Frequent hysteria upon the floor,
The bare floor without a rug
Or mat to soften the loud tread
Of neighbours crossing the uneasy boards
To peer at Davies with gruff words
Of meaningless comfort, before they turned
Heartless away from the stale smell
Of death in league with those dank walls.

EVANS

Evans? Yes, many a time
I came down his bare flight
Of stairs into the gaunt kitchen
With its wood fire, where crickets sang
Accompaniment to the black kettle's
Whine, and so into the cold
Dark to smother in the thick tide
Of night that drifted about the walls
Of his stark farm on the hill ridge.

It was not the dark filling my eyes
And mouth appalled me; not even the drip
Of rain like blood from the one tree
Weather-tortured. It was the dark
Silting the veins of that sick man
I left stranded upon the vast
And lonely shore of his bleak bed.

THE COUNTRY CLERGY

I see them working in old rectories
By the sun's light, by candlelight,
Venerable men, their black cloth
A little dusty, a little green
With holy mildew. And yet their skulls,
Ripening over so many prayers,
Toppled into the same grave
With oafs and yokels. They left no books,
Memorial to their lonely thought
In grey parishes; rather they wrote
On men's hearts and in the minds
Of young children sublime words
Too soon forgotten. God in his time
Or out of time will correct this.

MICHAEL ROBERTS

TIME'S OTHER COUNTRY

I walked, frowning, across the Cathedral Square,
I was late, and I had another appointment later,
The city crowded upon me, the walls narrowed;
And suddenly traffic, walls, loudspeakers vanished.

I have only to stop hurrying, and a seed springs up
Making a green place in the city, sweeping away the
clock,
Fountains burst up through pavements hard as habit,
Lightly I walk through a wall, and the sky is open.

Here again is truth, and infinite honesty,
The long unhurried diligence of childhood,
Measuring the exact length of a shadow, or chasing
butterflies,
With the house dead quiet, and only a blackbird in the
garden.

Out of the traffic, out of the tinkling glass,
There comes the apocalyptic galloping of horses;
I have seen the still water, like the eyes of heroes,
Here, on the other side of the wall, within six inches.

ASSAULT OF ANGELS

The mind trembles from the assault of angels;
Running in familiar light it sees the sea,
It remembers the dark subway and the lost fields of
childhood,
It remembers the loneliness of first love and the end of a
summer:
These are familiar and small.

But the assault of angels is more terrible; angels are
invisible,
Angels cast no shadow, and their unpredicted motion
Moves the familiar shadows into light.
Angels cannot burn the fingers: unacknowledged,
They pass unseen. No one will ever know.
Refuse them: they have no claim to charity,
To ignore them offers a key to omniscience.
Angels breed darkness out of light, angels rejoice
In things we hate and fear.

Angels are the launching of a new ship,
Angels offer to inhabit the landscape of your body,
Angels will let you grow as a child grows,
They are your enemy: they will destroy you.

And a time comes when a man is afraid to grow,
A time comes when the house is comfortable and narrow.
A time when the spirit of life contracts.
Angels are at the door: admit them, now.

KATHLEEN RAINE

THE MARRIAGE OF PSYCHE

I. THE HOUSE

In my love's house
There are hills and pastures carpeted with flowers,
His roof is the blue sky, his lamp the evening star,
The doors of his house are the winds, and the rain his
  curtain.
In his house are many mountains, each alone,
And islands where the sea-birds home.

In my love's house
There is a waterfall that flows all night
Down from the mountain summit where the snow lies
White in the shimmering blue of everlasting summer,
Down from the high crag where the eagle flies.
At his threshold the tides of ocean rise,
And the porpoise follows the shoals into still bays
Where starfish gleam on brown weed under still water.

In sleep I was borne here
And waking found rivers and waves my servants,
Sun and cloud and winds, bird-messengers,
And all the flocks of his hills and shoals of his seas.
I rest, in the heat of the day, in the light shadow of leaves
And voices of air and water speak to me.
All this he has given me, whose face I have never seen,
But into whose all-enfolding arms I sink in sleep.

2. THE RING

He has married me with a ring, a ring of bright water
Whose ripples travel from the heart of the sea,
He has married me with a ring of light, the glitter
Broadcast on the swift river.

He has married me with the sun's circle
Too dazzling to see, traced in summer sky.
He has crowned me with the wreath of white cloud
That gathers on the snowy summit of the mountain,
Ringed me round with the world-circling wind,
Bound me to the whirlwind's centre.
He has married me with the orbit of the moon
And with the boundless circle of the stars,
With the orbits that measure years, months, days and
nights,
Set the tides flowing,
Command the winds to travel or be at rest.

At the ring's centre,
Spirit, or angel troubling the still pool,
Causality not in nature,
Finger's touch that summons at a point, a moment
Stars and planets, life and light
Or gathers cloud about an apex of cold,
Transcendent touch of love summons my world to being.

THE HOLY SHROUD

Face of the long-dead
Floating up from under the deep waves
Of time, that we try to see,
To draw towards us by closer looking, that fades
And will not become more clear than shadow,
Mist gathering always like dusk round a dead king,
That face, however closely we look, is always departing,
Neither questions nor answers us. It is still,
It is whole, has known, loved, suffered all,
And un-known all again.
That face of man
Un-knows us now; whatever being passed
Beyond that holy shroud into the mind of God
No longer sees this earth: we are alone.

ANNE RIDLER

BATHING IN THE WINDRUSH

Their lifted arms disturb the pearl
And hazel stream
And move like swanbeams through the yielding
Pool above the water's whirl
As water swirls and falls through the torn field.

Earth bears its bodies as a burden:
Arms on a bright
Surface are from their shadows parted,
Not as the stream transforms these children
But as time divides the echo from the start.

Smiling above the water's brim
The daylight creatures
Trail their moonshine limbs below;
That melt and waver as they swim
And yet are treasures more possessed than shadows.

This wonder is only submarine:
Drawn to the light
Marble is stone and moons are eyes.
These are like symbols, where half-seen
The meaning swims, and drawn to the surface, dies.

1949

ST. ISHMAEL'S

This valley waits. For whom is it waiting?
This valley is holding its breath. Till when?

Not far off, the gnashing sea,
Gobbled rock and wind-lashed headland;

Here, a calm viridian valley,
Sap and silence.

Down in the deep wood stand the fruit-trees
Laden with apples. Who will pick them?
Thick wood crowds against the wall,
Within the wall is woodland crowding
Outwards: where is the house, the garden?
Gone. Where is the wonder who
Should make his entrance? Not yet come.

The valley is waiting. Not for us.

No one stirs, not a bird; only
An idiot down in the cove jabbers
And fights his shadow: cocks a snook,
With Peep Bo behind the wall.
His part's designed: the Anti-Masque
To a solemn drama—mocks the hero
Still awaited. Rusty rocks
That dip in a level estuary sea
Hundreds of million years have waited.

Part the bamboo thicket: there
Is the grey chapel you thought to find,
Eyebrow-deep in rhododendrons,
Dittany-of-Crete with dangling crimson,
Flaring pokers, pallid fuchsia.

The valley is waiting.

So our lives wait for the blaze of glory
Always expected. Each with a secret,
Cluttered with leaves, with flowers and fruit,
Silence caught by the sleeve, to stay
Till the new glory enters the scene.
But when, or how, is out of sight;
Or whether it is for death we wait,
And his the called-for, marvellous entrance.

NORMAN MACCAIG

WET SNOW

White tree on black tree,
Ghostly appearance fastened on another,
Called up by harsh spells of this wintry weather
You stand in the night as though to speak to me.

I could almost
Say what you do not fail to say; that's why
I turn away, in terror, not to see
A tree stand there hugged by its own ghost.

YOU WENT AWAY

Suddenly, in my world of you,
You created time.
I walked about in its bitter lanes
Looking for whom I'd lost, afraid to go home.

You stole yourself and gave me this
Torturer for my friend
Who shows me gardens rotting in air
And tells me what I no longer understand.

The birds sing still in the apple trees,
But not in mine, I hear
Only the clock whose wintry strokes
Say, 'Now is now', the same lie over and over.

If I could kill this poem, sticking
My thin pen through its throat,
It would stand crying by your bed
And haunt your cruelty every empty night.

EXPLORER

He went no further than he could not go.
Holding the waver of light in his green hand
He disappeared beyond the impossible. No
Word could befriend him in that friendless land.

Then the impossible grew its usual fruits,
The monsters withdrew beyond his ring of light.
We found him talking to us—the old disputes;
For we had been waiting for him, all the night.

And so we met ourselves again. And so
Once more we were one of him; until one day
Wanting to meet us, he prepared to go
Further impossibilities away.

JUG

With a toad belly and a horny lip,
It madly flourishes flowers
On an ill-lit shelf; as though trying to hop and skip
Into the beautiful world of allegories.

Plain reason sensibly deploys
Its furniture around
This odd neurosis that explodes its joys
Like a wild vice in the bosom of Mrs. Grundy.

The revolution of the ugly, or
Only its pathos? Switch
The darkness on, that toads love; shut the door
On a midden-rose, on a Chaconne by Bach.

VERNON WATKINS

DISCOVERIES

The poles are flying where the two eyes set:
America has not found Columbus yet.

Ptolemy's planets, playing fast and loose,
Foretell the wisdom of Copernicus.

Dante calls Primum Mobile, the First Cause:
'Love that moves the world and the other stars.'

Great Galileo, twisted by the rack,
Groans the bright sun from heaven, then breathes it back.

Blake, on the world alighting, holds the skies,
And all the stars shine down through human eyes.

Donne sees those stars, yet will not let them lie:
'We're tapers, too, and at our own cost die.'

The shroud-lamp catches. Lips are smiling there.
'Les flammes—déjà?'—The world dies, or Voltaire.

Swift, a cold mourner at his burial-rite,
Burns to the world's heart like a meteorite.

Beethoven deaf, in deafness hearing all,
Unwinds all music from sound's funeral.

Three prophets fall, the litter of one night:
Blind Milton gazes in fixed deeps of light.

Beggar of those Minute Particulars,
Yeats lights again the turmoil of the stars.

Motionless motion! Come, Tiresias,
The eternal flies, what's passing cannot pass.

'Solace in flight,' old Heraclitus cries;
Light changing to Von Hugel's butterflies.

Rilke bears all, thinks like a tree, believes,
Sinks in the hand that bears the falling leaves.

The stars! The signs! Great Angelo hurls them back.
His whirling ceiling draws the zodiac.

The pulse of Keats testing the axiom;
The second music when the sound is dumb.

The Christian Paradox, bringing its great reward
By loss; the moment known to Kierkegaard.

THE MARE

The mare lies down in the grass where the nest of the
skylark is hidden.
Her eyes drink the delicate horizon moving behind the
song.
Deep sink the skies, a well of voices. Her sleep is the
vessel of Summer.
That climbing music requires the hidden music at rest.

Her body is utterly given to the light, surrendered in
perfect abandon
To the heaven above her shadow, still as her first-born
day.
Softly the wind runs over her. Circling the meadow, her
hooves
Rest in a race of daisies, halted where butterflies stand.

Do not pass her too close. It is easy to break the circle
And lose that indolent fullness rounded under the ray
Falling on light-eared grasses your footstep must not yet
    wake.
It is easy to darken the sun of her unborn foal at play.

JOHN BERRYMAN

THREE DREAM SONGS

I

Henry's pelt was put on sundry walls
where it did much resemble Henry and
them persons was delighted.
Especially his long & glowing tail
by all them was admired, and visitors.
They whistled: This is *it*!

Golden, whilst your frozen daiquiris
whir at midnight, gleams on you his fur
& silky & black.
Mission accomplished, pal.
My molten yellow & moonless bag,
drained, hangs at rest.

Collect in the cold depths barracuda. Ay,
in Sealdah Station some possessionless
hundreds exist & die.
The Chinese communes hum. Two daiquiris
withdrew into a corner of the gorgeous room
and one told the other a lie.

II

Spellbound held subtle Henry all his four
hearers in the racket of the market
with ancient signs, infamous characters,
new rhythms. On the steps he was belov'd,
hours a day, by all his four, or more,
depending. And they paid him.

It was not, so, like no one listening
but critics famed & Henry's pals or other
writers at all
chiefly in another country. No.
He by the heart & brains & tail, because
of their love for it, had them.

Junk he said to all them open-mouth'd.
Weather would govern. When the monsoon spread
its floods, few came, two.
Came a day when none, though he began
in his accustomed way on the filthy steps
in a crash of waters, came.

III

In a motion of night they massed nearer my post.
I hummed a short blues. When the stars went out
I studied my weapons system.
Grenades, the portable rack, the yellow spout
of the anthrax-ray: in order. Yes, and most
of my pencils were sharp.

This edge of the galaxy has often seen
a defence so stiff, but it could only go
one way.
—Mr Bones, your troubles give me vertigo,
& backache. Somehow, when I make your scene,
I cave to feel as if

de roses of dawn & pearls of dusks, made up
by some ol' writer-man, got right forgot
& greennesses of ours.
Springwater grow so thick it gonna clot
and the pleasing ladies cease. I figure, yup,
you is bad powers.

From HOMAGE TO MISTRESS BRADSTREET

17

The winters close, Springs open, no child stirs
under my withering heart, O seasoned heart
God grudged his aid.
All things else soil like a shirt.
Simon is much away. My executive stales.
The town came through for the cartway by the pales,
but my patience is short,
I revolt from, I am like, these savage foresters

18

whose passionless dicker in the shade, whose glance
impassive & scant, belie their murderous cries
when quarry seems to show.
Again I must have been wrong, twice.
Unwell in a new way. Can that begin?
God brandishes. O love, O I love, Kin,
gather. My world is strange
and merciful, ingrown months, blessing a swelling trance.

19

So squeezed, wince you I scream? I love you & hate
off with you. Ages! *Useless*. Below my waist
he has me in Hell's vise.
Stalling. He let go. Come back: brace
me somewhere. No. No. Yes! everything down
hardens I press with horrible joy down
my back cracks like a wrist
shame I am voiding oh behind it is too late

20

hide me forever I work thrust I must free
now I all muscles & bones concentrate

what is living from dying?
Simon I must leave you so untidy
Monster you are killing me Be sure
I'll have you later Women do endure
I can *can* no longer
and it passes the wretched trap whelming and I am me

21

drencht & powerful, I did it with my body!
One proud tug greets Heaven. Marvellous,
unforbidding Majesty.
Swell, imperious bells. I fly.
Mountainous, woman not breaks and will bend:
sways God nearby: anguish comes to an end.
Blossomed Sarah, and I
blossom. Is that thing alive? I hear a famisht howl.

ROBERT LOWELL

THE QUAKER GRAVEYARD IN NANTUCKET

(*For Warren Winslow, Dead at Sea*)

Let man have dominion over the fishes of the sea and the fowls of the air and the beasts and the whole earth, and every creeping creature that moveth upon the earth.

I

A brackish reach of shoal off Madaket,—
The sea was breaking violently and night
Had steamed into our North Atlantic Fleet,
When the drowned sailor clutched the drag-net. Light
Flashed from his matted head and marble feet,
He grappled at the net
With the coiled, hurdling muscles of his thighs:
The corpse was bloodless, a botch of reds and whites,
Its open, staring eyes
Were lustreless dead-lights
Or cabin-windows on a stranded hulk
Heavy with sand. We weight the body, close
Its eyes and heave it seaward whence it came,
Where the heel-headed dogfish barks its nose
On Ahab's void and forehead; and the name
Is blocked in yellow chalk.
Sailors, who pitch this portent at the sea
Where dreadnoughts shall confess
Its hell-bent deity,
When you are powerless
To sand-bag this Atlantic bulwark, faced
By the earth-shaker, green, unwearied, chaste
In his steel scales: ask for no Orphean lute

To pluck life back. The guns of the steeled fleet
Recoil and then repeat
The hoarse salute.

2

Whenever winds are moving and their breath
Heaves at the roped-in bulwarks of this pier,
The terns and sea-gulls tremble at your death
In these home waters. Sailor, can you hear
The Pequod's sea wings, beating landward, fall
Headlong and break on our Atlantic wall
Off 'Sconset, where the yawing S-boats splash
The bellbuoy, with ballooning spinnakers,
As the entangled, screeching mainsheet clears
The blocks: off Madaket, where lubbers lash
The heavy surf and throw their long lead squids
For blue-fish? Sea-gulls blink their heavy lids
Seaward. The winds' wings beat upon the stones,
Cousin, and scream for you and the claws rush
At the sea's throat and wring it in the slush
Of this old Quaker graveyard where the bones
Cry out in the long night for the hurt beast
Bobbing by Ahab's whaleboats in the East.

3

All you recovered from Poseidon died
With you, my cousin, and the harrowed brine
Is fruitless on the blue beard of the god.
Stretching beyond us to the castles in Spain,
Nantucket's westward haven. To Cape Cod
Guns, cradled on the tide,
Blast the eelgrass about a waterclock
Of bilge and backwash, roil the salt and sand
Lashing earth's scaffold, rock
Our warships in the hand
Of the great God, where time's contrition blues
Whatever it was these Quaker sailors lost

In the mad scramble of their lives. They died
When time was open-eyed,
Wooden and childish; only bones abide
There, in the nowhere, where their boats were tossed
Sky-high, where mariners had fabled news
Of IS, the whited monster. What it cost
Them is their secret. In the sperm-whale's slick
I see the Quakers drown and hear their cry:
'If God himself had not been on our side,
If God himself had not been on our side,
When the Atlantic rose against us, why,
Then it had swallowed us up quick.'

4

This is the end of the whaleroad and the whale
Who spewed Nantucket bones on the thrashed swell
And stirred the troubled waters to whirlpools
To send the Pequod packing off to hell:
This is the end of them, three-quarters fools,
Snatching at straws to sail
Seaward and seaward on the turntail whale,
Spouting out blood and water as it rolls,
Sick as a dog to these Atlantic shoals:
Clamavimus, O depths. Let the sea-gulls wail

For water, for the deep where the high tide
Mutters to its hurt self, mutters and ebbs.
Waves wallow in their wash, go out and out,
Leave only the death-rattle of the crabs,
The beach increasing, its enormous snout
Sucking the ocean's side.
This is the end of running on the waves;
We are poured out like water. Who will dance
The mast-lashed master of Leviathans
Up from this field of Quakers in their unstoned graves?

5

When the whale's viscera go and the roll
Of its corruption overruns this world
Beyond tree-swept Nantucket and Wood's Hole
And Martha's Vineyard, Sailor, will your sword
Whistle and fall and sink into the fat?
In the great ash-pit of Jehoshaphat
The bones cry for the blood of the white whale,
The fat flukes arch and whack about its ears,
The death-lance churns into the sanctuary, tears
The gun-blue swingle, heaving like a flail,
And hacks the coiling life out: it works and drags
And rips the sperm-whale's midriff into rags,
Gobbets of blubber spill to wind and weather,
Sailor, and gulls go round the stoven timbers
Where the morning stars sing out together
And thunder shakes the white surf and dismembers
The red flag hammered in the mast-head. Hide,
Our steel, Jonas Messias, in Thy side.

6

Our Lady of Walsingham

There once the penitents took off their shoes
And then walked barefoot the remaining mile;
And the small trees, a stream and hedgerows file
Slowly along the munching English lane,
Like cows to the old shrine, until you lose
Track of your dragging pain.
The stream flows down under the druid tree,
Shiloah's whirlpools gurgle and make glad
The castle of God. Sailor, you were glad
And whistled Sion by that stream. But see:

Our Lady, too small for her canopy,
Sits near the altar. There's no comeliness
At all or charm in that expressionless

Face with its heavy eyelids. As before,
This face, for centuries a memory,
Non est species, neque decor,
Expressionless, expresses God: it goes
Past castled Sion. She knows what God knows,
Not Calvary's Cross nor crib at Bethlehem
Now, and the world shall come to Walsingham.

7

The empty winds are creaking and the oak
Splatters and splatters on the cenotaph,
The boughs are trembling and a gaff
Bobs on the untimely stroke
Of the greased wash exploding on a shoal-bell
In the old mouth of the Atlantic. It's well;
Atlantic, you are fouled with the blue sailors,
Sea-monsters, upward angel, downward fish:
Unmarried and corroding, spare of flesh
Mart once of supercilious, wing'd clippers,
Atlantic, where your bell-trap guts its spoil
You could cut the brackish winds with a knife
Here in Nantucket, and cast up the time
When the Lord God formed man from the sea's slime
And breathed into his face the breath of life,
And blue-lung'd combers lumbered to the kill.
The Lord survives the rainbow of His will.

NEW YEAR'S DAY

Again and then again . . . the year is born
To ice and death, and it will never do
To skulk behind storm-windows by the stove
To hear the postgirl sounding her French horn
When the thin tidal ice is wearing through.
Here is the understanding not to love
Each other, or tomorrow that will sieve
Our resolutions. While we live, we live

To snuff the smoke of victims. In the snow
The kitten heaved its hindlegs, as if fouled,
And died. We bent it in a Christmas box
And scattered blazing weeds to scare the crow
Until the snake-tailed sea-winds coughed and howled
For alms outside the church whose double locks
Wait for St. Peter, the distorted key.
Under St. Peter's bell the parish sea

Swells with its smelt into the burlap shack
Where Joseph plucks his hand-lines like a harp,
And hears the fearful *Puer natus est*
Of Circumcision, and relives the wrack
And howls of Jesus whom he holds. How sharp
The burden of the Law before the beast:
Time and the grindstone and the knife of God.
The Child is born in blood, O child of blood.

SKUNK HOUR

(*For Elizabeth Bishop*)

Nautilus Island's hermit
heiress still lives through winter in her Spartan cottage;
her sheep still graze above the sea.
Her son's a bishop. Her farmer
is first selectman in our village;
she's in her dotage.

Thirsting for
the hierarchic privacy
of Queen Victoria's century,
she buys up all
the eyesores facing her shore,
and lets them fall.

The season's ill—
we've lost our summer millionaire,
who seemed to leap from an L. L. Bean
catalogue. His nine-knot yawl
was auctioned off to lobstermen.
A red fox stain covers Blue Hill.

And now our fairy
decorator brightens his shop for fall;
his fishnet's filled with orange cork,
orange, his cobbler's bench and awl;
there is no money in his work,
he'd rather marry.

One dark night,
my Tudor Ford climbed the hill's skull;
I watched for love-cars. Lights turned down,
they lay together, hull to hull,
where the graveyard shelves on the town. . . .
My mind's not right.

A car radio bleats,
'Love, O careless Love. . . .' I hear
my ill-spirit sob in each blood cell,
as if my hand were at its throat. . . .
I myself am hell;
nobody's here—

only skunks, that search
in the moonlight for a bite to eat.
They march on their soles up Main Street:
white stripes, moonstruck eyes' red fire
under the chalk-dry and spar spire
of the Trinitarian Church.

I stand on top
of our back steps and breathe the rich air—
a mother skunk with her column of kittens swills the
garbage pail.
She jabs her wedge-head in a cup
of sour cream, drops her ostrich tail,
and will not scare.

W. S. GRAHAM

LISTEN. PUT ON MORNING

Listen. Put on morning.
Waken into falling light.
A man's imagining
Suddenly may inherit
The handclapping centuries
Of his one minute on earth.
And hear the virgin juries
Talk with his own breath
To the corner boys of his street.
And hear the Black Maria
Searching the town at night.
And hear the playropes caa
The sister Mary in.
And hear Willie and Davie
Among bracken of Marnain
Sing in a mist heavy
With myrtle and listeners.
And hear the higher town
Weep a petition of fears
At the poorhouse close upon
The public heartbeat.
And hear the children tig
And run with my own feet
Into the netting drag
Of a suiciding principle.
Listen. Put on lightbreak.
Waken into miracle.
The audience lies awake
Under the tenements
Under the sugar docks
Under the printed moments.
The centuries turn their locks

And open under the hill
Their inherited books and doors
All gathered to distil
Like happy berry pickers
One voice to talk to us.
Yes listen. It carries away
The second and the years
Till the heart's in a jacket of snow
And the head's in a helmet white
And the song sleeps to be wakened
By the morning ear bright.
Listen. Put on morning.
Waken into falling light.

GIGHA

That firewood pale with salt and burning green
Outfloats its men who waved with a sound of drowning
Their saltcut hands over mazes of this rough bay.

Quietly this morning beside the subsided herds
Of water I walk. The children wade the shallows.
The sun with long legs wades into the sea.

HOWARD NEMEROV

BRAINSTORM

The house was shaken by a rising wind
That rattled window and door. He sat alone
In an upstairs room and heard these things: a blind
Ran up with a bang, a door slammed, a groan
Came from some hidden joist, a leaky tap,
At any silence of the wind walked like
A blind man through the house. Timber and sap
Revolt, he thought, from washer, baulk and spike.
Bent to his book, continued unafraid
Until the crows came down from their loud flight
To walk along the rooftree overhead.
Their horny feet, so near but out of sight,
Scratched on the slate; when they were blown away
He heard their wings beat till they came again,
While the wind rose, and the house seemed to sway,
And window panes began to blind with rain.
The house was talking, not to him, he thought,
But to the crows; the crows were talking back
In their black voices. The secret might be out:
Houses are only trees stretched on the rack.
And once the crows knew, all nature would know.
Fur, leaf and feather would invade the form,
Nail rust with rain and shingle warp with snow,
Vine tear the wall, till any straw-borne storm
Could rip both roof and rooftree off and show
Naked to nature what they had kept warm.
He came to feel the crows walk on his head
As if he were the house, their crooked feet
Scratched, through the hair, his scalp. He might be dead,
It seemed, and all the noises underneath
Be but the cooling of the sinews, veins,
Juices, and sodden sacks suddenly let go;

While in his ruins of wiring, his burst mains,
The rainy wind had been set free to blow
Until the green uprising and mob rule
That ran the world had taken over him,
Split him like seed, and set him in the school
Where any crutch can learn to be a limb.

Inside his head he heard the stormy crows.

THE IRON CHARACTERS

The iron characters, keepers of the public confidence,
The sponsors, fund raisers, and members of the board,
Who naturally assume their seats among the governors,
Who place their names behind the issue of bonds
And are consulted in the formation of cabinets,
The catastrophes of war, depression, and natural disaster:
They represent us in responsibilities many and great.
It is no wonder, then, if in a moment of crisis,
Before the microphones, under the lights, on a great
    occasion,
One of them will break down in hysterical weeping
Or fall in an epileptic seizure, or if one day
We read in the papers of one's having been found
Naked and drunk in a basement with three high school
    boys,
Of one who jumped from the window of his hospital
    room.
For are they not as ourselves in these things also?
Let the orphan, the pauper, the thief, the derelict drunk
And all those of no fixed address, shed tears of rejoicing
For the broken minds of the strong, the torn flesh of the
    just.

JOHN HEATH-STUBBS

NOT BEING OEDIPUS

Not being Oedipus he did not question the Sphinx
Nor allow it to question him. He thought it expedient
To make friends and try to influence it.
In this he entirely succeeded,

And continued his journey to Thebes. The abominable thing
Now tame as a kitten (though he was not unaware
That its destructive claws were merely sheathed)
Lolloped along beside him—

To the consternation of the Reception Committee.
It posed a nice problem: he had certainly overcome
But not destroyed the creature—was he or was he not
Entitled to the hand of the Princess

Dowager Jocasta? Not being Oedipus
He saw it as a problem too. For frankly he was not
By natural instinct at all attracted to her.
The question was soon solved—

Solved itself, you might say; for while they argued
The hungry Sphinx, which had not been fed all day,
Sneaked off unobserved, penetrated the royal apartments,
And softly consumed the lady.

So he ascended the important throne of Cadmus,
Beginning a distinguished and uneventful reign.
Celibate, he had nothing to fear from ambitious sons;
Although he was lonely at nights,

With only the Sphinx, curled up upon his eiderdown.
Its body exuded a sort of unearthly warmth
(Though in fact cold-blooded) but its capacity
For affection was strictly limited.

Granted, after his death it was inconsolable,
And froze into its own stone effigy
Upon his tomb. But this was self-love, really—
It felt it had failed in its mission.

While Thebes, by common consent of the people, adopted
His extremely liberal and reasonable constitution,
Which should have enshrined his name—but not being
Oedipus,
It vanished from history, as from legend.

THE SPHINX

It is not feminine: this crouching cat-beast
Kneading a vacant temple between its claws—
Napoleon and the rest
Can fire their guns in its face. In the vicinity
Of the pyramidical Pyramids, where the lanner
Nested, and boys can easily scale,
For a few piastres, an old cove's tombstone,
It will stay, it will gaze
At the rising, rising sun, until the sun
Forgets to rise, and Time ruins, and it, too,
Crumbles—the implacable image
Of male power that smoothly worships itself.

RICHARD WILBUR

JUGGLER

A ball will bounce, but less and less. It's not
A light-hearted thing, resents its own resilience.
Falling is what it loves, and the earth falls
So in our hearts from brilliance,
Settles and is forgot.
It takes a sky-blue juggler with five red balls

To shake our gravity up. Whee, in the air
The balls roll round, wheel on his wheeling hands,
Learning the ways of lightness, alter to spheres
Grazing his finger ends,
Cling to their courses there,
Swinging a small heaven about his ears.

But a heaven is easier made of nothing at all
Than the earth regained, and still and sole within
The spin of worlds, with a gesture sure and noble
He reels that heaven in,
Landing it ball by ball,
And trades it all for a broom, a plate, a table.

Oh, on his toe the table is turning, the broom's
Balancing up on his nose, and the plate whirls
On the tip of the broom! Damn, what a show, we cry:
The boys stamp, and the girls
Shriek, and the drum booms
And all comes down, and he bows and says good-bye.

If the juggler is tired now, if the broom stands
In the dust again, if the table starts to drop
Through the daily dark again, and though the plate
Lies flat on the table top,
For him we batter our hands
Who has won for once over the world's weight.

YEARS'-END

Now winter downs the dying of the year,
And night is all a settlement of snow;
From the soft street the rooms of houses show
A gathered light, a shapen atmosphere,
Like frozen-over lakes whose ice is thin
And still allows some stirring down within.

I've known the wind by water banks to shake
The late leaves down, which frozen where they fell
And held in ice as dancers in a spell
Fluttered all winter long into a lake;
Graved on the dark in gestures of descent,
They seemed their own most perfect monument.

There was perfection in the death of ferns
Which laid their fragile cheeks against the stone
A million years. Great mammoths overthrown
Composedly have made their long sojourns,
Like palaces of patience, in the grey
And changeless lands of ice. And at Pompeii

The little dog lay curled and did not rise
But slept the deeper as the ashes rose
And found the people incomplete, and froze
The random hands, the loose unready eyes
Of men expecting yet another sun
To do the shapely thing they had not done.

These sudden ends of time must give us pause.
We fray into the future, rarely wrought
Save in the tapestries of afterthought.
More time, more time. Barrages of applause
Come muffled from a buried radio.
The New-year bells are wrangling with the snow.

MIND

Mind in its purest play is like some bat
That beats about in caverns all alone,
Contriving by a kind of senseless wit
Not to conclude against a wall of stone.

It has no need to falter or explore;
Darkly it knows what obstacles are there,
And so may weave and flitter, dip and soar
In perfect courses through the blackest air.

And has this simile a like perfection?
The mind is like a bat. Precisely. Save
That in the very happiest intellection
A graceful error may correct the cave.

'A WORLD WITHOUT OBJECTS IS A SENSIBLE EMPTINESS'

The tall camels of the spirit
Steer for their deserts, passing the last groves loud
With the sawmill shrill of the locust, to the whole honey
of the arid
Sun. They are slow, proud,

And move with a stilted stride
To the land of sheer horizon, hunting Traherne's
Sensible emptiness, there where the brain's lantern-slide
Revels in vast returns.

O connoisseurs of thirst,
Beasts of my soul who long to learn to drink
Of pure mirage, those prosperous islands are accurst
That shimmer on the brink

Of absence; auras, lustres,
And all shinings need to be shaped and borne.
Think of those painted saints, capped by the early masters
With bright, jauntily-worn

Aureate plates, or even
Merry-go-round rings. Turn, O turn
From the fine sleights of the sand, from the long empty oven
Where flames in flamings burn

Back to the trees arrayed
In bursts of glare, to the halo-dialling run
Of the country creeks, and the hills' bracken tiaras made
Gold in the sunken sun,

Wisely watch for the sight
Of the supernova burgeoning over the barn,
Lampshine blurred in the steam of beasts, the spirit's right
Oasis, light incarnate.

MERLIN ENTHRALLED

In a while they rose and went out aimlessly riding,
Leaving their drained cups on the table round.
Merlin, Merlin, their hearts cried, where are you hiding?
In all the world was no unnatural sound.

Mystery watched them riding glade by glade;
They saw it darkle from under leafy brows;
But leaves were all its voice, and squirrels made
An alien fracas in the ancient boughs.

Once by a lake-edge something made them stop.
Yet what they found was the thumping of a frog,

Bugs skating on the shut water-top,
Some hairlike algae bleaching on a log.

Gawen thought for a moment that he heard
A whitethorn breathe *Niniane*. That Siren's daughter
Rose in a fort of dreams and spoke the word
Sleep, her voice like dark diving water;

And Merlin slept, who had imagined her
Of water-sounds and the deep unsoundable swell
A creature to bewitch a sorcerer,
And lay there now within her towering spell.

Slowly the shapes of searching men and horses
Escaped him as he dreamt on that high bed:
History died; he gathered in its forces;
The mists of time condensed in the still head

Until his mind, as clear as mountain water,
Went raveling toward the deep transparent dream
Who bade him sleep. And then the Siren's daughter
Received him as the sea receives a stream.

Fate would be fated; dreams desire to sleep.
This the forsaken will not understand.
Arthur upon the road began to weep
And said to Gawen *Remember when this hand*

Once haled a sword from stone; now no less strong
It cannot dream of such a thing to do.
Their mail grew quainter as they clopped along.
The sky became a still and woven blue.

SHAME

It is a cramped little state with no foreign policy,
Save to be thought inoffensive. The grammar of the
    language
Has never been fathomed, owing to the national habit

Of allowing each sentence to trail off in confusion.
Those who have visited Scusi, the capital city,
Report that the railway-route from Schuldig passes
Through country best described as unrelieved.
Sheep are the national product. The faint inscription
Over the city gates may perhaps be rendered,
'I'm afraid you won't find much of interest here.'
Census-reports which give the population
As zero are, of course, not to be trusted,
Save as reflecting the natives' flustered insistence
That they do not count, as well as their modest horror
Of letting one's sex be known in so many words.
The uniform grey of the nondescript buildings, the absence
Of churches or comfort-stations, have given observers
An odd impression of ostentatious meanness,
And it must be said of the citizens (muttering by
In their ratty sheepskins, shying at cracks in the sidewalk)
That they lack the peace of mind of the truly humble.
The tenor of life is careful, even in the stiff
Unsmiling carelessness of the border-guards
And *douaniers*, who admit, whenever they can,
Not merely the usual carloads of deodorant
But gypsies, g-strings, hasheesh, and contraband pigments.
Their complete negligence is reserved, however,
For the hoped-for invasion, at which time the happy people
(Sniggering, ruddily naked, and shamelessly drunk)
Will stun the foe by their overwhelming submission,
Corrupt the generals, infiltrate the staff,
Usurp the throne, proclaim themselves to be sun-gods,
And bring about the collapse of the whole empire.

KEITH DOUGLAS

VERGISSMEINICHT

Three weeks gone and the combatants gone,
returning over the nightmare ground
we found the place again, and found
the soldier sprawling in the sun.

The frowning barrel of his gun
overshadowing. As we came on
that day, he hit my tank with one
like the entry of a demon.

Look. Here in the gunpit spoil
the dishonoured picture of his girl
who has put: *Steffi. Vergissmeinicht*
in a copybook gothic script.

We see him almost with content
abased, and seeming to have paid
and mocked at by his own equipment
that's hard and good when he's decayed.

But she would weep to see to-day
how on his skin the swart flies move;
the dust upon the paper eye
And the burst stomach like a cave.

For here the lover and killer are mingled
who had one body and one heart.
And death who had the soldier singled
has done the lover mortal hurt.

Homs, Tripolitania, 1943.

ARISTOCRATS

'I think I am becoming a God'

The noble horse with courage in his eye
clean in the bone, looks up at a shellburst:
away fly the images of the shires
but he puts the pipe back in his mouth.

Peter was unfortunately killed by an 88:
it took his leg away, he died in the ambulance.
I saw him crawling on the sand; he said
It's most unfair, they've shot my foot off.

How can I live among this gentle
obsolescent breed of heroes, and not weep?
Unicorns, almost,
for they are falling into two legends
in which their stupidity and chivalry
are celebrated. Each, fool and hero, will be an immortal.

The plains were their cricket pitch
and in the mountains the tremendous drop fences
brought down some of the runners. Here then
under the stones and earth they dispose themselves,
I think with their famous unconcern.
It is not gunfire I hear but a hunting horn.

Enfidaville, Tunisia, 1943.

ON A RETURN FROM EGYPT

To stand here in the wings of Europe
disheartened, I have come away
from the sick land where in the sun lay
the gentle sloe-eyed murderers
of themselves, exquisites under a curse;
here to exercise my depleted fury.

For the heart is a coal, growing colder
when jewelled cerulean seas change
into grey rocks, grey water-fringe,
sea and sky altering like a cloth
till colour and sheen are gone both:
cold is an opiate of the soldier.

And all my endeavours are unlucky explorers
come back, abandoning the expedition;
the specimens, the lilies of ambition
still spring in their climate, still unpicked:
but time, time is all I lacked
to find them, as the great collectors before me.

The next month, then, is a window
and with a crash I'll split the glass.
Behind it stands one I must kiss,
person of love or death
a person or a wraith,
I fear what I shall find.

Egypt-England, 1943-44.

SNAKESKIN AND STONE

I praise a snakeskin or a stone:
a bald head or a public speech
I hate: the serpent's lozenges
are a calligraphy, and it is
truth these cryptograms teach,
the pebble is truth alone.
Complication belonging to the snake
who is as subtle as his gold, black, green—
it is right the stone is old
and smooth, utterly cruel and old.
These two are two pillars. Between
stand all the buildings truth can make,

a whole city, inhabited by lovers,
murderers, workmen and artists
not much recognized: all
who have no memorial
but are mere men. Even the lowest
never made himself a mask of words or figures.
The bald head is a desert
between country of life and country of death;
between the desolate projecting ears
move the wicked explorers, the flies
who know the dead bone is beneath
and from the skin the life half out
and dead words tumbled in heaps
in the papers lie in rows
awaiting burial. The speakers mouth
like a cold sea that sucks and spews them out
with insult to their bodies. Tangled they cruise
like mariners' bodies in the grave of ships.
Borrow hair for the bald crown,
borrow applause for the dead words;
for you who think the desert hidden
or the words, like the dry bones, living
are fit to profit from the world.
And God help the lover of snakeskin and stone.

DONALD DAVIE

GARDENS NO EMBLEMS

Man with a scythe: the torrent of his swing
Finds its own level; and is not hauled back
But gathers fluently, like water rising
Behind the watergates that close a lock.

The gardener eased his foot into a boot;
Which action like the mower's had its mould,
Being itself a sort of taking root,
Feeling for lodgment in the leather's fold.

But forms of thought move in another plane
Whose matrices no natural forms afford
Unless subjected to prodigious strain:
Say, light proceeding edgewise, like a sword.

HEARING RUSSIAN SPOKEN

Unsettled again and hearing Russian spoken
I think of brokenness perversely planned
By Dostoievsky's debauchees; recall
The 'visible brokenness' that is the token
Of the true believer; and connect it all
With speaking a language I cannot command.

If broken means unmusical I speak
Even in English brokenly, a man
Wretched enough, yet one who cannot borrow
Their hunger for indignity nor, weak,
Abet my weakness, drink to drown a sorrow
Or write in metres that I cannot scan.

Unsettled again at hearing Russian spoken,
'Abjure politic brokenness for good,'
I tell myself. 'Recall what menaces,
What self-loathings must be re-awoken:
This girl and that, and all your promises
Your pidgin that they too well understood.'

Not just in Russian but in any tongue
Abandonment, morality's soubrette
Of lyrical surrender and excess,
Knows the weak endings equal to the strong;
She trades on broken English with success
And, disenchanted, I'm enamoured yet.

THE MUSHROOM GATHERERS

after Mickiewicz

Strange walkers! See their processional
Perambulations under low boughs,
The birches white, and the green turf under.
These should be ghosts by moonlight wandering.

Their attitudes strange: the human tree
Slowly revolves on its bole. All around
Downcast looks; and the direct dreamer
Treads out in trance his lane, unwavering.

Strange decorum: so prodigal of bows,
Yet lost in thought and self-absorbed, they meet
Impassively, without acknowledgment.
A courteous nation, but unsociable.

Field full of folk, in their immunity
From human ills, crestfallen and serene.
Who would have thought these shades our lively friends?
Surely these acres are Elysian Fields.

PHILIP LARKIN

NEXT, PLEASE

Always too eager for the future, we
Pick up bad habits of expectancy.
Something is always approaching; every day
Till then we say,

Watching from a bluff the tiny, clear
Sparkling armada of promises draw near.
How slow they are! And how much time they waste,
Refusing to make haste!

Yet still they leave us holding wretched stalks
Of disappointment, for, though nothing balks
Each big approach, leaning with brasswork prinked,
Each rope distinct,

Flagged, and the figurehead with golden tits
Arching our way, it never anchors; it's
No sooner present that it turns to past.
Right to the last

We think each one will heave to and unload
All good into our lives, all we are owed
For waiting so devoutly and so long.
But we are wrong:

Only one ship is seeking us, a black-
Sailed unfamiliar, towing at her back
A huge and birdless silence. In her wake
No waters breed or break.

DECEPTIONS

'Of course I was drugged, and so heavily I did not regain my consciousness till the next morning. I was horrified to discover that I had been ruined, and for some days I was inconsolable, and cried like a child to be killed or sent back to my aunt.'—Mayhew, *London Labour and the London Poor.*

Even so distant, I can taste the grief,
Bitter and sharp with stalks, he made you gulp.
The sun's occasional print, the brisk brief
Worry of wheels along the street outside
Where bridal London bows the other way,
And light, unanswerable and tall and wide,
Forbids the scar to heal, and drives
Shame out of hiding. All the unhurried day
Your mind lay open like a drawer of knives.

Slums, years, have buried you. I would not dare
Console you if I could. What can be said,
Except that suffering is exact, but where
Desire takes charge, readings will grow erratic?
For you would hardly care
That you were less deceived, out on that bed,
Than he was, stumbling up the breathless stair
To burst into fulfilment's desolate attic.

TOADS

Why should I let the toad *work*
  Squat on my life?
Can't I use my wit as a pitchfork
  And drive the brute off?

Six days of the week it soils
  With its sickening poison—
Just for paying a few bills!
  That's out of proportion.

Lots of folk live on their wits:
  Lecturers, lispers,
Losels, loblolly-men, louts—
  They don't end as paupers;

Lots of folk live up lanes
  With fires in a bucket,
Eat windfalls and tinned sardines—
  They seem to like it.

Their nippers have got bare feet,
  Their unspeakable wives
Are skinny as whippets—and yet
  No one actually *starves*.

Ah, were I courageous enough
  To shout *Stuff your pension!*
But I know, all too well, that's the stuff
  That dreams are made on:

For something sufficiently toad-like
  Squats in me, too;
Its hunkers are heavy as hard luck,
  And cold as snow,

And will never allow me to blarney
  My way to getting
The fame and the girl and the money
  All at one sitting.

I don't say, one bodies the other
  One's spiritual truth;
But I do say it's hard to lose either,
  When you have both.

MR. BLEANEY

'This was Mr. Bleaney's room. He stayed
The whole time he was at the Bodies, till
They moved him.' Flowered curtains, thin and frayed,
Fall to within five inches of the sill,

Whose window shows a strip of building land,
Tussocky, littered. 'Mr. Bleaney took
My bit of garden properly in hand.'
Bed, upright chair, sixty-watt bulb, no hook

Behind the door, no room for books or bags—
'I'll take it.' So it happens that I lie
Where Mr. Bleaney lay, and stub my fags
On the same saucer-souvenir, and try

Stuffing my ears with cotton-wool, to drown
The jabbering set he egged her on to buy.
I know his habits—what time he came down,
His preference for sauce to gravy, why

He kept on plugging at the four aways—
Likewise their yearly frame: the Frinton folk
Who put him up for summer holidays,
And Christmas at his sister's house in Stoke.

But if he stood and watched the frigid wind
Tousling the clouds, lay on the fusty bed
Telling himself that this was home, and grinned,
And shivered, without shaking off the dread

That how we live measures our own nature,
And at his age having no more to show
Than one hired box should make him pretty sure
He warranted no better, I don't know.

AFTERNOONS

Summer is fading:
The leaves fall in ones and twos
From trees bordering
The new recreation ground.
In the hollows of afternoons
Young mothers assemble
At swing and sandpit
Setting free their children.

Behind them, at intervals,
Stand husbands in skilled trades,
An estateful of washing,
And the albums, lettered
Our Wedding, lying
Near the television:
Before them, the wind
Is ruining their courting-places

That are still courting-places
(But the lovers are all in school),
And their children, so intent on
Finding more unripe acorns,
Expect to be taken home.
Their beauty has thickened.
Something is pushing them
To the side of their own lives.

DAYS

What are days for?
Days are where we live.
They come, they wake us
Time and time over.

They are to be happy in:
Where can we live but days?

Ah, solving that question
Brings the priest and the doctor
In their long coats
Running over the fields.

CHARLES TOMLINSON

PARING THE APPLE

There are portraits and still-lives.

And there is paring the apple.

And then? Paring it slowly,
From under cool-yellow
Cold-white emerging. And . . . ?

The spring of concentric peel
Unwinding off white,
The blade hidden, dividing.

There are portraits and still-lives
And the first, because 'human'
Does not excel the second, and
Neither is less weighted
With a human gesture, than paring the apple
With a human stillness.

The cool blade
Severs between coolness, apple-rind
Compelling a recognition.

A MEDITATION ON JOHN CONSTABLE

'Painting is a science, and should be pursued as an inquiry into the laws of nature. Why, then, may not landscape painting be considered as a branch of natural philosophy, of which pictures are but the experiments?'

JOHN CONSTABLE, The History of Landscape

He replied to his own question, and with the unmannered
  Exactness of art; enriched his premises
By confirming his practice: the labour of observation

In face of meteorological fact. Clouds
Followed by others, temper the sun in passing
Over and off it. Massed darks
Blotting it back, scattered and mellowed shafts
Break damply out of them, until the source
Unmasks, floods its retreating bank
With raw fire. One perceives (though scarcely)
The remnant clouds trailing across it
In rags, and thinned to a gauze.
But the next will dam it. They loom past
And narrow its blaze. It shrinks to a crescent
Crushed out, a still lengthening ooze
As the mass thickens, though it cannot exclude
Its silvered-yellow. The eclipse is sudden,
Seen first on the darkening grass, then complete
In a covered sky.
Facts. And what are they?
He admired accidents, because governed by laws,
Representing them (since the illusion was not his end)
As governed by feeling. The end is our approval
Freely accorded, the illusion persuading us
That it exists as a human image. Caught
By a wavering sun, or under a wind
Which moistening among the outlines of banked foliage
Prepares to dissolve them, it must grow constant;
Though there, ruffling and parted, the disturbed
Trees let through the distance, like white fog
Into their broken ranks. It must persuade
And with a constancy, not to be swept back
To reveal what it half-conceals. Art is itself
Once we accept it. The day veers. He would have judged
Exactly in such a light, that strides down
Over the quick stains of could-shadows
Expunged now, by its conflagration of colour.
A descriptive painter? If delight
Describes, which wrings from the brush
The errors of a mind, so tempered,

It can forgo all pathos; for what he saw
  Discovered what he was, and the hand—unswayed
By the dictation of a single sense—
  Bodied the accurate and total knowledge
In a calligraphy of present pleasure. Art
  Is complete when it is human. It is human
Once the looped pigments, the pin-heads of light
  Securing space under their deft restrictions
Convince, as the index of a possible passion,
  As the adequate gauge, both of the passion
And its object. The artist lies
  For the improvement of truth. Believe him.

THE HAND AT CALLOW HILL FARM

Silence. The man defined
The quality, ate at his separate table
Silent, not because silence was enjoined
But was his nature. It shut him round
Even at outdoor tasks, his speech
Following upon a pause, as though
A hesitance to comply had checked it—
Yet comply he did, and willingly:
Pause and silence: both
Were essential graces, a reticence
Of the blood, whose calm concealed
The tutelary of that upland field.

JAMES DICKEY

THE HEAVEN OF ANIMALS

Here they are. The soft eyes open.
If they have lived in a wood
It is a wood.
If they have lived on plains
It is grass rolling
Under their feet forever.

Having no souls, they have come,
Anyway, beyond their knowing.
Their instincts wholly bloom
And they rise.
The soft eyes open.

To match them, the landscape flowers,
Outdoing, desperately
Outdoing what is required:
The richest wood,
The deepest field.

For some of these,
It could not be the place
It is, without blood.
These hunt, as they have done,
But with claws and teeth grown perfect,

More deadly than they can believe.
They stalk more silently,
And crouch on the limbs of trees,
And their descent
Upon the bright backs of their prey

May take years
In a sovereign floating of joy.
And those that are hunted
Know this as their life,
Their reward: to walk

Under such trees in full knowledge
Of what is in glory above them,
And to feel no fear,
But acceptance, compliance.
Fulfilling themselves without pain

At the cycle's center,
They tremble, they walk
Under the tree,
They fall, they are torn,
They rise, they walk again.

IN THE TREE HOUSE AT NIGHT

And now the green household is dark.
The half-moon completely is shining
On the earth-lighted tops of the trees.
To be dead, a house must be still.
The floor and the walls wave me slowly;
I am deep in them over my head.
The needles and pine cones about me

Are full of small birds at their roundest,
Their fists without mercy gripping
Hard down through the tree to the roots
To sing back at light when they feel it.
We lie here like angels in bodies,
My brothers and I, one dead,
The other asleep from much living,

In mid-air huddled beside me.
Dark climbed to us here as we climbed
Up the nails I have hammered all day
Through the sprained, comic rungs of the ladder
Of broom handles, crate slats, and laths
Foot by foot up the trunk to the branches
Where we came out at last over lakes

Of leaves, of fields disencumbered of earth
That move with the moves of the spirit.
Each nail that sustains us I set here;
Each nail in the house is now steadied
By my dead brother's huge, freckled hand.
Through the years, he has pointed his hammer
Up into these limbs, and told us

That we must ascend, and all lie here.
Step after step he has brought me,
Embracing the trunk as his body,
Shaking its limbs with my heartbeat,
Till the pine cones danced without wind
And fell from the branches like apples.
In the arm-slender forks of our dwelling

I breathe my live brother's light hair.
The blanket around us becomes
As solid as stone, and it sways.
With all my heart, I close
The blue, timeless eye of my mind.
Wind springs, as my dead brother smiles
And touches the tree at the root;

A shudder of joy runs up
The trunk; the needles tingle;
One bird uncontrollably cries.
The wind changes round, and I stir
Within another's life. Whose life?
Who is dead? Whose presence is living?
When may I fall strangely to earth,

Who am nailed to this branch by a spirit?
Can two bodies make up a third?
To sing, must I feel the world's light?
My green, graceful bones fill the air
With sleeping birds. Alone, alone
And with them I move gently.
I move at the heart of the world.

LOUIS SIMPSON

WALT WHITMAN AT BEAR MOUNTAIN

'. . . *life which does not give the preference to any other life, of any previous period, which therefore prefers its own existence*. . . .'—Ortega Y Gasset

Neither on horseback nor seated,
But like himself, squarely on two feet,
The poet of death and lilacs
Loafs by the footpath. Even the bronze looks alive
Where it is folded like cloth. And he seems friendly.

'Where is the Mississippi panorama
And the girl who played the piano?
Where are you, Walt?
The Open Road goes to the used-car lot.

'Where is the nation you promised?
These houses built of wood sustain
Colossal snows,
And the light above the street is sick to death.

'As for the people—see how they neglect you!
Only a poet pauses to read the inscription.'

'I am here,' he answered.
'It seems you have found me out.
Yet, did I not warn you that it was Myself
I advertised? Were my words not sufficiently plain?

'I gave no prescriptions,
And those who have taken my moods for prophecies
Mistake the matter.'
Then, vastly amused—'Why do you reproach me?

I freely confess I am wholly disreputable.
Yet I am happy, because you have found me out.'

A crocodile in wrinkled metal loafing . . .

Then all the realtors,
Pickpockets, salesmen, and the actors performing
Official scenarios,
Turned a deaf ear, for they had contracted
American dreams.

But the man who keeps a store on a lonely road,
And the housewife who knows she's dumb,
And the earth, are relieved.

All that grave weight of America
Cancelled! Like Greece and Rome.
The future in ruins!
The castles, the prisons, the cathedrals
Unbuilding, and roses
Blossoming from the stones that are not there . . .

The clouds are lifting from the high Sierras,
The Bay mists clearing;
And the angel in the gate, the flowering plum,
Dances like Italy, imagining red.

I DREAMED THAT IN A CITY DARK AS PARIS

I dreamed that in a city dark as Paris
I stood alone in a deserted square.
The night was trembling with a violet
Expectancy. At the far edge it moved
And rumbled; on that flickering horizon
The guns were pumping color in the sky.

There was the Front. But I was lonely here,
Left behind, abandoned by the army.
The empty city and the empty square
Was my inhabitation, my unrest.
The helmet with its vestige of a crest,
The rifle in my hands, long out of date,
The belt I wore, the trailing overcoat
And hobnail boots, were those of a *poilu.*
I was the man, as awkward as a bear.

Over the rooftops where cathedrals loomed
In speaking majesty, two aeroplanes
Forlorn as birds, appeared. Then growing large,
The German *Taube* and the *Nieuport Scout,*
They chased each other tumbling through the sky,
Till one streamed down on fire to the earth.

These wars have been so great, they are forgotten
Like the Egyptian dynasts. My confrere
In whose thick boots I stood, were you amazed
To wander through my brain four decades later
As I have wandered in a dream through yours?

The violence of waking life disrupts
The order of our death. Strange dreams occur,
For dreams are licensed as they never were.

DENISE LEVERTOV

TO THE SNAKE

Green Snake, when I hung you round my neck
and stroked your cold, pulsing throat
as you hissed to me, glinting
arrowy gold scales, and I felt
the weight of you on my shoulders,
and the whispering silver of your dryness
sounded close at my ears—

Green Snake—I swore to my companions that certainly
you were harmless! But truly
I had no certainty, and no hope, only desiring
to hold you, for that joy,
which left
a long wake of pleasure, as the leaves moved
and you faded into the pattern
of grass and shadows, and I returned
smiling and haunted, to a dark morning.

THE RAINWALKERS

An old man whose black face
shines golden-brown as wet pebbles
under the streetlamp, is walking
two mongrel dogs of dis-
proportionate size, in the rain,
in the relaxed early-evening avenue.

The small sleek one wants to stop,
docile to the imploring soul of the trashbasket,
but the young tall curly one

wants to walk on; the glistening sidewalk
entices him to arcane happenings.

Increasing rain. The old bareheaded man
smiles and grumbles to himself.
The lights change: the avenue's
endless nave echoes notes of liturgical red. He drifts

between his dogs' desires.
The three of them are enveloped—
turning now to go crosstown—in their
sense of each other, of pleasure,
of weather, of corners,
of leisurely tensions between them
and private silence.

W. D. SNODGRASS

APRIL INVENTORY

The green catalpa tree has turned
All white; the cherry blooms once more.
In one whole year I haven't learned
A blessed thing they pay you for.
The blossoms snow down in my hair;
The trees and I will soon be bare.

The trees have more than I to spare.
The sleek, expensive girls I teach,
Younger and pinker every year,
Bloom gradually out of reach.
The pear tree lets its petals drop
Like dandruff on a tabletop.

The girls have grown so young by now
I have to nudge myself to stare.
This year they smile and mind me how
My teeth are falling with my hair.
In thirty years I may not get
Younger, shrewder, or out of debt.

The tenth time, just a year ago,
I made myself a little list
Of all the things I'd ought to know;
Then told my parents, analyst,
And everyone who's trusted me
I'd be substantial, presently.

I haven't read one book about
A book or memorized one plot.
Or found a mind I didn't doubt.

I learned one date. And then forgot.
And one by one the solid scholars
Get the degrees, the jobs, the dollars.

And smile above their starchy collars.
I taught my classes Whitehead's notions;
One lovely girl, a song of Mahler's.
Lacking a source-book or promotions,
I showed one child the colors of
A luna moth and how to love.

I taught myself to name my name,
To bark back, loosen love and crying;
To ease my woman so she came,
To ease an old man who was dying.
I have not learned how often I
Can win, can love, but choose to die.

I have not learned there is a lie
Love shall be blonder, slimmer, younger;
That my equivocating eye
Loves only by my body's hunger;
That I have poems, true to feel,
Or that the lovely world is real.

While scholars speak authority
And wear their ulcers on their sleeves,
My eyes in spectacles shall see
These trees procure and spend their leaves.
There is a value underneath
The gold and silver in my teeth.

Though trees turn bare and girls turn wives,
We shall afford our costly seasons;
There is a gentleness survives
That will outspeak and has its reasons.
There is a loveliness exists,
Preserves us. Not for specialists.

MONET: 'LES NYMPHÉAS'

The eyelids glowing, some chill morning.
O world half-known through opening, twilit lids
Before the vague face clenches into light;
O universal waters like a cloud,
Like those first clouds of half-created matter;
O all things rising, rising like the fumes
From waters falling, O forever falling;
Infinite, the skeletal shells that fall, relinquished,
The snowsoft sift of the diatoms, like selves
Downdrifting age upon age through milky oceans;
O slow downdrifting of the atoms;
O island nebulae and O the nebulous islands
Wandering these mists like falsefires, which are true,
Bobbing like milkweed, like warm lanterns bobbing
Through the snowfilled windless air, blinking and
passing
As we pass into the memory of women
Who are passing. Within those depths
What ravening? What devouring rage?
How shall our living know its ends of yielding?
These things have taken me as the mouth an orange—
That acrid sweet juice entering every cell;
And I am shared out. I become these things:
These lilies, if these things *are* waterlilies
Which are dancers growing dim across no floor;
These mayflies; whirled dust orbiting in the sun;
This blossoming diffused as rushlights; galactic vapours;
Fluorescence into which we pass and penetrate;
O soft as the thighs of women;
O radiance, into which I go on dying. . . .

CHRISTOPHER MIDDLETON

THE THOUSAND THINGS

Dry vine leaves burn in an angle of the wall.
Dry vine leaves and a sheet of paper, overhung by the
green vine.
From an open grate in an angle of the wall
dry vine leaves and dead flies send smoke up
into the green vine where grape clusters go
ignored by lizards. Dry vine leaves
and a few dead flies on fire
and a Spanish toffee spat
into an angle of the wall
make a smell that calls to mind
the thousand things. Dead flies go,
paper curls and flares,
Spanish toffee sizzles and the smell
has soon gone over the wall.

A naked child jumps over the threshold,
waving a green spray of leaves of vine.

MALE TORSO

Before I woke, the customed thews
Alighted on strangeness.
Crammed over booms of vine,
The once buxom canvas quilled.

From his hot nest, before I woke,
The snowgoose flew, in skyward rings;
And funnelled air that filled my mouth
Rang with his wingbeat.

The customed eyes, before I woke, were glass:
A bleating queen whose legs were sheaths
Of hammered moon fed swill to pigs;
With needle oars they swept her bark

Through floes of starfruit, dolphins cutting
Under her eyelid's bow blue arcs in air;
And the beat of their oars like drums
Fanned my hushabye head.

Before I woke, no savour was;
But three birds sang that song they piped as girls,
Of sweetness, golden-rinded, and the fountaintree,
For mortal grapes cooled in my hands.

Then down the quartz-walled galleries of ears I coiled,
Before I woke; cymbals clashing sliced their hill,
And there with bulls my skew-wigged mother trod
Her crocus dance around its axle;

Counterwheeling Horn and Bear
Shared in her coronal the thud of fingertips on flutes,
Until my customed silence dipped and rose,
And gall was mine and darkness was,

I live now in a hutch of mud,
Without a floor, nailed by the sun,
Now for the interminable writhing sea
A fair food housed in roofless marble.

But if I wake to sniff the air of clustered stars,
I'm clothed in dew, for babes to drink,
The snowgoose moors her nest on light,
And the small horned worms walk high with hope.

ROBERT BLY

A MAN WRITES TO A PART OF HIMSELF

What cave are you in, hiding, rained on?
Like a wife, starving, without care,
Water dripping from your head, bent
Over ground corn . . .

You raise your face into the rain
That drives over the valley—
Forgive me, your husband,
On the streets of a distant city, laughing,
With many appointments,
Though at night going also
To a bare room, a room of poverty,
To sleep among a bare pitcher and basin
In a room with no heat—

Which of us two then is the worse off?
And how did this separation come about?

'TAKING THE HANDS'

Taking the hands of someone you love,
You see they are delicate cages . . .
Tiny birds are singing
In the secluded prairies
And in the deep valleys of the hand.

LAZINESS AND SILENCE

I

On a Saturday afternoon in the football season,
I lie in a bed near the lake,
And dream of moles with golden wings.

While the depth of the water trembles on the ceiling,
Like the tail of an enraged bird,
I watch the dust floating above the bed, content.

I think of ships leaving lonely harbors,
Dolphins playing far at sea,
Fish with the faces of old men come in from a blizzard.

II

A dream of moles with golden wings
Is not so bad; it is like imagining
Waterfalls of stone deep in mountains,
Or a wing flying alone beneath the earth.

I know that far out in the Minnesota lake
Fish are nosing the mouths of cold springs,
Whose water causes ripples in the sleeping sand,
Like a spirit moving in a body.

It is Saturday afternoon. Crowds are gathered,
Warmed by the sun, and the pure air.
I thought of this strange mole this morning,
After sleeping all night by the lake.

W. S. MERWIN

THE ICEBERG

It is not its air but our own awe
That freezes us. Hardest of all to believe
That so fearsome a destroyer can be
Dead, with those lights moving in it,
With the sea all around it charged
With its influence. It seems that only now
We realize the depth of the waters, the
Abyss over which we float among such
Clouds. And still not understanding
The coldness of most elegance, even
With so vast and heartless a splendor
Before us, stare, caught in the magnetism
Of great silence, thinking: this is the terror
That cannot be charted, this is only
A little of it. And recall how many
Mariners, watching the sun set, have seen
These peaks on the horizon and made sail
Through the darkness for islands that no map
Had promised, floating blessed in
The west. These must dissolve
Before they can again grow apple trees.

DEPARTURE'S GIRL-FRIEND

Loneliness leapt in the mirrors, but all week
I kept them covered like cages. Then I thought
Of a better thing.

And though it was late night in the city
There I was on my way
To my boat, feeling good to be going, hugging

This big wreath with the words like real
Silver: *Bon Voyage.*

The night
Was mine but everyone's, like a birthday.
Its fur touched my face in passing. I was going
Down to my boat, my boat,
To see it off, and glad at the thought.
Some leaves of the wreath were holding my hands
And the rest waved good-bye as I walked, as though
They were still alive.

And all went well till I came to the wharf, and no one.

I say no one, but I mean
There was this young man, maybe
Out of the merchant marine,
In some uniform, and I knew who he was; just the same
When he said to me where do you think you're going,
I was happy to tell him.

But he said to me, it isn't your boat,
You don't have one. I said, it's mine, I can prove it:
Look at this wreath, I'm carrying to it,
Bon Voyage. He said, This is the stone wharf, lady,
You don't own anything here.

And as I
Was turning away, the injustice of it
Lit up the buildings, and there I was
In the other and hated city
Where I was born, where nothing is moored, where
The lights crawl over the stone like flies, spelling now,
Now, and the same fat chances roll
Their many eyes; and I step once more
Through a hoop of tears and walk on, holding this
Buoy of flowers in front of my beauty,
Wishing myself the good voyage.

JAMES WRIGHT

LYING IN A HAMMOCK AT WILLIAM DUFFY'S FARM IN PINE ISLAND, MINNESOTA

Over my head, I see the bronze butterfly,
Asleep on the black trunk,
Blowing like a leaf in green shadow.
Down the ravine behind the empty house,
The cowbells follow one another
Into the distances of the afternoon.
To my right,
In a field of sunlight between two pines,
The droppings of last year's horses
Blaze up into golden stones.
I lean back, as the evening darkens and comes on.
A chicken hawk floats over, looking for home.
I have wasted my life.

HOW MY FEVER LEFT

I can still hear her.
She hobbles downstairs to the kitchen.
She is swearing at the dishes.
She slaps her grease rags
Into a basket,
And slings it over her skinny forearm, crooked
With hatred, and stomps outside.
I can hear my father downstairs,
Standing without a coat in the open back door,
Calling to the old bat across the snow.
She's forgotten her black shawl,
But I see her through my window, sneering,

Flapping upward
Toward some dark church on the hill.
She has to meet somebody else, and
It's no use, she won't listen,
She's gone.

EISENHOWER'S VISIT TO FRANCO, 1959

'. . . *we die of cold, and not of darkness.*'
—Unamuno

The American hero must triumph over
The forces of darkness.
He has flown through the very light of heaven
And come down in the slow dusk
Of Spain.

Franco stands in a shining circle of police.
His arms open in welcome.
He promises all dark things
Will be hunted down.

State police yawn in the prisons.
Antonio Machado follows the moon
Down a road of white dust,
To a cave of silent children
Under the Pyrenees.
Wine darkens in stone jars in villages.
Wine sleeps in the mouths of old men, it is a dark red
color.

Smiles glitter in Madrid.
Eisenhower has touched hands with Franco, embracing
In a glare of photographers.
Clean new bombers from America muffle their engines
And glide down now.

Their wings shine in the searchlights
Of bare fields,
In Spain.

THOM GUNN

THE NATURE OF AN ACTION

I

Here is a room with heavy-footed chairs,
A glass bell loaded with wax grapes and pears,

A polished table, holding down the look
Of bracket, mantelpiece, and marbled book.

Staying within the cluttered square of fact,
I cannot slip the clumsy fond contact:

So step into the corridor and start,
Directed by the compass of my heart.

II

Although the narrow corridor appears
So short, the journey took me twenty years.

Each gesture that my habit taught me fell
Down to the boards and made an obstacle.

I paused to watch the fly marks on a shelf,
And found the great obstruction of myself.

I reached the end but, pacing back and forth,
I could not see what reaching it was worth.

In corridors the rooms are undefined:
I groped to feel a handle in the mind.

Testing my faculties I found a stealth
Of passive illness lurking in my health.

And though I saw the corridor stretch bare,
Dusty, and hard, I doubted it was there;

Doubted myself, what final evidence
Lay in perceptions or in common sense?

III

My cause lay in the will, that opens straight
Upon an act for the most desperate.

That simple handle found, I entered in
The other room, where I had never been.

I found within it heavy-footed chairs,
A glass bell loaded with wax grapes and pears,

A polished table, holding down the look
Of bracket, mantelpiece, and marbled book.

Much like the first, this room in which I went.
Only my being there is different.

IN SANTA MARIA DEL POPOLO

Waiting for when the sun an hour or less
Conveniently oblique makes visible
The painting on one wall of this recess
By Caravaggio, of the Roman School,
I see how shadow in the painting brims
With a real shadow, drowning all shapes out
But a dim horse's haunch and various limbs,
Until the very subject is in doubt.

But evening gives the act, beneath the horse
And one indifferent groom, I see him sprawl,
Foreshortened from the head, with hidden face,
Where he has fallen, Saul becoming Paul.

O wily painter, limiting the scene
From a cacophony of dusty forms
To the one convulsion, what is it you mean
In that wide gesture of the lifting arms?

No Ananias croons a mystery yet,
Casting the pain out under name of sin.
The painter saw what was, an alternate
Candour and secrecy inside the skin.
He painted, elsewhere, that firm insolent
Young whore in Venus' clothes, those pudgy cheats,
Those sharpers; and was strangled, as things went,
For money, by one such picked off the streets.

I turn, hardly enlightened, from the chapel
To the dim interior of the church instead,
In which there kneel already several people,
Mostly old women: each head closeted
In tiny fists holds comfort as it can.
Their poor arms are too tired for more than this
—For the large gesture of solitary man,
Resisting, by embracing, nothingness.

INNOCENCE

(to Tony White)

He ran the course and as he ran he grew,
And smelt his fragrance in the field. Already,
Running he knew the most he ever knew,
The egotism of a healthy body.

Ran into manhood, ignorant of the past:
Culture of guilt and guilt's vague heritage,
Self-pity and the soul; what he possessed
Was rich, potential, like the bud's tipped rage.

The Corps developed, it was plain to see,
Courage, endurance, loyalty and skill
To a morale firm as morality,
Hardening him to an instrument, until

The finitude of virtues that were there
Bodied within the swarthy uniform
A compact innocence, child-like and clear,
No doubt could penetrate, no act could harm.

When he stood near the Russian partisan
Being burned alive, he therefore could behold
The ribs wear gently through the darkening skin
And sicken only at the Northern cold,

Could watch the fat burn with a violet flame
And feel disgusted only at the smell,
And judge that all pain finishes the same
As melting quietly by his boots it fell.

CONSIDERING THE SNAIL

The snail pushes through a green
night, for the grass is heavy
with water and meets over
the bright path he makes, where rain
has darkened the earth's dark. He
moves in a wood of desire,

pale antlers barely stirring
as he hunts. I cannot tell
what power is at work, drenched there
with purpose, knowing nothing.
What is a snail's fury? all
I think is that if later

I parted the blades above
the tunnel and saw the thin
train of broken white across
litter, I would never have
imagined the slow passion
to that deliberate progress.

MY SAD CAPTAINS

One by one they appear in
the darkness: a few friends, and
a few with historical
names. How late they start to shine!
but before they fade they stand
perfectly embodied, all

the past lapping them like a
cloak of chaos. They were men
who, I thought, lived only to
renew the wasteful force they
spent with each hot convulsion.
They remind me, distant now.

True, they are not at rest yet,
but now that they are indeed
apart, winnowed from failures,
they withdraw to an orbit
and turn with disinterested
hard energy, like the stars.

TED HUGHES

NOVEMBER

The month of the drowned dog. After long rain the land
Was sodden as the bed of an ancient lake,
Treed with iron and birdless. In the sunk lane
The ditch—a seep silent all summer—

Made brown foam with a big voice: that, and my boots
On the lane's scrubbed stones, in the gulleyed leaves,
Against the hill's hanging silence;
Mist silvering the droplets on the bare thorns

Slower than the change of daylight.
In a let of the ditch a tramp was bundled asleep:
Face tucked down into beard, drawn in
Under its hair like a hedgehog's. I took him for dead,

But his stillness separated from the death
Of the rotting grass and the ground. A wind chilled,
And a fresh comfort tightened through him,
Each hand stuffed deeper into the other sleeve.

His ankles, bound with sacking and hairy band,
Rubbed each other, resettling. The wind hardened;
A puff shook a glittering from the thorns,
And again the rains' dragging grey columns

Smudged the farms. In a moment
The fields were jumping and smoking; the thorns
Quivered, riddled with the glassy verticals.
I stayed on under the welding cold

Watching the tramp's face glisten and the drops on his
coat
Flash and darken. I thought what strong trust

Slept in him—as the trickling furrows slept,
And the thorn-roots in their grip on darkness;

And the buried stones, taking the weight of winter;
The hill where the hare crouched with clenched teeth.
Rain plastered the land till it was shining
Like hammered lead, and I ran, and in the rushing wood

Shuttered by a black oak leaned.
The keeper's gibbet had owls and hawks
By the neck, weasels, a gang of cats, crows:
Some, stiff, weightless, twirled like dry bark bits

In the drilling rain. Some still had their shape,
Had their pride with it; hung, chins on chests,
Patient to outwait these worst days that beat
Their crowns bare and dripped from their feet.

THRUSHES

Terrifying are the attent sleek thrushes on the lawn,
More coiled steel than living—a poised
Dark deadly eye, those delicate legs
Triggered to stirrings beyond sense—with a start, a
 bounce, a stab
Overtake the instant and drag out some writhing thing.
No indolent procrastinations and no yawning states,
No sighs or head-scratchings. Nothing but bounce and
 stab
And a ravening second.

Is it their single-mind-sized skulls, or a trained
Body, or genius, or a nestful of brats
Gives their days this bullet and automatic
Purpose? Mozart's brain had it, and the shark's mouth

That hungers down the blood-smell even to a leak of its own
Side and devouring of itself: efficiency wnich
Strikes too streamlined for any doubt to pluck at it
Or obstruction deflect.

With a man it is otherwise. Heroisms on horseback,
Outstripping his desk-diary at a broad desk,
Carving at a tiny ivory ornament
For years: his act worships itself—while for him,
Though he bends to be blent in the prayer, how loud and above what
Furious spaces of fire do the distracting devils
Orgy and hosannah, under what wilderness
Of black silent waters weep.

PIKE

Pike, three inches long, perfect
Pike in all parts, green tigering the gold.
Killers from the egg: the malevolent aged grin.
They dance on the surface among the flies.

Or move, stunned by their own grandeur,
Over a bed of emerald, silhouette
Of submarine delicacy and horror.
A hundred feet long in their world.

In ponds, under the heat-struck lily pads—
Gloom of their stillness:
Logged on last year's black leaves, watching upwards.
Or hung in an amber cavern of weeds

The jaws' hooked clamp and fangs
Not to be changed at this date;

A life subdued to its instrument;
The gills kneading quietly, and the pectorals.

Three we kept behind glass,
Jungled in weed: three inches, four,
And four and a half: fed fry to them—
Suddenly there were two. Finally one

With a sag belly and the grin it was born with.
And indeed they spare nobody.
Two, six pounds each, over two feet long,
High and dry and dead in the willow-herb—

One jammed past its gills down the other's gullet:
The outside eye stared: as a vice locks—
The same iron in this eye
Though its film shrank in death.

A pond I fished, fifty yards across,
Whose lilies and muscular tench
Had outlasted every visible stone
Of the monastery that planted them—

Stilled legendary depth:
It was as deep as England. It held
Pike too immense to stir, so immense and old
That past nightfall I dared not cast

But silently cast and fished
With the hair frozen on my head
For what might move, for what eye might move.
The still splashes on the dark pond,

Owls hushing the floating woods
Frail on my ear against the dream
Darkness beneath night's darkness had freed,
That rose slowly towards me, watching.

PIBROCH

The sea cries with its meaningless voice,
Treating alike its dead and its living,
Probably bored with the appearance of heaven
After so many millions of nights without sleep,
Without purpose, without self-deception.

Stone likewise. A pebble is imprisoned
Like nothing in the Universe.
Created for black sleep. Or growing
Conscious of the sun's red spot occasionally,
Then dreaming it is the foetus of God.

Over the stone rushes the wind,
Able to mingle with nothing,
Like the hearing of the blind stone itself.
Or turns, as if the stone's mind came feeling
A fantasy of directions.

Drinking the sea and eating the rock
A tree struggles to make leaves—
An old woman fallen from space
Unprepared for these conditions.
She hangs on, because her mind's gone completely.

Minute after minute, aeon after aeon,
Nothing lets up or develops.
And this is neither a bad variant nor a tryout.
This is where the staring angels go through.
This is where all the stars bow down.

SNOWDROP

Now is the globe shrunk tight
Round the mouse's dulled wintering heart.
Weasel and crow, as if moulded in brass,
Move through an outer darkness
Not in their right minds,
With the other deaths. She, too, pursues her ends,
Brutal as the stars of this month,
Her pale head heavy as metal.

SYLVIA PLATH

MIRROR

I am silver and exact. I have no preconceptions.
Whatever I see I swallow immediately
Just as it is, unmisted by love or dislike.
I am not cruel, only truthful—
The eye of a little god, four-cornered.
Most of the time I meditate on the opposite wall.
It is pink, with speckles. I have looked at it so long
I think it is a part of my heart. But it flickers.
Faces and darkness separate us over and over.

Now I am a lake. A woman bends over me,
Searching my reaches for what she really is.
Then she turns to those liars, the candles or the moon.
I see her back, and reflect it faithfully.
She rewards me with tears and an agitation of hands.
I am important to her. She comes and goes.
Each morning it is her face that replaces the darkness.
In me she has drowned a young girl, and in me an old
woman
Rises toward her day after day, like a terrible fish.

DEATH & CO.

Two. Of course there are two.
It seems perfectly natural now—
The one who never looks up, whose eyes are lidded
And balled, like Blake's,
Who exhibits

The birthmarks that are his trademark—
The scald scar of water,
The nude
Verdigris of the condor.
I am red meat. His beak

Claps sidewise: I am not his yet
He tells me how badly I photograph.
He tells me how sweet
The babies look in their hospital
Icebox, a simple

Frill at the neck,
Then the flutings of their Ionian
Death-gowns,
Then two little feet.
He does not smile or smoke.

The other does that,
His hair long and plausive.
Bastard
Masturbating a glitter,
He wants to be loved.

I do not stir.
The frost makes a flower,
The dew makes a star.
The dead bell,
The dead bell.

Somebody's done for.

GEOFFREY HILL

OF COMMERCE AND SOCIETY

Variations on a theme

Then hang this picture for a calendar,
As sheep for goat, and pray most fixedly
For the cold martial progress of your star,
With thoughts of commerce and society,
Well-milked Chinese, Negroes who cannot sing,
The Huns gelded and feeding in a ring.
—Allen Tate: More Sonnets at Christmas, 1942

I. THE APOSTLES: VERSAILLES, 1919

They sat. They stood about.
They were estranged. The air,
As water curdles from clear,
Fleshed the silence. They sat.

They were appalled. The bells
In hollowed Europe spilt
To the gods of coin and salt.
The sea creaked with worked vessels.

II. THE LOWLANDS OF HOLLAND

Europe, the much-scarred, much-scoured terrain,
Its attested liberties, home-produce,
Labelled and looking up, invites use,
Stuffed with artistry and substantial gain:

Shrunken, magnified—(nest, holocaust)—
Not half innocent and not half undone;
Profiting from custom: its replete strewn
Cities such ample monuments to lost

Nations and generations: its cultural
Or trade skeletons such hand-picked bone:
Flaws in the best, revised science marks down:
Witness many devices; the few natural

Corruptions, graftings; witness classic falls;
(The dead subtracted; the greatest resigned;)
Witness earth fertilised, decently drained,
The sea decent again behind walls.

III. THE DEATH OF SHELLEY

i

Slime; the residues of refined tears;
And salt-bristled, blown on a drying sea,
The sunned and risen faces.
                    There's Andromeda
Depicted in relief, after the fashion.

'His guarded eyes under his shielded brow'
Through poisonous baked sea-things Perseus
Goes—clogged sword, clear, aimless mirror—
With nothing to strike at or blind
                    in the frothed shallows.

ii

Rivers bring down. The sea
Brings away;
Voids, sucks back, its pearls and auguries.
Eagles or vultures churn the fresh made skies.

Over the statues, unchanging features
Of commerce and quaint love, soot lies.
Earth steams. The bull and the great mute swan
Strain into life with their notorious cries.

IV

Statesmen have known visions. And, not alone,
Artistic men prod dead men from their stone:

Some of us have heard the dead speak:
The dead are my obsession this week

But may be lifted away. In summer
Thunder may strike, or, as a tremor
Of remote adjustment, pass on the far side
From us: however deified and defied

By those it does strike. Many have died. Auschwitz,
Its furnace chambers and lime pits
Half-erased, is half-dead; a fable
Unbelievable in fatted marble.

There is, at times, some need to demonstrate
Jehovah's touchy methods, that create
The connoisseur of blood, the smitten man.
At times it seems not common to explain.

V. ODE ON THE LOSS OF THE 'TITANIC'

Thriving against facades the ignorant sea
Souses our public baths, statues, waste ground:
Archaic earth-shaker, fresh enemy:
('The tables of exchange being overturned');

Drowns Babel in upheaval and display;
Unswerving, as were the admired multitudes
Silenced from time to time under its sway.
By all means let us appease the terse gods.

VI. THE MARTYRDOM OF SAINT SEBASTIAN

Homage to Henry James
'But then face to face'

Naked, as if for swimming, the martyr
Catches his death in a little flutter
Of plain arrows. A grotesque situation,
But priceless, and harmless to the nation.

Consider such pains 'crystalline': then fine art
Persists where most crystals accumulate.
History can be scraped clean of its old price.
Engrossed in the cold blood of sacrifice,

The provident and self-healing gods
Destroy only to save. Well-stocked with foods,
Enlarged and deep-oiled, America
Detects music, apprehends the day-star

Where, sensitive and half-under a cloud,
Europe muddles her dreaming, is loud
And critical beneath the varied domes
Resonant with tribute and with commerce.

ACKNOWLEDGEMENTS

For permission to reprint copyright material, the following acknowledgements are made:

For poems by Conrad Aiken, to the author, Charles Scribner's Sons and A. M. Heath & Co. Ltd.

Preludes for Memnon (Scribners) 1931.

For poems by W. H. Auden, to the author, Faber & Faber Ltd. and Curtis Brown Ltd.

Collected Shorter Poems (Faber) 1950.

Nones (Faber) 1952.

In *Collected Shorter Poems*, 'Prologue' appears under the title of 'Perhaps', 'Watch any day' under the title of 'A Free One' and 'Sir, no man's enemy' under the title of 'Petition'.

For poems by George Barker, to the author and Faber & Faber Ltd.

Collected Poems 1930–1955 (Faber) 1957.

For poems by John Berryman, to the author, Faber & Faber Ltd. and Farrar, Straus & Co. Inc.

Homage to Mistress Bradstreet (Faber) 1959; (Farrar, Straus) 1956. © 1956 by John Berryman.

77 Dream Songs (Faber) 1964; (Farrar, Straus) 1964. © 1959, 1962, 1963, 1964 by John Berryman.

For poems by Robert Bly, to the author.

Silence in the Snowy Fields (Wesleyan University Press) 1962.

For poems by Hart Crane, to the poet's family and Mr. Horace Liveright.

Collected Poems (Liveright) 1933.

For poems by E. E. Cummings, to his literary executors and Mr. Horace Liveright.

is 5 (Boni & Liveright) 1926.

For poems by Donald Davie, to the author and Routledge & Kegan Paul Ltd.

A Winter Talent and other Poems (Routledge) 1957.

For poems by James Dickey, to the author and the Wesleyan University Press.

Drowning with Others (Wesleyan University Press) 1961. © 1961 by James Dickey.

For poems by H. D., to her literary executors, Mr. Horace Liveright and Chatto & Windus Ltd.

Collected Poems (Boni & Liveright) 1925.

Red Roses for Bronze (Chatto & Windus) 1931.

For poems by Keith Douglas, to Mrs. Marie Douglas.

Collected Poems (Editions Poetry London) 1951.

For poems by Richard Eberhart, to the author and Chatto & Windus Ltd.

Collected Poems 1930–1960 (Chatto & Windus) 1960.

For poems by T. S. Eliot, to Mrs Eliot and Faber & Faber Ltd.

Collected Poems 1909–1962 (Faber) 1963.

For poems by William Empson, to the author and Chatto & Windus Ltd.

Collected Poems (Chatto & Windus) 1962.

For poems by David Gascoyne, to the author.

'Landscape' appeared in *The Year's Poetry* (Bodley Head) 1934 and 'In Defence of Humanism' in *A Little Treasury of Modern Poetry* (Scribners) 1950.

For poems by W. S. Graham, to the author and Faber & Faber Ltd.

The White Threshold (Faber) 1949.

For poems by Robert Graves, to the author, the Seizin Press, Cassell & Co. Ltd., A. P. Watt & Son and International Authors N.V.

Collected Poems (Cassell) 1938.

Collected Poems (Cassell) 1959.

For poems by Thom Gunn, to the author and Faber & Faber Ltd.

The Sense of Movement (Faber) 1957.

My Sad Captains (Faber) 1961.

For poems by John Heath-Stubbs, to the author and the Oxford University Press.

Blue Fly in His Head (O.U.P.) 1962.

For poems by Geoffrey Hill, to the author and André Deutsch Ltd.

For the Unfallen — Poems 1952–1958 (Deutsch) 1959.

For poems by Gerard Manley Hopkins, to the poet's family and the Oxford University Press.

Poems: Edited by Robert Bridges. Second Edition (O.U.P.) 1930.

For poems by T. E. Hulme, to Mr. Herbert Read and Routledge & Kegan Paul Ltd.

Speculations (Kegan Paul) 1924. Hulme's five poems had previously been printed as an addendum to Ezra Pound's *Ripostes* (Elkin Mathews).

For poems by Ted Hughes, to the author and Faber & Faber Ltd.

Lupercal (Faber) 1960.

'Pibroch' has not previously been printed in book form.

For extracts from the poem by David Jones, to the author and Faber & Faber Ltd.

In Parenthesis (Faber) 1937.

For poems by Philip Larkin, to the author, The Marvell Press and Faber & Faber Ltd.

The Less Deceived (Marvell Press) 1958.

The Whitsun Weddings (Faber) 1964.

For poems by D. H. Lawrence, to his literary executors and William Heinemann Ltd.

Collected Poems (Secker) 1932.

Last Poems (Secker) 1933.

For poems by C. Day Lewis, to the author, The Hogarth Press Ltd. and Jonathan Cape Ltd.

Collected Poems (Hogarth Press) 1935.

A Time to Dance (Hogarth Press) 1935.

Overtures to Death (Cape) 1938.

Poems 1943–1947 (Cape) 1948.

For poems by Denise Levertov, to the author and New Directions.

The Jacob's Ladder (New Directions) 1958. © 1958 by Denise Levertov.

For poems by Robert Lowell, to the author, Faber & Faber Ltd., Harcourt, Brace & World Inc. and Farrar, Straus & Co. Inc.

Poems 1938–1949 (Faber) 1950.

Lord Weary's Castle (Harcourt, Brace) 1946.

Life Studies (Faber) 1959; (Farrar, Straus) 1956. © 1956, 1959 by Robert Lowell.

For poems by Norman MacCaig, to the author and The Hogarth Press.

Riding Lights (Hogarth Press) 1955.

A Common Grace (Hogarth Press) 1960.

A Round of Applause (Hogarth Press) 1962.

For poems by Hugh MacDiarmid, to the author and The Macmillan Company.

Collected Poems (Macmillan Co.) 1962. © 1962 by Christopher Murray Grieve.

For poems by Louis MacNeice, to Mrs MacNeice and Faber & Faber Ltd.

Collected Poems 1925–1948 (Faber) 1949.

Solstices (Faber) 1961.

For poems by Charles Madge, to the author and Faber & Faber Ltd.

The Disappearing Castle (Faber) 1937.

The Father Found (Faber) 1941.

'Blocking the Pass' appeared in *Poems of Tomorrow* (Chatto & Windus) 1935.

'Lusty Juventus' and 'At War' appeared in *New Verse* (August and December 1934).

For poems by W. S. Merwin, to the author and David Higham Associates Ltd.

The Drunk in the Furnace (Hart-Davis) 1960.

The Moving Target (Atheneum) 1963.

For poems by Christopher Middleton, to the author and Longmans, Green & Co. Ltd.

Torse Three (Longmans) 1962.

For poems by Harold Monro, to Mrs. Alida Monro and Mr. Cobden-Sanderson.

Collected Poems (Cobden-Sanderson) 1933.

For poems by Marianne Moore, to the author and Faber & Faber Ltd.

Collected Poems (Faber) 1951.

In *Collected Poems*, 'Black Earth' appears under the title of 'Melancthon'.

For poems by Edwin Muir, to Mrs Muir and Faber & Faber Ltd.

Collected Poems (Faber) 1963.

For poems by Howard Nemerov, to the author and Margot Johnson Agency.

New and Selected Poems (University of Chicago Press) 1960.

The Next Room of the Dream (University of Chicago Press) 1963.

For poems by Charles Olson, to the author, Jargon Books and Corinth Books Inc.

The Maximus Poems (Jargon and Corinth) 1960. © 1960 by Charles Olson.

For poems by Wilfred Owen, to his literary executors and Chatto & Windus Ltd.

Poems (Chatto & Windus) 1931.

For poems by Sylvia Plath, to Mr. Ted Hughes.

Ariel (Faber) 1965.

'Mirror' has not previously been printed in book form.

For poems by Ezra Pound, to the author, Mr. A. V. Moore and Faber & Faber Ltd.

Selected Poems (Faber) 1948.

Homage to Sextus Propertius (Faber) 1934.

The Cantos of Ezra Pound (Faber) 1964.

'Canto 115' appeared in No 28 of *The Paris Review*.

For poems by F. T. Prince, to the author and Faber & Faber Ltd.

Poems (Faber) 1938.

For poems by Kathleen Raine, to the author and Hamish Hamilton Ltd.

Collected Poems (Hamish Hamilton) 1955.

For poems by John Crowe Ransom, to the author, Alfred

A. Knopf, Inc., Eyre & Spottiswoode Ltd. and Laurence Pollinger Ltd.

Selected Poems (Eyre & Spottiswoode) 1947.

For poems by Herbert Read, to the author and Faber & Faber Ltd.

Collected Poems (Faber) 1946.

For poems by Laura Riding, to the author, the Seizin Press and Cassell & Co. Ltd.

Collected Poems (Cassell) 1938.

For poems by Anne Ridler, to the author and Faber & Faber Ltd.

The Golden Bird (Faber) 1951.

A Matter of Life and Death (Faber) 1959.

For poems by Michael Roberts, to Mrs. Michael Roberts and Faber & Faber Ltd.

Collected Poems (Faber) 1958.

For poems by Theodore Roethke, to Mrs. Beatrice Roethke, A. M. Heath & Co. Ltd. and Doubleday & Co. Inc.

Words for the Wind (Secker & Warburg) 1957; (Doubleday) 1958. © 1948, 1942, 1947, 1954 by Theodore Roethke.

For poems by Isaac Rosenberg, to his literary executors and Chatto & Windus Ltd.

Collected Poems (Chatto & Windus) 1950.

For poems by Louis Simpson, to the author and the Wesleyan University Press.

A Dream of Governors (Wesleyan University Press) 1959. © 1956 by Louis Simpson.

At the End of the Open Road (Wesleyan University Press) 1963. © 1963 by Louis Simpson.

For poems by Edith Sitwell, to her literary executors, Mr. Basil Blackwell and Duckworth & Co. Ltd.

The Wooden Pegasus (Blackwell) 1920.

Collected Poems (Duckworth) 1930.

For poems by W. D. Snodgrass, to the author and The Marvell Press.

Heart's Needle (Marvell Press) 1960.

'Monet: Les Nymphéas' has not previously been printed in book form.

For poems by Stephen Spender, to the author and Faber & Faber Ltd.

Collected Poems (Faber) 1955.

For poems by Wallace Stevens, to his literary executors, Faber & Faber Ltd. and Alfred A. Knopf Inc.

Collected Poems (Faber) 1955; (Knopf) 1954. © 1952, 1954 by Wallace Stevens.

Opus Posthumous (Faber) 1959; (Knopf) 1957. © 1957 by Elsie Stevens and Holly Stevens.

For poems by Allen Tate, to the author and Eyre & Spottiswoode Ltd.

Selected Poems (Eyre & Spottiswoode) 1947.

For poems by Dylan Thomas, to his literary executors and J. M. Dent & Sons Ltd.

Collected Poems 1934–1952 (Dent) 1952.

For poems by R. S. Thomas, to the author and Rupert Hart-Davis Ltd.

Song at the Year's Turning (Hart-Davis) 1955.

Poetry for Supper (Hart-Davis) 1958.

For poems by Charles Tomlinson, to the author, the Oxford University Press and Ivan Obolensky Inc., New York.

Seeing is Believing (O.U.P.) 1960; (Obolensky) 1958. © 1958 by Charles Tomlinson.

A Peopled Landscape (O.U.P.) 1963.

For poems by Vernon Watkins, to the author and Faber & Faber Ltd.

Ballad of the Mari Lwyd (Faber) 1941.

The Lady with the Unicorn (Faber) 1948.

Cypress and Acacia (Faber) 1959.

For poems by Richard Wilbur, to the author, Faber & Faber Ltd. and Harcourt, Brace & World Inc.

Poems 1943–1956 (Faber) 1957.

Ceremony and Other Poems (Harcourt, Brace) 1950.

Things of this World (Harcourt, Brace) 1956.

Advice to a Prophet and Other Poems (Faber) 1962; (Harcourt, Brace) 1961.

For poems by William Carlos Williams, to his literary executors, Laurence Pollinger Ltd., MacGibbon & Kee Ltd. and New Directions.

Collected Earlier Poems of William Carlos Williams (New Directions) 1951.

Collected Later Poems of William Carlos Williams (New Directions) 1962.

Pictures from Breughel (MacGibbon & Kee) 1964; (New Directions) 1962.

MacGibbon & Kee Ltd. will be publishing *Collected Earlier Poems* and *Collected Later Poems* in this country.

For poems by James Wright, to the author, Longmans, Green & Co. Ltd. and the Wesleyan University Press.

The Branch will not Break (Longmans) 1963; (Wesleyan University Press) 1963. © 1962, 1961, 1962 by James Wright.

For poems by W. B. Yeats, to Mrs. W. B. Yeats and Macmillan & Co. Ltd.

Collected Poems of W. B. Yeats (Macmillan) 1950.

Collins gem

Collins Spanish Grammar

HarperCollins Publishers
Westerhill Road
Bishopbriggs
Glasgow
G64 2QT
Great Britain

Fourth edition 2006

Reprint 10 9 8 7 6

ISBN 978-0-00-722420-3

www.collinsdictionary.com
www.collins.co.uk

A catalogue record for this book is available from the British Library

Typeset by Davidson Publishing Solutions

Printed and bound in China by South China Printing Co., Ltd

A de Benito de Harland
I F Ariza

EDITOR
Jeremy Butterfield

EDITORIAL STAFF
Linda Chestnutt
Joyce Littlejohn
Enrique González Sardinero

EDITORIAL MANAGEMENT
Vivian Marr

INTRODUCTION

Your **Collins Gem Spanish Verb Tables and Grammar** is designed to offer students of Spanish of all ages and at all levels an uncluttered, step-by-step guide to the grammar of the language. For beginners, the book provides a clear introduction to all the basic rules and structures, and more advanced learners will find it an invaluable guide for reference and revision.

For ease of use, each part of speech (nouns, verbs, adjectives etc) has been treated separately (see the list of contents on the next page).

A special feature of this book is the clear demarcation of grammatical points, each treated on a left-hand page, and illustrated by examples in up-to-date Spanish on the opposite right-hand page. The appropriate example is clearly indicated by a system of boxed numbers e.g. → 1, → 2 etc, corresponding to an example number on the facing page.

Special attention has been paid throughout to areas in which Spanish and English usage differ, thus helping the user to avoid the mistake of trying to translate English structures by identical structures in Spanish.

The tables of irregular verbs complement the extensive treatment of regular verbs in the grammar section of the book. In them 80 major irregular verbs are conjugated in their simple tenses so you can see where they differ from regular verbs. In addition, the verb index, in which all verbs are cross-referred to the appropriate conjugation model, enables you to check how over 2,800 Spanish verbs are conjugated.

A comprehensive index, containing key words in both Spanish and English, as well as subject references, completes the grammar.

ABBREVIATIONS

algn	alguien	**masc**	masculine	**sing**	singular
cond	conditional	**p(p)**	page(s)	**sth**	something
fem	feminine	**plur**	plural	**subj**	subjunctive
ff	and following pages	**sb**	somebody		

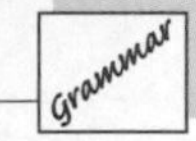

CONTENTS

CONTENTS

❐ Simple Tenses: Formation

In Spanish the simple tenses are:

Present	→ 1
Imperfect	→ 2
Future	→ 3
Conditional	→ 4
Preterite	→ 5
Present Subjunctive	→ 6
Imperfect Subjunctive	→ 7

They are formed by adding endings to a verb stem. The endings show the number and person of the subject of the verb → 8

The stem and endings of regular verbs are totally predictable. The following sections show all the patterns for regular verbs. For irregular verbs see pp 80 ff.

Regular Verbs

There are three regular verb patterns (called conjugations), each identifiable by the ending of the infinitive:

- First conjugation verbs end in **-ar** e.g. **hablar** to speak.
- Second conjugation verbs end in **-er** e.g. **comer** to eat.
- Third conjugation verbs end in **-ir** e.g. **vivir** to live.

These three conjugations are treated in order on the following pages. The subject pronouns will appear in brackets because they are not always necessary in Spanish (see p 226).

Examples

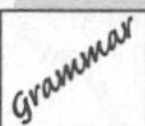

1	**(yo) hablo**	I speak I am speaking I do speak
2	**(yo) hablaba**	I spoke I was speaking I used to speak
3	**(yo) hablaré**	I shall speak I shall be speaking
4	**(yo) hablaría**	I should/would speak I should/would be speaking
5	**(yo) hablé**	I spoke
6	**(que) (yo) hable**	(that) I speak
7	**(que) (yo) hablara** *or* **hablase**	(that) I speak
8	**(yo) hablo** **(nosotros) hablamos** **(yo) hablaría** **(nosotros) hablaríamos**	I speak we speak I would speak we would speak

❐ Simple Tenses: First Conjugation

- The stem is formed as follows:

TENSE	FORMATION	EXAMPLE
Present Imperfect Preterite Present Subjunctive Imperfect Subjunctive*	infinitive minus **-ar** * For irregular verbs see p 80	**habl-**
Future Conditional	infinitive	**hablar-**

- To the appropriate stem add the following endings:

		PRESENT → 1	IMPERFECT → 2	PRETERITE → 3
sing	1st person	**-o**	**-aba**	**-é**
	2nd person	**-as**	**-abas**	**-aste**
	3rd person	**-a**	**-aba**	**-ó**
plur	1st person	**-amos**	**-ábamos**	**-amos**
	2nd person	**-áis**	**-abais**	**-asteis**
	3rd person	**-an**	**-aban**	**-aron**

		PRESENT SUBJUNCTIVE → 4	IMPERFECT SUBJUNCTIVE → 5
sing	1st person	**-e**	**-ara** *or* **-ase**
	2nd person	**-es**	**-aras** *or* **-ases**
	3rd person	**-e**	**-ara** *or* **-ase**
plur	1st person	**-emos**	**-áramos** *or* **-ásemos**
	2nd person	**-éis**	**-arais** *or* **-aseis**
	3rd person	**-en**	**-aran** *or* **-asen**

		FUTURE → 6	CONDITIONAL → 7
sing	1st person	**-é**	**-ía**
	2nd person	**-ás**	**-ías**
	3rd person	**-á**	**-ía**
plur	1st person	**-emos**	**-íamos**
	2nd person	**-éis**	**-íais**
	3rd person	**-án**	**-ían**

Examples

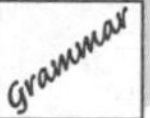

	1 PRESENT	2 IMPERFECT	3 PRETERITE
(yo)	habl**o**	habl**aba**	habl**é**
(tú)	habl**as**	habl**abas**	habl**aste**
(él/ella/Vd)	habl**a**	habl**aba**	habl**ó**
(nosotros/as)	habl**amos**	habl**ábamos**	habl**amos**
(vosotros/as)	habl**áis**	habl**abais**	habl**asteis**
(ellos/as/Vds)	habl**an**	habl**aban**	habl**aron**

	4 PRESENT SUBJUNCTIVE	5 IMPERFECT SUBJUNCTIVE
(yo)	habl**e**	habl**ara** *or* habl**ase**
(tú)	habl**es**	habl**aras** *or* habl**ases**
(él/ella/Vd)	habl**e**	habl**ara** *or* habl**ase**
(nosotros/as)	habl**emos**	habl**áramos** *or* habl**ásemos**
(vosotros/as)	habl**éis**	habl**arais** *or* habl**aseis**
(ellos/as/Vds)	habl**en**	habl**aran** *or* habl**asen**

	6 FUTURE	7 CONDITIONAL
(yo)	hablar**é**	hablar**ía**
(tú)	hablar**ás**	hablar**ías**
(él/ella/Vd)	hablar**á**	hablar**ía**
(nosotros/as)	hablar**emos**	hablar**íamos**
(vosotros/as)	hablar**éis**	hablar**íais**
(ellos/as/Vds)	hablar**án**	hablar**ían**

Simple Tenses: Second Conjugation

- The stem is formed as follows:

TENSE	FORMATION	EXAMPLE
Present Imperfect Preterite Present Subjunctive Imperfect Subjunctive*	infinitive minus **-er** *For irregular verbs see p80	**com-**
Future Conditional	infinitive	**comer-**

- To the appropriate stem add the following endings:

		PRESENT → 1	IMPERFECT → 2	PRETERITE → 3
sing	1st person	**-o**	**-ía**	**-í**
	2nd person	**-es**	**-ías**	**-iste**
	3rd person	**-e**	**-ía**	**-ió**
plur	1st person	**-emos**	**-íamos**	**-imos**
	2nd person	**-éis**	**-íais**	**-isteis**
	3rd person	**-en**	**-ían**	**-ieron**

		PRESENT SUBJUNCTIVE → 4	IMPERFECT SUBJUNCTIVE → 5
sing	1st person	**-a**	**-iera** *or* **-iese**
	2nd person	**-as**	**-ieras** *or* **-ieses**
	3rd person	**-a**	**-iera** *or* **-iese**
plur	1st person	**-amos**	**-iéramos** *or* **-iésemos**
	2nd person	**-áis**	**-ierais** *or* **-ieseis**
	3rd person	**-an**	**-ieran** *or* **-iesen**

		FUTURE → 6	CONDITIONAL → 7
sing	1st person	**-é**	**-ía**
	2nd person	**-ás**	**-ías**
	3rd person	**-á**	**-ía**
plur	1st person	**-emos**	**-íamos**
	2nd person	**-éis**	**-íais**
	3rd person	**-án**	**-ían**

11 Examples

	1 PRESENT	2 IMPERFECT	3 PRETERITE
(yo)	com**o**	com**ía**	com**í**
(tú)	com**es**	com**ías**	com**iste**
(él/ella/Vd)	com**e**	com**ía**	com**ió**
(nosotros/as)	com**emos**	com**íamos**	com**imos**
(vosotros/as)	com**éis**	com**íais**	com**isteis**
(ellos/as/Vds)	com**en**	com**ían**	com**ieron**

	4 PRESENT SUBJUNCTIVE	5 IMPERFECT SUBJUNCTIVE
(yo)	com**a**	com**iera** *or* com**iese**
(tú)	com**as**	com**ieras** *or* com**ieses**
(él/ella/Vd)	com**a**	com**iera** *or* com**iese**
(nosotros/as)	com**amos**	com**iéramos** *or* com**iésemos**
(vosotros/as)	com**áis**	com**ierais** *or* com**ieseis**
(ellos/as/Vds)	com**an**	com**ieran** *or* com**iesen**

	6 FUTURE	7 CONDITIONAL
(yo)	comer**é**	comer**ía**
(tú)	comer**ás**	comer**ías**
(él/ella/Vd)	comer**á**	comer**ía**
(nosotros/as)	comer**emos**	comer**íamos**
(vosotros/as)	comer**éis**	comer**íais**
(ellos/as/Vds)	comer**án**	comer**ían**

❒ Simple Tenses: Third Conjugation

- The stem is formed as follows:

TENSE	FORMATION	EXAMPLE
Present Imperfect Preterite Present Subjunctive Imperfect Subjunctive*	infinitive minus **-ir** *For irregular verbs see p80	**viv-**
Future Conditional	infinitive	**vivir-**

- To the appropriate stem add the following endings:

		PRESENT → 1	IMPERFECT → 2	PRETERITE → 3
sing	1st person	**-o**	**-ía**	**-í**
	2nd person	**-es**	**-ías**	**-iste**
	3rd person	**-e**	**-ía**	**-ió**
plur	1st person	**-imos**	**-íamos**	**-imos**
	2nd person	**-ís**	**-íais**	**-isteis**
	3rd person	**-en**	**-ían**	**-ieron**

		PRESENT SUBJUNCTIVE → 4	IMPERFECT SUBJUNCTIVE → 5
sing	1st person	**-a**	**-iera** *or* **-iese**
	2nd person	**-as**	**-ieras** *or* **-ieses**
	3rd person	**-a**	**-iera** *or* **-iese**
plur	1st person	**-amos**	**-iéramos** *or* **-iésemos**
	2nd person	**-áis**	**-ierais** *or* **-ieseis**
	3rd person	**-an**	**-ieran** *or* **-iesen**

		FUTURE → 6	CONDITIONAL → 7
sing	1st person	**-é**	**-ía**
	2nd person	**-ás**	**-ías**
	3rd person	**-á**	**-ía**
plur	1st person	**-emos**	**-íamos**
	2nd person	**-éis**	**-íais**
	3rd person	**-án**	**-ían**

Examples

	1 PRESENT	2 IMPERFECT	3 PRETERITE
(yo)	viv**o**	viv**ía**	viv**í**
(tú)	viv**es**	viv**ías**	viv**iste**
(él/ella/Vd)	viv**e**	viv**ía**	viv**ió**
(nosotros/as)	viv**imos**	viv**íamos**	viv**imos**
(vosotros/as)	viv**ís**	viv**íais**	viv**isteis**
(ellos/as/Vds)	viv**en**	viv**ían**	viv**ieron**

	4 PRESENT SUBJUNCTIVE	5 IMPERFECT SUBJUNCTIVE
(yo)	viv**a**	viv**iera** or viv**iese**
(tú)	viv**as**	viv**ieras** or viv**ieses**
(él/ella/Vd)	viv**a**	viv**iera** or viv**iese**
(nosotros/as)	viv**amos**	viv**iéramos** or viv**iésemos**
(vosotros/as)	viv**áis**	viv**ierais** or viv**ieseis**
(ellos/as/Vds)	viv**an**	viv**ieran** or viv**iesen**

	6 FUTURE	7 CONDITIONAL
(yo)	vivir**é**	vivir**ía**
(tú)	vivir**ás**	vivir**ías**
(él/ella/Vd)	vivir**á**	vivir**ía**
(nosotros/as)	vivir**emos**	vivir**íamos**
(vosotros/as)	vivir**éis**	vivir**íais**
(ellos/as/Vds)	vivir**án**	vivir**ían**

❐ The Imperative

The imperative is the form of the verb used to give commands or orders. It can be used politely, as in English 'Shut the door, please'.

In POSITIVE commands, the imperative forms for **Vd, Vds** and **nosotros** are the same as the subjunctive. The other forms are as follows:

tú (same as 3rd person singular present indicative)
vosotros (final **-r** of infinitive changes to **-d**) → [1]

(tú)	**habla**	**come**	**vive**
	speak	*eat*	*live*
(Vd)	**hable**	**coma**	**viva**
	speak	*eat*	*live*
(nosotros)	**hablemos**	**comamos**	**vivamos**
	let's speak	*let's eat*	*let's live*
(vosotros)	**hablad**	**comed**	**vivid**
	speak	*eat*	*live*
(Vds)	**hablen**	**coman**	**vivan**
	speak	*eat*	*live*

In NEGATIVE commands, all the imperative forms are exactly the same as the present subjunctive.

- The imperative of irregular verbs is given in the verb tables, pp 82 ff.

Position of object pronouns with the imperative

In POSITIVE commands: they follow the verb and are attached to it. An accent is needed to show the correct position for stress (see p 292) → [2]

In NEGATIVE commands: they precede the verb and are not attached to it → [3]

- For the order of object pronouns, see page 232.

Examples

1 **cantar**
to sing

cantad
sing

2 **Perdóneme**
Excuse me

Elíjanos
Choose us

Esperémosla
Let's wait for her/it

Enviémoselos
Let's send them to him/her/them

Explíquemelo
Explain it to me

Devuélvaselo
Give it back to him/her/them

3 **No me molestes**
Don't disturb me

No les castiguemos
Let's not punish them

No las conteste
Don't answer them

No se la devolvamos
Let's not give it back to him/her/them

No me lo mandes
Don't send it to me

No nos lo hagan
Don't do it to us

❒ The Imperative *(Continued)*

- For reflexive verbs – e.g. **levantarse** *to get up* – the object pronoun is the reflexive pronoun. It should be noted that the imperative forms need an accent to show the correct position for stress (see p 292). The forms **nosotros** and **vosotros** also drop the final **-s** and **-d** respectively before the pronoun → [1]

BUT: **idos (vosotros)** *go*

⚠ NOTE: For general instructions, the infinitive is used instead of the imperative →[2], but when it is preceded by **vamos a** it often translates *let's* … → [3]

Examples

1 **Levántate**
Get up
Levántese (Vd)
Get up
Levantémonos
Let's get up
Levantaos
Get up
Levántense (Vds)
Get up

No te levantes
Don't get up
No se levante (Vd)
Don't get up
No nos levantemos
Let's not get up
No os levantéis
Don't get up
No se levanten (Vds)
Don't get up

2 **Ver pág ...**
See page
No pasar
Do not pass ...

3 **Vamos a ver**
Let's see
Vamos a empezar
Let's start

❐ Compound Tenses: Formation

In Spanish the compound tenses are:

Perfect → [1]
Pluperfect → [2]
Future Perfect → [3]
Conditional Perfect → [4]
Past Anterior → [5]
Perfect Subjunctive → [6]
Pluperfect Subjunctive → [7]

They consist of the past participle of the verb together with the auxiliary verb **haber**.

Compound tenses are formed in exactly the same way for both regular and irregular verbs, the only difference being that irregular verbs may have an irregular past participle.

The Past Participle

For all compound tenses you need to know how to form the past participle of the verb. For regular verbs this is as follows:

- 1st conjugation: replace the **-ar** of the infinitive by **-ado** → [8]
- 2nd conjugation: replace the **-er** of the infinitive by **-ido** → [9]
- 3rd conjugation: replace the **-ir** of the infinitive by **-ido** → [10]

Examples

1 **(yo) he hablado**
I have spoken

2 **(yo) había hablado**
I had spoken

3 **(yo) habré hablado**
I shall have spoken

4 **(yo) habría hablado**
I should/would have spoken

5 **(yo) hube hablado**
I had spoken

6 **(que) (yo) haya hablado**
(that) I spoke, have spoken

7 **(que) (yo) hubiera/hubiese hablado**
(that) I had spoken

8 **cantar** → **cantado**
to sing sung

9 **comer** → **comido**
to eat eaten

10 **vivir** → **vivido**
to live lived

❒ Compound Tenses: Formation *(Continued)*

Perfect tense: the present tense of **haber** plus the past participle → [1]

Pluperfect tense: the imperfect tense of **haber** plus the past participle → [2]

Future Perfect: the future tense of **haber** plus the past participle → [3]

Conditional Perfect: the conditional of **haber** plus the past participle → [4]

Examples

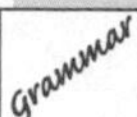

1 PERFECT	(yo) (tú) (él/ella/Vd) (nosotros/as) (vosotros/as) (ellos/as/Vds)	**he** habl**ado** **has** habl**ado** **ha** habl**ado** **hemos** habl**ado** **habéis** habl**ado** **han** habl**ado**

2 PLUPERFECT	(yo) (tú) (él/ella/Vd) (nosotros/as) (vosotros/as) (ellos/as/Vds)	**había** habl**ado** **habías** habl**ado** **había** habl**ado** **habíamos** habl**ado** **habíais** habl**ado** **habían** habl**ado**

3 FUTURE PERFECT	(yo) (tú) (él/ella/Vd) (nosotros/as) (vosotros/as) (ellos/as/Vds)	**habré** habl**ado** **habrás** habl**ado** **habrá** habl**ado** **habremos** habl**ado** **habréis** habl**ado** **habrán** habl**ado**

4 CONDITIONAL PERFECT	(yo) (tú) (él/ella/Vd) (nosotros/as) (vosotros/as) (ellos/as/Vds)	**habría** habl**ado** **habrías** habl**ado** **habría** habl**ado** **habríamos** habl**ado** **habríais** habl**ado** **habrían** habl**ado**

❒ Compound Tenses: Formation *(Continued)*

Past Anterior:	the preterite of **haber** plus the past participle → [1]
Perfect Subjunctive:	the present subjunctive of **haber** plus the past participle → [2]
Pluperfect Subjunctive:	the imperfect subjunctive of **haber** plus the past participle → [3]

- For how to form the past participle of regular verbs see p 18. The past participle of irregular verbs is given for each verb in the verb tables, pp 82 to 161.

Examples

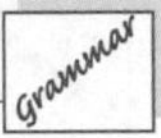

1 PAST ANTERIOR	(yo)	**hube** hablado
	(tú)	**hubiste** hablado
	(él/ella/Vd)	**hubo** hablado
	(nosotros/as)	**hubimos** hablado
	(vosotros/as)	**hubisteis** hablado
	(ellos/as/Vds)	**hubieron** hablado

2 PERFECT SUBJUNCTIVE	(yo)	**haya** hablado
	(tú)	**hayas** hablado
	(él/ella/Vd)	**haya** hablado
	(nosotros/as)	**hayamos** hablado
	(vosotros/as)	**hayáis** hablado
	(ellos/as/Vds)	**hayan** hablado

3 PLUPERFECT SUBJUNCTIVE	(yo)	**hubiera** or **hubiese** hablado
	(tú)	**hubieras** or **hubieses** hablado
	(él/ella/Vd)	**hubiera** or **hubiese** hablado
	(nosotros/as)	**hubiéramos** or **hubiésemos** hablado
	(vosotros/as)	**hubierais** or **hubieseis** hablado
	(ellos/as/Vds)	**hubieran** or **hubiesen** hablado

❐ Reflexive Verbs

A reflexive verb is one accompanied by a reflexive pronoun. The infinitive of a reflexive verb ends with the pronoun **se**, which is added to the verb form e.g.

levantarse *to get up*; **lavarse** *to wash (oneself)*

The reflexive pronouns are:

PERSON	SINGULAR	PLURAL
1st	**me**	**nos**
2nd	**te**	**os**
3rd	**se**	**se**

- The reflexive pronoun 'reflects back' to the subject, but it is not always translated in English → [1]

The plural pronouns are sometimes translated as *one another*, *each other* (the 'reciprocal' meaning) → [2]

The reciprocal meaning may be emphasized by **el uno al otro/la una a la otra (los unos a los otros/las unas a las otras)** → [3]

- Both simple and compound tenses of reflexive verbs are conjugated in exactly the same way as those of non-reflexive verbs, except that the reflexive pronoun is always used.

The only irregularity is in the 1st and 2nd person plural of the affirmative imperative (see p 16). A sample reflexive verb is conjugated in full on pp 28 to 31.

Position of reflexive pronouns

- Except with the infinitive, gerund and positive commands, the pronoun comes before the verb → [4]
- In the infinitive, gerund and positive commands, the pronoun follows the verb and is attached to it (but see also p 228) → [5]

Examples

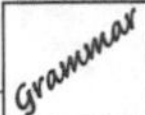

1 **Me visto**
I'm dressing (myself)

Nos lavamos
We're washing (ourselves)

Se levanta
He gets up

2 **Nos queremos**
We love each other

Se parecen
They resemble one another

3 **Se miraban el uno al otro**
They were looking at each other

4 **Me acuesto temprano**
I go to bed early

No se ha despertado
He hasn't woken up

¿Cómo se llama Vd?
What is your name?

No te levantes
Don't get up

5 **Quiero irme**
I want to go away

Siéntense
Sit down

Estoy levantándome
I am getting up

Vámonos
Let's go

❒ Reflexive Verbs *(Continued)*

Some verbs have both a reflexive and non-reflexive form. When used reflexively, they have a different but closely related meaning, as shown in the following examples.

NON-REFLEXIVE	REFLEXIVE
acostar *to put to bed*	**acostarse** *to go to bed*
casar *to marry (off)*	**casarse** *to get married*
detener *to stop*	**detenerse** *to come to a halt*
dormir *to sleep*	**dormirse** *to go to sleep*
enfadar *to annoy*	**enfadarse** *to get annoyed*
hacer *to make*	**hacerse** *to become*
ir *to go*	**irse** *to leave, go away*
lavar *to wash*	**lavarse** *to get washed*
levantar *to raise*	**levantarse** *to get up*
llamar *to call*	**llamarse** *to be called*
poner *to put*	**ponerse** *to put on (clothing), to become*
sentir *to feel (something)*	**sentirse** *to feel (sick, tired, etc)*
vestir *to dress (someone)*	**vestirse** *to get dressed*
volver *to return*	**volverse** *to turn round*

- Some other verbs exist only in the reflexive:

  arrepentirse *to repent* — **jactarse** *to boast*
  atreverse *to dare* — **quejarse** *to complain*

- Some verbs acquire a different nuance when used reflexively:

  caer *to fall* → 1 — **caerse** *to fall down (by accident)* → 2
  morir *to die, be killed (by accident or on purpose)* → 3 — **morirse** *to die (from natural causes)* → 4

- Often a reflexive verb can be used:
  — to avoid the passive (see p 34) → 5
  — in impersonal expressions (see p 40) → 6

Examples

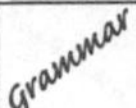

1 **El agua caía desde las rocas**
Water fell from the rocks

2 **Me caí y me rompí el brazo**
I fell and broke my arm

3 **Tres personas han muerto en un accidente/atentado terrorista**
Three people were killed in an accident/a terrorist attack

4 **Mi abuelo se murió a los ochenta años**
My grandfather died at the age of eighty

5 **Se perdió la batalla**
The battle was lost

No se veían las casas
The houses could not be seen

6 **Se dice que …**
It is said that …, People say that …

No se puede entrar
You/One can't go in

No se permite
It is not allowed

❒ Reflexive Verbs *(Continued)*

Conjugation of: **lavarse** *to wash oneself*

I SIMPLE TENSES

PRESENT	
(yo)	**me** lav**o**
(tú)	**te** lav**as**
(él/ella/Vd)	**se** lav**a**
(nosotros/as)	**nos** lav**amos**
(vosotros/as)	**os** lav**áis**
(ellos/as/Vds)	**se** lav**an**
IMPERFECT	
(yo)	**me** lav**aba**
(tú)	**te** lav**abas**
(él/ella/Vd)	**se** lav**aba**
(nosotros/as)	**nos** lav**ábamos**
(vosotros/as)	**os** lav**abais**
(ellos/as/Vds)	**se** lav**aban**
FUTURE	
(yo)	**me** lavar**é**
(tú)	**te** lavar**ás**
(él/ella/Vd)	**se** lavar**á**
(nosotros/as)	**nos** lavar**emos**
(vosotros/as)	**os** lavar**éis**
(ellos/as/Vds)	**se** lavar**án**
CONDITIONAL	
(yo)	**me** lavar**ía**
(tú)	**te** lavar**ías**
(él/ella/Vd)	**se** lavar**ía**
(nosotros/as)	**nos** lavar**íamos**
(vosotros/as)	**os** lavar**íais**
(ellos/as/Vds)	**se** lavar**ían**

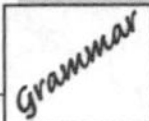

❒ **Reflexive Verbs** *(Continued)*

Conjugation of: **lavarse** *to wash oneself*

I SIMPLE TENSES

PRETERITE	
(yo)	**me** lav**é**
(tú)	**te** lav**aste**
(él/ella/Vd)	**se** lav**ó**
(nosotros/as)	**nos** lav**amos**
(vosotros/as)	**os** lav**asteis**
(ellos/as/Vds)	**se** lav**aron**
PRESENT SUBJUNCTIVE	
(yo)	**me** lav**e**
(tú)	**te** lav**es**
(él/ella/Vd)	**se** lav**e**
(nosotros/as)	**nos** lav**emos**
(vosotros/as)	**os** lav**éis**
(ellos/as/Vds)	**se** lav**en**
IMPERFECT SUBJUNCTIVE	
(yo)	**me** lav**ara** *or* lav**ase**
(tú)	**te** lav**aras** *or* lav**ases**
(él/ella/Vd)	**se** lav**ara** *or* lav**ase**
(nosotros/as)	**nos** lav**áramos** *or* lav**ásemos**
(vosotros/as)	**os** lav**arais** *or* lav**aseis**
(ellos/as/Vds)	**se** lav**aran** *or* lav**asen**

❒ Reflexive Verbs *(Continued)*

Conjugation of: **lavarse** *to wash oneself*

II COMPOUND TENSES

PERFECT	
(yo)	**me he** lavado
(tú)	**te has** lavado
(él/ella/Vd)	**se ha** lavado
(nosotros/as)	**nos hemos** lavado
(vosotros/as)	**os habéis** lavado
(ellos/as/Vds)	**se han** lavado
PLUPERFECT	
(yo)	**me había** lavado
(tú)	**te habías** lavado
(él/ella/Vd)	**se había** lavado
(nosotros/as)	**nos habíamos** lavado
(vosotros/as)	**os habíais** lavado
(ellos/as/Vds)	**se habían** lavado
FUTURE PERFECT	
(yo)	**me habré** lavado
(tú)	**te habrás** lavado
(él/ella/Vd)	**se habrá** lavado
(nosotros/as)	**nos habremos** lavado
(vosotros/as)	**os habréis** lavado
(ellos/as/Vds)	**se habrán** lavado

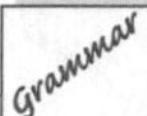

❒ Reflexive Verbs *(Continued)*

Conjugation of: **lavarse** *to wash oneself*

II COMPOUND TENSES

PAST ANTERIOR	
(yo)	**me hube** lavado
(tú)	**te hubiste** lavado
(él/ella/Vd)	**se hubo** lavado
(nosotros/as)	**nos hubimos** lavado
(vosotros/as)	**os hubisteis** lavado
(ellos/as/Vds)	**se hubieron** lavado
PERFECT SUBJUNCTIVE	
(yo)	**me haya** lavado
(tú)	**te hayas** lavado
(él/ella/Vd)	**se haya** lavado
(nosotros/as)	**nos hayamos** lavado
(vosotros/as)	**os hayáis** lavado
(ellos/as/Vds)	**se hayan** lavado
PLUPERFECT SUBJUNCTIVE	
(yo)	**me hubiera** *or* **hubiese** lavado
(tú)	**te hubieras** *or* **hubieses** lavado
(él/ella/Vd)	**se hubiera** *or* **hubiese** lavado
(nosotros/as)	**nos hubiéramos** *or* **hubiésemos** lavado
(vosotros/as)	**os hubierais** *or* **hubieseis** lavado
(ellos/as/Vds)	**se hubieran** *or* **hubiesen** lavado

❐ The Passive

In active sentences, the subject of a verb carries out the action of that verb, but in passive sentences the subject receives the action. Compare the following:

The car hit Jane (subject: *the car*)
Jane was hit by the car (subject: *Jane*)

- English uses the verb *'to be'* with the past participle to form passive sentences. Spanish forms them in the same way, i.e.:

  a tense of **ser** + past participle

  The past participle agrees in number and gender with the subject → [1]

  A sample verb is conjugated in the passive voice on pp 36 to 39.

- In English, the word *'by'* usually introduces the agent through which the action of a passive sentence is performed. In Spanish this agent is preceded by **por** → [2]

- The passive voice is used much less frequently in Spanish than English. It is, however, often used in expressions where the identity of the agent is unknown or unimportant → [3]

Examples

1 **Pablo ha sido despedido**
Paul has been sacked
Su madre era muy admirada
His mother was greatly admired
El palacio será vendido
The palace will be sold
Las puertas habían sido cerradas
The doors had been closed

2 **La casa fue diseñada por mi hermano**
The house was designed by my brother

3 **La ciudad fue conquistada tras un largo asedio**
The city was conquered after a long siege
Ha sido declarado el estado de excepción
A state of emergency has been declared

❐ The Passive *(Continued)*

In English the indirect object in an active sentence can become the subject of the related passive sentence, e.g.

His mother gave him the book (indirect object: *him*)
He was given the book by his mother

This is not possible in Spanish. The indirect object remains as such, while the object of the active sentence becomes the subject of the passive sentence → 1

Other ways to express a passive meaning

Since modern Spanish tends to avoid the passive, it uses various other constructions to replace it:

- If the agent (person or object performing the action) is known, the active is often preferred where English might prefer the passive → 2
- The 3rd person plural of the active voice can be used. The meaning is equivalent to *they* + verb → 3
- When the action of the sentence is performed on a person, the reflexive form of the verb can be used in the 3rd person singular, and the person becomes the object → 4
- When the action is performed on a thing, this becomes the subject of the sentence and the verb is made reflexive, agreeing in number with the subject → 5

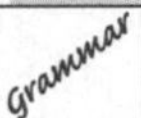

1 **Su madre le regaló el libro**
His mother gave him the book

becomes

El libro le fue regalado por su madre
The book was given to him by his mother

2 **La policía interrogó al sospechoso**
The police questioned the suspect

rather than

El sospechoso fue interrogado por la policía

3 **Usan demasiada publicidad en la televisión**
Too much advertising is used on television

4 **Últimamente no se le/les ha visto mucho en público**
He has/they have not been seen much in public recently

5 **Esta palabra ya no se usa**
This word is no longer used
Todos los libros se han vendido
All the books have been sold

❐ The Passive *(Continued)*

Conjugation of: **ser amado** *to be loved*

PRESENT	
(yo)	**soy** amado(a)
(tú)	**eres** amado(a)
(él/ella/Vd)	**es** amado(a)
(nosotros/as)	**somos** amado(a)s
(vosotros/as)	**sois** amado(a)s
(ellos/as/Vds)	**son** amado(a)s
IMPERFECT	
(yo)	**era** amado(a)
(tú)	**eras** amado(a)
(él/ella/Vd)	**era** amado(a)
(nosotros/as)	**éramos** amado(a)s
(vosotros/as)	**erais** amado(a)s
(ellos/as/Vds)	**eran** amado(a)s
FUTURE	
(yo)	**seré** amado(a)
(tú)	**serás** amado(a)
(él/ella/Vd)	**será** amado(a)
(nosotros/as)	**seremos** amado(a)s
(vosotros/as)	**seréis** amado(a)s
(ellos/as/Vds)	**serán** amado(a)s
CONDITIONAL	
(yo)	**sería** amado(a)
(tú)	**serías** amado(a)
(él/ella/Vd)	**sería** amado(a)
(nosotros/as)	**seríamos** amado(a)s
(vosotros/as)	**seríais** amado(a)s
(ellos/as/Vds)	**serían** amado(a)s

❐ The Passive *(Continued)*

Conjugation of: **ser amado** *to be loved*

PRETERITE	
(yo)	**fui** amad**o(a)**
(tú)	**fuiste** amad**o(a)**
(él/ella/Vd)	**fue** amad**o(a)**
(nosotros/as)	**fuimos** amad**o(a)s**
(vosotros/as)	**fuisteis** amad**o(a)s**
(ellos/as/Vds)	**fueron** amad**o(a)s**
PRESENT SUBJUNCTIVE	
(yo)	**sea** amad**o(a)**
(tú)	**seas** amad**o(a)**
(él/ella/Vd)	**sea** amad**o(a)**
(nosotros/as)	**seamos** amad**o(a)s**
(vosotros/as)	**seáis** amad**o(a)s**
(ellos/as/Vds)	**sean** amad**o(a)s**
IMPERFECT SUBJUNCTIVE	
(yo)	**fuera** *or* **fuese** amad**o(a)**
(tú)	**fueras** *or* **fueses** amad**o(a)**
(él/ella/Vd)	**fuera** *or* **fuese** amad**o(a)**
(nosotros/as)	**fuéramos** *or* **fuésemos** amad**o(a)s**
(vosotros/as)	**fuerais** *or* **fueseis** amad**o(a)s**
(ellos/as/Vds)	**fueran** *or* **fuesen** amad**o(a)s**

❒ The Passive *(Continued)*

Conjugation of: **ser amado** *to be loved*

PERFECT	
(yo)	**he sido** amado(a)
(tú)	**has sido** amado(a)
(él/ella/Vd)	**ha sido** amado(a)
(nosotros/as)	**hemos sido** amado(a)s
(vosotros/as)	**habéis sido** amado(a)s
(ellos/as/Vds)	**han sido** amado(a)s
PLUPERFECT	
(yo)	**había sido** amado(a)
(tú)	**habías sido** amado(a)
(él/ella/Vd)	**había sido** amado(a)
(nosotros/as)	**habíamos sido** amado(a)s
(vosotros/as)	**habíais sido** amado(a)s
(ellos/as/Vds)	**habían sido** amado(a)s
FUTURE PERFECT	
(yo)	**habré sido** amado(a)
(tú)	**habrás sido** amado(a)
(él/ella/Vd)	**habrá sido** amado(a)
(nosotros/as)	**habremos sido** amado(a)s
(vosotros/as)	**habréis sido** amado(a)s
(ellos/as/Vds)	**habrán sido** amado(a)s
CONDITIONAL PERFECT	
(yo)	**habría sido** amado(a)
(tú)	**habrías sido** amado(a)
(él/ella/Vd)	**habría sido** amado(a)
(nosotros/as)	**habríamos sido** amado(a)s
(vosotros/as)	**habríais sido** amado(a)s
(ellos/as/Vds)	**habrían sido** amado(a)s

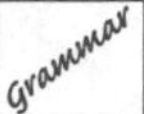

❐ The Passive *(Continued)*

Conjugation of: **ser amado** *to be loved*

PAST ANTERIOR	
(yo)	**hube sido** amado(a)
(tú)	**hubiste sido** amado(a)
(él/ella/Vd)	**hubo sido** amado(a)
(nosotros/as)	**hubimos sido** amado(a)s
(vosotros/as)	**hubisteis sido** amado(a)s
(ellos/as/Vds)	**hubieron sido** amado(a)s
PERFECT SUBJUNCTIVE	
(yo)	**haya sido** amado(a)
(tú)	**hayas sido** amado(a)
(él/ella/Vd)	**haya sido** amado(a)
(nosotros/as)	**hayamos sido** amado(a)s
(vosotros/as)	**hayáis sido** amado(a)s
(ellos/as/Vds)	**hayan sido** amado(a)s
PLUPERFECT SUBJUNCTIVE	
(yo)	**hubiera/-se sido** amado(a)
(tú)	**hubieras/-ses sido** amado(a)
(él/ella/Vd)	**hubiera/-se sido** amado(a)
(nosotros/as)	**hubiéramos/-semos sido** amado(a)s
(vosotros/as)	**hubierais/-seis sido** amado(a)s
(ellos/as/Vds)	**hubieran/-sen sido** amado(a)s

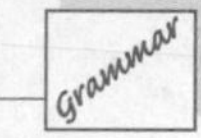

❒ Impersonal Verbs

Impersonal verbs are used only in the infinitive, the gerund, and in the 3rd person (usually singular); unlike English, Spanish does not use the subject pronoun with impersonal verbs, e.g.

llueve
it's raining

es fácil decir que ...
it's easy to say that ...

The most common impersonal verbs are:

INFINITIVE	CONSTRUCTION	
amanecer	**amanece/está amaneciendo** *it's daybreak*	
anochecer	**anochece/está anocheciendo** *it's getting dark*	
granizar	**graniza/está granizando** *it's hailing*	
llover	**llueve/está lloviendo** *it's raining*	→ 1
lloviznar	**llovizna/está lloviznando** *it's drizzling*	
nevar	**nieva/está nevando** *it's snowing*	
tronar	**truena/está tronando** *it's thundering*	

Some reflexive verbs are also used impersonally.
The most common are:

INFINITIVE	CONSTRUCTION
creerse	**se cree que*** + indicative → 2 *it is thought that; people think that*
decirse	**se dice que*** + indicative → 3 *it is said that; people say that*

Examples

1 **Llovía a cántaros**
It was raining cats and dogs
Estaba nevando cuando salieron
It was snowing when they left

2 **Se cree que llegarán mañana**
It is thought they will arrive tomorrow

3 **Se dice que ha sido el peor invierno en 50 años**
People say it's been the worst winter in 50 years

❒ Impersonal Verbs *(Continued)*

INFINITIVE	CONSTRUCTION
poderse	**se puede** + infinitive → [1] *one/people can, it is possible to*
tratarse de	**se trata de** + noun → [2] *it's a question/matter of something* *it's about something* **se trata de** + infinitive → [3] *it's a question/matter of doing; somebody must do*
venderse	**se vende*** + noun → [4] *to be sold; for sale*

* This impersonal construction conveys the same meaning as the 3rd person plural of these verbs; **creen que, dicen que, venden**

The following verbs are also commonly used in impersonal constructions:

INFINITIVE	CONSTRUCTION
bastar	**basta con** + infinitive → [5] *it is enough to do* **basta con** + noun → [6] *something is enough, it only takes something*
faltar	**falta** + infinitive → [7] *we still have to/one still has to*
haber	**hay** + noun → [8] *there is/are* **hay que** + infinitive → [9] *one has to/we have to*
hacer	**hace** + noun/adjective depicting weather/ dark/light etc → [10] *it is* **hace** + time expression + **que** + indicative → [11] *somebody has done* OR *been doing something since …* **hace** + time expression + **que** + negative indicative → [12] *it is … since*

Examples

1 **Aquí se puede aparcar**
One can park here

2 **No se trata de dinero**
It isn't a question/matter of money

3 **Se trata de poner fin al asunto**
We must put an end to the matter

4 **Se vende coche**
Car for sale

5 **Basta con telefonear para reservar un asiento**
You need only phone to reserve a seat

6 **Basta con un error para que todo se estropee**
One single error is enough to ruin everything

7 **Aún falta cerrar las maletas**
We/One still have/has to close the suitcases

8 **Hay una habitación libre**
There is one spare room

No había cartas esta mañana
There were no letters this morning

9 **Hay que cerrar las puertas**
We have/One has to shut the doors

10 **Hace calor/viento/sol**
It is hot/windy/sunny

Mañana hará bueno
It'll be nice (weather) tomorrow

11 **Hace seis meses que vivo/vivimos aquí**
I/We have lived *or* been living here for six months

12 **Hace tres años que no le veo**
It is three years since I last saw him

❒ Impersonal Verbs *(Continued)*

INFINITIVE	CONSTRUCTION
hacer falta	**hace falta** + noun object (+ indirect object) → 1 *(somebody) needs something, something is necessary (to somebody)* **hace falta** + infinitive (+ indirect object) → 2 *it is necessary to do* **hace falta que** + subjunctive → 3 *it is necessary to do, somebody must do*
parecer	**parece que** (+ indirect object) + indicative → 4 *it seems/appears that*
ser	**es/son** + time expression → 5 *it is* **es** + **de día/noche** → 6 *it is* **es** + adjective + infinitive → 7 *it is*
ser mejor	**es mejor** + infinitive → 8 *it's better to do* **es mejor que** + subjunctive → 9 *it's better if/that*
valer más	**más vale** + infinitive → 10 *it's better to do* **más vale que** + subjunctive → 11 *it's better to do/that somebody does*

Examples

1 **Hace falta valor para hacer eso**
One needs courage to do that, Courage is needed to do that

Me hace falta otro vaso más
I need an extra glass

2 **Hace falta volver**
It is necessary to return, We/I/You must return*

Me hacía falta volver
I had to return

3 **Hace falta que Vd se vaya**
You have to/must leave

4 **(Me) parece que estás equivocado**
It seems (to me) you are wrong

5 **Son las tres y media**
It is half past three

Ya es primavera
It is spring now

6 **Era de noche cuando llegamos**
It was night when we arrived

7 **Era inútil protestar**
It was useless to complain

8 **Es mejor no decir nada**
It's better to keep quiet

9 **Es mejor que lo pongas aquí**
It's better if/that you put it here

10 **Más vale prevenir que curar**
Prevention is better than cure

11 **Más valdría que no fuéramos**
It would be better if we didn't go/We'd better not go

* The translation here obviously depends on context

❐ The Infinitive

The infinitive is the form of the verb found in dictionary entries meaning *'to ...'*, e.g. **hablar** *to speak*, **vivir** *to live*.

The infinitive is used in the following ways:

- After a preposition → [1]
- As a verbal noun → [2]
  In this use the article may precede the infinitive, especially when the infinitive is the subject and begins the sentence → [3]
- As a dependent infinitive, in the following verbal constructions:
  — with no linking preposition → [4]

  — with the linking preposition **a** → [5]
  (see also p 66)

  — with the linking preposition **de** → [6]
  (see also p 66)

  — with the linking preposition **en** → [7]
  (see also p 66)

  — with the linking preposition **con** → [8]
  (see also p 66)

  — with the linking preposition **por** → [9]
  (see also p 66)
- The following construction should also be noted: indefinite pronoun + **que** + infinitive → [10]
- The object pronouns generally follow the infinitive and are attached to it. For exceptions see p 228.

Examples

1 **Después de acabar el desayuno, salió de casa**
After finishing her breakfast she went out

Al enterarse de lo ocurrido se puso furiosa
When she found out what had happened she was furious

Me hizo daño sin saberlo
She hurt me without her knowing

2 **Su deporte preferido es montar a caballo**
Her favourite sport is horse riding

Ver es creer
Seeing is believing

3 **El viajar tanto me resulta cansado**
I find so much travelling tiring

4 **¿Quiere Vd esperar?**
Would you like to wait?

5 **Aprenderán pronto a nadar**
They will soon learn to swim

6 **Pronto dejará de llover**
It'll stop raining soon

7 **La comida tarda en hacerse**
The meal is taking a long time to cook

8 **Amenazó con denunciarles**
He threatened to report them (to the police)

9 **Comience Vd por decirme su nombre**
Please start by giving me your name

10 **Tengo algo que decirte**
I have something to tell you

❐ The Infinitive *(Continued)*

The verbs set out below are followed by the infinitive with no linking preposition.

- **deber, poder, saber, querer** and **tener que** (**hay que** in impersonal constructions) → [1]
- **valer más, hacer falta**: see Impersonal Verbs, p 44.
- verbs of seeing or hearing, e.g. **ver** to see, **oír** to hear → [2]
- **hacer** → [3]
- **dejar** to let, allow → [3]
- The following common verbs:

aconsejar	to advise → [4]
conseguir	to manage to → [5]
decidir	to decide
desear	to wish, want → [6]
esperar	to hope → [7]
evitar	to avoid → [8]
impedir	to prevent → [9]
intentar	to try → [10]
lograr	to manage to → [5]
necesitar	to need → [11]
odiar	to hate
olvidar	to forget → [12]
pensar	to think → [13]
preferir	to prefer → [14]
procurar	to try → [10]
prohibir	to forbid → [15]
prometer	to promise → [16]
proponer	to propose → [17]

Examples

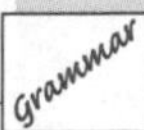

1 **¿Quiere Vd esperar?**
Would you like to wait?
No puede venir
She can't come

2 **Nos ha visto llegar**
She saw us arriving
Se les oye cantar
You can hear them singing

3 **No me hagas reír**
Don't make me laugh
Déjeme pasar
Let me past

4 **Le aconsejamos dejarlo para mañana**
We advise you to leave it until tomorrow

5 **Aún no he conseguido/logrado entenderlo**
I still haven't managed to understand it

6 **No desea tener más hijos**
She doesn't want to have any more children

7 **Esperamos ir de vacaciones este verano**
We are hoping to go on holiday this summer

8 **Evite beber cuando conduzca**
Avoid drinking and driving

9 **No pudo impedirle hablar**
He couldn't prevent him from speaking

10 **Intentamos/procuramos pasar desapercibidos**
We tried not to be noticed

11 **Necesitaba salir a la calle**
I/he/she needed to go out

12 **Olvidó dejar su dirección**
He/she forgot to leave his/her address

13 **¿Piensan venir por Navidad?**
Are you thinking of coming for Christmas?

14 **Preferiría elegirlo yo mismo**
I'd rather choose it myself

15 **Prohibió fumar a los alumnos**
He forbade the pupils to smoke

16 **Prometieron volver pronto**
They promised to come back soon

17 **Propongo salir cuanto antes**
I propose to leave as soon as possible

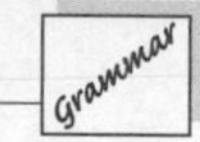

❒ The Infinitive: Set Expressions

The following are set in Spanish with the meaning shown:

dejar caer	*to drop* → 1
hacer entrar	*to show in* → 2
hacer saber	*to let know, make known* → 3
hacer salir	*to let out* → 4
hacer venir	*to send for* → 5
ir(se) a buscar	*to go for, go and get* → 6
mandar hacer	*to order* → 7
mandar llamar	*to send for* → 8
oír decir que	*to hear it said that* → 9
oír hablar de	*to hear of/about* → 10
querer decir	*to mean* → 11

The Perfect Infinitive

- The perfect infinitive is formed using the auxiliary verb **haber** with the past participle of the verb → 12
- The perfect infinitive is found:
  — following certain prepositions, especially **después de** *after* → 13
  — following certain verbal constructions → 14

Examples

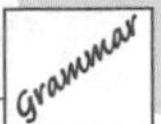

1 **Al verlo, dejó caer lo que llevaba en las manos**
When he saw him he dropped what he was carrying

2 **Haz entrar a nuestros invitados**
Show our guests in

3 **Quiero hacerles saber que no serán bien recibidos**
I want to let them know that they won't be welcome

4 **Hágale salir, por favor**
Please let him out

5 **Le he hecho venir a Vd porque ...**
I sent for you because ...

6 **Vete a buscar los guantes**
Go and get your gloves

7 **Me he mandado hacer un traje**
I have ordered a suit

8 **Mandaron llamar al médico**
They sent for the doctor

9 **He oído decir que está enfermo**
I've heard it said that he's ill

10 **No he oído hablar más de él**
I haven't heard anything more (said) of him

11 **¿Qué quiere decir eso?**
What does that mean?

12 **haber terminado**
to have finished

haberse vestido
to have got dressed

13 **Después de haber comprado el regalo, volvió a casa**
After buying/having bought the present, he went back home

Después de haber madrugado tanto, el taxi se retrasó
After she got up so early, the taxi arrived late

14 **perdonar a alguien por haber hecho**
to forgive somebody for doing/having done

dar las gracias a alguien por haber hecho
to thank somebody for doing/having done

pedir perdón por haber hecho
to be sorry for doing/having done

❐ The Gerund

Formation

- 1st conjugation
  Replace the **-ar** of the infinitive by **-ando** → [1]
- 2nd conjugation
  Replace the **-er** of the infinitive by **-iendo** → [2]
- 3rd conjugation
  Replace the **-ir** of the infinitive by **-iendo** → [3]
- For irregular gerunds, see irregular verbs, p 80 ff.

Uses

- After the verb **estar**, to form the continuous tenses → [4]
- After the verbs **seguir** and **continuar** *to continue*, and **ir** when meaning *to happen gradually* → [5]
- In time constructions, after **llevar** → [6]
- When the action in the main clause needs to be complemented by another action → [7]
- The position of object pronouns is the same as for the infinitive (see p 46).
- The gerund is invariable and strictly verbal in sense.

❐ The Present Participle

- It is formed by replacing the **-ar** of the infinitive of 1st conjugation verbs by **-ante**, and the **-er** and **-ir** of the 2nd and 3rd conjugations by **-iente** → [8]
- A very limited number of verbs have a present participle, which is either used as an adjective or a noun → [9]/ [10]

Examples

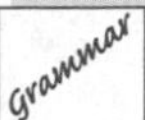

1	**cantar**	→	**cantando**
	to sing		singing
2	**temer**	→	**temiendo**
	to fear		fearing
3	**partir**	→	**partiendo**
	to leave		leaving

4 **Estoy escribiendo una carta**
I am writing a letter
Estaban esperándonos
They were waiting for us

5 **Sigue viniendo todos los días**
He/she is still coming every day
Continuarán subiendo los precios
Prices will continue to go up
El ejército iba avanzando poco a poco
The army was gradually advancing

6 **Lleva dos años estudiando inglés**
He/she has been studying English for two years

7 **Pasamos el día tomando el sol en la playa**
We spent the day sunbathing on the beach
Iba cojeando
He/she/I was limping
Salieron corriendo
They ran out

8	**cantar**	→	**cantante**
	to sing		singing/singer
	pender	→	**pendiente**
	to hang		hanging
	seguir	→	**siguiente**
	to follow		following

9 **agua corriente**
running water

10 **un estudiante**
a student

❐ Use of Tenses

The Present

- Unlike English, Spanish often uses the same verb form for the simple present (e.g. *I smoke, he reads, we live*) and the continuous present (e.g. *I am smoking, he is reading, we are living*) → [1]

- Normally, however, the continuous present is used to translate the English:

  to be doing **estar haciendo** → [2]

- Spanish uses the present tense where English uses the perfect in the following cases:

  — with certain prepositions of time – notably **desde** *for/since* – when an action begun in the past is continued in the present → [3]

  ⚠ NOTE: The perfect can be used as in English when the verb is negative → [4]

  — in the construction **acabar de hacer** *to have just done* → [5]

- Like English, Spanish often uses the present where a future action is implied → [6]

The Future

The future is generally used as in English → [7], but note the following:

- Immediate future time is often expressed by means of the present tense of **ir** + **a** + infinitive → [8]
- When *'will'* or *'shall'* mean *'wish to', 'are willing to'*, **querer** is used → [9]

The Future Perfect

- Used as in English *shall/will have done* → [10]
- It can also express conjecture, usually about things in the recent past → [11]

Examples

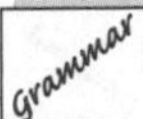

1 **Fumo** I smoke OR: I am smoking
Lee He reads OR: He is reading
Vivimos We live OR: We are living

2 **Está fumando**
He is smoking

3 **Linda estudia español desde hace seis meses**
Linda's been learning Spanish for six months (*and still is*)
Estoy de pie desde las siete
I've been up since seven
¿Hace mucho que esperan?
Have you been waiting long?
Ya hace dos semanas que estamos aquí
That's two weeks we've been here (now)

4 **No se han visto desde hace meses**
They haven't seen each other for months

5 **Isabel acaba de salir**
Isabel has just left

6 **Mañana voy a Madrid**
I am going to Madrid tomorrow

7 **Lo haré mañana**
I'll do it tomorrow

8 **Te vas a caer si no tienes cuidado**
You'll fall if you're not careful
Va a perder el tren
He's going to miss the train
Va a llevar una media hora
It'll take about half an hour

9 **¿Me quieres esperar un momento, por favor?**
Will you wait for me a second, please?

10 **Lo habré acabado para mañana**
I will have finished it for tomorrow

11 **Ya habrán llegado a casa**
They must have arrived home by now

❒ Use of Tenses *(Continued)*

The Imperfect

- The imperfect describes:
  - — an action or state in the past without definite limits in time → 1
  - — habitual action(s) in the past (often expressed in English by means of *would* or *used to*) → 2
- Spanish uses the imperfect tense where English uses the pluperfect in the following cases:
  - — with certain prepositions of time – notably **desde** *for/since* – when an action begun in the remoter past was continued in the more recent past → 3

  ⚠ NOTE: The pluperfect is used as in English when the verb is negative or the action has been completed → 4

  - — in the construction **acabar de hacer** *to have just done* → 5
- Both the continuous and simple forms in English can be translated by the Spanish simple imperfect, but the continuous imperfect is used when the emphasis is on the fact that an action was going on at a precise moment in the past → 6

The Perfect

- The perfect is generally used as in English → 7

The Preterite

- The preterite generally corresponds to the English simple past in both written and spoken Spanish → 8

However, while English can use the simple past to describe habitual actions or settings, Spanish uses the imperfect (see above) → 9

The Past Anterior

- This tense is only ever used in written, literary Spanish, to replace the pluperfect in time clauses where the verb in the main clause is in the preterite → 10

Examples

1 **Todos mirábamos en silencio**
We were all watching in silence
Nuestras habitaciones daban a la playa
Our rooms overlooked the beach

2 **En su juventud se levantaba de madrugada**
In his youth he got up at dawn
Hablábamos sin parar durante horas
We would talk non-stop for hours on end
Mi hermano siempre me tomaba el pelo
My brother always used to tease me

3 **Hacía dos años que vivíamos en Irlanda**
We had been living in Ireland for two years
Estaba enfermo desde 1990
He had been ill since 1990
Hacía mucho tiempo que salían juntos
They had been going out together for a long time

4 **Hacía un año que no le había visto**
I hadn't seen him for a year
Hacía una hora que había llegado
She had arrived an hour before

5 **Acababa de encontrármelos**
I had just met them

6 **Cuando llegué, todos estaban fumando**
When I arrived, they were all smoking

7 **Todavía no han salido**
They haven't come out yet

8 **Me desperté y salté de la cama**
I woke up and jumped out of bed

9 **Siempre iban en coche al trabajo**
They always travelled to work by car

10 **Apenas hubo acabado, se oyeron unos golpes en la puerta**
She had scarcely finished when there was a knock at the door

❐ The Subjunctive: when to use it

(For how to form the subjunctive see pp 6 ff.)

- After verbs of:

— 'wishing'

querer que
desear que } to wish that, want → [1]

— 'emotion' (e.g. regret, surprise, shame, pleasure, etc)
sentir que to be sorry that → [2]
sorprender que to be surprised that → [3]
alegrarse de que to be pleased that → [4]

— 'asking' and 'advising'
pedir que to ask that → [5]
aconsejar que to advise that → [6]

In all the above constructions, when the subject of the verbs in the main and subordinate clause is the same, the infinitive is used, and the conjunction **que** omitted → [7]

— 'ordering', 'forbidding', 'allowing'

mandar que*
ordenar que } to order that → [8]

permitir que*
dejar que* } to allow that → [9]

prohibir que* to forbid that → [10]
impedir que* to prevent that → [11]

* With these verbs either the subjunctive or the infinitive is used when the object of the main verb is the subject of the subordinate verb → [12]

- Always after verbs expressing doubt or uncertainty, and verbs of opinion used negatively

dudar que to doubt that → [13]

no creer que
no pensar que } not to think that → [14]

Examples

1 **Queremos que esté contenta**
We want her to be happy (literally: We want that she is happy)
¿Desea Vd que lo haga yo?
Do you want me to do it?

2 **Sentí mucho que no vinieran**
I was very sorry that they didn't come

3 **Nos sorprendió que no les vieran Vds**
We were surprised you didn't see them

4 **Me alegro de que te gusten**
I'm pleased that you like them

5 **Sólo les pedimos que tengan cuidado**
We're only asking you to take care

6 **Le aconsejé que no llegara tarde**
I advised him not to be late

7 **Quiero que lo termines pronto**
I want you to finish it soon
⚠ BUT: **Quiero terminarlo pronto**
I want to finish it soon

8 **Ha mandado que vuelvan**
He has ordered them to come back
Ordenó que fueran castigados
He ordered them to be punished

9 **No permitas que te tomen el pelo**
Don't let them pull your leg
No me dejó que la llevara a casa
She didn't allow me to take her home

10 **Te prohíbo que digas eso**
I forbid you to say that

11 **No les impido que vengan**
I am not preventing them from coming

12 **Les ordenó que salieran** OR: **Les ordenó salir**
She ordered them to go out

13 **Dudo que lo sepan hacer**
I doubt they can do it

14 **No creo que sean tan listos**
I don't think they are as clever as that

❐ The Subjunctive: when to use it *(Continued)*

- In impersonal constructions which express necessity, possibility, etc:

hace falta que **es necesario que**	*it is necessary that* → 1
es posible que	*it is possible that* → 2
más vale que	*it is better that* → 3
es una lástima que	*it is a pity that* → 4

⚠ NOTE: In impersonal constructions which state a fact or express certainty the indicative is used when the impersonal verb is affirmative. When it is negative, the subjunctive is used → 5

- After certain conjunctions

para que **a fin de que***	*so that* → 6
como si	*as if* → 7
sin que*	*without* → 8
a condición de que* **con tal (de) que*** **siempre que**	*provided that,* *on condition that* → 9
a menos que **a no ser que**	*unless* → 10
antes (de) que*	*before* → 11
no sea que	*lest/in case* → 12
mientras (que) **siempre que**	*as long as* → 13
(el) que	*the fact that* → 14

* When the subject of both verbs is the same, the infinitive is used, and the final **que** is omitted → 8

Examples

1 **¿Hace falta que vaya Jaime?**
Does James have to go?

2 **Es posible que tengan razón**
It's possible that they are right

3 **Más vale que se quede Vd en su casa**
It's better that you stay at home

4 **Es una lástima que haya perdido su perrito**
It's a shame/pity that she has lost her puppy

5 **Es verdad que va a venir**
It's true that he's coming

⚠ BUT: **No es verdad que vayan a hacerlo**
It's not true that they are going to do it

6 **Átalas bien para que no se caigan**
Tie them up tightly so that they won't fall

7 **Hablaba como si no creyera en sus propias palabras**
He talked as if he didn't believe in his own words

8 **Salimos sin que nos vieran**
We left without them seeing us

⚠ BUT: **Me fui sin esperarla**
I went without waiting for her

9 **Lo haré con tal de que me cuentes todo lo que pasó**
I'll do it provided you tell me all that happened

10 **Saldremos de paseo a menos que esté lloviendo**
We'll go for a walk unless it's raining

11 **Avísale antes de que sea demasiado tarde**
Warn him before it's too late

12 **Habla en voz baja, no sea que alguien nos oiga**
Speak softly in case anyone hears us

13 **Eso no pasará mientras yo sea el jefe aquí**
That won't happen as long as I am the boss here

14 **El que no me escribiera no me importaba demasiado**
The fact that he didn't write didn't matter to me too much

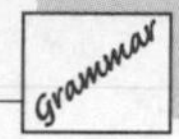

❐ The Subjunctive: when to use it *(Continued)*

- After the conjunctions

de modo que **de forma que** **de manera que**	*so that* (indicating a purpose) → [1]

⚠ NOTE: When these conjunctions introduce a result and not a purpose the subjunctive is not used → [2]

- In relative clauses with an antecedent which is:

  — negative → [3]

  — indefinite → [4]

  — non-specific → [5]

- In main clauses, to express a wish or exhortation. The verb may be preceded by expressions like **ojalá** or **que** → [6]
- In the **si** clause of conditions where the English sentence contains a conditional tense → [7]
- In set expressions → [8]
- In the following constructions which translate *however*:

  — **por** + adjective + subjunctive → [9]

  — **por** + adverb + subjunctive → [10]

  — **por** + **mucho** + subjunctive → [11]

Examples

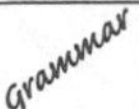

1 **Vuélvanse de manera que les vea bien**
Turn round so that I can see you properly

2 **No quieren hacerlo, de manera que tendré que hacerlo yo**
They won't do it, so I'll have to do it myself

3 **No he encontrado a nadie que la conociera**
I haven't met anyone who knows her
No dijo nada que no supiéramos ya
He/she didn't say anything we didn't already know

4 **Necesito alguien que sepa conducir**
I need someone who can drive
Busco algo que me distraiga
I'm looking for something to take my mind off it

5 **Busca una casa que tenga calefacción central**
He/she's looking for a house which has central heating
(*subjunctive used since such a house may or may not exist*)
El que lo haya visto tiene que decírmelo
Anyone who has seen it must tell me
(*subjunctive used since it is not known who has seen it*)

6 **¡Ojalá haga buen tiempo!**
Let's hope the weather will be good!
¡Que te diviertas!
Have a good time!

7 **Si fuéramos en coche llegaríamos a tiempo**
If we went by car we'd be there in time

8 **Diga lo que diga ...**
Whatever he may say ...
Pase lo que pase ...
Come what may ...
Sea lo que sea ...
Be that as it may ...
Sea como sea ...
One way or another ...

9 **Por cansado que esté, seguirá trabajando**
No matter how/however tired he may be, he'll go on working

10 **Por lejos que viva, iremos a buscarle**
No matter how/however far away he lives, we'll go and look for him

11 **Por mucho que lo intente, nunca lo conseguirá**
No matter how/however hard he tries, he'll never succeed

❐ The Subjunctive: when to use it *(Continued)*

Clauses taking either a subjunctive or an indicative

In certain constructions, a subjunctive is needed when the action refers to future events or hypothetical situations, whereas an indicative is used when stating a fact or experience → [1]

The commonest of these are:

- The conjunctions

cuando	*when* → [1]
en cuanto / **tan pronto como**	*as soon as* → [2]
después (de) que*	*after* → [3]
hasta que	*until* → [4]
mientras	*while* → [5]
siempre que	*whenever* → [6]
aunque	*even though* → [7]

All conjunctions and pronouns ending in **-quiera** (*-ever*) → [8]

* ⚠ NOTE: If the subject of both verbs is the same, the subjunctive introduced by **después (de) que** may be replaced by **después de** + infinitive → [9]

Sequence of tenses in Subordinate Clauses

- If the verb in the main clause is in the present, future or imperative, the verb in the dependent clause will be in the present or perfect subjunctive → [10]
- If the verb in the main clause is in the conditional or any past tense, the verb in the dependent clause will be in the imperfect or pluperfect subjunctive → [11]

Examples

1 **Le aconsejé que oyera música cuando estuviera nervioso**
I advised him to listen to music when he felt nervous
Me gusta nadar cuando hace calor
I like to swim when it is warm

2 **Te devolveré el libro tan pronto como lo haya leído**
I'll give you back the book as soon as I have read it

3 **Te lo diré después de que te hayas sentado**
I'll tell you after you've sat down

4 **Quédate aquí hasta que volvamos**
Stay here until we come back

5 **No hablen en voz alta mientras estén ellos aquí**
Don't speak loudly while they are here

6 **Vuelvan por aquí siempre que quieran**
Come back whenever you wish to

7 **No le creeré aunque diga la verdad**
I won't believe him even if he tells the truth

8 **La encontraré dondequiera que esté**
I will find her wherever she might be

9 **Después de cenar nos fuimos al cine**
After dinner we went to the cinema

10 **Quiero que lo hagas** (*pres + pres subj*)
I want you to do it
Temo que no haya venido (*pres + perf subj*)
I fear he hasn't come (might not have come)
Iremos por aquí para que no nos vean
(*future + pres subj*)
We'll go this way so that they won't see us

11 **Me gustaría que llegaras temprano**
(*cond + imperf subj*)
I'd like you to arrive early
Les pedí que me esperaran (*preterite + imperf subj*)
I asked them to wait for me
Sentiría mucho que hubiese muerto
(*cond + pluperf subj*)
I would be very sorry if he were dead

❒ Verbs governing a, de, con, en, por and para

The following lists (pp 66 to 73) contain common verbal constructions using the prepositions **a, de, con, en, por** and **para**.

Note the following abbreviations:

infin	infinitive
perf infin	perfect infinitive*
algn	alguien
sb	somebody
sth	something

* For formation see p 50

aburrirse de + infin	*to get bored with doing* → [1]
acabar con algo/algn	*to put an end to sth/finish with sb* → [2]
acabar de* + infin	*to have just done* → [3]
acabar por + infin	*to end up doing* → [4]
acercarse a algo/algn	*to approach sth/sb*
acordarse de algo/algn/de + infin	*to remember sth/sb/doing* → [5]
acostumbrarse a algo/algn/a + infin	*to get used to sth/sb/to doing* → [6]
acusar a algn de algo/de + perf infin	*to accuse sb of sth/of doing, having done* → [7]
advertir a algn de algo	*to notify, warn sb about sth* → [8]
aficionarse a algo/a + infin	*to grow fond of sth/of doing* → [9]
alegrarse de algo/de + perf infin	*to be glad about sth/of doing, having done* → [10]
alejarse de algn/algo	*to move away from sb/sth*
amenazar a algn con algo/con + infin	*to threaten sb with sth/to do* → [11]
animar a algn a + infin	*to encourage sb to do*
apresurarse a + infin	*to hurry to do* → [12]

* See also Use of Tenses, pp 54 and 56

Examples

1 **Me aburría de no poder salir de casa**
I used to get bored with not being able to leave the house

2 **Quiso acabar con su vida**
He wanted to put an end to his life

3 **Acababan de llegar cuando ...**
They had just arrived when ...

4 **El acusado acabó por confesarlo todo**
The accused ended up by confessing everything

5 **Nos acordamos muy bien de aquellas vacaciones**
We remember that holiday very well

6 **Me he acostumbrado a levantarme temprano**
I've got used to getting up early

7 **Le acusó de haber mentido**
She accused him of lying

8 **Advertí a mi amigo del peligro que corría**
I warned my friend about the danger he was in

9 **Nos hemos aficionado a la música clásica**
We've grown fond of classical music

10 **Me alegro de haberle conocido**
I'm glad I met him

11 **Amenazó con denunciarles**
He threatened to report them

12 **Se apresuraron a coger sitio**
They hurried to find a seat

❐ Verbs governing a, de, con, en, por and para *(Continued)*

aprender a + infin	*to learn to do* → [1]
aprovecharse de algo/algn	*to take advantage of sth/sb*
aproximarse a algn/algo	*to approach sb/sth*
asistir a algo	*to attend sth, be at sth*
asomarse a/por	*to lean out of* → [2]
asombrarse de + infin	*to be surprised at doing* → [3]
atreverse a + infin	*to dare to do*
avergonzarse de algo/algn/de + perf infin	*to be ashamed of sth/sb/of doing, having done* → [4]
ayudar a algn a + infin	*to help sb to do* → [5]
bajarse de (+ place/vehicle)	*to get off/out of* → [6]
burlarse de algn	*to make fun of sb*
cansarse de algo/algn/de + infin	*to tire of sth/sb/of doing*
carecer de algo	*to lack sth* → [7]
cargar de algo	*to load with sth* → [8]
casarse con algn	*to get married to sb* → [9]
cesar de + infin	*to stop doing*
chocar con algo	*to crash/bump into sth* → [10]
comenzar a + infin	*to begin to do*
comparar con algn/algo	*to compare with sb/sth*
consentir en + infin	*to agree to do*
consistir en + infin	*to consist of doing* → [11]
constar de algo	*to consist of sth* → [12]
contar con algn/algo	*to rely on sb/sth* → [13]
convenir en + infin	*to agree to do* → [14]
darse cuenta de algo	*to realize sth*
dejar de + infin	*to stop doing* → [15]
depender de algo/algn	*to depend on sth/sb* → [16]
despedirse de algn	*to say goodbye to sb*
dirigirse a + place/**a algn**	*to head for/address sb*
disponerse a + infin	*to get ready to do*
empezar a + infin	*to begin to do*
empezar por + infin	*to begin by doing* → [17]

Examples

1 **Me gustaría aprender a nadar**
I'd like to learn to swim

2 **No te asomes a la ventana**
Don't lean out of the window

3 **Nos asombramos mucho de verles ahí**
We were very surprised at seeing them there

4 **No me avergüenzo de haberlo hecho**
I'm not ashamed of having done it

5 **Ayúdeme a llevar estas maletas**
Help me to carry these cases

6 **Se bajó del coche**
He got out of the car

7 **La casa carecía de jardín**
The house lacked (did not have) a garden

8 **El carro iba cargado de paja**
The cart was loaded with straw

9 **Se casó con Andrés**
She married Andrew

10 **Enciende la luz, o chocarás con la puerta**
Turn the light on, or you'll bump into the door

11 **Mi plan consistía en vigilarles de cerca**
My plan consisted of keeping a close eye on them

12 **El examen consta de tres partes**
The exam consists of three parts

13 **Cuento contigo para que me ayudes a hacerlo**
I rely on you to help me do it

14 **Convinieron en reunirse al día siguiente**
They agreed to meet the following day

15 **¿Quieres dejar de hablar?**
Will you stop talking?

16 **No depende de mí**
It doesn't depend on me

17 **Empieza por enterarte de lo que se trata**
Begin by finding out what it is about

❐ Verbs governing a, de, con, en, por and para *(Continued)*

encontrarse con algn	*to meet sb (by chance)* → 1
enfadarse con algn	*to get annoyed with sb*
enseñar a algn a + infin	*to teach sb to* → 2
enterarse de algo	*to find out about sth* → 3
entrar en (+ place)	*to enter, go into*
esperar a + infin	*to wait until* → 4
estar de acuerdo con algn/algo	*to agree with sb/sth*
fiarse de algn/algo	*to trust sb/sth*
fijarse en algo/algn	*to notice sth/sb* → 5
hablar con algn	*to talk to sb* → 6
hacer caso a algn	*to pay attention to sb*
hartarse de algo/algn/de + infin	*to get fed up with sth/sb/with doing* → 7
interesarse por algo/algn	*to be interested in sth/sb* → 8
invitar a algn a + infin	*to invite sb to do*
jugar a (+ sports, games)	*to play*
luchar por algo/por + infin	*to fight, strive for/to do* → 9
llegar a (+ place)**/a** + infin	*to reach/to manage to do* → 10
llenar de algo	*to fill with sth*
negarse a + infin	*to refuse to do* → 11
obligar a algn a + infin	*to make sb do* → 12
ocuparse de algn/algo	*to take care of sb/attend to sth*
oler a algo	*to smell of sth* → 13
olvidarse de algo/algn/de + infin	*to forget sth/sb/to do* → 14
oponerse a algo/a + infin	*to be opposed to sth/to doing*
parecerse a algn/algo	*to resemble sb/sth*
pensar en algo/algn/en + infin	*to think about sth/sb/about doing* → 15
preguntar por algn	*to ask for/about sb*
preocuparse de *or* **por algo/algn**	*to worry about sth/sb* → 16

Examples

1 **Me encontré con ella al entrar en el banco**
I met her as I was entering the bank

2 **Le estoy enseñando a nadar**
I am teaching him to swim

3 **¿Te has enterado del sitio adonde hay que ir?**
Have you found out where we have to go?

4 **Espera a saber lo que quiere antes de comprar el regalo**
Wait until you know what he wants before buying the present

5 **Me fijé en él cuando subía a su coche**
I noticed him when he was getting into his car

6 **¿Puedo hablar con Vd un momento?**
May I talk to you for a moment?

7 **Me he hartado de escribirle**
I've got fed up with writing to him

8 **Me interesaba mucho por la arqueología**
I was very interested in archaeology

9 **Hay que luchar por mantener la paz**
One must strive to preserve peace

10 **Lo intenté sin llegar a conseguirlo**
I tried without managing to do it

11 **Se negó a hacerlo**
He refused to do it

12 **Le obligó a sentarse**
He made him sit down

13 **Este perfume huele a jazmín**
This perfume smells of jasmine

14 **Siempre me olvido de cerrar la puerta**
I always forget to shut the door

15 **No quiero pensar en eso**
I don't want to think about that

16 **Se preocupa mucho de/por su apariencia**
He worries a lot about his appearance

❒ Verbs governing a, de, con, en, por and para *(Continued)*

prepararse a + infin	*to prepare to do*
probar a + infin	*to try to do*
quedar en + infin	*to agree to do* → 1
quedar por + infin	*to remain to be done* → 2
quejarse de algo	*to complain of sth*
referirse a algo	*to refer to sth*
reírse de algo/algn	*to laugh at sth/sb*
rodear de	*to surround with* → 3
romper a + infin	*to (suddenly) start to do* → 4
salir de (+ place)	*to leave*
sentarse a (+ table etc)	*to sit down at*
subir(se) a (+ vehicle/place)	*to get on, into/to climb* → 5
servir de algo a algn	*to be useful to/serve sb as sth* → 6
servir para algo/para + infin	*to be good as sth/for doing* → 7
servirse de algo	*to use sth* → 8
soñar con algn/algo/con + infin	*to dream about/of sb/sth/of doing*
sorprenderse de algo	*to be surprised at sth*
tardar en + infin	*to take time to do* → 9
tener ganas de algo/de + infin	*to want sth/to do* → 10
tener miedo de algo	*to be afraid of sth* → 11
tener miedo a algn	*to be afraid of sb* → 12
terminar por + infin	*to end by doing*
tirar de algo/algn	*to pull sth/sb*
trabajar de (+ occupation)	*to work as* → 13
trabajar en (+ place of work)	*to work at/in* → 14
traducir a (+ language)	*to translate into*
tratar de + infin	*to try to do* → 15
tratarse de algo/algn/de + infin	*to be a question of sth/about sb/about doing* → 16
vacilar en + infin	*to hesitate to do* → 17
volver a + infin	*to do again* → 18

Examples

1 **Habíamos quedado en encontrarnos a las 8**
We had agreed to meet at 8

2 **Queda por averiguar dónde se ocultan**
It remains to be discovered where they are hiding

3 **Habían rodeado el jardín de un seto de cipreses**
They had surrounded the garden with a hedge of cypress trees

4 **Al apagarse la luz, el niño rompió a llorar**
When the lights went out, the little boy suddenly started to cry

5 **¡De prisa, sube al coche!** Get into the car, quick!

6 **Esto me servirá de bastón**
This will serve me as a walking stick

7 **No sirvo para (ser) jardinero**
I'm no good as a gardener

8 **Se sirvió de un destornillador para abrirlo**
She used a screwdriver to open it

9 **Tardaron mucho en salir**
They took a long time to come out

10 **Tengo ganas de volver a España**
I want to go back to Spain

11 **Mi hija tiene miedo de la oscuridad**
My daughter is afraid of the dark

12 **Nunca tuvieron miedo a su padre**
They were never afraid of their father

13 **Pedro trabaja de camarero en Londres**
Peter works as a waiter in London

14 **Trabajaba en una oficina**
I used to work in an office

15 **No trates de engañarme**
Don't try to fool me

16 **Se trata de nuestro nuevo vecino**
It's about our new neighbour

17 **Nunca vacilaban en pedir dinero**
They never hesitated to borrow money

18 **No vuelvas a hacerlo nunca más**
Don't ever do it again

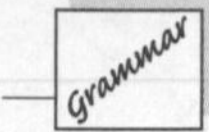

❒ Ser and Estar

Spanish has two verbs – **ser** and **estar** – for *to be*.

They are not interchangeable and each one is used in defined contexts.

ser is used:

- With an adjective, to express a permanent or inherent quality → 1
- To express occupation or nationality → 2
- To express possession → 3
- To express origin or the material from which something is made → 4
- With a noun, pronoun or infinitive following the verb → 5
- To express the time and date → 6
- To form the passive, with the past participle (see p 32).

  ⚠ NOTE: This use emphasizes the action of the verb. If, however, the resultant state or condition needs to be emphasized, **estar** is used. The past participle then functions as an adjective (see p 204) and has to agree in gender and in number with the noun → 7

estar is used:

- Always, to indicate place or location → 8
- With an adjective or adjectival phrase, to express a quality or state seen by the speaker as subject to change or different from expected → 9
- When speaking of a person's state of health → 10
- To form the continuous tenses, used with the gerund (see p 52) → 11
- With **de** + noun, to indicate a temporary occupation → 12

Examples

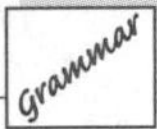

1 **Mi hermano es alto**
My brother is tall
María es inteligente
Mary is intelligent

2 **Javier es aviador**
Javier is an airman
Sus padres son italianos
His parents are Italian

3 **La casa es de Miguel**
The house belongs to Michael

4 **Mi hermana es de Granada**
My sister is from Granada
Las paredes son de ladrillo
The walls are made of brick

5 **Andrés es un niño travieso**
Andrew is a naughty boy
Soy yo, Enrique
It's me, Henry
Todo es proponérselo
It's all a question of putting your mind to it

6 **Son las tres y media**
It's half past three
Mañana es sábado
Tomorrow is Saturday

7 **Las puertas eran cerradas sigilosamente**
The doors were being silently closed
Las puertas estaban cerradas
The doors were closed (*resultant action*)

8 **La comida está en la mesa**
The meal is on the table

9 **Su amigo está enfermo**
Her friend is ill
Hoy estoy de mal humor
I'm in a bad mood today
El lavabo está ocupado
The toilet is engaged
Las tiendas están cerradas
The shops are closed

10 **¿Cómo están Vds?**
How are you?
Estamos todos bien
We are all well

11 **Estamos aprendiendo mucho**
We are learning a great deal

12 **Mi primo está de médico en un pueblo**
My cousin works as a doctor in a village

❒ Ser and Estar *(Continued)*

With certain adjectives, both **ser** and **estar** can be used, although they are not interchangeable when used in this way:

— **ser** will express a permanent or inherent quality → 1

— **estar** will express a temporary state or quality → 2

Both **ser** and **estar** may also be used in set expressions.

The commonest of these are:

- With **ser**

Sea como sea	*Be that as it may*
Es igual/Es lo mismo	*It's all the same*
llegar a ser	*to become*
¿Cómo fue eso?	*How did that happen?*
¿Qué ha sido de él?	*What has become of him?*
ser para (with the idea of purpose)	*to be for* → 3

- With **estar**

estar de pie/de rodillas	*to be standing/kneeling*
estar de viaje	*to be travelling*
estar de vacaciones	*to be on holiday*
estar de vuelta	*to be back*
estar de moda	*to be in fashion*
Está bien	*It's all right*
estar para	*to be about to do sth/to be in a mood for* → 4
estar por	*to be inclined to/to be (all) for* → 5
estar a punto de	*to be just about to do sth* → 6

Examples

1 **Su hermana es muy joven/vieja**
His sister is very young/old
Son muy ricos/pobres
They are very rich/poor
Su amigo era un enfermo
His friend was an invalid
Es un borracho
He is a drunkard
Mi hijo es bueno/malo
My son is good/naughty
Viajar es cansado
Travelling is tiring

2 **Está muy joven/vieja con ese vestido**
She looks very young/old in that dress
Ahora están muy ricos/pobres
They have become very rich/poor lately
Estaba enfermo
He was ill
Está borracho
He is drunk
Está bueno/malo
He is well/ill
Hoy estoy cansada
I am tired today

3 **Este paquete es para Vd**
This parcel is for you
Esta caja es para guardar semillas
This box is for keeping seeds in

4 **Están para llegar**
They're about to arrive

5 **Estoy por irme a vivir a España**
I'm inclined to go and live in Spain

6 **Las rosas están a punto de salir**
The roses are about to come out

❒ Verbal Idioms

Special Intransitive Verbs

With the following verbs the Spanish construction is the opposite of the English. The subject in English becomes the indirect object of the Spanish verb, while the object in English becomes the subject of the Spanish verb.

Compare the following:

I like that house (subject: *I*, object: *that house*)
Esa casa me gusta (subject: **esa casa**, indirect object: **me**)

The commonest of these verbs are:

gustar	*to like* → [1]
gustar más	*to prefer* → [2]
encantar	(colloquial) *to love* → [3]
faltar	*to need/to be short of/to have missing* → [4]
quedar	*to be/have left* → [5]
doler	*to have a pain in/to hurt, ache* → [6]
interesar	*to be interested in* → [7]
importar	*to mind* → [8]

Examples

1 **Me gusta este vestido**
I like this dress (This dress pleases me)

2 **Me gustan más éstas**
I prefer these

3 **Nos encanta hacer deporte**
We love sport

4 **Me faltaban cinco euros**
I was five euros short

Sólo le falta el toque final
It just needs the finishing touch

Le faltaban tres dientes
He/she had three teeth missing

5 **Sólo nos quedan dos kilómetros**
We only have two kilometres (left) to go

6 **Me duele la cabeza**
I have a headache

7 **Nos interesa mucho la política**
We are very interested in politics

8 **No me importa la lluvia**
I don't mind the rain

❒ Irregular Verbs

The verbs listed opposite and conjugated on pp 82 to 161 provide the main patterns for irregular verbs. The verbs are grouped opposite according to their infinitive ending and are shown in the following tables in alphabetical order.

In the tables, the most important irregular verbs are given in their most common simple tenses, together with the imperative and the gerund.

The past participle is also shown for each verb, to enable you to form all the compound tenses, as on pp 18 to 23.

The pronouns **ella** and **Vd** take the same verb endings as **él**, while **ellas** and **Vds** take the same endings as **ellos**.

- All the verbs included in the tables differ from the three conjugations set out on pp 8 to 13. Many – e.g. **contar** – serve as models for groups of verbs, while others – e.g. **ir** – are unique. On pp 162 to 186 you will find over 2,800 commonly used verbs listed alphabetically and cross-referred either to the relevant basic conjugation or to the appropriate model in the verb tables.

Imperfect Subjunctive of Irregular Verbs

For verbs with an irregular root form in the preterite tense – e.g. **andar** → **anduvieron** – the imperfect subjunctive is formed by using the root form of the 3rd person plural of the preterite tense, and adding the imperfect subjunctive endings **-iera/-iese** etc where the verb has an 'i' in the preterite ending – e.g. anduv**ieron** → anduv**iera/iese**. Where the verb has no 'i' in the preterite ending, add **-era/-ese** etc – e.g. produj**eron** → produj**era/ese**.

'-ar':
actuar
almorzar
andar
aunar
avergonzar
averiguar
contar
cruzar
dar
empezar
enviar
errar
estar
jugar
negar
pagar
pensar
rehusar
rogar
sacar
volcar

'-er':
caber
caer
cocer
coger
crecer
entender
haber
hacer
hay
leer
llover
mover
nacer
oler
poder
poner
querer
resolver
romper
saber
satisfacer
ser
tener
torcer
traer
valer
vencer
ver
volver

'-ir':
abolir
abrir
adquirir
bendecir
conducir
construir
cubrir
decir
dirigir
distinguir
dormir
elegir
erguir
escribir
freír
gruñir
ir
lucir
morir
oír
pedir
prohibir
reír
reñir
reunir
salir
seguir
sentir
venir
zurcir

abolir *to abolish*

PAST PARTICIPLE	IMPERATIVE
aboli**do**	aboli**d**
GERUND	
aboli**endo**	

PRESENT*		PRESENT SUBJUNCTIVE	
nosotros	aboli**mos**	*not used*	
vosotros	abol**ís**		
* Present tense only used in persons shown			

FUTURE		CONDITIONAL	
yo	abolir**é**	**yo**	abolir**ía**
tú	abolir**ás**	**tú**	abolir**ías**
él	abolir**á**	**él**	abolir**ía**
nosotros	abolir**emos**	**nosotros**	abolir**íamos**
vosotros	abolir**éis**	**vosotros**	abolir**íais**
ellos	abolir**án**	**ellos**	abolir**ían**

IMPERFECT		PRETERITE	
yo	abol**ía**	**yo**	abol**í**
tú	abol**ías**	**tú**	aboli**ste**
él	abol**ía**	**él**	aboli**ó**
nosotros	abol**íamos**	**nosotros**	aboli**mos**
vosotros	abol**íais**	**vosotros**	aboli**steis**
ellos	abol**ían**	**ellos**	aboli**eron**

abrir *to open*

PAST PARTICIPLE	IMPERATIVE
abierto	abre
GERUND	abrid
abriendo	

PRESENT		PRESENT SUBJUNCTIVE	
yo	abro	**yo**	abra
tú	abres	**tú**	abras
él	abre	**él**	abra
nosotros	abrimos	**nosotros**	abramos
vosotros	abrís	**vosotros**	abráis
ellos	abren	**ellos**	abran
FUTURE		CONDITIONAL	
yo	abriré	**yo**	abriría
tú	abrirás	**tú**	abrirías
él	abrirá	**él**	abriría
nosotros	abriremos	**nosotros**	abriríamos
vosotros	abriréis	**vosotros**	abriríais
ellos	abrirán	**ellos**	abrirían
IMPERFECT		PRETERITE	
yo	abría	**yo**	abrí
tú	abrías	**tú**	abriste
él	abría	**él**	abrió
nosotros	abríamos	**nosotros**	abrimos
vosotros	abríais	**vosotros**	abristeis
ellos	abrían	**ellos**	abrieron

actuar *to act*

PAST PARTICIPLE

actu**ado**

GERUND

actu**ando**

IMPERATIVE

actúa
actua**d**

PRESENT		PRESENT SUBJUNCTIVE	
yo	**actúo**	**yo**	**actúe**
tú	**actúas**	**tú**	**actúes**
él	**actúa**	**él**	**actúe**
nosotros	actu**amos**	**nosotros**	actu**emos**
vosotros	actu**áis**	**vosotros**	actu**éis**
ellos	**actúan**	**ellos**	**actúen**

FUTURE		CONDITIONAL	
yo	actuar**é**	**yo**	actuar**ía**
tú	actuar**ás**	**tú**	actuar**ías**
él	actuar**á**	**él**	actuar**ía**
nosotros	actuar**emos**	**nosotros**	actuar**íamos**
vosotros	actuar**éis**	**vosotros**	actuar**íais**
ellos	actuar**án**	**ellos**	actuar**ían**

IMPERFECT		PRETERITE	
yo	actu**aba**	**yo**	actu**é**
tú	actu**abas**	**tú**	actu**aste**
él	actu**aba**	**él**	actu**ó**
nosotros	actu**ábamos**	**nosotros**	actu**amos**
vosotros	actu**abais**	**vosotros**	actu**asteis**
ellos	actu**aban**	**ellos**	actu**aron**

adquirir *to acquire*

PAST PARTICIPLE

adquiri**do**

GERUND

adquiri**endo**

IMPERATIVE

adquiere
adquiri**d**

PRESENT		PRESENT SUBJUNCTIVE	
yo	**adquiero**	**yo**	**adquiera**
tú	**adquieres**	**tú**	**adquieras**
él	**adquiere**	**él**	**adquiera**
nosotros	adquiri**mos**	**nosotros**	adquir**amos**
vosotros	adquir**ís**	**vosotros**	adquir**áis**
ellos	**adquieren**	**ellos**	**adquieran**

FUTURE		CONDITIONAL	
yo	adquirir**é**	**yo**	adquirir**ía**
tú	adquirir**ás**	**tú**	adquirir**ías**
él	adquirir**á**	**él**	adquirir**ía**
nosotros	adquirir**emos**	**nosotros**	adquirir**íamos**
vosotros	adquirir**éis**	**vosotros**	adquirir**íais**
ellos	adquirir**án**	**ellos**	adquirir**ían**

IMPERFECT		PRETERITE	
yo	adquir**ía**	**yo**	adquir**í**
tú	adquir**ías**	**tú**	adquiri**ste**
él	adquir**ía**	**él**	adquiri**ó**
nosotros	adquir**íamos**	**nosotros**	adquiri**mos**
vosotros	adquir**íais**	**vosotros**	adquiri**steis**
ellos	adquir**ían**	**ellos**	adquiri**eron**

almorzar *to have lunch*

PAST PARTICIPLE	IMPERATIVE
almorzado	almuerza
	almorzad
GERUND	
almorzando	

PRESENT		PRESENT SUBJUNCTIVE	
yo	almuerzo	**yo**	almuerce
tú	almuerzas	**tú**	almuerces
él	almuerza	**él**	almuerce
nosotros	almorzamos	**nosotros**	almorcemos
vosotros	almorzáis	**vosotros**	almorcéis
ellos	almuerzan	**ellos**	almuercen

FUTURE		CONDITIONAL	
yo	almorzaré	**yo**	almorzaría
tú	almorzarás	**tú**	almorzarías
él	almorzará	**él**	almorzaría
nosotros	almorzaremos	**nosotros**	almorzaríamos
vosotros	almorzaréis	**vosotros**	almorzaríais
ellos	almorzarán	**ellos**	almorzarían

IMPERFECT		PRETERITE	
yo	almorzaba	**yo**	almorcé
tú	almorzabas	**tú**	almorzaste
él	almorzaba	**él**	almorzó
nosotros	almorzábamos	**nosotros**	almorzamos
vosotros	almorzabais	**vosotros**	almorzasteis
ellos	almorzaban	**ellos**	almorzaron

andar *to walk*

PAST PARTICIPLE	IMPERATIVE
and**ado**	and**a**
	and**ad**
GERUND	
and**ando**	

PRESENT		PRESENT SUBJUNCTIVE	
yo	and**o**	**yo**	and**e**
tú	and**as**	**tú**	and**es**
él	and**a**	**él**	and**e**
nosotros	and**amos**	**nosotros**	and**emos**
vosotros	and**áis**	**vosotros**	and**éis**
ellos	and**an**	**ellos**	and**en**
FUTURE		CONDITIONAL	
yo	andar**é**	**yo**	andar**ía**
tú	andar**ás**	**tú**	andar**ías**
él	andar**á**	**él**	andar**ía**
nosotros	andar**emos**	**nosotros**	andar**íamos**
vosotros	andar**éis**	**vosotros**	andar**íais**
ellos	andar**án**	**ellos**	andar**ían**
IMPERFECT		PRETERITE	
yo	and**aba**	**yo**	**anduve**
tú	and**abas**	**tú**	**anduviste**
él	and**aba**	**él**	**anduvo**
nosotros	and**ábamos**	**nosotros**	**anduvimos**
vosotros	and**abais**	**vosotros**	**anduvisteis**
ellos	and**aban**	**ellos**	**anduvieron**

aunar *to join together*

PAST PARTICIPLE	IMPERATIVE
aun**ado**	**aúna**
	aun**ad**
GERUND	
aun**ando**	

PRESENT		PRESENT SUBJUNCTIVE	
yo	**aúno**	**yo**	**aúne**
tú	**aúnas**	**tú**	**aúnes**
él	**aúna**	**él**	**aúne**
nosotros	aun**amos**	**nosotros**	aun**emos**
vosotros	aun**áis**	**vosotros**	aun**éis**
ellos	**aúnan**	**ellos**	**aúnen**
FUTURE		CONDITIONAL	
yo	aunar**é**	**yo**	aunar**ía**
tú	aunar**ás**	**tú**	aunar**ías**
él	aunar**á**	**él**	aunar**ía**
nosotros	aunar**emos**	**nosotros**	aunar**íamos**
vosotros	aunar**éis**	**vosotros**	aunar**íais**
ellos	aunar**án**	**ellos**	aunar**ían**
IMPERFECT		PRETERITE	
yo	aun**aba**	**yo**	aun**é**
tú	aun**abas**	**tú**	aun**aste**
él	aun**aba**	**él**	aun**ó**
nosotros	aun**ábamos**	**nosotros**	aun**amos**
vosotros	aun**abais**	**vosotros**	aun**asteis**
ellos	aun**aban**	**ellos**	aun**aron**

avergonzar *to shame*

PAST PARTICIPLE	IMPERATIVE
avergonz**ado**	**avergüenza**
	avergonza**d**
GERUND	
avergonz**ando**	

PRESENT		PRESENT SUBJUNCTIVE	
yo	**avergüenzo**	**yo**	**avergüence**
tú	**avergüenzas**	**tú**	**avergüences**
él	**avergüenza**	**él**	**avergüence**
nosotros	avergonz**amos**	**nosotros**	**avergoncemos**
vosotros	avergonz**áis**	**vosotros**	**avergoncéis**
ellos	**avergüenzan**	**ellos**	**avergüencen**
FUTURE		CONDITIONAL	
yo	avergonzar**é**	**yo**	avergonzar**ía**
tú	avergonzar**ás**	**tú**	avergonzar**ías**
él	avergonzar**á**	**él**	avergonzar**ía**
nosotros	avergonzar**emos**	**nosotros**	avergonzar**íamos**
vosotros	avergonzar**éis**	**vosotros**	avergonzar**íais**
ellos	avergonzar**án**	**ellos**	avergonzar**ían**
IMPERFECT		PRETERITE	
yo	avergonz**aba**	**yo**	**avergoncé**
tú	avergonz**abas**	**tú**	avergonz**aste**
él	avergonz**aba**	**él**	avergonz**ó**
nosotros	avergonz**ábamos**	**nosotros**	avergonz**amos**
vosotros	avergonz**abais**	**vosotros**	avergonz**asteis**
ellos	avergonz**aban**	**ellos**	avergonz**aron**

averiguar *to find out*

PAST PARTICIPLE

averigu**ado**

GERUND

averigu**ando**

IMPERATIVE

averigu**a**
averigu**ad**

PRESENT		PRESENT SUBJUNCTIVE	
yo	averiguo	**yo**	**averigüe**
tú	averiguas	**tú**	**averigües**
él	averigua	**él**	**averigüe**
nosotros	averigu**amos**	**nosotros**	**averigüemos**
vosotros	averigu**áis**	**vosotros**	**averigüéis**
ellos	averigu**an**	**ellos**	**averigüen**

FUTURE		CONDITIONAL	
yo	averiguar**é**	**yo**	averiguar**ía**
tú	averiguar**ás**	**tú**	averiguar**ías**
él	averiguar**á**	**él**	averiguar**ía**
nosotros	averiguar**emos**	**nosotros**	averiguar**íamos**
vosotros	averiguar**éis**	**vosotros**	averiguar**íais**
ellos	averiguar**án**	**ellos**	averiguar**ían**

IMPERFECT		PRETERITE	
yo	averigu**aba**	**yo**	**averigüé**
tú	averigu**abas**	**tú**	averigu**aste**
él	averigu**aba**	**él**	averigu**ó**
nosotros	averigu**ábamos**	**nosotros**	averigu**amos**
vosotros	averigu**abais**	**vosotros**	averigu**asteis**
ellos	averigu**aban**	**ellos**	averigu**aron**

bendecir *to bless*

PAST PARTICIPLE

bendec**ido**

GERUND

bendiciendo

IMPERATIVE

bendice
bendecid

PRESENT		PRESENT SUBJUNCTIVE	
yo	**bendigo**	**yo**	**bendiga**
tú	**bendices**	**tú**	**bendigas**
él	**bendice**	**él**	**bendiga**
nosotros	bendec**imos**	**nosotros**	**bendigamos**
vosotros	bendec**ís**	**vosotros**	**bendigáis**
ellos	**bendicen**	**ellos**	**bendigan**

FUTURE		CONDITIONAL	
yo	bendecir**é**	**yo**	bendecir**ía**
tú	bendecir**ás**	**tú**	bendecir**ías**
él	bendecir**á**	**él**	bendecir**ía**
nosotros	bendecir**emos**	**nosotros**	bendecir**íamos**
vosotros	bendecir**éis**	**vosotros**	bendecir**íais**
ellos	bendecir**án**	**ellos**	bendecir**ían**

IMPERFECT		PRETERITE	
yo	bendec**ía**	**yo**	**bendije**
tú	bendec**ías**	**tú**	**bendijiste**
él	bendec**ía**	**él**	**bendijo**
nosotros	bendec**íamos**	**nosotros**	**bendijimos**
vosotros	bendec**íais**	**vosotros**	**bendijisteis**
ellos	bendec**ían**	**ellos**	**bendijeron**

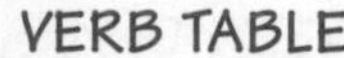

caber *to fit*

PAST PARTICIPLE	IMPERATIVE
cab**ido**	cabe
	cabed
GERUND	
cab**iendo**	

PRESENT		PRESENT SUBJUNCTIVE	
yo	**quepo**	**yo**	**quepa**
tú	cabes	**tú**	**quepas**
él	cabe	**él**	**quepa**
nosotros	cabemos	**nosotros**	**quepamos**
vosotros	cabéis	**vosotros**	**quepáis**
ellos	caben	**ellos**	**quepan**

FUTURE		CONDITIONAL	
yo	**cabré**	**yo**	**cabría**
tú	**cabrás**	**tú**	**cabrías**
él	**cabrá**	**él**	**cabría**
nosotros	**cabremos**	**nosotros**	**cabríamos**
vosotros	**cabréis**	**vosotros**	**cabríais**
ellos	**cabrán**	**ellos**	**cabrían**

IMPERFECT		PRETERITE	
yo	cabía	**yo**	**cupe**
tú	cabías	**tú**	**cupiste**
él	cabía	**él**	**cupo**
nosotros	cabíamos	**nosotros**	**cupimos**
vosotros	cabíais	**vosotros**	**cupisteis**
ellos	cabían	**ellos**	**cupieron**

caer *to fall*

PAST PARTICIPLE	IMPERATIVE
caído	cae
GERUND	caed
cayendo	

PRESENT		PRESENT SUBJUNCTIVE	
yo	caigo	**yo**	caiga
tú	caes	**tú**	caigas
él	cae	**él**	caiga
nosotros	caemos	**nosotros**	caigamos
vosotros	caéis	**vosotros**	caigáis
ellos	caen	**ellos**	caigan

FUTURE		CONDITIONAL	
yo	caeré	**yo**	caería
tú	caerás	**tú**	caerías
él	caerá	**él**	caería
nosotros	caeremos	**nosotros**	caeríamos
vosotros	caeréis	**vosotros**	caeríais
ellos	caerán	**ellos**	caerían

IMPERFECT		PRETERITE	
yo	caía	**yo**	caí
tú	caías	**tú**	caíste
él	caía	**él**	cayó
nosotros	caíamos	**nosotros**	caímos
vosotros	caíais	**vosotros**	caísteis
ellos	caían	**ellos**	cayeron

cocer *to boil*

PAST PARTICIPLE
coc**ido**

GERUND
coc**iendo**

IMPERATIVE
cuece
coce**d**

PRESENT		PRESENT SUBJUNCTIVE	
yo	**cuezo**	**yo**	**cueza**
tú	**cueces**	**tú**	**cuezas**
él	**cuece**	**él**	**cueza**
nosotros	coc**emos**	**nosotros**	**cozamos**
vosotros	coc**éis**	**vosotros**	**cozáis**
ellos	**cuecen**	**ellos**	**cuezan**

FUTURE		CONDITIONAL	
yo	coce**ré**	**yo**	coce**ría**
tú	coce**rás**	**tú**	coce**rías**
él	coce**rá**	**él**	coce**ría**
nosotros	coce**remos**	**nosotros**	coce**ríamos**
vosotros	coce**réis**	**vosotros**	coce**ríais**
ellos	coce**rán**	**ellos**	coce**rían**

IMPERFECT		PRETERITE	
yo	coc**ía**	**yo**	coc**í**
tú	coc**ías**	**tú**	coc**iste**
él	coc**ía**	**él**	coc**ió**
nosotros	coc**íamos**	**nosotros**	coc**imos**
vosotros	coc**íais**	**vosotros**	coc**isteis**
ellos	coc**ían**	**ellos**	coc**ieron**

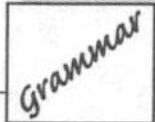

coger *to catch*

PAST PARTICIPLE	IMPERATIVE
cogido	coge
	coged
GERUND	
cogiendo	

PRESENT		PRESENT SUBJUNCTIVE	
yo	cojo	**yo**	coja
tú	coges	**tú**	cojas
él	coge	**él**	coja
nosotros	cogemos	**nosotros**	cojamos
vosotros	cogéis	**vosotros**	cojáis
ellos	cogen	**ellos**	cojan

FUTURE		CONDITIONAL	
yo	cogeré	**yo**	cogería
tú	cogerás	**tú**	cogerías
él	cogerá	**él**	cogería
nosotros	cogeremos	**nosotros**	cogeríamos
vosotros	cogeréis	**vosotros**	cogeríais
ellos	cogerán	**ellos**	cogerían

IMPERFECT		PRETERITE	
yo	cogía	**yo**	cogí
tú	cogías	**tú**	cogiste
él	cogía	**él**	cogió
nosotros	cogíamos	**nosotros**	cogimos
vosotros	cogíais	**vosotros**	cogisteis
ellos	cogían	**ellos**	cogieron

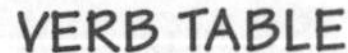

conducir *to drive, to lead*

PAST PARTICIPLE	IMPERATIVE
conduc**ido**	conduce conduc**id**
GERUND	
conduc**iendo**	

PRESENT		PRESENT SUBJUNCTIVE	
yo	**conduzco**	**yo**	**conduzca**
tú	conduces	**tú**	**conduzcas**
él	conduce	**él**	**conduzca**
nosotros	conduc**imos**	**nosotros**	**conduzcamos**
vosotros	conduc**ís**	**vosotros**	**conduzcáis**
ellos	conducen	**ellos**	**conduzcan**

FUTURE		CONDITIONAL	
yo	conduciré	**yo**	conduciría
tú	conducirás	**tú**	conducirías
él	conducirá	**él**	conduciría
nosotros	conduci**remos**	**nosotros**	conduci**ríamos**
vosotros	conduci**réis**	**vosotros**	conduci**ríais**
ellos	conducirán	**ellos**	conducirían

IMPERFECT		PRETERITE	
yo	conducía	**yo**	**conduje**
tú	conducías	**tú**	**condujiste**
él	conducía	**él**	**condujo**
nosotros	conducíamos	**nosotros**	**condujimos**
vosotros	conducíais	**vosotros**	**condujisteis**
ellos	conducían	**ellos**	**condujeron**

construir *to build*

PAST PARTICIPLE
construi**do**

GERUND
construyendo

IMPERATIVE
construye
construi**d**

PRESENT		PRESENT SUBJUNCTIVE	
yo	**construyo**	**yo**	**construya**
tú	**construyes**	**tú**	**construyas**
él	**construye**	**él**	**construya**
nosotros	constru**imos**	**nosotros**	**construyamos**
vosotros	constru**ís**	**vosotros**	**construyáis**
ellos	**construyen**	**ellos**	**construyan**

FUTURE		CONDITIONAL	
yo	constru**iré**	**yo**	constru**iría**
tú	constru**irás**	**tú**	constru**irías**
él	constru**irá**	**él**	constru**iría**
nosotros	constru**iremos**	**nosotros**	constru**iríamos**
vosotros	constru**iréis**	**vosotros**	constru**iríais**
ellos	constru**irán**	**ellos**	constru**irían**

IMPERFECT		PRETERITE	
yo	constru**ía**	**yo**	constru**í**
tú	constru**ías**	**tú**	constru**iste**
él	constru**ía**	**él**	**construyó**
nosotros	constru**íamos**	**nosotros**	constru**imos**
vosotros	constru**íais**	**vosotros**	constru**isteis**
ellos	constru**ían**	**ellos**	**construyeron**

contar *to tell, to count*

PAST PARTICIPLE	IMPERATIVE
cont**ado**	**cuenta**
	cont**ad**
GERUND	
cont**ando**	

PRESENT		PRESENT SUBJUNCTIVE	
yo	**cuento**	**yo**	**cuente**
tú	**cuentas**	**tú**	**cuentes**
él	**cuenta**	**él**	**cuente**
nosotros	cont**amos**	**nosotros**	cont**emos**
vosotros	cont**áis**	**vosotros**	cont**éis**
ellos	**cuentan**	**ellos**	**cuenten**

FUTURE		CONDITIONAL	
yo	contar**é**	**yo**	contar**ía**
tú	contar**ás**	**tú**	contar**ías**
él	contar**á**	**él**	contar**ía**
nosotros	contar**emos**	**nosotros**	contar**íamos**
vosotros	contar**éis**	**vosotros**	contar**íais**
ellos	contar**án**	**ellos**	contar**ían**

IMPERFECT		PRETERITE	
yo	cont**aba**	**yo**	cont**é**
tú	cont**abas**	**tú**	cont**aste**
él	cont**aba**	**él**	cont**ó**
nosotros	cont**ábamos**	**nosotros**	cont**amos**
vosotros	cont**abais**	**vosotros**	cont**asteis**
ellos	cont**aban**	**ellos**	cont**aron**

crecer *to grow*

PAST PARTICIPLE	IMPERATIVE
crec**ido**	crec**e**
	crece**d**
GERUND	
crec**iendo**	

PRESENT		PRESENT SUBJUNCTIVE	
yo	**crezco**	**yo**	**crezca**
tú	crec**es**	**tú**	**crezcas**
él	crec**e**	**él**	**crezca**
nosotros	crec**emos**	**nosotros**	**crezcamos**
vosotros	crec**éis**	**vosotros**	**crezcáis**
ellos	crec**en**	**ellos**	**crezcan**

FUTURE		CONDITIONAL	
yo	crecer**é**	**yo**	crecer**ía**
tú	crecer**ás**	**tú**	crecer**ías**
él	crecer**á**	**él**	crecer**ía**
nosotros	crecer**emos**	**nosotros**	crecer**íamos**
vosotros	crecer**éis**	**vosotros**	crecer**íais**
ellos	crecer**án**	**ellos**	crecer**ían**

IMPERFECT		PRETERITE	
yo	crec**ía**	**yo**	crec**í**
tú	crec**ías**	**tú**	crec**iste**
él	crec**ía**	**él**	crec**ió**
nosotros	crec**íamos**	**nosotros**	crec**imos**
vosotros	crec**íais**	**vosotros**	crec**isteis**
ellos	crec**ían**	**ellos**	crec**ieron**

cruzar *to cross*

PAST PARTICIPLE

cruz**ado**

GERUND

cruz**ando**

IMPERATIVE

cruz**a**

cruz**ad**

PRESENT		PRESENT SUBJUNCTIVE	
yo	cruz**o**	**yo**	**cruce**
tú	cruz**as**	**tú**	**cruces**
él	cruz**a**	**él**	**cruce**
nosotros	cruz**amos**	**nosotros**	**crucemos**
vosotros	cruz**áis**	**vosotros**	**crucéis**
ellos	cruz**an**	**ellos**	**crucen**

FUTURE		CONDITIONAL	
yo	cruzar**é**	**yo**	cruzar**ía**
tú	cruzar**ás**	**tú**	cruzar**ías**
él	cruzar**á**	**él**	cruzar**ía**
nosotros	cruzar**emos**	**nosotros**	cruzar**íamos**
vosotros	cruzar**éis**	**vosotros**	cruzar**íais**
ellos	cruzar**án**	**ellos**	cruzar**ían**

IMPERFECT		PRETERITE	
yo	cruz**aba**	**yo**	**crucé**
tú	cruz**abas**	**tú**	cruz**aste**
él	cruz**aba**	**él**	cruz**ó**
nosotros	cruz**ábamos**	**nosotros**	cruz**amos**
vosotros	cruz**abais**	**vosotros**	cruz**asteis**
ellos	cruz**aban**	**ellos**	cruz**aron**

cubrir *to cover*

PAST PARTICIPLE

cubierto

GERUND

cubr**iendo**

IMPERATIVE

cubr**e**
cubr**id**

PRESENT		PRESENT SUBJUNCTIVE	
yo	cubr**o**	**yo**	cubr**a**
tú	cubr**es**	**tú**	cubr**as**
él	cubr**e**	**él**	cubr**a**
nosotros	cubr**imos**	**nosotros**	cubr**amos**
vosotros	cubr**ís**	**vosotros**	cubr**áis**
ellos	cubr**en**	**ellos**	cubr**an**

FUTURE		CONDITIONAL	
yo	cubrir**é**	**yo**	cubrir**ía**
tú	cubrir**ás**	**tú**	cubrir**ías**
él	cubrir**á**	**él**	cubrir**ía**
nosotros	cubrir**emos**	**nosotros**	cubrir**íamos**
vosotros	cubrir**éis**	**vosotros**	cubrir**íais**
ellos	cubrir**án**	**ellos**	cubrir**ían**

IMPERFECT		PRETERITE	
yo	cubr**ía**	**yo**	cubr**í**
tú	cubr**ías**	**tú**	cubr**iste**
él	cubr**ía**	**él**	cubr**ió**
nosotros	cubr**íamos**	**nosotros**	cubr**imos**
vosotros	cubr**íais**	**vosotros**	cubr**isteis**
ellos	cubr**ían**	**ellos**	cubr**ieron**

dar *to give*

PAST PARTICIPLE	IMPERATIVE
dado	da
	dad
GERUND	
dando	

PRESENT		PRESENT SUBJUNCTIVE	
yo	doy	**yo**	dé
tú	das	**tú**	des
él	da	**él**	dé
nosotros	damos	**nosotros**	demos
vosotros	dais	**vosotros**	deis
ellos	dan	**ellos**	den

FUTURE		CONDITIONAL	
yo	daré	**yo**	daría
tú	darás	**tú**	darías
él	dará	**él**	daría
nosotros	daremos	**nosotros**	daríamos
vosotros	daréis	**vosotros**	daríais
ellos	darán	**ellos**	darían

IMPERFECT		PRETERITE	
yo	daba	**yo**	di
tú	dabas	**tú**	diste
él	daba	**él**	dio
nosotros	dábamos	**nosotros**	dimos
vosotros	dabais	**vosotros**	disteis
ellos	daban	**ellos**	dieron

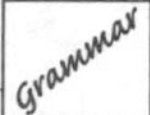

decir *to say*

PAST PARTICIPLE	IMPERATIVE
dicho	**di**
GERUND	decid
diciendo	

PRESENT		PRESENT SUBJUNCTIVE	
yo	**digo**	**yo**	**diga**
tú	**dices**	**tú**	**digas**
él	**dice**	**él**	**diga**
nosotros	decimos	**nosotros**	**digamos**
vosotros	decís	**vosotros**	**digáis**
ellos	**dicen**	**ellos**	**digan**

FUTURE		CONDITIONAL	
yo	**diré**	**yo**	**diría**
tú	**dirás**	**tú**	**dirías**
él	**dirá**	**él**	**diría**
nosotros	**diremos**	**nosotros**	**diríamos**
vosotros	**diréis**	**vosotros**	**diríais**
ellos	**dirán**	**ellos**	**dirían**

IMPERFECT		PRETERITE	
yo	decía	**yo**	**dije**
tú	decías	**tú**	**dijiste**
él	decía	**él**	**dijo**
nosotros	decíamos	**nosotros**	**dijimos**
vosotros	decíais	**vosotros**	**dijisteis**
ellos	decían	**ellos**	**dijeron**

dirigir *to direct*

PAST PARTICIPLE	IMPERATIVE
dirigido	dirige
	dirigid
GERUND	
dirigiendo	

PRESENT		PRESENT SUBJUNCTIVE	
yo	dirijo	**yo**	dirija
tú	diriges	**tú**	dirijas
él	dirige	**él**	dirija
nosotros	dirigimos	**nosotros**	dirijamos
vosotros	dirigís	**vosotros**	dirijáis
ellos	dirigen	**ellos**	dirijan
FUTURE		CONDITIONAL	
yo	dirigiré	**yo**	dirigiría
tú	dirigirás	**tú**	dirigirías
él	dirigirá	**él**	dirigiría
nosotros	dirigiremos	**nosotros**	dirigiríamos
vosotros	dirigiréis	**vosotros**	dirigiríais
ellos	dirigirán	**ellos**	dirigirían
IMPERFECT		PRETERITE	
yo	dirigía	**yo**	dirigí
tú	dirigías	**tú**	dirigiste
él	dirigía	**él**	dirigió
nosotros	dirigíamos	**nosotros**	dirigimos
vosotros	dirigíais	**vosotros**	dirigisteis
ellos	dirigían	**ellos**	dirigieron

distinguir *to distinguish*

PAST PARTICIPLE

distingu**ido**

GERUND

distingu**iendo**

IMPERATIVE

distingu**e**
distingu**id**

PRESENT		PRESENT SUBJUNCTIVE	
yo	**distingo**	**yo**	**distinga**
tú	distingu**es**	**tú**	**distingas**
él	distingu**e**	**él**	**distinga**
nosotros	distingu**imos**	**nosotros**	**distingamos**
vosotros	distingu**ís**	**vosotros**	**distingáis**
ellos	distingu**en**	**ellos**	**distingan**

FUTURE		CONDITIONAL	
yo	distinguir**é**	**yo**	distinguir**ía**
tú	distinguir**ás**	**tú**	distinguir**ías**
él	distinguir**á**	**él**	distinguir**ía**
nosotros	distinguir**emos**	**nosotros**	distinguir**íamos**
vosotros	distinguir**éis**	**vosotros**	distinguir**íais**
ellos	distinguir**án**	**ellos**	distinguir**ían**

IMPERFECT		PRETERITE	
yo	distingu**ía**	**yo**	distingu**í**
tú	distingu**ías**	**tú**	distingu**iste**
él	distingu**ía**	**él**	distingu**ió**
nosotros	distingu**íamos**	**nosotros**	distingu**imos**
vosotros	distingu**íais**	**vosotros**	distingu**isteis**
ellos	distingu**ían**	**ellos**	distingu**ieron**

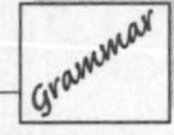

dormir *to sleep*

PAST PARTICIPLE

dorm**ido**

GERUND

durmiendo

IMPERATIVE

duerme
dormi**d**

PRESENT		PRESENT SUBJUNCTIVE	
yo	**duermo**	**yo**	**duerma**
tú	**duermes**	**tú**	**duermas**
él	**duerme**	**él**	**duerma**
nosotros	dorm**imos**	**nosotros**	**durmamos**
vosotros	dorm**ís**	**vosotros**	**durmáis**
ellos	**duermen**	**ellos**	**duerman**

FUTURE		CONDITIONAL	
yo	dormir**é**	**yo**	dormir**ía**
tú	dormir**ás**	**tú**	dormir**ías**
él	dormir**á**	**él**	dormir**ía**
nosotros	dormir**emos**	**nosotros**	dormir**íamos**
vosotros	dormir**éis**	**vosotros**	dormir**íais**
ellos	dormir**án**	**ellos**	dormir**ían**

IMPERFECT		PRETERITE	
yo	dorm**ía**	**yo**	dorm**í**
tú	dorm**ías**	**tú**	dorm**iste**
él	dorm**ía**	**él**	**durmió**
nosotros	dorm**íamos**	**nosotros**	dorm**imos**
vosotros	dorm**íais**	**vosotros**	dorm**isteis**
ellos	dorm**ían**	**ellos**	**durmieron**

elegir *to choose*

PAST PARTICIPLE	IMPERATIVE
elegido	elige
	elegid

GERUND

eligiendo

PRESENT		PRESENT SUBJUNCTIVE	
yo	elijo	**yo**	elija
tú	eliges	**tú**	elijas
él	elige	**él**	elija
nosotros	elegimos	**nosotros**	elijamos
vosotros	elegís	**vosotros**	elijáis
ellos	eligen	**ellos**	elijan

FUTURE		CONDITIONAL	
yo	elegiré	**yo**	elegiría
tú	elegirás	**tú**	elegirías
él	elegirá	**él**	elegiría
nosotros	elegiremos	**nosotros**	elegiríamos
vosotros	elegiréis	**vosotros**	elegiríais
ellos	elegirán	**ellos**	elegirían

IMPERFECT		PRETERITE	
yo	elegía	**yo**	elegí
tú	elegías	**tú**	elegiste
él	elegía	**él**	eligió
nosotros	elegíamos	**nosotros**	elegimos
vosotros	elegíais	**vosotros**	elegisteis
ellos	elegían	**ellos**	eligieron

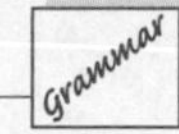
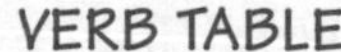

empezar *to begin*	
PAST PARTICIPLE	IMPERATIVE
empez**ado**	**empieza**
	empeza**d**
GERUND	
empez**ando**	

PRESENT		PRESENT SUBJUNCTIVE	
yo	**empiezo**	**yo**	**empiece**
tú	**empiezas**	**tú**	**empieces**
él	**empieza**	**él**	**empiece**
nosotros	empez**amos**	**nosotros**	**empecemos**
vosotros	empez**áis**	**vosotros**	**empecéis**
ellos	**empiezan**	**ellos**	**empiecen**

FUTURE		CONDITIONAL	
yo	empezar**é**	**yo**	empezar**ía**
tú	empezar**ás**	**tú**	empezar**ías**
él	empezar**á**	**él**	empezar**ía**
nosotros	empezar**emos**	**nosotros**	empezar**íamos**
vosotros	empezar**éis**	**vosotros**	empezar**íais**
ellos	empezar**án**	**ellos**	empezar**ían**

IMPERFECT		PRETERITE	
yo	empez**aba**	**yo**	**empecé**
tú	empez**abas**	**tú**	empez**aste**
él	empez**aba**	**él**	empez**ó**
nosotros	empez**ábamos**	**nosotros**	empez**amos**
vosotros	empez**abais**	**vosotros**	empez**asteis**
ellos	empez**aban**	**ellos**	empez**aron**

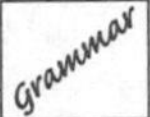

entender *to understand*

PAST PARTICIPLE

entend**ido**

GERUND

entend**iendo**

IMPERATIVE

entiende
entende**d**

PRESENT		PRESENT SUBJUNCTIVE	
yo	**entiendo**	**yo**	**entienda**
tú	**entiendes**	**tú**	**entiendas**
él	**entiende**	**él**	**entienda**
nosotros	entend**emos**	**nosotros**	entend**amos**
vosotros	entend**éis**	**vosotros**	entend**áis**
ellos	**entienden**	**ellos**	**entiendan**

FUTURE		CONDITIONAL	
yo	entender**é**	**yo**	entender**ía**
tú	entender**ás**	**tú**	entender**ías**
él	entender**á**	**él**	entender**ía**
nosotros	entender**emos**	**nosotros**	entender**íamos**
vosotros	entender**éis**	**vosotros**	entender**íais**
ellos	entender**án**	**ellos**	entender**ían**

IMPERFECT		PRETERITE	
yo	entend**ía**	**yo**	entend**í**
tú	entend**ías**	**tú**	entend**iste**
él	entend**ía**	**él**	entend**ió**
nosotros	entend**íamos**	**nosotros**	entend**imos**
vosotros	entend**íais**	**vosotros**	entend**isteis**
ellos	entend**ían**	**ellos**	entend**ieron**

enviar *to send*

PAST PARTICIPLE

envi**ado**

GERUND

envi**ando**

IMPERATIVE

envía

envia**d**

PRESENT		PRESENT SUBJUNCTIVE	
yo	**envío**	**yo**	**envíe**
tú	**envías**	**tú**	**envíes**
él	**envía**	**él**	**envíe**
nosotros	envi**amos**	**nosotros**	envi**emos**
vosotros	envi**áis**	**vosotros**	envi**éis**
ellos	**envían**	**ellos**	**envíen**

FUTURE		CONDITIONAL	
yo	enviar**é**	**yo**	enviar**ía**
tú	enviar**ás**	**tú**	enviar**ías**
él	enviar**á**	**él**	enviar**ía**
nosotros	enviar**emos**	**nosotros**	enviar**íamos**
vosotros	enviar**éis**	**vosotros**	enviar**íais**
ellos	enviar**án**	**ellos**	enviar**ían**

IMPERFECT		PRETERITE	
yo	envi**aba**	**yo**	envi**é**
tú	envi**abas**	**tú**	envi**aste**
él	envi**aba**	**él**	envi**ó**
nosotros	envi**ábamos**	**nosotros**	envi**amos**
vosotros	envi**abais**	**vosotros**	envi**asteis**
ellos	envi**aban**	**ellos**	envi**aron**

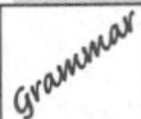

erguir *to erect*

PAST PARTICIPLE	IMPERATIVE
erguido	yergue
	erguid
GERUND	
irguiendo	

PRESENT		PRESENT SUBJUNCTIVE	
yo	yergo	**yo**	yerga
tú	yergues	**tú**	yergas
él	yergue	**él**	yerga
nosotros	erguimos	**nosotros**	irgamos
vosotros	erguís	**vosotros**	irgáis
ellos	yerguen	**ellos**	yergan

FUTURE		CONDITIONAL	
yo	erguiré	**yo**	erguiría
tú	erguirás	**tú**	erguirías
él	erguirá	**él**	erguiría
nosotros	erguiremos	**nosotros**	erguiríamos
vosotros	erguiréis	**vosotros**	erguiríais
ellos	erguirán	**ellos**	erguirían

IMPERFECT		PRETERITE	
yo	erguía	**yo**	erguí
tú	erguías	**tú**	erguiste
él	erguía	**él**	irguió
nosotros	erguíamos	**nosotros**	erguimos
vosotros	erguíais	**vosotros**	erguisteis
ellos	erguían	**ellos**	irguieron

errar *to err*

PAST PARTICIPLE	IMPERATIVE
errado	yerra
	errad
GERUND	
errando	

PRESENT		PRESENT SUBJUNCTIVE	
yo	yerro	**yo**	yerre
tú	yerras	**tú**	yerres
él	yerra	**él**	yerre
nosotros	erramos	**nosotros**	erremos
vosotros	erráis	**vosotros**	erréis
ellos	yerran	**ellos**	yerren

FUTURE		CONDITIONAL	
yo	erraré	**yo**	erraría
tú	errarás	**tú**	errarías
él	errará	**él**	erraría
nosotros	erraremos	**nosotros**	erraríamos
vosotros	erraréis	**vosotros**	erraríais
ellos	errarán	**ellos**	errarían

IMPERFECT		PRETERITE	
yo	erraba	**yo**	erré
tú	errabas	**tú**	erraste
él	erraba	**él**	erró
nosotros	errábamos	**nosotros**	erramos
vosotros	errabais	**vosotros**	errasteis
ellos	erraban	**ellos**	erraron

escribir *to write*

PAST PARTICIPLE

escrito

GERUND

escrib**iendo**

IMPERATIVE

escrib**e**
escrib**id**

PRESENT		PRESENT SUBJUNCTIVE	
yo	escrib**o**	**yo**	escrib**a**
tú	escrib**es**	**tú**	escrib**as**
él	escrib**e**	**él**	escrib**a**
nosotros	escrib**imos**	**nosotros**	escrib**amos**
vosotros	escrib**ís**	**vosotros**	escrib**áis**
ellos	escrib**en**	**ellos**	escrib**an**

FUTURE		CONDITIONAL	
yo	escribir**é**	**yo**	escribir**ía**
tú	escribir**ás**	**tú**	escribir**ías**
él	escribir**á**	**él**	escribir**ía**
nosotros	escribir**emos**	**nosotros**	escribir**íamos**
vosotros	escribir**éis**	**vosotros**	escribir**íais**
ellos	escribir**án**	**ellos**	escribir**ían**

IMPERFECT		PRETERITE	
yo	escrib**ía**	**yo**	escrib**í**
tú	escrib**ías**	**tú**	escrib**iste**
él	escrib**ía**	**él**	escrib**ió**
nosotros	escrib**íamos**	**nosotros**	escrib**imos**
vosotros	escrib**íais**	**vosotros**	escrib**isteis**
ellos	escrib**ían**	**ellos**	escrib**ieron**

estar *to be*	
PAST PARTICIPLE estado GERUND estando	IMPERATIVE está estad

PRESENT		PRESENT SUBJUNCTIVE	
yo	estoy	**yo**	esté
tú	estás	**tú**	estés
él	está	**él**	esté
nosotros	estamos	**nosotros**	estemos
vosotros	estáis	**vosotros**	estéis
ellos	están	**ellos**	estén
FUTURE		CONDITIONAL	
yo	estaré	**yo**	estaría
tú	estarás	**tú**	estarías
él	estará	**él**	estaría
nosotros	estaremos	**nosotros**	estaríamos
vosotros	estaréis	**vosotros**	estaríais
ellos	estarán	**ellos**	estarían
IMPERFECT		PRETERITE	
yo	estaba	**yo**	estuve
tú	estabas	**tú**	estuviste
él	estaba	**él**	estuvo
nosotros	estábamos	**nosotros**	estuvimos
vosotros	estabais	**vosotros**	estuvisteis
ellos	estaban	**ellos**	estuvieron

freír *to fry*

PAST PARTICIPLE	IMPERATIVE
frito	**fríe** freíd
GERUND	
friendo	

PRESENT		PRESENT SUBJUNCTIVE	
yo	**frío**	**yo**	**fría**
tú	**fríes**	**tú**	**frías**
él	**fríe**	**él**	**fría**
nosotros	freímos	**nosotros**	**friamos**
vosotros	freís	**vosotros**	**friáis**
ellos	**fríen**	**ellos**	**frían**
FUTURE		CONDITIONAL	
yo	freiré	**yo**	freiría
tú	freirás	**tú**	freirías
él	freirá	**él**	freiría
nosotros	freiremos	**nosotros**	freiríamos
vosotros	freiréis	**vosotros**	freiríais
ellos	freirán	**ellos**	freirían
IMPERFECT		PRETERITE	
yo	freía	**yo**	freí
tú	freías	**tú**	freíste
él	freía	**él**	**frio**
nosotros	freíamos	**nosotros**	freímos
vosotros	freíais	**vosotros**	freísteis
ellos	freían	**ellos**	**frieron**

gruñir *to grunt*

PAST PARTICIPLE

gruñ**ido**

GERUND

gruñendo

IMPERATIVE

gruñ**e**
gruñ**id**

PRESENT		PRESENT SUBJUNCTIVE	
yo	gruñ**o**	**yo**	gruñ**a**
tú	gruñ**es**	**tú**	gruñ**as**
él	gruñ**e**	**él**	gruñ**a**
nosotros	gruñ**imos**	**nosotros**	gruñ**amos**
vosotros	gruñ**ís**	**vosotros**	gruñ**áis**
ellos	gruñ**en**	**ellos**	gruñ**an**

FUTURE		CONDITIONAL	
yo	gruñir**é**	**yo**	gruñir**ía**
tú	gruñir**ás**	**tú**	gruñir**ías**
él	gruñir**á**	**él**	gruñir**ía**
nosotros	gruñir**emos**	**nosotros**	gruñir**íamos**
vosotros	gruñir**éis**	**vosotros**	gruñir**íais**
ellos	gruñir**án**	**ellos**	gruñir**ían**

IMPERFECT		PRETERITE	
yo	gruñ**ía**	**yo**	gruñ**í**
tú	gruñ**ías**	**tú**	gruñ**iste**
él	gruñ**ía**	**él**	**gruñó**
nosotros	gruñ**íamos**	**nosotros**	gruñ**imos**
vosotros	gruñ**íais**	**vosotros**	gruñ**isteis**
ellos	gruñ**ían**	**ellos**	**gruñeron**

haber *to have (auxiliary)*

PAST PARTICIPLE	IMPERATIVE
hab**ido**	*not used*
GERUND	
hab**iendo**	

PRESENT		PRESENT SUBJUNCTIVE	
yo	**he**	**yo**	**haya**
tú	**has**	**tú**	**hayas**
él	**ha**	**él**	**haya**
nosotros	**hemos**	**nosotros**	**hayamos**
vosotros	hab**éis**	**vosotros**	**hayáis**
ellos	**han**	**ellos**	**hayan**

FUTURE		CONDITIONAL	
yo	**habré**	**yo**	**habría**
tú	**habrás**	**tú**	**habrías**
él	**habrá**	**él**	**habría**
nosotros	**habremos**	**nosotros**	**habríamos**
vosotros	**habréis**	**vosotros**	**habríais**
ellos	**habrán**	**ellos**	**habrían**

IMPERFECT		PRETERITE	
yo	hab**ía**	**yo**	**hube**
tú	hab**ías**	**tú**	**hubiste**
él	hab**ía**	**él**	**hubo**
nosotros	hab**íamos**	**nosotros**	**hubimos**
vosotros	hab**íais**	**vosotros**	**hubisteis**
ellos	hab**ían**	**ellos**	**hubieron**

hacer *to do, to make*

PAST PARTICIPLE	IMPERATIVE
hecho	**haz**
	haced

GERUND

haciendo

PRESENT		PRESENT SUBJUNCTIVE	
yo	hago	**yo**	**haga**
tú	haces	**tú**	**hagas**
él	hace	**él**	**haga**
nosotros	hacemos	**nosotros**	**hagamos**
vosotros	hacéis	**vosotros**	**hagáis**
ellos	hacen	**ellos**	**hagan**

FUTURE		CONDITIONAL	
yo	**haré**	**yo**	**haría**
tú	**harás**	**tú**	**harías**
él	**hará**	**él**	**haría**
nosotros	**haremos**	**nosotros**	**haríamos**
vosotros	**haréis**	**vosotros**	**haríais**
ellos	**harán**	**ellos**	**harían**

IMPERFECT		PRETERITE	
yo	hacía	**yo**	**hice**
tú	hacías	**tú**	**hiciste**
él	hacía	**él**	**hizo**
nosotros	hacíamos	**nosotros**	**hicimos**
vosotros	hacíais	**vosotros**	**hicisteis**
ellos	hacían	**ellos**	**hicieron**

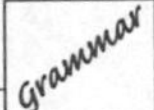

hay *there is, there are*

PAST PARTICIPLE

hab**ido**

GERUND

hab**iendo**

IMPERATIVE

not used

PRESENT	PRESENT SUBJUNCTIVE
hay	**haya**

FUTURE	CONDITIONAL
habrá	**habría**

IMPERFECT	PRETERITE
había	**hubo**

ir *to go*

PAST PARTICIPLE

ido

GERUND

yendo

IMPERATIVE

ve
id

PRESENT		PRESENT SUBJUNCTIVE	
yo	**voy**	**yo**	**vaya**
tú	**vas**	**tú**	**vayas**
él	**va**	**él**	**vaya**
nosotros	**vamos**	**nosotros**	**vayamos**
vosotros	**vais**	**vosotros**	**vayáis**
ellos	**van**	**ellos**	**vayan**

FUTURE		CONDITIONAL	
yo	iré	**yo**	iría
tú	irás	**tú**	irías
él	irá	**él**	iría
nosotros	iremos	**nosotros**	iríamos
vosotros	iréis	**vosotros**	iríais
ellos	irán	**ellos**	irían

IMPERFECT		PRETERITE	
yo	**iba**	**yo**	**fui**
tú	**ibas**	**tú**	**fuiste**
él	**iba**	**él**	**fue**
nosotros	**íbamos**	**nosotros**	**fuimos**
vosotros	**ibais**	**vosotros**	**fuisteis**
ellos	**iban**	**ellos**	**fueron**

jugar *to play*

PAST PARTICIPLE

jug**ado**

GERUND

jug**ando**

IMPERATIVE

juega
jug**ad**

PRESENT		PRESENT SUBJUNCTIVE	
yo	**juego**	**yo**	**juegue**
tú	**juegas**	**tú**	**juegues**
él	**juega**	**él**	**juegue**
nosotros	jug**amos**	**nosotros**	**juguemos**
vosotros	jug**áis**	**vosotros**	**juguéis**
ellos	**juegan**	**ellos**	**jueguen**

FUTURE		CONDITIONAL	
yo	jugar**é**	**yo**	jugar**ía**
tú	jugar**ás**	**tú**	jugar**ías**
él	jugar**á**	**él**	jugar**ía**
nosotros	jugar**emos**	**nosotros**	jugar**íamos**
vosotros	jugar**éis**	**vosotros**	jugar**íais**
ellos	jugar**án**	**ellos**	jugar**ían**

IMPERFECT		PRETERITE	
yo	jug**aba**	**yo**	**jugué**
tú	jug**abas**	**tú**	jug**aste**
él	jug**aba**	**él**	jug**ó**
nosotros	jug**ábamos**	**nosotros**	jug**amos**
vosotros	jug**abais**	**vosotros**	jug**asteis**
ellos	jug**aban**	**ellos**	jug**aron**

leer *to read*

PAST PARTICIPLE	IMPERATIVE
leído	**lee**
	leed
GERUND	
leyendo	

PRESENT		PRESENT SUBJUNCTIVE	
yo	leo	**yo**	lea
tú	lees	**tú**	leas
él	lee	**él**	lea
nosotros	leemos	**nosotros**	leamos
vosotros	leéis	**vosotros**	leáis
ellos	leen	**ellos**	lean
FUTURE		CONDITIONAL	
yo	leeré	**yo**	leería
tú	leerás	**tú**	leerías
él	leerá	**él**	leería
nosotros	leeremos	**nosotros**	leeríamos
vosotros	leeréis	**vosotros**	leeríais
ellos	leerán	**ellos**	leerían
IMPERFECT		PRETERITE	
yo	leía	**yo**	**leí**
tú	leías	**tú**	**leíste**
él	leía	**él**	**leyó**
nosotros	leíamos	**nosotros**	**leímos**
vosotros	leíais	**vosotros**	**leísteis**
ellos	leían	**ellos**	**leyeron**

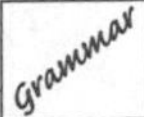

lucir *to shine*

PAST PARTICIPLE

luc**ido**

GERUND

luc**iendo**

IMPERATIVE

luce
lucid

PRESENT		PRESENT SUBJUNCTIVE	
yo	**luzco**	**yo**	**luzca**
tú	luces	**tú**	**luzcas**
él	luce	**él**	**luzca**
nosotros	lucimos	**nosotros**	**luzcamos**
vosotros	lucís	**vosotros**	**luzcáis**
ellos	lucen	**ellos**	**luzcan**

FUTURE		CONDITIONAL	
yo	luciré	**yo**	luciría
tú	lucirás	**tú**	lucirías
él	lucirá	**él**	luciría
nosotros	luciremos	**nosotros**	luciríamos
vosotros	luciréis	**vosotros**	luciríais
ellos	lucirán	**ellos**	lucirían

IMPERFECT		PRETERITE	
yo	lucía	**yo**	lucí
tú	lucías	**tú**	luciste
él	lucía	**él**	lució
nosotros	lucíamos	**nosotros**	lucimos
vosotros	lucíais	**vosotros**	lucisteis
ellos	lucían	**ellos**	lucieron

llover *to rain*

PAST PARTICIPLE

llov**ido**

GERUND

llov**iendo**

IMPERATIVE

not used

PRESENT	PRESENT SUBJUNCTIVE
llueve	**llueva**

FUTURE	CONDITIONAL
llover**á**	llover**ía**

IMPERFECT	PRETERITE
llov**ía**	llov**ió**

morir *to die*

PAST PARTICIPLE

muerto

GERUND

muriendo

IMPERATIVE

muere
morid

PRESENT		PRESENT SUBJUNCTIVE	
yo	**muero**	**yo**	**muera**
tú	**mueres**	**tú**	**mueras**
él	**muere**	**él**	**muera**
nosotros	morimos	**nosotros**	**muramos**
vosotros	morís	**vosotros**	**muráis**
ellos	**mueren**	**ellos**	**mueran**

FUTURE		CONDITIONAL	
yo	moriré	**yo**	moriría
tú	morirás	**tú**	morirías
él	morirá	**él**	moriría
nosotros	moriremos	**nosotros**	moriríamos
vosotros	moriréis	**vosotros**	moriríais
ellos	morirán	**ellos**	morirían

IMPERFECT		PRETERITE	
yo	moría	**yo**	morí
tú	morías	**tú**	moriste
él	moría	**él**	**murió**
nosotros	moríamos	**nosotros**	morimos
vosotros	moríais	**vosotros**	moristeis
ellos	morían	**ellos**	**murieron**

mover *to move*

PAST PARTICIPLE	IMPERATIVE
mov**ido**	**mueve**
	mov**ed**
GERUND	
mov**iendo**	

PRESENT		PRESENT SUBJUNCTIVE	
yo	**muevo**	**yo**	**mueva**
tú	**mueves**	**tú**	**muevas**
él	**mueve**	**él**	**mueva**
nosotros	mov**emos**	**nosotros**	mov**amos**
vosotros	mov**éis**	**vosotros**	mov**áis**
ellos	**mueven**	**ellos**	**muevan**

FUTURE		CONDITIONAL	
yo	mover**é**	**yo**	mover**ía**
tú	mover**ás**	**tú**	mover**ías**
él	mover**á**	**él**	mover**ía**
nosotros	mover**emos**	**nosotros**	mover**íamos**
vosotros	mover**éis**	**vosotros**	mover**íais**
ellos	mover**án**	**ellos**	mover**ían**

IMPERFECT		PRETERITE	
yo	mov**ía**	**yo**	mov**í**
tú	mov**ías**	**tú**	mov**iste**
él	mov**ía**	**él**	mov**ió**
nosotros	mov**íamos**	**nosotros**	mov**imos**
vosotros	mov**íais**	**vosotros**	mov**isteis**
ellos	mov**ían**	**ellos**	mov**ieron**

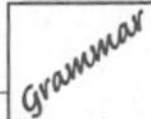

nacer *to be born*

PAST PARTICIPLE	IMPERATIVE
nacido	nace
	naced
GERUND	
naciendo	

PRESENT		PRESENT SUBJUNCTIVE	
yo	nazco	**yo**	nazca
tú	naces	**tú**	nazcas
él	nace	**él**	nazca
nosotros	nacemos	**nosotros**	nazcamos
vosotros	nacéis	**vosotros**	nazcáis
ellos	nacen	**ellos**	nazcan
FUTURE		**CONDITIONAL**	
yo	naceré	**yo**	nacería
tú	nacerás	**tú**	nacerías
él	nacerá	**él**	nacería
nosotros	naceremos	**nosotros**	naceríamos
vosotros	naceréis	**vosotros**	naceríais
ellos	nacerán	**ellos**	nacerían
IMPERFECT		**PRETERITE**	
yo	nacía	**yo**	nací
tú	nacías	**tú**	naciste
él	nacía	**él**	nació
nosotros	nacíamos	**nosotros**	nacimos
vosotros	nacíais	**vosotros**	nacisteis
ellos	nacían	**ellos**	nacieron

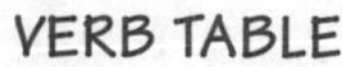

negar *to deny*

PAST PARTICIPLE	IMPERATIVE
neg**ado**	**niega**
	neg**ad**
GERUND	
neg**ando**	

PRESENT		PRESENT SUBJUNCTIVE	
yo	**niego**	**yo**	**niegue**
tú	**niegas**	**tú**	**niegues**
él	**niega**	**él**	**niegue**
nosotros	neg**amos**	**nosotros**	**neguemos**
vosotros	neg**áis**	**vosotros**	**neguéis**
ellos	**niegan**	**ellos**	**nieguen**

FUTURE		CONDITIONAL	
yo	negar**é**	**yo**	negar**ía**
tú	negar**ás**	**tú**	negar**ías**
él	negar**á**	**él**	negar**ía**
nosotros	negar**emos**	**nosotros**	negar**íamos**
vosotros	negar**éis**	**vosotros**	negar**íais**
ellos	negar**án**	**ellos**	negar**ían**

IMPERFECT		PRETERITE	
yo	neg**aba**	**yo**	**negué**
tú	neg**abas**	**tú**	neg**aste**
él	neg**aba**	**él**	neg**ó**
nosotros	neg**ábamos**	**nosotros**	neg**amos**
vosotros	neg**abais**	**vosotros**	neg**asteis**
ellos	neg**aban**	**ellos**	neg**aron**

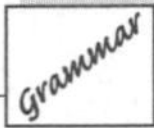

oír *to hear*

PAST PARTICIPLE	IMPERATIVE
oído	**oye**
	oíd
GERUND	
oyendo	

PRESENT		PRESENT SUBJUNCTIVE	
yo	oigo	**yo**	oiga
tú	oyes	**tú**	oigas
él	oye	**él**	oiga
nosotros	oímos	**nosotros**	oigamos
vosotros	oís	**vosotros**	oigáis
ellos	oyen	**ellos**	oigan

FUTURE		CONDITIONAL	
yo	oiré	**yo**	oiría
tú	oirás	**tú**	oirías
él	oirá	**él**	oiría
nosotros	oiremos	**nosotros**	oiríamos
vosotros	oiréis	**vosotros**	oiríais
ellos	oirán	**ellos**	oirían

IMPERFECT		PRETERITE	
yo	oía	**yo**	oí
tú	oías	**tú**	oíste
él	oía	**él**	oyó
nosotros	oíamos	**nosotros**	oímos
vosotros	oíais	**vosotros**	oísteis
ellos	oían	**ellos**	oyeron

oler *to smell*

PAST PARTICIPLE

ol**ido**

GERUND

ol**iendo**

IMPERATIVE

huele
ol**ed**

PRESENT		PRESENT SUBJUNCTIVE	
yo	**huelo**	**yo**	**huela**
tú	**hueles**	**tú**	**huelas**
él	**huele**	**él**	**huela**
nosotros	ol**emos**	**nosotros**	ol**amos**
vosotros	ol**éis**	**vosotros**	ol**áis**
ellos	**huelen**	**ellos**	**huelan**

FUTURE		CONDITIONAL	
yo	ol**eré**	**yo**	ol**ería**
tú	ol**erás**	**tú**	ol**erías**
él	ol**erá**	**él**	ol**ería**
nosotros	ol**eremos**	**nosotros**	ol**eríamos**
vosotros	ol**eréis**	**vosotros**	ol**eríais**
ellos	ol**erán**	**ellos**	ol**erían**

IMPERFECT		PRETERITE	
yo	ol**ía**	**yo**	ol**í**
tú	ol**ías**	**tú**	ol**iste**
él	ol**ía**	**él**	ol**ió**
nosotros	ol**íamos**	**nosotros**	ol**imos**
vosotros	ol**íais**	**vosotros**	ol**isteis**
ellos	ol**ían**	**ellos**	ol**ieron**

pagar *to pay*

PAST PARTICIPLE	IMPERATIVE
pagado	paga
	pagad
GERUND	
pagando	

PRESENT		PRESENT SUBJUNCTIVE	
yo	pago	**yo**	pague
tú	pagas	**tú**	pagues
él	paga	**él**	pague
nosotros	pagamos	**nosotros**	paguemos
vosotros	pagáis	**vosotros**	paguéis
ellos	pagan	**ellos**	paguen

FUTURE		CONDITIONAL	
yo	pagaré	**yo**	pagaría
tú	pagarás	**tú**	pagarías
él	pagará	**él**	pagaría
nosotros	pagaremos	**nosotros**	pagaríamos
vosotros	pagaréis	**vosotros**	pagaríais
ellos	pagarán	**ellos**	pagarían

IMPERFECT		PRETERITE	
yo	pagaba	**yo**	pagué
tú	pagabas	**tú**	pagaste
él	pagaba	**él**	pagó
nosotros	pagábamos	**nosotros**	pagamos
vosotros	pagabais	**vosotros**	pagasteis
ellos	pagaban	**ellos**	pagaron

pedir *to ask for*

PAST PARTICIPLE

ped**ido**

GERUND

pidiendo

IMPERATIVE

pide

pedid

PRESENT		PRESENT SUBJUNCTIVE	
yo	**pido**	**yo**	**pida**
tú	**pides**	**tú**	**pidas**
él	**pide**	**él**	**pida**
nosotros	ped**imos**	**nosotros**	**pidamos**
vosotros	ped**ís**	**vosotros**	**pidáis**
ellos	**piden**	**ellos**	**pidan**

FUTURE		CONDITIONAL	
yo	pedir**é**	**yo**	pedir**ía**
tú	pedir**ás**	**tú**	pedir**ías**
él	pedir**á**	**él**	pedir**ía**
nosotros	pedir**emos**	**nosotros**	pedir**íamos**
vosotros	pedir**éis**	**vosotros**	pedir**íais**
ellos	pedir**án**	**ellos**	pedir**ían**

IMPERFECT		PRETERITE	
yo	ped**ía**	**yo**	ped**í**
tú	ped**ías**	**tú**	ped**iste**
él	ped**ía**	**él**	**pidió**
nosotros	ped**íamos**	**nosotros**	ped**imos**
vosotros	ped**íais**	**vosotros**	ped**isteis**
ellos	ped**ían**	**ellos**	**pidieron**

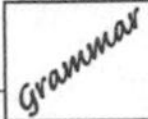

pensar *to think*

PAST PARTICIPLE

pens**ado**

GERUND

pens**ando**

IMPERATIVE

piensa
pensa**d**

PRESENT		PRESENT SUBJUNCTIVE	
yo	**pienso**	**yo**	**piense**
tú	**piensas**	**tú**	**pienses**
él	**piensa**	**él**	**piense**
nosotros	pens**amos**	**nosotros**	pens**emos**
vosotros	pens**áis**	**vosotros**	pens**éis**
ellos	**piensan**	**ellos**	**piensen**

FUTURE		CONDITIONAL	
yo	pensar**é**	**yo**	pensar**ía**
tú	pensar**ás**	**tú**	pensar**ías**
él	pensar**á**	**él**	pensar**ía**
nosotros	pensar**emos**	**nosotros**	pensar**íamos**
vosotros	pensar**éis**	**vosotros**	pensar**íais**
ellos	pensar**án**	**ellos**	pensar**ían**

IMPERFECT		PRETERITE	
yo	pens**aba**	**yo**	pens**é**
tú	pens**abas**	**tú**	pens**aste**
él	pens**aba**	**él**	pens**ó**
nosotros	pens**ábamos**	**nosotros**	pens**amos**
vosotros	pens**abais**	**vosotros**	pens**asteis**
ellos	pens**aban**	**ellos**	pens**aron**

poder *to be able*

PAST PARTICIPLE	IMPERATIVE
podido	**puede**
GERUND	poded
pudiendo	

PRESENT		PRESENT SUBJUNCTIVE	
yo	**puedo**	**yo**	**pueda**
tú	**puedes**	**tú**	**puedas**
él	**puede**	**él**	**pueda**
nosotros	podemos	**nosotros**	podamos
vosotros	podéis	**vosotros**	podáis
ellos	**pueden**	**ellos**	**puedan**
FUTURE		CONDITIONAL	
yo	**podré**	**yo**	**podría**
tú	**podrás**	**tú**	**podrías**
él	**podrá**	**él**	**podría**
nosotros	**podremos**	**nosotros**	**podríamos**
vosotros	**podréis**	**vosotros**	**podríais**
ellos	**podrán**	**ellos**	**podrían**
IMPERFECT		PRETERITE	
yo	podía	**yo**	**pude**
tú	podías	**tú**	**pudiste**
él	podía	**él**	**pudo**
nosotros	podíamos	**nosotros**	**pudimos**
vosotros	podíais	**vosotros**	**pudisteis**
ellos	podían	**ellos**	**pudieron**

poner *to put*

PAST PARTICIPLE

puesto

GERUND

pon**iendo**

IMPERATIVE

pon
poned

PRESENT		PRESENT SUBJUNCTIVE	
yo	pon**go**	**yo**	**ponga**
tú	pones	**tú**	**pongas**
él	pone	**él**	**ponga**
nosotros	ponemos	**nosotros**	**pongamos**
vosotros	ponéis	**vosotros**	**pongáis**
ellos	ponen	**ellos**	**pongan**

FUTURE		CONDITIONAL	
yo	**pondré**	**yo**	**pondría**
tú	**pondrás**	**tú**	**pondrías**
él	**pondrá**	**él**	**pondría**
nosotros	**pondremos**	**nosotros**	**pondríamos**
vosotros	**pondréis**	**vosotros**	**pondríais**
ellos	**pondrán**	**ellos**	**pondrían**

IMPERFECT		PRETERITE	
yo	ponía	**yo**	**puse**
tú	ponías	**tú**	**pusiste**
él	ponía	**él**	**puso**
nosotros	poníamos	**nosotros**	**pusimos**
vosotros	poníais	**vosotros**	**pusisteis**
ellos	ponían	**ellos**	**pusieron**

prohibir *to forbid*	
PAST PARTICIPLE	IMPERATIVE
prohib**ido**	**prohíbe**
	prohib**id**
GERUND	
prohib**iendo**	

PRESENT		PRESENT SUBJUNCTIVE	
yo	**prohíbo**	**yo**	**prohíba**
tú	**prohíbes**	**tú**	**prohíbas**
él	**prohíbe**	**él**	**prohíba**
nosotros	prohib**imos**	**nosotros**	prohib**amos**
vosotros	prohib**ís**	**vosotros**	prohib**áis**
ellos	**prohíben**	**ellos**	**prohíban**

FUTURE		CONDITIONAL	
yo	prohibir**é**	**yo**	prohibir**ía**
tú	prohibir**ás**	**tú**	prohibir**ías**
él	prohibir**á**	**él**	prohibir**ía**
nosotros	prohibir**emos**	**nosotros**	prohibir**íamos**
vosotros	prohibir**éis**	**vosotros**	prohibir**íais**
ellos	prohibir**án**	**ellos**	prohibir**ían**

IMPERFECT		PRETERITE	
yo	prohib**ía**	**yo**	prohib**í**
tú	prohib**ías**	**tú**	prohib**iste**
él	prohib**ía**	**él**	prohib**ió**
nosotros	prohib**íamos**	**nosotros**	prohib**imos**
vosotros	prohib**íais**	**vosotros**	prohib**isteis**
ellos	prohib**ían**	**ellos**	prohib**ieron**

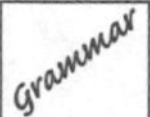

querer *to want*

PAST PARTICIPLE
quer**ido**

GERUND
quer**iendo**

IMPERATIVE
quiere
quered

PRESENT		PRESENT SUBJUNCTIVE	
yo	**quiero**	**yo**	**quiera**
tú	**quieres**	**tú**	**quieras**
él	**quiere**	**él**	**quiera**
nosotros	quer**emos**	**nosotros**	quer**amos**
vosotros	quer**éis**	**vosotros**	quer**áis**
ellos	**quieren**	**ellos**	**quieran**

FUTURE		CONDITIONAL	
yo	**querré**	**yo**	**querría**
tú	**querrás**	**tú**	**querrías**
él	**querrá**	**él**	**querría**
nosotros	**querremos**	**nosotros**	**querríamos**
vosotros	**querréis**	**vosotros**	**querríais**
ellos	**querrán**	**ellos**	**querrían**

IMPERFECT		PRETERITE	
yo	quer**ía**	**yo**	**quise**
tú	quer**ías**	**tú**	**quisiste**
él	quer**ía**	**él**	**quiso**
nosotros	quer**íamos**	**nosotros**	**quisimos**
vosotros	quer**íais**	**vosotros**	**quisisteis**
ellos	quer**ían**	**ellos**	**quisieron**

rehusar *to refuse*

PAST PARTICIPLE

rehus**ado**

GERUND

rehus**ando**

IMPERATIVE

rehúsa

rehusa**d**

PRESENT		PRESENT SUBJUNCTIVE	
yo	**rehúso**	**yo**	**rehúse**
tú	**rehúsas**	**tú**	**rehúses**
él	**rehúsa**	**él**	**rehúse**
nosotros	rehus**amos**	**nosotros**	rehus**emos**
vosotros	rehus**áis**	**vosotros**	rehus**éis**
ellos	**rehúsan**	**ellos**	**rehúsen**

FUTURE		CONDITIONAL	
yo	rehusar**é**	**yo**	rehusar**ía**
tú	rehusar**ás**	**tú**	rehusar**ías**
él	rehusar**á**	**él**	rehusar**ía**
nosotros	rehusar**emos**	**nosotros**	rehusar**íamos**
vosotros	rehusar**éis**	**vosotros**	rehusar**íais**
ellos	rehusar**án**	**ellos**	rehusar**ían**

IMPERFECT		PRETERITE	
yo	rehus**aba**	**yo**	rehus**é**
tú	rehus**abas**	**tú**	rehus**aste**
él	rehus**aba**	**él**	rehus**ó**
nosotros	rehus**ábamos**	**nosotros**	rehus**amos**
vosotros	rehus**abais**	**vosotros**	rehus**asteis**
ellos	rehus**aban**	**ellos**	rehus**aron**

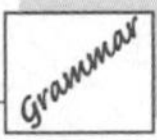

reír *to laugh*

PAST PARTICIPLE	IMPERATIVE
reído	**rie**
	reíd

GERUND

riendo

PRESENT		PRESENT SUBJUNCTIVE	
yo	**río**	**yo**	**ría**
tú	**ríes**	**tú**	**rías**
él	**ríe**	**él**	**ría**
nosotros	**reímos**	**nosotros**	**riamos**
vosotros	**reís**	**vosotros**	**riáis**
ellos	**ríen**	**ellos**	**rían**

FUTURE		CONDITIONAL	
yo	**reiré**	**yo**	**reiría**
tú	**reirás**	**tú**	**reirías**
él	**reirá**	**él**	**reiría**
nosotros	**reiremos**	**nosotros**	**reiríamos**
vosotros	**reiréis**	**vosotros**	**reiríais**
ellos	**reirán**	**ellos**	**reirían**

IMPERFECT		PRETERITE	
yo	**reía**	**yo**	**reí**
tú	**reías**	**tú**	**reíste**
él	**reía**	**él**	**rio**
nosotros	**reíamos**	**nosotros**	**reímos**
vosotros	**reíais**	**vosotros**	**reísteis**
ellos	**reían**	**ellos**	**rieron**

reñir *to scold*

PAST PARTICIPLE	IMPERATIVE
reñido	riñe
	reñid
GERUND	
riñendo	

PRESENT		PRESENT SUBJUNCTIVE	
yo	riño	**yo**	riña
tú	riñes	**tú**	riñas
él	riñe	**él**	riña
nosotros	reñimos	**nosotros**	riñamos
vosotros	reñís	**vosotros**	riñáis
ellos	riñen	**ellos**	riñan

FUTURE		CONDITIONAL	
yo	reñiré	**yo**	reñiría
tú	reñirás	**tú**	reñirías
él	reñirá	**él**	reñiría
nosotros	reñiremos	**nosotros**	reñiríamos
vosotros	reñiréis	**vosotros**	reñiríais
ellos	reñirán	**ellos**	reñirían

IMPERFECT		PRETERITE	
yo	reñía	**yo**	reñí
tú	reñías	**tú**	reñiste
él	reñía	**él**	riñó
nosotros	reñíamos	**nosotros**	reñimos
vosotros	reñíais	**vosotros**	reñisteis
ellos	reñían	**ellos**	riñeron

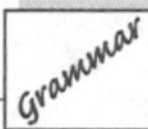

resolver *to solve*

PAST PARTICIPLE	IMPERATIVE
resuelto	resuelve
	resolved
GERUND	
resolviendo	

PRESENT		PRESENT SUBJUNCTIVE	
yo	resuelvo	yo	resuelva
tú	resuelves	tú	resuelvas
él	resuelve	él	resuelva
nosotros	resolvemos	nosotros	resolvamos
vosotros	resolvéis	vosotros	resolváis
ellos	resuelven	ellos	resuelvan

FUTURE		CONDITIONAL	
yo	resolveré	yo	resolvería
tú	resolverás	tú	resolverías
él	resolverá	él	resolvería
nosotros	resolveremos	nosotros	resolveríamos
vosotros	resolveréis	vosotros	resolveríais
ellos	resolverán	ellos	resolverían

IMPERFECT		PRETERITE	
yo	resolvía	yo	resolví
tú	resolvías	tú	resolviste
él	resolvía	él	resolvió
nosotros	resolvíamos	nosotros	resolvimos
vosotros	resolvíais	vosotros	resolvisteis
ellos	resolvían	ellos	resolvieron

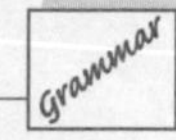

reunir *to put together, to gather*

PAST PARTICIPLE	IMPERATIVE
reun**ido**	**reúne**
	reun**id**
GERUND	
reun**iendo**	

PRESENT		PRESENT SUBJUNCTIVE	
yo	**reúno**	**yo**	**reúna**
tú	**reúnes**	**tú**	**reúnas**
él	**reúne**	**él**	**reúna**
nosotros	reun**imos**	**nosotros**	reun**amos**
vosotros	reun**ís**	**vosotros**	reun**áis**
ellos	**reúnen**	**ellos**	**reúnan**

FUTURE		CONDITIONAL	
yo	reunir**é**	**yo**	reunir**ía**
tú	reunir**ás**	**tú**	reunir**ías**
él	reunir**á**	**él**	reunir**ía**
nosotros	reunir**emos**	**nosotros**	reunir**íamos**
vosotros	reunir**éis**	**vosotros**	reunir**íais**
ellos	reunir**án**	**ellos**	reunir**ían**

IMPERFECT		PRETERITE	
yo	reun**ía**	**yo**	reun**í**
tú	reun**ías**	**tú**	reun**iste**
él	reun**ía**	**él**	reun**ió**
nosotros	reun**íamos**	**nosotros**	reun**imos**
vosotros	reun**íais**	**vosotros**	reun**isteis**
ellos	reun**ían**	**ellos**	reun**ieron**

rogar *to beg*

PAST PARTICIPLE	IMPERATIVE
rogado	ruega
	rogad
GERUND	
rogando	

PRESENT		PRESENT SUBJUNCTIVE	
yo	ruego	**yo**	ruegue
tú	ruegas	**tú**	ruegues
él	ruega	**él**	ruegue
nosotros	rogamos	**nosotros**	roguemos
vosotros	rogáis	**vosotros**	roguéis
ellos	ruegan	**ellos**	rueguen

FUTURE		CONDITIONAL	
yo	rogaré	**yo**	rogaría
tú	rogarás	**tú**	rogarías
él	rogará	**él**	rogaría
nosotros	rogaremos	**nosotros**	rogaríamos
vosotros	rogaréis	**vosotros**	rogaríais
ellos	rogarán	**ellos**	rogarían

IMPERFECT		PRETERITE	
yo	rogaba	**yo**	rogué
tú	rogabas	**tú**	rogaste
él	rogaba	**él**	rogó
nosotros	rogábamos	**nosotros**	rogamos
vosotros	rogabais	**vosotros**	rogasteis
ellos	rogaban	**ellos**	rogaron

romper *to break*

PAST PARTICIPLE	IMPERATIVE
roto	rompe
GERUND	romped
rompiendo	

PRESENT		PRESENT SUBJUNCTIVE	
yo	rompo	**yo**	rompa
tú	rompes	**tú**	rompas
él	rompe	**él**	rompa
nosotros	rompemos	**nosotros**	rompamos
vosotros	rompéis	**vosotros**	rompáis
ellos	rompen	**ellos**	rompan
FUTURE		**CONDITIONAL**	
yo	romperé	**yo**	rompería
tú	romperás	**tú**	romperías
él	romperá	**él**	rompería
nosotros	romperemos	**nosotros**	romperíamos
vosotros	romperéis	**vosotros**	romperíais
ellos	romperán	**ellos**	romperían
IMPERFECT		**PRETERITE**	
yo	rompía	**yo**	rompí
tú	rompías	**tú**	rompiste
él	rompía	**él**	rompió
nosotros	rompíamos	**nosotros**	rompimos
vosotros	rompíais	**vosotros**	rompisteis
ellos	rompían	**ellos**	rompieron

saber *to know*

PAST PARTICIPLE	IMPERATIVE
sab**ido**	sab**e**
	sab**ed**
GERUND	
sab**iendo**	

PRESENT		PRESENT SUBJUNCTIVE	
yo	sé	**yo**	**sepa**
tú	sab**es**	**tú**	**sepas**
él	sab**e**	**él**	**sepa**
nosotros	sab**emos**	**nosotros**	**sepamos**
vosotros	sab**éis**	**vosotros**	**sepáis**
ellos	sab**en**	**ellos**	**sepan**

FUTURE		CONDITIONAL	
yo	**sabré**	**yo**	**sabría**
tú	**sabrás**	**tú**	**sabrías**
él	**sabrá**	**él**	**sabría**
nosotros	**sabremos**	**nosotros**	**sabríamos**
vosotros	**sabréis**	**vosotros**	**sabríais**
ellos	**sabrán**	**ellos**	**sabrían**

IMPERFECT		PRETERITE	
yo	sab**ía**	**yo**	**supe**
tú	sab**ías**	**tú**	**supiste**
él	sab**ía**	**él**	**supo**
nosotros	sab**íamos**	**nosotros**	**supimos**
vosotros	sab**íais**	**vosotros**	**supisteis**
ellos	sab**ían**	**ellos**	**supieron**

sacar *to take out*

PAST PARTICIPLE	IMPERATIVE
sacado	saca
	sacad
GERUND	
sacando	

PRESENT		PRESENT SUBJUNCTIVE	
yo	saco	**yo**	saque
tú	sacas	**tú**	saques
él	saca	**él**	saque
nosotros	sacamos	**nosotros**	saquemos
vosotros	sacáis	**vosotros**	saqueís
ellos	sacan	**ellos**	saquen

FUTURE		CONDITIONAL	
yo	sacaré	**yo**	sacaría
tú	sacarás	**tú**	sacarías
él	sacará	**él**	sacaría
nosotros	sacaremos	**nosotros**	sacaríamos
vosotros	sacaréis	**vosotros**	sacaríais
ellos	sacarán	**ellos**	sacarían

IMPERFECT		PRETERITE	
yo	sacaba	**yo**	saqué
tú	sacabas	**tú**	sacaste
él	sacaba	**él**	sacó
nosotros	sacábamos	**nosotros**	sacamos
vosotros	sacabais	**vosotros**	sacasteis
ellos	sacaban	**ellos**	sacaron

salir *to go out*

PAST PARTICIPLE	IMPERATIVE
salido	**sal**
	salid
GERUND	
saliendo	

PRESENT		PRESENT SUBJUNCTIVE	
yo	salgo	**yo**	salga
tú	sales	**tú**	salgas
él	sale	**él**	salga
nosotros	salimos	**nosotros**	salgamos
vosotros	salís	**vosotros**	salgáis
ellos	salen	**ellos**	salgan

FUTURE		CONDITIONAL	
yo	saldré	**yo**	saldría
tú	saldrás	**tú**	saldrías
él	saldrá	**él**	saldría
nosotros	saldremos	**nosotros**	saldríamos
vosotros	saldréis	**vosotros**	saldríais
ellos	saldrán	**ellos**	saldrían

IMPERFECT		PRETERITE	
yo	salía	**yo**	salí
tú	salías	**tú**	saliste
él	salía	**él**	salió
nosotros	salíamos	**nosotros**	salimos
vosotros	salíais	**vosotros**	salisteis
ellos	salían	**ellos**	salieron

satisfacer *to satisfy*

PAST PARTICIPLE

satisfecho

GERUND

satisfac**iendo**

IMPERATIVE

satisfaz/satisface
satisfaced

PRESENT		PRESENT SUBJUNCTIVE	
yo	**satisfago**	**yo**	**satisfaga**
tú	satisfaces	**tú**	**satisfagas**
él	satisface	**él**	**satisfaga**
nosotros	satisfac**emos**	**nosotros**	**satisfagamos**
vosotros	satisfac**éis**	**vosotros**	**satisfagáis**
ellos	satisfac**en**	**ellos**	**satisfagan**

FUTURE		CONDITIONAL	
yo	**satisfaré**	**yo**	**satisfaría**
tú	**satisfarás**	**tú**	**satisfarías**
él	**satisfará**	**él**	**satisfaría**
nosotros	**satisfaremos**	**nosotros**	**satisfaríamos**
vosotros	**satisfaréis**	**vosotros**	**satisfaríais**
ellos	**satisfarán**	**ellos**	**satisfarían**

IMPERFECT		PRETERITE	
yo	satisfacía	**yo**	**satisfice**
tú	satisfacías	**tú**	**satisficiste**
él	satisfacía	**él**	**satisfizo**
nosotros	satisfacíamos	**nosotros**	**satisficimos**
vosotros	satisfacíais	**vosotros**	**satisficisteis**
ellos	satisfacían	**ellos**	**satisficieron**

seguir *to follow*

PAST PARTICIPLE	IMPERATIVE
seguido	**sigue**
GERUND	seguid
siguiendo	

PRESENT		PRESENT SUBJUNCTIVE	
yo	**sigo**	**yo**	**siga**
tú	**sigues**	**tú**	**sigas**
él	**sigue**	**él**	**siga**
nosotros	seguimos	**nosotros**	**sigamos**
vosotros	seguís	**vosotros**	**sigáis**
ellos	**siguen**	**ellos**	**sigan**

FUTURE		CONDITIONAL	
yo	seguiré	**yo**	seguiría
tú	seguirás	**tú**	seguirías
él	seguirá	**él**	seguiría
nosotros	seguiremos	**nosotros**	seguiríamos
vosotros	seguiréis	**vosotros**	seguiríais
ellos	seguirán	**ellos**	seguirían

IMPERFECT		PRETERITE	
yo	seguía	**yo**	seguí
tú	seguías	**tú**	seguiste
él	seguía	**él**	**siguió**
nosotros	seguíamos	**nosotros**	seguimos
vosotros	seguíais	**vosotros**	seguisteis
ellos	seguían	**ellos**	**siguieron**

sentir *to feel*

PAST PARTICIPLE	IMPERATIVE
sentido	**siente**
GERUND	sentid
sintiendo	

PRESENT		PRESENT SUBJUNCTIVE	
yo	**siento**	**yo**	**sienta**
tú	**sientes**	**tú**	**sientas**
él	**siente**	**él**	**sienta**
nosotros	sentimos	**nosotros**	**sintamos**
vosotros	sentís	**vosotros**	**sintáis**
ellos	**sienten**	**ellos**	**sientan**
FUTURE		**CONDITIONAL**	
yo	sentiré	**yo**	sentiría
tú	sentirás	**tú**	sentirías
él	sentirá	**él**	sentiría
nosotros	sentiremos	**nosotros**	sentiríamos
vosotros	sentiréis	**vosotros**	sentiríais
ellos	sentirán	**ellos**	sentirían
IMPERFECT		**PRETERITE**	
yo	sentía	**yo**	sentí
tú	sentías	**tú**	sentiste
él	sentía	**él**	**sintió**
nosotros	sentíamos	**nosotros**	sentimos
vosotros	sentíais	**vosotros**	sentisteis
ellos	sentían	**ellos**	**sintieron**

ser *to be*

PAST PARTICIPLE

sido

GERUND

siendo

IMPERATIVE

sé
sed

PRESENT		PRESENT SUBJUNCTIVE	
yo	**soy**	**yo**	**sea**
tú	**eres**	**tú**	**seas**
él	**es**	**él**	**sea**
nosotros	**somos**	**nosotros**	**seamos**
vosotros	**sois**	**vosotros**	**seáis**
ellos	**son**	**ellos**	**sean**

FUTURE		CONDITIONAL	
yo	seré	**yo**	sería
tú	serás	**tú**	serías
él	será	**él**	sería
nosotros	seremos	**nosotros**	seríamos
vosotros	seréis	**vosotros**	seríais
ellos	serán	**ellos**	serían

IMPERFECT		PRETERITE	
yo	**era**	**yo**	**fui**
tú	**eras**	**tú**	**fuiste**
él	**era**	**él**	**fue**
nosotros	**éramos**	**nosotros**	**fuimos**
vosotros	**erais**	**vosotros**	**fuisteis**
ellos	**eran**	**ellos**	**fueron**

tener *to have*

PAST PARTICIPLE

ten**ido**

GERUND

ten**iendo**

IMPERATIVE

ten

tene**d**

PRESENT		PRESENT SUBJUNCTIVE	
yo	**tengo**	**yo**	**tenga**
tú	**tienes**	**tú**	**tengas**
él	**tiene**	**él**	**tenga**
nosotros	ten**emos**	**nosotros**	**tengamos**
vosotros	ten**éis**	**vosotros**	**tengáis**
ellos	**tienen**	**ellos**	**tengan**
FUTURE		CONDITIONAL	
yo	**tendré**	**yo**	**tendría**
tú	**tendrás**	**tú**	**tendrías**
él	**tendrá**	**él**	**tendría**
nosotros	**tendremos**	**nosotros**	**tendríamos**
vosotros	**tendréis**	**vosotros**	**tendríais**
ellos	**tendrán**	**ellos**	**tendrían**
IMPERFECT		PRETERITE	
yo	tenía	**yo**	**tuve**
tú	tenías	**tú**	**tuviste**
él	tenía	**él**	**tuvo**
nosotros	teníamos	**nosotros**	**tuvimos**
vosotros	teníais	**vosotros**	**tuvisteis**
ellos	tenían	**ellos**	**tuvieron**

torcer *to twist*

PAST PARTICIPLE	IMPERATIVE
torc**ido**	**tuerce**
GERUND	torce**d**
torc**iendo**	

PRESENT		PRESENT SUBJUNCTIVE	
yo	**tuerzo**	**yo**	**tuerza**
tú	**tuerces**	**tú**	**tuerzas**
él	**tuerce**	**él**	**tuerza**
nosotros	torc**emos**	**nosotros**	**torzamos**
vosotros	torc**éis**	**vosotros**	**torzáis**
ellos	**tuercen**	**ellos**	**tuerzan**

FUTURE		CONDITIONAL	
yo	torcer**é**	**yo**	torcer**ía**
tú	torcer**ás**	**tú**	torcer**ías**
él	torcer**á**	**él**	torcer**ía**
nosotros	torcer**emos**	**nosotros**	torcer**íamos**
vosotros	torcer**éis**	**vosotros**	torcer**íais**
ellos	torcer**án**	**ellos**	torcer**ían**

IMPERFECT		PRETERITE	
yo	torc**ía**	**yo**	torc**í**
tú	torc**ías**	**tú**	torc**iste**
él	torc**ía**	**él**	torc**ió**
nosotros	torc**íamos**	**nosotros**	torc**imos**
vosotros	torc**íais**	**vosotros**	torc**isteis**
ellos	torc**ían**	**ellos**	torc**ieron**

traer *to bring*

PAST PARTICIPLE	IMPERATIVE
traído	trae
	traed
GERUND	
trayendo	

PRESENT		PRESENT SUBJUNCTIVE	
yo	**traigo**	**yo**	**traiga**
tú	**traes**	**tú**	**traigas**
él	**trae**	**él**	**traiga**
nosotros	**traemos**	**nosotros**	**traigamos**
vosotros	**traéis**	**vosotros**	**traigáis**
ellos	**traen**	**ellos**	**traigan**

FUTURE		CONDITIONAL	
yo	traeré	**yo**	traería
tú	traerás	**tú**	traerías
él	traerá	**él**	traería
nosotros	traeremos	**nosotros**	traeríamos
vosotros	traeréis	**vosotros**	traeríais
ellos	traerán	**ellos**	traerían

IMPERFECT		PRETERITE	
yo	traía	**yo**	**traje**
tú	traías	**tú**	**trajiste**
él	traía	**él**	**trajo**
nosotros	traíamos	**nosotros**	**trajimos**
vosotros	traíais	**vosotros**	**trajisteis**
ellos	traían	**ellos**	**trajeron**

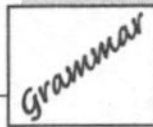

valer *to be worth*

PAST PARTICIPLE	IMPERATIVE
valido	vale
	valed
GERUND	
valiendo	

PRESENT		PRESENT SUBJUNCTIVE	
yo	valgo	**yo**	valga
tú	vales	**tú**	valgas
él	vale	**él**	valga
nosotros	valemos	**nosotros**	valgamos
vosotros	valéis	**vosotros**	valgáis
ellos	valen	**ellos**	valgan

FUTURE		CONDITIONAL	
yo	valdré	**yo**	valdría
tú	valdrás	**tú**	valdrías
él	valdrá	**él**	valdría
nosotros	valdremos	**nosotros**	valdríamos
vosotros	valdréis	**vosotros**	valdríais
ellos	valdrán	**ellos**	valdrían

IMPERFECT		PRETERITE	
yo	valía	**yo**	valí
tú	valías	**tú**	valiste
él	valía	**él**	valió
nosotros	valíamos	**nosotros**	valimos
vosotros	valíais	**vosotros**	valisteis
ellos	valían	**ellos**	valieron

vencer *to win*

PAST PARTICIPLE	IMPERATIVE
venc**ido**	vence
GERUND	venced
venc**iendo**	

PRESENT		PRESENT SUBJUNCTIVE	
yo	venzo	**yo**	venza
tú	vences	**tú**	venzas
él	vence	**él**	venza
nosotros	vencemos	**nosotros**	venzamos
vosotros	vencéis	**vosotros**	venzáis
ellos	vencen	**ellos**	venzan
FUTURE		CONDITIONAL	
yo	venceré	**yo**	vencería
tú	vencerás	**tú**	vencerías
él	vencerá	**él**	vencería
nosotros	venceremos	**nosotros**	venceríamos
vosotros	venceréis	**vosotros**	venceríais
ellos	vencerán	**ellos**	vencerían
IMPERFECT		PRETERITE	
yo	vencía	**yo**	vencí
tú	vencías	**tú**	venciste
él	vencía	**él**	venció
nosotros	vencíamos	**nosotros**	vencimos
vosotros	vencíais	**vosotros**	vencisteis
ellos	vencían	**ellos**	vencieron

venir *to come*

PAST PARTICIPLE

venido

GERUND

viniendo

IMPERATIVE

ven
venid

PRESENT		PRESENT SUBJUNCTIVE	
yo	vengo	yo	venga
tú	vienes	tú	vengas
él	viene	él	venga
nosotros	venimos	nosotros	vengamos
vosotros	venís	vosotros	vengáis
ellos	vienen	ellos	vengan

FUTURE		CONDITIONAL	
yo	vendré	yo	vendría
tú	vendrás	tú	vendrías
él	vendrá	él	vendría
nosotros	vendremos	nosotros	vendríamos
vosotros	vendréis	vosotros	vendríais
ellos	vendrán	ellos	vendrían

IMPERFECT		PRETERITE	
yo	venía	yo	vine
tú	venías	tú	viniste
él	venía	él	vino
nosotros	veníamos	nosotros	vinimos
vosotros	veníais	vosotros	vinisteis
ellos	venían	ellos	vinieron

ver *to see*

PAST PARTICIPLE	IMPERATIVE
visto	**ve**
	ved
GERUND	
viendo	

PRESENT		PRESENT SUBJUNCTIVE	
yo	**veo**	**yo**	**vea**
tú	**ves**	**tú**	**veas**
él	**ve**	**él**	**vea**
nosotros	**vemos**	**nosotros**	**veamos**
vosotros	**veis**	**vosotros**	**veáis**
ellos	**ven**	**ellos**	**vean**

FUTURE		CONDITIONAL	
yo	**veré**	**yo**	**vería**
tú	**verás**	**tú**	**verías**
él	**verá**	**él**	**vería**
nosotros	**veremos**	**nosotros**	**veríamos**
vosotros	**veréis**	**vosotros**	**veríais**
ellos	**verán**	**ellos**	**verían**

IMPERFECT		PRETERITE	
yo	**veía**	**yo**	**vi**
tú	**veías**	**tú**	**viste**
él	**veía**	**él**	**vio**
nosotros	**veíamos**	**nosotros**	**vimos**
vosotros	**veíais**	**vosotros**	**visteis**
ellos	**veían**	**ellos**	**vieron**

volcar *to overturn*

PAST PARTICIPLE	IMPERATIVE
volc**ado**	**vuelca**
GERUND	volc**ad**
volc**ando**	

PRESENT		PRESENT SUBJUNCTIVE	
yo	**vuelco**	**yo**	**vuelque**
tú	**vuelcas**	**tú**	**vuelques**
él	**vuelca**	**él**	**vuelque**
nosotros	volc**amos**	**nosotros**	**volquemos**
vosotros	volc**áis**	**vosotros**	**volquéis**
ellos	**vuelcan**	**ellos**	**vuelquen**

FUTURE		CONDITIONAL	
yo	volcar**é**	**yo**	volcar**ía**
tú	volcar**ás**	**tú**	volcar**ías**
él	volcar**á**	**él**	volcar**ía**
nosotros	volcar**emos**	**nosotros**	volcar**íamos**
vosotros	volcar**éis**	**vosotros**	volcar**íais**
ellos	volcar**án**	**ellos**	volcar**ían**

IMPERFECT		PRETERITE	
yo	volc**aba**	**yo**	**volqué**
tú	volc**abas**	**tú**	volc**aste**
él	volc**aba**	**él**	volc**ó**
nosotros	volc**ábamos**	**nosotros**	volc**amos**
vosotros	volc**abais**	**vosotros**	volc**asteis**
ellos	volc**aban**	**ellos**	volc**aron**

volver *to return*

PAST PARTICIPLE

vuelto

GERUND

volv**iendo**

IMPERATIVE

vuelve
volve**d**

PRESENT		PRESENT SUBJUNCTIVE	
yo	**vuelvo**	**yo**	**vuelva**
tú	**vuelves**	**tú**	**vuelvas**
él	**vuelve**	**él**	**vuelva**
nosotros	volv**emos**	**nosotros**	volv**amos**
vosotros	volv**éis**	**vosotros**	volv**áis**
ellos	**vuelven**	**ellos**	**vuelvan**

FUTURE		CONDITIONAL	
yo	volver**é**	**yo**	volver**ía**
tú	volver**ás**	**tú**	volver**ías**
él	volver**á**	**él**	volver**ía**
nosotros	volver**emos**	**nosotros**	volver**íamos**
vosotros	volver**éis**	**vosotros**	volver**íais**
ellos	volver**án**	**ellos**	volver**ían**

IMPERFECT		PRETERITE	
yo	volv**ía**	**yo**	volv**í**
tú	volv**ías**	**tú**	volv**iste**
él	volv**ía**	**él**	volv**ió**
nosotros	volv**íamos**	**nosotros**	volv**imos**
vosotros	volv**íais**	**vosotros**	volv**isteis**
ellos	volv**ían**	**ellos**	volv**ieron**

zurcir *to darn*

PAST PARTICIPLE	IMPERATIVE
zurcido	zurce
	zurcid
GERUND	
zurciendo	

PRESENT		PRESENT SUBJUNCTIVE	
yo	zurzo	**yo**	zurza
tú	zurces	**tú**	zurzas
él	zurce	**él**	zurza
nosotros	zurcimos	**nosotros**	zurzamos
vosotros	zurcís	**vosotros**	zurzáis
ellos	zurcen	**ellos**	zurzan
FUTURE		**CONDITIONAL**	
yo	zurciré	**yo**	zurciría
tú	zurcirás	**tú**	zurcirías
él	zurcirá	**él**	zurciría
nosotros	zurciremos	**nosotros**	zurciríamos
vosotros	zurciréis	**vosotros**	zurciríais
ellos	zurcirán	**ellos**	zurcirían
IMPERFECT		**PRETERITE**	
yo	zurcía	**yo**	zurcí
tú	zurcías	**tú**	zurciste
él	zurcía	**él**	zurció
nosotros	zurcíamos	**nosotros**	zurcimos
vosotros	zurcíais	**vosotros**	zurcisteis
ellos	zurcían	**ellos**	zurcieron

VERBS INDEX

The following pages, 163 to 186, contain an index of over 2,800 commonly used verbs cross-referred to the appropriate conjugation model.

- Regular verbs belonging to the first, second and third conjugation are numbered 1, 2 and 3 respectively. For the regular conjugations see pp 6 to 13.

- Irregular verbs are numerically cross-referred to the appropriate model as conjugated on pp 82 to 161. Thus, **alzar** is cross-referred to p 100 where **cruzar**, the model for this verb group, is conjugated.

- Verbs which are most commonly used in the reflexive form – e.g. **amodorrarse** – have been cross-referred to the appropriate non-reflexive model. For the full conjugation of a reflexive verb, see pp 28 to 31.

- Verbs printed in **bold** – e.g. **abrir** – are themselves models.

- Superior numbers refer you to notes on p 187 which indicate how the verb differs from its model.

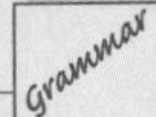
Grammar

Verb	No.
adscribir	113
aducir	96
adueñarse	1
adular	1
adulterar	1
advertir	150
afanarse	1
afear	1
afectar	1
afeitar	1
aferrar	1
afianzar	100
aficionar	1
afilar	1
afiliarse	1
afinar	1
afirmar	1
afligir	104
aflojar	1
afluir	97
afrentar	1
afrontar	1
agachar	1
agarrar	1
agarrotar	1
agasajar	1
agitar	1
aglomerarse	1
agobiar	1
agolparse	1
agonizar	100
agotar	1
agraciar	1
agradar	1
agradecer	99
agrandar	1
agravar	1
agraviar	1
agregar	131
agriar	110
agrietarse	1
agrupar	1
aguantar	1
aguar	90
aguardar	1
aguijonear	1
agujerear	1
aguzar	100
ahogar	131
ahondar	1
ahorcar	146
ahorrar	1
ahuecar	146
ahumar	1
ahuyentar	1
airarse	1
airear	1
aislar	88
ajar	1
ajustar	1
ajusticiar	1
alabar	1
alabear	1
alambicar	144
alardear	1
alargar	131
albergar	131
alborotar	1
alborozar	100
alcanzar	100
aleccionar	1
alegar	131
alegrar	1
alejar	1
alentar	133
aletargar	131
aletear	1
alfombrar	1
aliarse	110
aligerar	1
alimentar	1
alinear	1
aliñar	1
alisar	1
alistar	1
aliviar	1
almacenar	1
almidonar	1
almorzar	86
alojar	1
alquilar	1
alterar	1
alternar	1
alucinar	1
aludir	3
alumbrar	1
alunizar	100
alzar	100
allanar	1
amaestrar	1
amagar	131
amainar	1
amalgamar	1
amamantar	1
amanecer[1]	99
amanerarse	1
amansar	1
amar	1
amargar	131
amarrar	1
amartillar	1
ambicionar	1
amedrentar	1
amenazar	100
amenguar	90
amerizar	100
amilanar	1
aminorar	1
amnistiar	110
amodorrarse	1

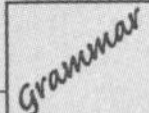

Verb	Model
amoldar	1
amonestar	1
amontonar	1
amordazar	100
amortajar	1
amortiguar	90
amortizar	100
amotinar	1
amparar	1
ampliar	110
amplificar	146
amputar	1
amueblar	1
amurallar	1
analizar	100
anclar	1
andar	87
anegar	131
anexionar	1
angustiar	1
anhelar	1
anidar	1
animar	1
aniquilar	1
anochecer[1]	199
anonadar	1
anotar	1
anquilosarse	1
ansiar	110
anteceder	2
anteponer	135
anticipar	1
antojarse	1
anudar	1
anular	1
anunciar	1
añadir	3
apabullar	1
apacentar	133
apaciguar	90
apadrinar	1
apagar	131
apalabrar	1
apalear	1
apañar	1
aparcar	146
aparecer	99
aparejar	1
aparentar	1
apartar	1
apasionarse	1
apearse	1
apedrear	1
apegarse	1
apelar	1
apellidar	1
apelotonarse	1
apenar	1
apercibir	3
apesadumbrar	1
apestar	1
apetecer	99
apiadarse	1
apiñarse	1
aplacar	146
aplanar	1
aplastar	1
aplaudir	3
aplazar	100
aplicar	146
apocar	146
apodar	1
apoderarse	1
aporrear	1
aportar	1
aposentarse	1
apostar	98
apoyar	1
apreciar	1
aprehender	2
apremiar	1
aprender	2
apresar	1
aprestarse	1
apresurarse	1
apretar	133
aprisionar	1
aprobar	98
apropiar	1
aprovechar	1
aproximar	1
apuntalar	1
apuntar	1
apuñalar	1
apurar	1
aquejar	1
aquietar	1
arañar	1
arar	1
arbitrar	1
arbolar	1
archivar	1
arder	2
arengar	1
argamasar	1
argüir	97
argumentar	1
armar	1
armonizar	100
arquear	1
arraigar	131
arrancar	146
arrasar	1
arrastrar	1
arrear	1
arrebatar	1
arreglar	1
arremangar	131
arremeter	2
arrendar	133

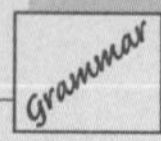
Grammar

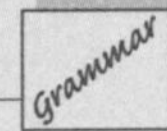
Grammar

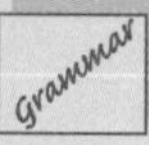

celar	1	cinchar	1	colorear	1
celebrar	1	circular	1	columbrar	1
cementar	1	circuncidar	1	columpiar	1
cenar	1	circundar	1	comadrear	1
censar	1	circunscribir	113	comandar	1
censurar	1	circunvalar	1	comarcar	146
centellear	1	citar	1	combar	1
centralizar	100	civilizar	100	combatir	3
centrar	1	clamar	1	combinar	1
centrifugar	131	clamorear	1	comedirse	132
ceñir	140	clarear	1	comentar	1
cepillar	1	clarificar	146	comenzar	108
cercar	146	clasificar	146	comer	2
cerciorarse	1	claudicar	146	comercializar	100
cerner	109	clavar	1	comerciar	1
cerrar	133	coartar	1	cometer	2
certificar	146	cobijar	1	comisionar	1
cesar	1	cobrar	1	compadecer	99
chamuscar	146	cocear	1	comparar	1
chantajear	1	**cocer**	94	comparecer	99
chapotear	1	cocinar	1	compartir	3
chapurrear	1	codear	1	compeler	2
chapuzarse	100	codiciar	1	compendiar	1
charlar	1	codificar	146	compensar	1
chasquear	1	coexistir	3	competer[1]	2
chequear	1	**coger**	95	competir	132
chiflar	1	cohabitar	1	compilar	1
chillar	1	cohibir	136	complacer	127
chirriar	110	coincidir	3	completar	1
chisporrotear	1	cojear	1	complicar	146
chispear	1	colaborar	1	componer	135
chocar	146	colar	98	comportarse	1
chochear	1	colear	1	comprar	1
chorrear	1	coleccionar	1	comprender	2
chupar	1	colegir	107	comprimir	3
cicatrizar	100	colgar	143	comprobar	98
cifrar	1	colindar	1	comprometer	2
cimbrear	1	colmar	1	computar	1
cimentar	133	colocar	146	comulgar	131
cincelar	1	colonizar	100	comunicar	146

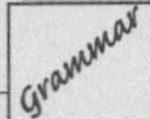
Grammar

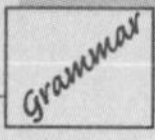
Grammar

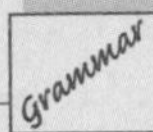
Grammar

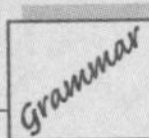
Grammar

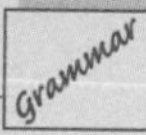

Grammar

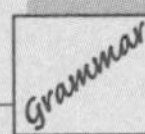
Grammar

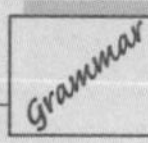
Grammar

Grammar

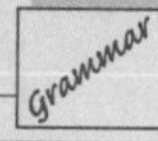

VERBS INDEX

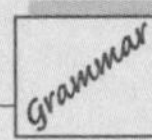
Grammar

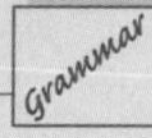
Grammar

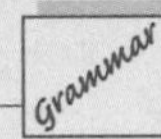
Grammar

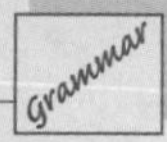
Grammar

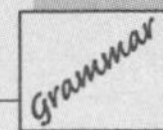
Grammar

Verb	Model
trincar	146
trinchar	1
tripular	1
triturar	1
triunfar	1
trivializar	100
trocar	159
tronar[1]	98
tronchar	1
tropezar	108
trotar	1
truncar	146
tullir	116
tumbar	1
turbar	1
turnarse	1
tutear	1
ubicar	146
ufanarse	1
ulcerar	1
ultimar	1
ultrajar	1
ulular	1
uncir	161
ungir	104
unificar	146
uniformar	1
unir	3
untar	1
urbanizar	100
urdir	3
urgir	104
usar	1
usurpar	1
utilizar	100
vaciar	110
vacilar	1
vacunar	1
vadear	1
vagar	131
valer	155
validar	1
valorar	1
valuar	84
vallar	1
vanagloriarse	1
vaporizar	100
varear	1
variar	110
vedar	1
vejar	1
velar	1
vencer	156
vendar	1
vender	2
venerar	1
vengar	131
venir	157
ventear	1
ventilar	1
ventosear	1
ver	158
veranear	1
verdear[1]	1
verdecer[1]	99
verificar	146
versar	1
verter	109
vestir	132
vetar	1
viajar	1
vibrar	1
viciar	1
vigilar	1
vilipendiar	1
vincular	1
vindicar	146
violar	1
violentar	1
virar	1
visitar	1
vislumbrar	1
vitalizar	100
vitorear	1
vituperar	1
vivificar	146
vivir	3
vocalizar	100
vocear	1
vociferar	1
volar	98
volatilizar	100
volcar	159
voltear	1
volver	160
vomitar	1
votar	1
vulgarizar	100
vulnerar	1
yacer[15]	2
yuxtaponer	135
zafarse	1
zaherir	150
zambullirse	116
zampar	1
zanjar	1
zapatear	1
zarandear	1
zarpar	1
zigzaguear	1
zozobrar	1
zumbar	1
zurcir	161
zurrar	1

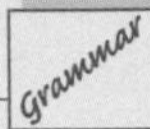

❒ Notes

The notes below indicate special peculiarities of individual verbs. When only some forms of a given tense are affected, all these are shown. When all forms of the tense are affected, only the 1st and 2nd persons are shown, followed by *etc.*

1 Gerund *2* Past Participle *3* Present *4* Preterite *5* Present Subjunctive *6* Imperfect Subjunctive

1) **acaecer, acontecer, amanecer, anochecer, atardecer, competer, deshelar, escampar, granizar, helar, llover, lloviznar, nevar, neviscar, nublarse, relampaguear, tronar, verdear, verdecer**: used almost exclusively in infinitive and 3rd person singular

2) **asir** *3* asgo *5* asga, asgas *etc*

3) **atañer** *1* atañendo *4* atañó: see also **1)** above

4) **balbucir** *3* balbuceo *5* balbucee, balbucees *etc*

5) **concernir** *3* concierne, conciernen *5* concierna, conciernan: only used in 3rd person

6) **degollar** *3* degüello, degüellas, degüella, degüellan *5* degüelle, degüelles, degüellen

7) **delinquir** *3* delinco *5* delinca, delincas *etc*

8) **desasir** *3* desasgo *5* desasga, desasgas *etc*

9) **discernir** *3* discierno, disciernes, discierne, disciernen *5* discierna, disciernas, disciernan

10) **enraizar** *3* enraízo, enraízas, enraíza, enraízan *5* enraíce, enraíces, enraícen

11) **pudrir** *2* podrido

12) **rehuir** *3* rehúyo, rehúyes, rehúye, rehúyen *5* rehúya, rehúyas, rehúyan

13) **roer** *4* royó, royeron *6* royera, royeras *etc*

14) **soler**: used only in present and imperfect indicative

15) **yacer** *3* yazgo *or* yazco *or* yago *5* yazga *etc or* yazca *etc or* yaga *etc*

❐ The Gender of Nouns

In Spanish, all nouns are either masculine or feminine, whether denoting people, animals or things. Gender is largely unpredictable and has to be learnt for each noun. However, the following guidelines will help you determine the gender for certain types of nouns.

- Nouns denoting male people and animals are usually – but not always – masculine, e.g.

un hombre	**un toro**
a man	*a bull*
un enfermero	**un semental**
a (male) nurse	*a stallion*

- Nouns denoting female people and animals are usually – but not always – feminine, e.g.

una niña	**una vaca**
a girl	*a cow*
una enfermera	**una yegua**
a nurse	*a mare*

- Some nouns are masculine *or* feminine depending on the sex of the person to whom they refer, e.g.

un camarada	**una camarada**
a (male) comrade	*a (female) comrade*
un belga	**una belga**
a Belgian (man)	*a Belgian (woman)*
un marroquí	**una marroquí**
a Moroccan (man)	*a Moroccan (woman)*

- Other nouns referring to either men or women have only one gender which applies to both, e.g.

una persona	**una visita**
a person	*a visitor*
una víctima	**una estrella**
a victim	*a star*

- Often the ending of a noun indicates its gender. Shown below are some of the most important to guide you.

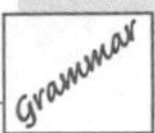

Masculine endings

-o	**un clavo** *a nail*, **un plátano** *a banana* EXCEPTIONS: **mano** *hand*, **foto** *photograph*, **moto(cicleta)** *motorbike*
-l	**un tonel** *a barrel*, **un hotel** *a hotel* EXCEPTIONS: **cal** *lime*, **cárcel** *prison*, **catedral** *cathedral*, **col** *cabbage*, **miel** *honey*, **piel** *skin*, **sal** *salt*, **señal** *sign*
-r	**un tractor** *a tractor*, **el altar** *the altar* EXCEPTIONS: **coliflor** *cauliflower*, **flor** *flower*, **labor** *task*
-y	**el rey** *the king*, **un buey** *an ox* EXCEPTION: **ley** *law*

Feminine endings

-a	**una casa** *a house*, **la cara** *the face* EXCEPTIONS: **día** *day*, **mapa** *map*, **planeta** *planet*, **tranvía** *tram*, and most words ending in **-ma** (**tema** *subject*, **problema** *problem*, etc)
-ión	**una canción** *a song*, **una procesión** *a procession* EXCEPTIONS: most nouns not ending in **-ción** or **-sión**, e.g. **avión** *aeroplane*, **camión** *lorry*, **gorrión** *sparrow*
-dad, -tad, -tud	**una ciudad** *a town*, **la libertad** *freedom*, **una multitud** *a crowd*
-ed	**una pared** *a wall*, **la sed** *thirst* EXCEPTION: **césped** *lawn*
-itis	**una faringitis** *pharyngitis*, **la celulitis** *cellulitis*
-iz	**una perdiz** *a partridge*, **una matriz** *a matrix* EXCEPTIONS: **lápiz** *pencil*, **maíz** *corn*, **tapiz** *tapestry*
-sis	**una tesis** *a thesis*, **una dosis** *a dose* EXCEPTIONS: **análisis** *analysis*, **énfasis** *emphasis*, **paréntesis** *parenthesis*
-umbre	**la podredumbre** *rot*, **la muchedumbre** *crowd*

❒ Gender of nouns *(Continued)*

Some nouns change meaning according to gender. The most common are set out below:

	MASCULINE	FEMININE
capital	*capital* (money)	*capital* (city) → 1
clave	*harpsichord*	*clue*
cólera	*cholera*	*anger* → 2
cometa	*comet*	*kite*
corriente	*current month*	*current*
corte	*cut*	*court* (royal) → 3
coma	*coma*	*comma* → 4
cura	*priest*	*cure* → 5
frente	*front* (in war)	*forehead* → 6
guardia	*guard(sman)*	*guard* → 7
guía	*guide* (person)	*guide(book)* → 8
moral	*mulberry tree*	*morals*
orden	*order* (arrangement)	*order* (command) → 9
ordenanza	*office boy*	*ordinance*
papa	*Pope*	*potato*
parte	*dispatch*	*part* → 10
pendiente	*earring*	*slope*
pez	*fish*	*pitch*
policía	*policeman*	*police*
radio	*radius, radium*	*radio*

Examples

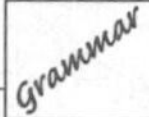

1	**Invirtieron mucho capital** They invested a lot of capital **La capital es muy fea** The capital city is very ugly	
2	**Es difícil luchar contra el cólera** Cholera is difficult to combat	**Montó en cólera** He got angry
3	**Me encanta tu corte de pelo** I love your haircut **Se trasladó la corte a Madrid** The court was moved to Madrid	
4	**Entró en un coma profundo** He went into a deep coma **Aquí hace falta una coma** You need to put a comma here	
5	**¿Quién es? – El cura** Who is it? – The priest	**No tiene cura** It's hopeless
6	**Han mandado a su hijo al frente** Her son has been sent to the front **Tiene la frente muy ancha** She has a very broad forehead	
7	**Vino un guardia de tráfico** A traffic policeman came **Están relevando la guardia ahora** They're changing the guard now	
8	**Nuestro guía nos hizo reír a carcajadas** Our guide had us falling about laughing **Busco una guía turística** I'm looking for a guidebook	
9	**Están en orden alfabético** They're in alphabetical order **No hemos recibido la orden de pago** We haven't had the payment order	
10	**Le mandó un parte al general** He sent a dispatch to the general **En alguna parte debe estar** It must be somewhere or other	

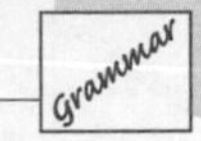

❒ Gender: the formation of feminines

As in English, male and female are sometimes differentiated by the use of two quite separate words, e.g.

mi marido	**mi mujer**
my husband	*my wife*
un toro	**una vaca**
a bull	*a cow*

There are, however, some words in Spanish which show this distinction by the form of their ending:

- Nouns ending in **-o** change to **-a** to form the feminine → [1]
- If the masculine singular form already ends in **-a**, no further **-a** is added to the feminine → [2]
- If the last letter of the masculine singular form is a consonant, an **-a** is normally added in the feminine* → [3]

Feminine forms to note

MASCULINE	FEMININE	
el abad	**la abadesa**	*abbot/abbess*
un actor	**una actriz**	*actor/actress*
el alcalde	**la alcaldesa**	*mayor/mayoress*
el conde	**la condesa**	*count/countess*
el duque	**la duquesa**	*duke/duchess*
el emperador	**la emperatriz**	*emperor/empress*
un poeta	**una poetisa**	*poet/poetess*
el príncipe	**la princesa**	*prince/princess*
el rey	**la reina**	*king/queen*
un sacerdote	**una sacerdotisa**	*priest/priestess*
un tigre	**una tigresa**	*tiger/tigress*
el zar	**la zarina**	*tzar/tzarina*

* If the last syllable has an accent, it disappears in the feminine (see p 292) → [4]

Examples

1

un amigo
a (male) friend
un empleado
a (male) employee
un gato
a cat

una amiga
a (female) friend
una empleada
a (female) employee
una gata
a (female) cat

2

un deportista
a sportsman
un colega
a (male) colleague
un camarada
a (male) comrade

una deportista
a sportswoman
una colega
a (female) colleague
una camarada
a (female) comrade

3

un español
a Spaniard, a Spanish man
un vendedor
a salesman
un jugador
a (male) player

una española
a Spanish woman
una vendedora
a saleswoman
una jugadora
a (female) player

4

un lapón
a Laplander (man)
un león
a lion
un neocelandés
a New Zealander (man)

una lapona
a Laplander (woman)
una leona
a lioness
una neocelandesa
a New Zealander (woman)

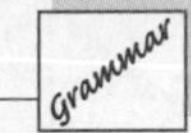

❐ The formation of plurals

- Nouns ending in an unstressed vowel add **-s** to the singular form → [1]

- Nouns ending in a consonant or a stressed vowel add **-es** to the singular form → [2]

⚠ BUT:

café	*coffee shop*	(plur: **cafés**)
mamá	*mummy*	(plur: **mamás**)
papá	*daddy*	(plur: **papás**)
pie	*foot*	(plur: **pies**)
sofá	*sofa*	(plur: **sofás**)
té	*tea*	(plur: **tes**)

and words of foreign origin ending in a consonant, e.g.:

coñac	*brandy*	(plur: **coñacs**)
jersey	*jumper*	(plur: **jerseys**)

⚠ NOTE:

— nouns ending in **-n** or **-s** with an accent on the last syllable drop this accent in the plural (see p 292) → [3]

— nouns ending in **-n** with the stress on the second-last syllable in the singular add an accent to that syllable in the plural in order to show the correct position for stress (see p 292) → [4]

— nouns ending in **-z** change this to **c** in the plural → [5]

- Nouns with an unstressed final syllable ending in **-s** do not change in the plural → [6]

Examples

1	**la casa** the house **el libro** the book	**las casas** the houses **los libros** the books
2	**un rumor** a rumour **un jabalí** a boar	**unos rumores** (some) rumours **unos jabalíes** (some) boars
3	**la canción** the song **el autobús** the bus	**las canciones** the songs **los autobuses** the buses
4	**un examen** an exam **un crimen** a crime	**unos exámenes** (some) exams **unos crímenes** (some) crimes
5	**la luz** the light	**las luces** the lights
6	**un paraguas** an umbrella **la dosis** the dose **el lunes** Monday	**unos paraguas** (some) umbrellas **las dosis** the doses **los lunes** Mondays

❐ The Definite Article

	WITH MASC NOUN	WITH FEM NOUN	
SING	**el**	**la**	*the*
PLUR	**los**	**las**	*the*

- The gender and number of the noun determine the form of the article → [1]

⚠ NOTE: However, if the article comes directly before a feminine singular noun which starts with a stressed **a-** or **ha-**, the masculine form **el** is used instead of the feminine **la** → [2]

- For uses of the definite article see p 199.
- **a** + **el** becomes **al** → [3]
- **de** + **el** becomes **del** → [4]

Examples

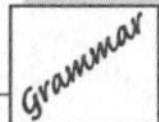

1	**el tren** the train		**la estación** the station
	el actor the actor		**la actriz** the actress
	los hoteles the hotels		**las escuelas** the schools
	los profesores the teachers		**las mujeres** the women
2	**el agua** the water	⚠ BUT:	**la misma agua** the same water
	el hacha the axe	⚠ BUT:	**la mejor hacha** the best axe
3	**al cine** to the cinema		
	al empleado to the employee		
	al hospital to the hospital		
4	**del departamento** from/of the department		
	del autor from/of the author		
	del presidente from/of the president		

❒ Uses of the definite article

While the definite article is used in much the same way in Spanish as it is in English, its use is more widespread in Spanish. Unlike English the definite article is also used:

- with abstract nouns, except when following certain prepositions → [1]

- in generalizations, especially with plural or uncountable* nouns → [2]

- with parts of the body → [3]

  'Ownership' is often indicated by an indirect object pronoun or a reflexive pronoun → [4]

- with titles/ranks/professions followed by a proper name → [5]

  ⚠ EXCEPTIONS: with **Don/Doña, San/Santo(a)** → [6]

- before nouns of official, academic and religious buildings, and names of meals and games → [7]

- The definite article is NOT used with nouns in apposition unless those nouns are individualized → [8]

* An uncountable noun is one which cannot be used in the plural or with an indefinite article, e.g. **el acero** *steel*, **la leche** *milk*.

Examples

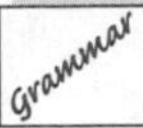

1 **Los precios suben**
Prices are rising
El tiempo es oro
Time is money
⚠ BUT:
con pasión
with passion
sin esperanza
without hope

2 **No me gusta el café**
I don't like coffee
Los niños necesitan ser queridos
Children need to be loved

3 **Vuelva la cabeza hacia la izquierda**
Turn your head to the left
No puedo mover las piernas
I can't move my legs

4 **La cabeza me da vueltas**
My head is spinning
Lávate las manos
Wash your hands

5 **El rey Jorge III**
King George III
el capitán Menéndez
Captain Menéndez
el doctor Ochoa
Doctor Ochoa
el señor Ramírez
Mr Ramírez

6 **Don Arturo Ruiz**
Mr Arturo Ruiz
Santa Teresa
Saint Teresa

7 **en la cárcel**
in prison
en la universidad
at university
en la iglesia
at church
la cena
dinner
el tenis
tennis
el ajedrez
chess

8 **Madrid, capital de España, es la ciudad que …**
Madrid, the capital of Spain, is the city which …
⚠ BUT:
Maria Callas, la famosa cantante de ópera …
Maria Callas, the famous opera singer …

❒ The Indefinite Article

	WITH MASC NOUN	WITH FEM NOUN	
SING	**un**	**una**	*a*
PLUR	**unos**	**unas**	*some*

The indefinite article is used in Spanish largely as it is in English.

⚠ BUT:

- There is no article when a person's profession is being stated → [1]

  The article is used, however, when the profession is qualified by an adjective → [2]

- The article is not used with the following words:

otro	*another*	→ [3]
cierto	*certain*	→ [4]
semejante	*such (a)*	→ [5]
tal	*such (a)*	→ [6]
cien	*a hundred*	→ [7]
mil	*a thousand*	→ [8]
sin	*without*	→ [9]
qué	*what a*	→ [10]

- There is no article with a noun in apposition → [11]. When an abstract noun is qualified by an adjective, the indefinite article is used, but is not translated in English → [12]

Examples

1 **Es profesor**
He's a teacher

Mi madre es enfermera
My mother is a nurse

2 **Es un buen médico**
He's a good doctor

Se hizo una escritora célebre
She became a famous writer

3 **otro libro**
another book

4 **cierta calle**
a certain street

5 **semejante ruido**
such a noise

6 **tal mentira**
such a lie

7 **cien soldados**
a hundred soldiers

8 **mil años**
a thousand years

9 **sin casa**
without a house

10 **¡Qué sorpresa!**
What a surprise!

11 **Baroja, gran escritor de la Generación del 98**
Baroja, a great writer of the 'Generación del 98'

12 **con una gran sabiduría/un valor admirable**
with great wisdom/admirable courage

Dieron pruebas de una sangre fría increíble
They showed incredible coolness

una película de un mal gusto espantoso
a film in appallingly bad taste

❐ The Article 'lo'

This is never used with a noun. Instead, it is used in the following ways:

- As an intensifier before an adjective or adverb in the construction

  lo + adjective/adverb + **que** → [1]

  ⚠ NOTE: The adjective agrees with the noun it refers to → [2]

- With an adjective or participle to form an abstract noun → [3]
- In the phrase **lo de** to refer to a subject of which speaker and listener are already aware. It can often be translated as *the business/affair of/about ...* → [4]
- In set expressions, the commonest of which are:

a lo mejor	*maybe, perhaps*	→ [5]
a lo lejos	*in the distance*	→ [6]
a lo largo de	*along, through*	→ [7]
por lo menos	*at least*	→ [8]
por lo tanto	*therefore, so*	→ [9]
por lo visto	*apparently*	→ [10]

Examples

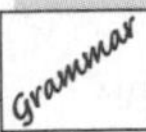

1 **No sabíamos lo pequeña que era la casa**
We didn't know how small the house was

Sé lo mucho que te gusta la música
I know how much you like music

2 **No te imaginas lo simpáticos que son**
You can't imagine how nice they are

Ya sabes lo buenas que son estas manzanas
You already know how good these apples are

3 **Lo bueno de eso es que …**
The good thing about it is that …

Sentimos mucho lo ocurrido
We are very sorry about what happened

4 **Lo de ayer es mejor que lo olvides**
It's better if you forget what happened yesterday

Lo de tu hermano me preocupa mucho
The business about your brother worries me very much

5 **A lo mejor ha salido**
Perhaps he's gone out

6 **A lo lejos se veían unas casas**
Some houses could be seen in the distance

7 **A lo largo de su vida**
Throughout his life

A lo largo de la carretera
Along the road

8 **Hubo por lo menos cincuenta heridos**
At least fifty people were injured

9 **No hemos recibido ninguna instrucción al respecto, y por lo tanto no podemos …**
We have not received any instructions about it, therefore we cannot …

10 **Por lo visto, no viene**
Apparently he's not coming OR: He's not coming, it seems

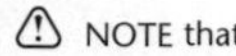

Most adjectives agree in number and in gender with the noun or pronoun.

⚠ NOTE that:

— if the adjective refers to two or more singular nouns of the same gender, a plural ending of that gender is required → 1

— if the adjective refers to two or more singular nouns of different genders, a masculine plural ending is required → 2

The formation of feminines

- Adjectives ending in **-o** change to **-a** → 3
- Some groups of adjectives add **-a**:
  - adjectives of nationality or geographical origin → 4
  - adjectives ending in **-or** (except irregular comparatives: see p 210), **-án, -ón, -ín** → 5

  ⚠ NOTE: When there is an accent on the last syllable, it disappears in the feminine (see p 292).

- Other adjectives do not change → 6

The formation of plurals

- Adjectives ending in an unstressed vowel add **-s** → 7
- Adjectives ending in a stressed vowel or a consonant add **-es** → 8

  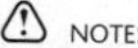

  – if there is an accent on the last syllable of a word ending in a consonant, it will disappear in the plural (see p 292) → 9

  – if the last letter is a **z** it will become a **c** in the plural → 10

Examples

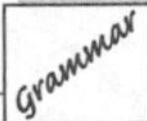

1 **la lengua y la literatura españolas**
(the) Spanish language and literature

2 **Me he comprado un abrigo y una camisa rojos**
I bought myself a red coat and shirt

3	**mi hermano pequeño** my little brother	**mi hermana pequeña** my little sister
4	**un chico español** a Spanish boy	**una chica española** a Spanish girl
	el equipo barcelonés the team from Barcelona	**la vida barcelonesa** the Barcelona way of life
5	**un niño encantador** a charming little boy	**una niña encantadora** a charming little girl
	un hombre holgazán an idle man	**una mujer holgazana** an idle woman
	un gesto burlón a mocking gesture	**una sonrisa burlona** a mocking smile
	un chico cantarín a boy fond of singing	**una chica cantarina** a girl fond of singing
6	**un final feliz** a happy ending	**una infancia feliz** a happy childhood
	mi amigo belga my Belgian (male) friend	**mi amiga belga** my Belgian (female) friend
	el vestido verde the green dress	**la blusa verde** the green blouse
7	**el último tren** the last train	**los últimos trenes** the last trains
	una casa vieja an old house	**unas casas viejas** (some) old houses
8	**un médico iraní** an Iranian doctor	**unos médicos iraníes** (some) Iranian doctors
	un examen fácil an easy exam	**unos exámenes fáciles** (some) easy exams
9	**un río francés** a French river	**unos ríos franceses** (some) French rivers
10	**un día feliz** a happy day	**unos días felices** (some) happy days

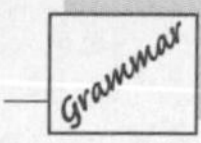

❒ Invariable Adjectives

Some adjectives and other parts of speech when used adjectivally never change in the feminine or plural.

The commonest of these are:

— nouns denoting colour → [1]

— compound adjectives → [2]

— nouns used as adjectives → [3]

Shortening of Adjectives

- The following drop the final **-o** before a masculine singular noun:

  bueno *good* → [4]

  malo *bad*

  alguno* *some* → [5]

  ninguno* *none*

  uno *one* → [6]

  primero *first* → [7]

  tercero *third*

  postrero *last* → [8]

  * ⚠ NOTE: An accent is required to show the correct position for stress.

- **Grande** *big, great* is usually shortened to **gran** before a masculine *or* feminine singular noun → [9]
- **Santo** *Saint* changes to **San** except with saints' names beginning with **Do-** or **To-** → [10]
- **Ciento** *a hundred* is shortened to **cien** before a masculine *or* feminine plural noun → [11]
- **Cualquiera** drops the final **-a** before a masculine *or* feminine singular noun → [12]

1 **los vestidos naranja**
the orange dresses

2 **las chaquetas azul marino**
the navy blue jackets

3 **bebés probeta**
test-tube babies

mujeres soldado
women soldiers

4 **un buen libro**
a good book

5 **algún libro**
some book

6 **un día**
one day

7 **el primer hijo**
the first child

8 **un postrer deseo**
a last wish

9 **un gran actor**
a great actor

una gran decepción
a great disappointment

10 **San Antonio**
Saint Anthony

Santo Tomás
Saint Thomas

11 **cien años**
a hundred years

cien millones
a hundred million

12 **cualquier día**
any day

a cualquier hora
any time

❐ Comparatives and Superlatives

Comparatives

These are formed using the following constructions:

más … (que)		*more … (than)*	→ 1
menos … (que)		*less … (than)*	→ 2
tanto … como		*as … as*	→ 3
tan … como		*as … as*	→ 4
tan … que		*so … that*	→ 5
demasiado …	**para**	*too …*	*to* → 6
bastante …	**para**	*enough …*	*to* → 6
suficiente …	**para**	*enough …*	*to* → 6

- *'Than'* followed by a clause is translated by **de lo que** → 7

Superlatives

These are formed using the following constructions:

el/la/los/las más … (que)	*the most … (that)*	→ 8
el/la/los/las menos … (que)	*the least … (that)*	→ 9

- After a superlative the preposition **de** is often translated as *in* → 10

- The absolute superlative (*very, most, extremely* + *adjective*) is expressed in Spanish by **muy** + adjective, or by adding **-ísimo/a/os/as** to the adjective when it ends in a consonant, or to its stem (adjective minus final vowel) when it ends in a vowel → 11

⚠ NOTE: It is sometimes necessary to change the spelling of the adjective when **-ísimo** is added, in order to maintain the same sound (see p 296) → 12

Examples

1 **una razón más seria**
a more serious reason
Es más alto que mi hermano
He's taller than my brother

2 **una película menos conocida**
a less well known film
Luis es menos tímido que tú
Luis is less shy than you

3 **Pablo tenía tanto miedo como yo**
Paul was as frightened as I was

4 **No es tan grande como creía**
It isn't as big as I thought

5 **El examen era tan difícil que nadie aprobó**
The exam was so difficult that nobody passed

6 **No tengo suficiente dinero para comprarlo**
I haven't got enough money to buy it

7 **Está más cansada de lo que parece**
She is more tired than she seems

8 **el caballo más veloz**
the fastest horse
los días más lluviosos
the wettest days
la casa más pequeña
the smallest house
las manzanas más maduras
the ripest apples

9 **el hombre menos simpático**
the least likeable man
los cuadros menos bonitos
the least attractive paintings
la niña menos habladora
the least talkative girl
las camisas menos viejas
the least old shirts

10 **la estación más ruidosa de Londres**
the noisiest station in London

11 **Este libro es muy interesante**
This book is very interesting
Era facilísimo de hacer
It was very easy to make
Tienen un coche rapidísimo
They have an extremely fast car

12 **Mi tío era muy rico**
My uncle was very rich
un león muy feroz
a very ferocious lion
Se hizo riquísimo
He became extremely rich
un tigre ferocísimo
an extremely ferocious tiger

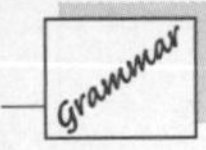

Comparatives and Superlatives *(Continued)*

Adjectives with irregular comparatives/superlatives

ADJECTIVE	COMPARATIVE	SUPERLATIVE
bueno *good*	**mejor** *better*	**el mejor** *the best*
malo *bad*	**peor** *worse*	**el peor** *the worst*
grande *big*	**mayor** OR: **más grande** *bigger; older*	**el mayor** OR: **el más grande** *the biggest; the oldest*
pequeño *small*	**menor** OR: **más pequeño** *smaller; younger; lesser*	**el menor** OR: **el más pequeño** *the smallest; the youngest; the least*

- The irregular comparative and superlative forms of **grande** and **pequeño** are used mainly to express:
  - — age, in which case they come after the noun → 1
  - — abstract size and degrees of importance, in which case they come before the noun → 2

  The regular forms are used mainly to express physical size → 3

- Irregular comparatives and superlatives have one form for both masculine and feminine, but always agree in number with the noun → 1

Examples

1 **mis hermanos mayores**
my older brothers
la hija menor
the youngest daughter

2 **el menor ruido**
the slightest sound
las mayores dificultades
the biggest difficulties

3 **Este plato es más grande que aquél**
This plate is bigger than that one
Mi casa es más pequeña que la tuya
My house is smaller than yours

❒ Demonstrative Adjectives

	MASCULINE	FEMININE	
SING	**este**	**esta**	*this*
	ese	**esa**	*that*
	aquel	**aquella**	
PLUR	**estos**	**estas**	*these*
	esos	**esas**	*those*
	aquellos	**aquellas**	

- Demonstrative adjectives normally precede the noun and always agree in number and in gender → [1]

- The forms **ese/a/os/as** are used:
  - — to indicate distance from the speaker but proximity to the person addressed → [2]
  - — to indicate a not too remote distance → [3]

- The forms **aquel/la/los/las** are used to indicate distance, in space or time → [4]

Examples

1 **Este bolígrafo no escribe**
This pen is not working
Esa revista es muy mala
That is a very bad magazine
Aquella montaña es muy alta
That mountain (over there) is very high
¿Conoces a esos señores?
Do you know those gentlemen?
Siga Vd hasta aquellos edificios
Carry on until you come to those buildings
¿Ves aquellas personas?
Can you see those people (over there)?

2 **Ese papel en donde escribes** …
That paper you are writing on …

3 **No me gustan esos cuadros**
I don't like those pictures

4 **Aquella calle parece muy ancha**
That street (over there) looks very wide
Aquellos años sí que fueron felices
Those were really happy years

Interrogative Adjectives

	MASCULINE	FEMININE	
SING	**¿qué?**	**¿qué?**	*what?, which?*
	¿cuánto?	**¿cuánta?**	*how much?; how many?*
PLUR	**¿qué?**	**¿qué?**	*what?, which?*
	¿cuántos?	**¿cuántas?**	*how much?; how many?*

- Interrogative adjectives, when not invariable, agree in number and gender with the noun → [1]

- The forms shown above are also used in indirect questions → [2]

Exclamatory Adjectives

	MASCULINE	FEMININE	
SING	**¡qué!**	**¡qué!**	*what (a)*
	¡cuánto!	**¡cuánta!**	*what (a lot of)*
PLUR	**¡qué!**	**¡qué!**	*what*
	¡cuántos!	**¡cuántas!**	*what (a lot of)*

- Exclamatory adjectives, when not invariable, agree in number and gender with the noun → [3]

Examples

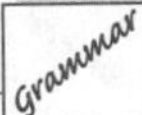

1 **¿Qué libro te gustó más?**
Which book did you like most?
¿Qué clase de hombre es?
What type of man is he?
¿Qué instrumentos toca Vd?
What instruments do you play?
¿Qué ofertas ha recibido Vd?
What offers have you received?
¿Cuánto dinero te queda?
How much money have you got left?
¿Cuánta lluvia ha caído?
How much rain have we had?
¿Cuántos vestidos quieres comprar?
How many dresses do you want to buy?
¿Cuántas personas van a venir?
How many people are coming?

2 **No sé a qué hora llegó**
I don't know at what time she arrived
Dígame cuántas postales quiere
Tell me how many postcards you'd like

3 **¡Qué pena!**
What a pity!
¡Qué tiempo tan/más malo!
What lousy weather!
¡Cuánto tiempo!
What a long time!
¡Cuánta pobreza!
What poverty!
¡Cuántos autobuses!
What a lot of buses!
¡Cuántas mentiras!
What a lot of lies!

❐ Possessive Adjectives

Weak forms

WITH SING NOUN		WITH PLUR NOUN		
MASC	*FEM*	*MASC*	*FEM*	
mi	**mi**	**mis**	**mis**	*my*
tu	**tu**	**tus**	**tus**	*your*
su	**su**	**sus**	**sus**	*his; her; its; your (of* **Vd***)*
nuestro	**nuestra**	**nuestros**	**nuestras**	*our*
vuestro	**vuestra**	**vuestros**	**vuestras**	*your*
su	**su**	**sus**	**sus**	*their; your (of* **Vds***)*

- All possessive adjectives agree in number and (when applicable) in gender with the noun, NOT WITH THE OWNER → [1]

- The weak forms always precede the noun → [1]

- Since the form **su(s)** can mean *his, her, your (of* **Vd, Vds***)* or *their*, clarification is often needed. This is done by adding **de él, de ella, de Vds** etc to the noun, and usually (but not always) changing the possessive to a definite article → [2]

Examples

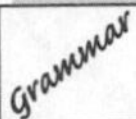

1 **Pilar no ha traído nuestros libros**
Pilar hasn't brought our books
Antonio irá a vuestra casa
Anthony will go to your house
¿Han vendido su coche tus vecinos?
Have your neighbours sold their car?
Mi hermano y tu primo no se llevan bien
My brother and your cousin don't get on

2 **su casa → la casa de él**
his house
sus amigos → los amigos de Vd
your friends
sus coches → los coches de ellos
their cars
su abrigo → el abrigo de ella
her coat

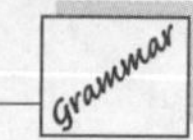

❒ Possessive Adjectives *(Continued)*

Strong forms

WITH SING NOUN		WITH PLUR NOUN		
MASC	*FEM*	*MASC*	*FEM*	
mío	**mía**	**míos**	**mías**	*my*
tuyo	**tuya**	**tuyos**	**tuyas**	*your*
suyo	**suya**	**suyos**	**suyas**	*his; her; its; your (of* **Vd***)*
nuestro	**nuestra**	**nuestros**	**nuestras**	*our*
vuestro	**vuestra**	**vuestros**	**vuestras**	*your*
suyo	**suya**	**suyos**	**suyas**	*their; your (of* **Vds***)*

- The strong forms agree in the same way as the weak forms (see p 216).

- The strong forms always follow the noun, and they are used:
  - — to translate the English *of mine, of yours,* etc → [1]
  - — to address people → [2]

Examples

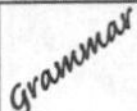

1 **Es un capricho suyo**
It's a whim of hers
un amigo nuestro
a friend of ours
una revista tuya
a magazine of yours

2 **Muy señor mío** (in letters)
Dear Sir
hija mía
my daughter
¡Dios mío!
My God!
Amor mío
Darling/My love

❐ Indefinite Adjectives

alguno(a)s	*some*
ambos(as)	*both*
cada	*each; every*
cierto(a)s	*certain; definite*
cualquiera, plur **cualesquiera**	*some; any*
los (las) demás	*the others; the remainder*
mismo(a)s	*same; -self*
mucho(a)s	*many; much*
ningún, ninguna plur **ningunos, ningunas**	*any; no*
otro(a)s	*other; another*
poco(a)s	*few; little*
tal(es)	*such (a)*
tanto(a)s	*so much; so many*
todo(a)s	*all; every*
varios(as)	*several; various*

Unless invariable, all indefinite adjectives agree in number and gender with the noun → [1]

- **alguno**

  Before a masculine singular noun it drops the final **-o** and adds an accent to show the correct position for stress → [2] (see also p 292)

- **ambos**

  Usually it is only used in written Spanish. The spoken language prefers the form **los dos/las dos** → [3]

- **cierto** and **mismo**

  They change their meaning according to their position in relation to the noun (see also **Position of Adjectives**, p 224) → [4]

- **cualquiera**

  It drops the final **-a** before a masculine *or* feminine noun → [5]

Examples

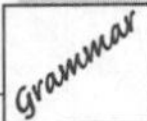

1 **el mismo día**
the same day
mucha/poca gente
many/few people

las mismas películas
the same films
mucho/poco dinero
much/little money

2 **algún día**
some day

alguna razón
some reason

3 **Me gustan los dos cuadros**
I like both pictures
¿Conoces a las dos enfermeras?
Do you know both nurses?

4 **cierto tiempo**
a certain time
⚠ BUT: **éxito cierto**
sure success

el mismo color
the same colour
⚠ BUT: **en la iglesia misma**
in the church itself

5 **cualquier casa**
any house
⚠ BUT: **una revista cualquiera**
any magazine

❐ Indefinite Adjectives *(Continued)*

- **ningún** is only used in negative sentences or phrases → [1]

- **otro**

  It is never preceded by an indefinite article → [2]

- **tal**

  It is never followed by an indefinite article → [3]

- **todo**

  It can be followed by a definite article, a demonstrative or possessive adjective or a place name → [4]

⚠ EXCEPTIONS:

— when **todo** in the singular means *any, every*, or *each* → [5]

— in some set expressions → [6]

Examples

1 **No es ninguna tonta**
She's no fool
¿No tienes parientes? – No, ninguno
Haven't you any relatives? – No, none

2 **¿Me das otra manzana?**
Will you give me another apple?
Prefiero estos otros zapatos
I prefer these other shoes

3 **Nunca dije tal cosa**
I never said such a thing

4 **Estudian durante toda la noche**
They study all night
Ha llovido toda esta semana
It has rained all this week
Pondré en orden todos mis libros
I'll sort out all my books
Lo sabe todo Madrid
All Madrid knows it

5 **Podrá entrar toda persona que lo desee**
Any person who wishes to enter may do so

⚠ BUT:

Vienen todos los días
They come every day

6 **de todos modos**
anyway
por todas partes
por todos lados
a/en todas partes
a/en todos lados
everywhere

a toda velocidad
at full/top speed

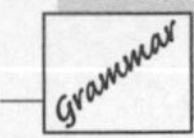

❒ Position of Adjectives

- Spanish adjectives usually follow the noun → 1, 2
- Note that when used figuratively or to express a quality already inherent in the noun, adjectives can precede the noun → 3
- As in English, demonstrative, possessive (weak forms), numerical, interrogative and exclamatory adjectives precede the noun → 4
- Indefinite adjectives also usually precede the noun → 5

⚠ NOTE: **alguno** *some* in negative expressions follows the noun → 6

- Some adjectives can precede or follow the noun, but their meaning varies according to their position:

	BEFORE NOUN	AFTER NOUN	
antiguo	*former*	*old, ancient*	→ 7
diferente	*various*	*different*	→ 8
grande	*great*	*big*	→ 9
medio	*half*	*average*	→ 10
mismo	*same*	*-self, very/precisely*	→ 11
nuevo	*new, another, fresh*	*brand new*	→ 12
pobre	*poor (wretched)*	*poor (not rich)*	→ 13
puro	*sheer, mere*	*pure (clear)*	→ 14
varios	*several*	*various, different*	→ 15
viejo	*old (long known, etc)*	*old (aged)*	→ 16

- Adjectives following the noun are linked by **y** → 17

Examples

1	**la página siguiente** the following page	**la hora exacta** the right time	
2	**una corbata azul** a blue tie	**una palabra española** a Spanish word	
3	**un dulce sueño** a sweet dream **un terrible desastre** (all disasters are terrible) a terrible disaster		
4	**este sombrero** this hat	**mi padre** my father	**¿qué hombre?** what man?
5	**cada día** every day	**otra vez** another time	**poco dinero** little money
6	**sin duda alguna** without any doubt		
7	**un antiguo colega** a former colleague	**la historia antigua** ancient history	
8	**diferentes capítulos** various chapters	**personas diferentes** different people	
9	**un gran pintor** a great painter	**una casa grande** a big house	
10	**medio melón** half a melon	**velocidad media** average speed	
11	**la misma respuesta** the same answer	**yo mismo** myself	**eso mismo** precisely that
12	**mi nuevo coche** my new car	**unos zapatos nuevos** (some) brand new shoes	
13	**esa pobre mujer** that poor woman	**un país pobre** a poor country	
14	**la pura verdad** the plain truth	**aire puro** fresh air	
15	**varios caminos** several ways/paths	**artículos varios** various items	
16	**un viejo amigo** an old friend	**esas toallas viejas** those old towels	
17	**una acción cobarde y falsa** a cowardly, deceitful act		

❒ Personal Pronouns

SUBJECT PRONOUNS

PERSON	SINGULAR	PLURAL
1st	**yo** *I*	**nosotros** *we* (masc/masc + fem) **nosotras** *we* (all fem)
2nd	**tú** *you*	**vosotros** *you* (masc/masc + fem) **vosotras** *you* (all fem)
3rd	**él** *he; it* **ella** *she; it* **usted (Vd)** *you*	**ellos** *they* (masc/masc + fem) **ellas** *they* (all fem) **ustedes (Vds)** *you*

- Subject pronouns have a limited usage in Spanish. Normally they are only used:

  — for emphasis → [1]

  — for clarity → [2]

  ⚠ BUT: **Vd** and **Vds** should always be used for politeness, whether they are otherwise needed or not → [3]

- *It* as subject and *they*, referring to things, are never translated into Spanish → [4]

- **tú/usted**

  As a general rule, you should use **tú** (or **vosotros,** if plural) when addressing a friend, a child, a relative, someone you know well, or when invited to do so. In all other cases, use **usted** (or **ustedes**)

- **nosotros/as; vosotros/as; él/ella; ellos/ellas**

  All these forms reflect the number and gender of the noun(s) they replace. **Nosotros, vosotros** and **ellos** also replace a combination of masculine and feminine nouns.

Examples

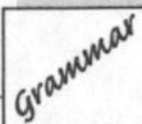

1 **Ellos sí que llegaron tarde**
They really did arrive late
Tú no tienes por qué venir
There is no reason for you to come
Ella jamás creería eso
She would never believe that

2 **Yo estudio español pero él estudia francés**
I study Spanish but he studies French
Ella era muy deportista pero él prefería jugar a las cartas
She was a sporty type but he preferred to play cards
Vosotros saldréis primero y nosotros os seguiremos
You leave first and we will follow you

3 **Pase Vd por aquí**
Please come this way
¿Habían estado Vds antes en esta ciudad?
Had you been to this town before?

4 **¿Qué es? – Es una sorpresa**
What is it? – It's a surprise
¿Qué son? – Son abrelatas
What are they? – They are tin-openers

❒ Personal Pronouns *(Continued)*

DIRECT OBJECT PRONOUNS

PERSON	SINGULAR	PLURAL
1st	**me** *me*	**nos** *us*
2nd	**te** *you*	**os** *you*
3rd (masculine)	**lo** *him; it; you* (of **Vd**)	**los** *them; you* (of **Vds**)
(feminine)	**la** *her; it; you* (of **Vd**)	**las** *them; you* (of **Vds**)

- **lo** sometimes functions as a 'neuter' pronoun, referring to an idea or information contained in a previous statement or question. It is often not translated → [1]

Position of direct object pronouns

- In constructions other than the imperative affirmative, infinitive or gerund, the pronoun always comes before the verb → [2]

  In the imperative affirmative, infinitive and gerund, the pronoun follows the verb and is attached to it. An accent is needed in certain cases to show the correct position for stress (see also p 292) → [3]

- Where an infinitive or gerund depends on a previous verb, the pronoun may be used either after the infinitive or gerund, or before the main verb → [4]

  ⚠ NOTE: see how this applies to reflexive verbs → [4]

- For further information, see **Order of Object Pronouns**, p 232.

Reflexive Pronouns

These are dealt with under reflexive verbs, p 24.

Examples

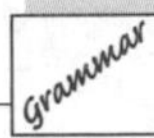

1 **¿Va a venir María? – No lo sé**
Is Maria coming? – I don't know
Hay que regar las plantas – Yo lo haré
The plants need watering – I'll do it
Habían comido ya pero no nos lo dijeron
They had already eaten, but they didn't tell us
Yo conduzco de prisa pero él lo hace despacio
I drive fast but he drives slowly

2 **Te quiero**
I love you
¿Las ve Vd?
Can you see them?
¿No me oyen Vds?
Can't you hear me?
Tu hija no nos conoce
Your daughter doesn't know us
No los toques
Don't touch them

3 **Ayúdame**
Help me
Acompáñenos
Come with us
Quiero decirte algo
I want to tell you something
Estaban persiguiéndonos
They were coming after us

4 **Lo está comiendo** OR: **Está comiéndolo**
She is eating it
Nos vienen a ver OR: **Vienen a vernos**
They are coming to see us
No quería levantarse OR: **No se quería levantar**
He didn't want to get up
Estoy afeitándome OR: **Me estoy afeitando**
I'm shaving

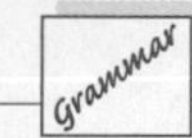

❐ Personal Pronouns *(Continued)*

INDIRECT OBJECT PRONOUNS

PERSON	SINGULAR	PLURAL
1st	**me**	**nos**
2nd	**te**	**os**
3rd	**le**	**les**

- The pronouns shown in the above table replace the preposition **a** + noun → [1]

Position of indirect object pronouns

- In constructions other than the imperative affirmative, the infinitive or the gerund, the pronoun comes before the verb → [2]

  In the imperative affirmative, infinitive and gerund, the pronoun follows the verb and is attached to it. An accent is needed in certain cases to show the correct position for stress (see also p 292) → [3]

- Where an infinitive or gerund depends on a previous verb, the pronoun may be used either after the infinitive or gerund, or before the main verb → [4]

- For further information, see **Order of Object Pronouns**, p 232.

Reflexive Pronouns

These are dealt with under reflexive verbs, p 24.

Examples

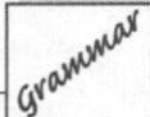

1 **Estoy escribiendo a Teresa** → **Le estoy escribiendo**
I am writing to Teresa — I am writing to her
Da de comer al gato → **Dale de comer**
Give the cat some food — Give it some food

2 **Sofía os ha escrito** — **¿Os ha escrito Sofía?**
Sophie has written to you — Has Sophie written to you?
Carlos no nos habla
Charles doesn't speak to us
¿Qué te pedían?
What were they asking you for?
No les haga caso Vd
Don't take any notice of them

3 **Respóndame Vd** — **Díganos Vd la respuesta**
Answer me — Tell us the answer
No quería darte la noticia todavía
I didn't want to tell you the news yet
Llegaron diciéndome que ...
They came telling me that ...

4 **Estoy escribiéndole** OR: **Le estoy escribiendo**
I am writing to him/her
Les voy a hablar OR: **Voy a hablarles**
I'm going to talk to them

❐ Personal Pronouns *(Continued)*

Order of object pronouns

- When two object pronouns of different persons are combined, the order is: indirect before direct, i.e.

me **te** **nos** **os**	before	**lo** **la** **los** **las**	→ [1]

  ⚠ NOTE: When two 3rd person object pronouns are combined, the first (i.e. the indirect object pronoun) becomes **se** → [2]

Points to note on object pronouns

- As **le/les** can refer to either gender, and **se** to either gender, singular or plural, sometimes clarification is needed. This is done by adding **a él** *to him*, **a ella** *to her*, **a Vd** *to you* etc to the phrase, usually after the verb → [3]

- When a noun object precedes the verb, the corresponding object pronoun must be used too → [4]

- Indirect object pronouns are often used instead of possessive adjectives with parts of the body or clothing to indicate 'ownership', and also in certain common constructions involving reflexive verbs (see also **The Indefinite Article**, p 198) → [5]

- **Le** and **les** are often used in Spanish instead of **lo** and **los** when referring to people. Equally **la** is sometimes used instead of **le** when referring to a feminine person or animal, although this usage is considered incorrect by some speakers of Spanish → [6]

Examples

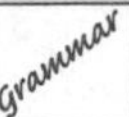

1 **Paloma os lo mandará mañana**
Paloma is sending it to you tomorrow
¿Te los ha enseñado mi hermana?
Has my sister shown them to you?
No me lo digas
Don't tell me (that)
Todos estaban pidiéndotelo
They were all asking you for it
No quiere prestárnosla
He won't lend it to us

2 **Se lo di ayer**
I gave it to him/her/them yesterday

3 **Le escriben mucho a ella**
They write to her often
Se lo van a mandar pronto a ellos
They will be sending it to them soon

4 **A tu hermano lo conozco bien**
I know your brother well
A María la vemos algunas veces
We sometimes see Maria

5 **La chaqueta le estaba ancha**
His jacket was too loose
Me duele el tobillo
My ankle is aching
Se me ha perdido el bolígrafo
I have lost my pen

6 **Le/lo encontraron en el cine**
They met him at the cinema
Les/los oímos llegar
We heard them coming
Le/la escribimos una carta
We wrote a letter to her

❐ Personal Pronouns *(Continued)*

Pronouns after prepositions

- These are the same as the subject pronouns, except for the forms **mí** *me*, **ti** *you* (sing), and the reflexive **sí** *himself, herself, themselves, yourselves* → [1]

- **Con** *with* combines with **mí, ti** and **sí** to form

  conmigo *with me* → [2]
  contigo *with you*
  consigo *with himself/herself etc*

- The following prepositions always take a subject pronoun:

entre	*between, among* → [3]
hasta / **incluso**	*even, including* → [4]
salvo / **menos**	*except* → [5]
según	*according to* → [6]

- These pronouns are used for emphasis, especially where contrast is involved → [7]

- **Ello** *it, that* is used after a preposition when referring to an idea already mentioned, but never to a concrete noun → [8]

- **A él, de él** NEVER contract → [9]

Examples

1 **Pienso en ti**
I think about you
Es para ella
This is for her
Volveréis sin nosotros
You'll come back without us
Hablaba para sí
He was talking to himself
¿Son para mí?
Are they for me?
Iban hacia ellos
They were going towards them
Volaban sobre vosotros
They were flying above you

2 **Venid conmigo**
Come with me
Lo trajeron consigo
They brought it/him with them
⚠ BUT: **¿Hablaron con vosotros?**
Did they talk to you?

3 **entre tú y ella**
between you and her

4 **Hasta yo puedo hacerlo**
Even I can do it

5 **todos menos yo**
everybody except me

6 **según tú**
according to you

7 **¿A ti no te escriben?**
Don't they write to you?
Me lo manda a mí, no a ti
She is sending it to me, not to you

8 **Nunca pensaba en ello**
He never thought about it
Por todo ello me parece que …
For all those reasons it seems to me that …

9 **A él no lo conozco**
I don't know him
No he sabido nada de él
I haven't heard from him

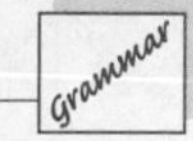

❒ Indefinite Pronouns

algo	*something, anything*	→ 1
alguien	*somebody, anybody*	→ 2
alguno/a/os/as	*some, a few*	→ 3
cada uno/a	*each (one)*	→ 4
	everybody	
cualquiera	*anybody; any*	→ 5
los/las demás	*the others*	
	the rest	→ 6
mucho/a/os/as	*many; much*	→ 7
nada	*nothing*	→ 8
nadie	*nobody*	→ 9
ninguno/a	*none, not any*	→ 10
poco/a/os/as	*few; little*	→ 11
tanto/a/os/as	*so much; so many*	→ 12
todo/a/os/as	*all; everything*	→ 13
uno ... (el) otro / **una ... (la) otra**	*(the) one ... the other*	→ 14
unos ... (los) otros / **unas ... (las) otras**	*some ... (the) others*	→ 14
varios/as	*several*	→ 15

- **algo, alguien, alguno**

  They can never be used after a negative. The appropriate negative pronouns are used instead: **nada, nadie, ninguno** (see also negatives, p 272) → 16

Examples

1 **Tengo algo para ti**
I have something for you
¿Viste algo?
Did you see anything?

2 **Alguien me lo ha dicho**
Somebody said it to me
¿Has visto a alguien?
Have you seen anybody?

3 **Algunos de los niños ya sabían leer**
Some of the children could read already

4 **Le dio una manzana a cada uno**
She gave each of them an apple
¡Cada uno a su casa!
Everybody go home!

5 **Cualquiera puede hacerlo**
Anybody can do it
Cualquiera de las explicaciones vale
Any of the explanations is a valid one

6 **Yo me fui, los demás se quedaron**
I went, the others stayed

7 **Muchas de las casas no tenían jardín**
Many of the houses didn't have a garden

8 **¿Qué tienes en la mano? – Nada**
What have you got in your hand? – Nothing

9 **¿A quién ves? – A nadie**
Who can you see? – Nobody

10 **¿Cuántas tienes? – Ninguna**
How many have you got? – None

11 **Había muchos cuadros, pero vi pocos que me gustaran**
There were many pictures, but I saw few I liked

12 **¿Se oía mucho ruido? – No tanto**
Was it very noisy? – Not so very

13 **Lo ha estropeado todo**
He has spoiled everything
Todo va bien
All is going well

14 **Unos cuestan 10 euros, los otros 15 euros**
Some cost 10 euros, the others 15 euros

15 **Varios de ellos me gustaron mucho**
I liked several of them very much

16 **Veo a alguien**
I can see somebody
No veo a nadie
I can't see anybody
Tengo algo que hacer
I have something to do
No tengo nada que hacer
I don't have anything to do

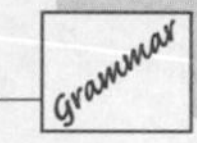

❐ Relative Pronouns

PEOPLE

SINGULAR	PLURAL	
que	**que**	*who, that* (subject) → 1
que	**que**	*who(m), that* (direct object) → 2
a quien	**a quienes**	
a quien	**a quienes**	*to whom, that* → 3
de que	**de que**	*of whom, that* → 4
de quien	**de quienes**	
cuyo/a	**cuyos/as**	*whose* → 5

THINGS

SINGULAR AND PLURAL		
que	*which, that* (subject)	→ 6
que	*which, that* (direct object)	→ 7
a que	*to which, that*	→ 8
de que	*of which, that*	→ 9
cuyo	*whose*	→ 10

⚠ NOTE: These forms can also refer to people.

- **cuyo** agrees with the noun it accompanies, NOT WITH THE OWNER → 5/ 10
- You cannot omit the relative pronoun in Spanish as you can in English → 2/7

Examples

1 **Mi hermano, que tiene veinte años, es el más joven**
My brother, who is twenty, is the youngest

2 **Los amigos que más quiero son ...**
The friends (that) I like best are ...

María, a quien Daniel admira tanto, es ...
Maria, whom Daniel admires so much, is ...

3 **Mis abogados, a quienes he escrito hace poco, están ...**
My lawyers, to whom I wrote recently, are ...

4 **La chica de que te hablé llega mañana**
The girl (that) I told you about is coming tomorrow

los niños de quienes se ocupa Vd
the children (that) you look after

5 **Vendrá la mujer cuyo hijo está enfermo**
The woman whose son is ill will be coming

6 **Hay una escalera que lleva a la buhardilla**
There's a staircase which leads to the loft

7 **La casa que hemos comprado tiene ...**
The house (which) we've bought has ...

Este es el regalo que me ha mandado mi amiga
This is the present (that) my friend has sent to me

8 **la tienda a que siempre va**
the shop (which) she always goes to

9 **las injusticias de que se quejan**
the injustices (that) they're complaining about

10 **la ventana cuyas cortinas están corridas**
the window whose curtains are drawn

❒ Relative Pronouns *(Continued)*

el cual, el que

- These are used when the relative is separated from the word it refers to, or when it would otherwise be unclear which word it referred to. The pronouns always agree in number and gender with the noun → [1]

  El cual may also be used when the verb in the relative clause is separated from the relative pronoun → [2]

lo que, lo cual

- The neuter form **lo** is normally used when referring to an idea, statement or abstract noun. In certain expressions, the form **lo cual** may also be used as the subject of the relative clause → [3]

Relative pronouns after prepositions

- **Que** and **quienes** are generally used after the prepositions:

a	*to*	→	[4]
con	*with*	→	[5]
de	*from, about, of*	→	[6]
en	*in, on, into*	→	[7]

  It should be noted that **en que** can sometimes be translated by:
  — *where.* In this case it can also be replaced by **en donde** or **donde** → [8]
  — *when.* Sometimes here it can be replaced by **cuando** → [9]

- **El que** or **el cual** are used after other prepositions, and they always agree → [10]

Examples

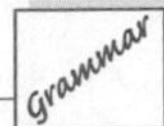

1 **El padre de Elena, el cual tiene mucho dinero, es ...**
Elena's father, who has a lot of money, is ...
(**el cual** is *used here since* **que** *or* **quien** *might equally refer to Elena*)
Su hermana, a la cual/la que hacía mucho que no veía, estaba también allí
His sister, whom I hadn't seen for a long time, was also there

2 **Vieron a su tio, el cual, después de levantarse, salió**
They saw their uncle, who, after having got up, went out

3 **No sabe lo que hace**
He doesn't know what he is doing
Lo que dijiste fue una tontería
What you said was foolish
Todo estaba en silencio, lo que (*or* **lo cual) me pareció muy raro**
All was silent, which I thought most odd

4 **las tiendas a (las) que íbamos**
the shops we used to go to

5 **la chica con quien (***or* **la que) sale**
the girl he's going out with

6 **el libro de(l) que te hablé**
the book I told you about

7 **el lío en (el) que te has metido**
the trouble you've got yourself into

8 **el sitio en que (en donde/donde) se escondía**
the place where he/she was hiding

9 **el año en que naciste**
the year (when) you were born

10 **el puente debajo del que/cual pasa el río**
the bridge under which the river flows
las obras por las cuales/que es famosa
the plays for which she is famous

❐ Relative Pronouns *(Continued)*

el que, la que; los que, las que

These mean *the one(s) who/which, those who* → [1]

⚠ NOTE: **quien(es)** can replace **el que** *etc* when used in a general sense → [2]

todos los que, todas las que

These mean *all who, all those/the ones which* → [3]

todo lo que

This translates *all that, everything that* → [4]

el de, la de; los de, las de

These can mean:

— *the one(s) of, that/those of* → [5]

— *the one(s) with* → [6]

Examples

1 **Esa película es la que quiero ver**
That film is the one I want to see
¿Te acuerdas de ese amigo? El que te presenté ayer
Do you remember that friend? The one I introduced you to yesterday
Los que quieran entrar tendrán que pagar
Those who want to go in will have to pay

2 **Quien** (*or* **el que**) **llegue antes ganará el premio**
He who arrives first will win the prize

3 **Todos los que salían iban de negro**
All those who were coming out were dressed in black
¿Qué autobuses puedo tomar? – Todos los que pasen por aquí
Which buses can I take? – Any (All those) that come this way

4 **Quiero saber todo lo que ha pasado**
I want to know all that has happened

5 **Trae la foto de tu novio y la de tu hermano**
Bring the photo of your boyfriend and the one of your brother
Viajamos en mi coche y en el de María
We travelled in my car and Maria's
Te doy estos libros y también los de mi hermana
I'll give you these books and my sister's too

6 **Tu amigo, el de las gafas, me lo contó**
Your friend, the one with glasses, told me

Interrogative Pronouns

¿qué?	*what?; which?*
¿cuál(es)?	*which?; what?*
¿quién(es)?	*who?*

qué

It always translates *what* → [1]

⚠ NOTE: **por + qué** is normally translated by *why* → [2]

cuál

It normally implies a choice, and translates *which* → [3]

⚠ EXCEPT when no choice is implied or more specific information is required → [4]

⚠ NOTE: Whilst the pronoun **qué** can also work as an adjective, **cuál** only works as a pronoun → [5]

quién

— **quién(es)** (subject or after preposition)	*who*	→ [6]
— **a quién(es)** (object)	*whom*	→ [7]
— **de quién(es)**	*whose*	→ [8]

- All the forms shown above are also used in indirect questions → [9]

Examples

1 **¿Qué estan haciendo?**
What are they doing?
¿Para qué lo quieres?
What do you want it for?
¿Qué dices?
What are you saying?

2 **¿Por qué no llegaron Vds antes?**
Why didn't you arrive earlier?

3 **¿Cuál de estos vestidos te gusta más?**
Which of these dresses do you like best?
¿Cuáles viste?
Which ones did you see?

4 **¿Cuál es la capital de España?**
What is the capital of Spain?
¿Cuál es tu concejo?
What is your advice?
¿Cuál es su fecha de nacimiento?
What is your date of birth?

5 **¿Qué libro es más interesante?**
Which book is more interesting?
¿Cuál (de estos libros) es más interesante?
Which (of these books) is more interesting?

6 **¿Quién ganó la carrera?**
Who won the race?
¿Con quiénes los viste?
Who did you see them with?

7 **¿A quiénes ayudaste?**
Who(m) did you help?
¿A quién se lo diste?
Who did you give it to?

8 **¿De quién es este libro?**
Whose is this book?

9 **Le pregunté para qué lo quería**
I asked him/her what he/she wanted it for
No me dijeron cuáles preferían
They didn't tell me which ones they preferred
No sabía a quién acudir
I didn't know who to turn to

❐ Possessive Pronouns

These are the same as the strong forms of the possessive adjectives, but they are always accompanied by the definite article.

SINGULAR		
MASCULINE	FEMININE	
el mío	**la mía**	*mine*
el tuyo	**la tuya**	*yours* (of **tú**)
el suyo	**la suya**	*his; hers; its; yours* (of **Vd**)
el nuestro	**la nuestra**	*ours*
el vuestro	**la vuestra**	*yours* (of **vosotros**)
el suyo	**la suya**	*theirs; yours* (of **Vds**)

PLURAL		
MASCULINE	FEMININE	
los míos	**las mías**	*mine*
los tuyos	**las tuyas**	*yours* (of **tú**)
los suyos	**las suyas**	*his; hers; its; yours* (of **Vd**)
los nuestros	**las nuestras**	*ours*
los vuestros	**las vuestras**	*yours* (of **vosotros**)
los suyos	**las suyas**	*theirs; yours* (of **Vds**)

- The pronoun agrees in number and gender with the noun it replaces, NOT WITH THE OWNER → [1]

- Alternative translations are *my own, your own,* etc → [2]

- After the prepositions **a** and **de** the article **el** is contracted in the normal way (see p 196)

  a + el mío → al mío → [3]

  de + el mío → del mío → [4]

Examples

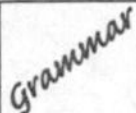

1 **Pregunta a Cristina si este bolígrafo es el suyo**
Ask Christine if this pen is hers
¿Qué equipo ha ganado, el suyo o el nuestro?
Which team won – theirs or ours?
Mi perro es más joven que el tuyo
My dog is younger than yours
Daniel pensó que esos libros eran los suyos
Daniel thought those books were his
Si no tienes discos, te prestaré los míos
If you don't have any records, I'll lend you mine
Las habitaciones son menos amplias que las vuestras
The rooms are smaller than yours

2 **¿Es su familia tan grande como la tuya?**
Is his/her/their family as big as your own?
Sus precios son más bajos que los nuestros
Their prices are lower than our own

3 **¿Por qué prefieres este sombrero al mío?**
Why do you prefer this hat to mine?
Su coche se parece al vuestro
His/her/their car looks like yours

4 **Mi libro está encima del tuyo**
My book is on top of yours
Su padre vive cerca del nuestro
His/her/their father lives near ours

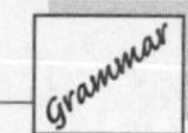

❒ Demonstrative Pronouns

	MASCULINE	FEMININE	NEUTER	
SING	**éste**	**ésta**	**esto**	*this*
	ése	**ésa**	**eso**	*that*
	aquél	**aquélla**	**aquello**	
PLUR	**éstos**	**éstas**		*these*
	ésos	**ésas**		*those*
	aquéllos	**aquéllas**		

- The pronoun agrees in number and gender with the noun it replaces → [1]

- The difference in meaning between the forms **ése** and **aquél** is the same as between the corresponding adjectives (see p 212)

- The masculine and feminine forms have an accent, which is the only thing that differentiates them from the corresponding adjectives.

- The neuter forms always refer to an idea or a statement or to an object when we want to identify it, etc, but never to specified nouns → [2]

- An additional meaning of **aquél** is *the former*, and of **éste** *the latter* → [3]

Examples

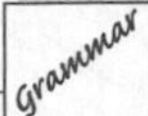

1 **¿Qué abrigo te gusta más? – Este de aquí**
Which coat do you like best? – This one here

Aquella casa era más grande que ésta
That house was bigger than this one

estos libros y aquéllos
these books and those (over there)

Quiero estas sandalias y ésas
I'd like these sandals and those ones

2 **No puedo creer que esto me esté pasando a mí**
I can't believe this is really happening to me

Eso de madrugar es algo que no le gusta
(This business of) getting up early is something she doesn't like

Aquello sí que me gustó
I really did like that

Esto es una bicicleta
This is a bicycle

3 **Hablaban Jaime y Andrés, éste a voces y aquél casi en un susurro**
James and Andrew were talking, the latter in a loud voice and the former almost in a whisper

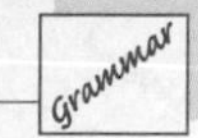

❒ Adverbs

Formation

- Most adverbs are formed by adding **-mente** to the feminine form of the adjective. Accents on the adjective are not affected since the suffix **-mente** is stressed independently → [1]

  ⚠ NOTE: **-mente** is omitted:

  — in the first of two or more of these adverbs when joined by a conjunction → [2]
  — in **recientemente** *recently* when immediately preceding a past participle → [3]
  An accent is then needed on the last syllable (see p 292)

- The following adverbs are formed in an irregular way:

  bueno → **bien**
  good *well*
  malo → **mal**
  bad *badly*

Adjectives used as adverbs

Certain adjectives are used adverbially. These include:
alto, bajo, barato, caro, claro, derecho, fuerte and **rápido** → [4]

⚠ NOTE: Other adjectives used as adverbs agree with the subject, and can normally be replaced by the adverb ending in **-mente** or an adverbial phrase → [5]

Position of Adverbs

- When the adverb accompanies a verb, it may either immediately follow it or precede it for emphasis → [6]

  ⚠ NOTE: The adverb can never be placed between **haber** and the past participle in compound tenses → [7]

- When the adverb accompanies an adjective or another adverb, it generally precedes the adjective or adverb → [8]

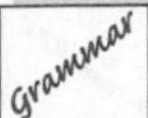

	FEM ADJECTIVE	ADVERB
1	**lenta** slow	**lentamente** slowly
	franca frank	**francamente** frankly
	feliz happy	**felizmente** happily
	fácil easy	**fácilmente** easily

2 **Lo hicieron lenta pero eficazmente**
They did it slowly but efficiently

3 **El pan estaba recién hecho**
The bread had just been baked

4 **hablar alto/bajo**
to speak loudly/softly
costar barato/caro
to be cheap/expensive
ver claro
to see clearly
cortar derecho
to cut (in a) straight (line)
Habla muy fuerte
He talks very loudly
correr rápido
to run fast

5 **Esperaban impacientes** (*or* **impacientemente/con impaciencia**)
They were waiting impatiently
Vivieron muy felices (*or* **muy felizmente**)
They lived very happily

6 **No conocemos aún al nuevo médico**
We still haven't met the new doctor
Aún estoy esperando
I'm still waiting
Han hablado muy bien
They have spoken very well
Siempre le regalaban flores
They always gave her flowers

7 **Lo he hecho ya**
I've already done it
No ha estado nunca en Italia
She's never been to Italy

8 **un sombrero muy bonito**
a very nice hat
mañana temprano
early tomorrow
hablar demasiado alto
to talk too loud
hoy mismo
today

❐ Comparatives and Superlatives

Comparatives

These are formed using the following constructions:

más ... (que)	*more ... (than)*	→ 1
menos ... (que)	*less ... (than)*	→ 2
tanto como	*as much as*	→ 3
tan ... como	*as ... as*	→ 4
tan ... que	*so ... that*	→ 5
demasiado ... para	*too ... to*	→ 6
(lo) bastante ... / **(lo) suficientemente ...** } **para**	*enough to*	→ 7
cada vez más/menos	*more and more/ less and less*	→ 8

Superlatives

- These are formed by placing **más/menos** *the most/the least* before the adverb → 9
- **lo** is added before a superlative which is qualified → 10
- The absolute superlative (*very, most, extremely* + adverb) is formed by placing **muy** before the adverb. The form **-ísimo** (see also p 292) is also occasionally found → 11

Adverbs with irregular comparatives/superlatives

ADVERB	COMPARATIVE	SUPERLATIVE
bien	**mejor***	**(lo) mejor**
well	*better*	*(the) best*
mal	**peor**	**(lo) peor**
badly	*worse*	*(the) worst*
mucho	**más**	**(lo) más**
a lot	*more*	*(the) most*
poco	**menos**	**(lo) menos**
little	*less*	*(the) least*

* **más bien** also exists, meaning *rather* → 12

Examples

1 **más de prisa** more quickly | **más abiertamente** more openly

Mi hermana canta más fuerte que yo
My sister sings louder than me

2 **menos fácilmente** less easily | **menos a menudo** less often

Nos vemos menos frecuentemente que antes
We see each other less frequently than before

3 **Daniel no lee tanto como Andrés**
Daniel doesn't read as much as Andrew

4 **Hágalo tan rápido como le sea posible**
Do it as quickly as you can

Ganan tan poco como nosotros
They earn as little as we do

5 **Llegaron tan pronto que tuvieron que esperarnos**
They arrived so early that they had to wait for us

6 **Es demasiado tarde para ir al cine**
It's too late to go to the cinema

7 **Eres (lo) bastante grande para hacerlo solo**
You're old enough to do it by yourself

8 **Me gusta el campo cada vez más**
I like the countryside more and more

9 **María es la que corre más rápido**
Maria is the one who runs fastest

El que llegó menos tarde fue Miguel
Miguel was the one to arrive the least late

10 **Lo hice lo más de prisa que pude**
I did it as quickly as I could

11 **muy lentamente** very slowly | **tempranísimo** extremely early | **muchísimo** very much

12 **Era un hombre más bien bajito**
He was a rather short man

Estaba más bien inquieta que impaciente
I was restless rather than impatient

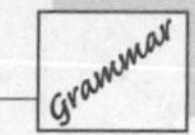

❒ Common Adverbs and their usage

bastante	*enough; quite*	→ 1
bien	*well*	→ 2
cómo	*how*	→ 3
cuánto	*how much*	→ 4
demasiado	*too much; too*	→ 5
más	*more*	→ 6
menos	*less*	→ 7
mucho	*a lot; much*	→ 8
poco	*little, not much; not very*	→ 9
siempre	*always*	→ 10
también	*also, too*	→ 11
tan	*as*	→ 12
tanto	*as much*	→ 13
todavía/aún	*still; yet; even*	→ 14
ya	*already*	→ 15

- **bastante, cuánto, demasiado, mucho, poco** and **tanto** are also used as adjectives that agree with the noun they qualify (see indefinite adjectives, p 220, and interrogative adjectives, p 214)

Examples

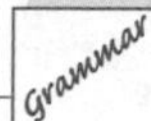

1 **Es bastante tarde**
It's quite late

2 **¡Bien hecho!**
Well done!

3 **¡Cómo me ha gustado!**
How I liked it!

4 **¿Cuánto cuesta este libro?**
How much is this book?

5 **He comido demasiado**
I've eaten too much

Es demasiado caro
It's too expensive

6 **Mi hermano trabaja más ahora**
My brother works more now

Es más tímida que Sofía
She is shyer than Sophie

7 **Se debe beber menos**
One must drink less

Estoy menos sorprendida que tú
I'm less surprised than you are

8 **¿Lees mucho?**
Do you read a lot?

¿Está mucho más lejos?
Is it much further?

9 **Comen poco**
They don't eat (very) much

María es poco decidida
Maria is not very daring

10 **Siempre dicen lo mismo**
They always say the same (thing)

11 **A mí también me gusta**
I like it too

12 **Ana es tan alta como yo**
Ana is as tall as I am

13 **Nos aburrimos tanto como vosotros**
We got as bored as you did

14 **Todavía/aún tengo dos**
I've still got two

Todavía/aún no han llegado
They haven't arrived yet

Mejor aún/todavía
Even better

15 **Ya lo he hecho**
I've done it already

On the following pages you will find some of the most frequent uses of prepositions in Spanish. Particular attention is paid to cases where usage differs markedly from English. It is often difficult to give an English equivalent for Spanish prepositions, since usage *does* vary so much between the two languages. In the list below, the broad meaning of the preposition is given on the left, with examples of usage following. Prepositions are dealt with in alphabetical order, except **a**, **de**, **en** and **por** which are shown first.

a

at	**echar algo a algn**	*to throw sth at sb*
	a un euro el kilo	*(at) one euro a kilo*
	a 100 km por hora	*at 100 km per hour*
	sentarse a la mesa	*to sit down at the table*
in	**al sol**	*in the sun*
	a la sombra	*in the shade*
onto	**cayeron al suelo**	*they fell onto the floor*
	pegar una foto al álbum	*to stick a photo into the album*
to	**ir al cine**	*to go to the cinema*
	dar algo a algn	*to give sth to sb*
	venir a hacer	*to come to do*
from	**quitarle algo a algn**	*to take sth from sb*
	robarle algo a algn	*to steal sth from sb*
	arrebatarle algo a algn	*to snatch sth from sb*
	comprarle algo a algn	*to buy sth from/for sb**
	esconderle algo a algn	*to hide sth from sb*
means	**a mano**	*by hand*
	a caballo	*on horseback* (but note other forms of transport used with **en** and **por**)
	a pie	*on foot*

* The translation here obviously depends on the context.

manner	**a la inglesa**	*in the English manner*
	a pasos lentos	*with slow steps*
	poco a poco	*little by little*
	a ciegas	*blindly*
time, date: *at, on*	**a medianoche**	*at midnight*
	a las dos y cuarto	*at quarter past two*
	a tiempo	*on time*
	a final/fines de mes	*at the end of the month*
	a veces	*at times*
distance	**a 8 km de aquí**	*(at a distance of) 8 kms from here*
	a dos pasos de mi casa	*just a step from my house*
	a lo lejos	*in the distance*
with **el** + infin	**al levantarse**	*on getting up*
	al abrir la puerta	*on opening the door*
after certain adjectives	**dispuesto a todo**	*ready for anything*
	parecido a esto	*similar to this*
	obligado a ello	*obliged to (do) that*
after certain verbs	see p 66	

Personal a

When the direct object of a verb is a person or pet animal, **a** must always be placed immediately before it.

EXAMPLES: **querían mucho a sus hijos**
they loved their children dearly
el niño miraba a su perro con asombro
the boy kept looking at his dog in astonishment

⚠ EXCEPTION: **tener** *to have* — **tienen dos hijos** *they have two children*

de

from	**venir de Londres**	*to come from London*
	un médico de Valencia	*a doctor from Valencia*
	de la mañana a la noche	*from morning till night*
	de 10 a 15	*from 10 to 15*
belonging to, of	**el sombrero de mi padre**	*my father's hat*
	las lluvias de abril	*April showers*
contents, composition, material	**una caja de cerillas**	*a box of matches*
	una taza de té	*a cup of tea; a tea-cup*
	un vestido de seda	*a silk dress*
destined for	**una silla de cocina**	*a kitchen chair*
	un traje de noche	*an evening dress*
descriptive	**la mujer del sombrero verde**	*the woman with the green hat*
	el vecino de al lad/lado	*the next door neighbour*
manner	**de manera irregular**	*in an irregular way*
	de una puñalada	*by stabbing*
quality	**una mujer de edad**	*an aged lady*
	objetos de valor	*valuable items*
comparative + number	**había más/menos de 100 personas**	*there were more/fewer than 100 people*
after superlatives: *in*	**la ciudad más/menos bonita del mundo**	*the most/least beautiful city in the world*
after certain adjectives	**contento de ver**	*pleased to see*
	fácil/difícil de entender	*easy/difficult to understand*
	capaz de hacer	*capable of doing*
after certain verbs	see p 66	

en

in, at	**en el campo**	*in the country*
	en Londres	*in London*
	en la cama	*in bed*
	con un libro en la mano	*with a book in his hand*
	en voz baja	*in a low voice*
	en la escuela	*in/at school*
into	**entra en la casa**	*go into the house*
	metió la mano en su bolso	*she put her hand into her handbag*
on	**un cuadro en la pared**	*a picture on the wall*
	sentado en una silla	*sitting on a chair*
	en la planta baja	*on the ground floor*
time, dates, months: *at, in*	**en este momento**	*at this moment*
	en 1994	*in 1994*
	en enero	*in January*
transport: *by*	**en coche**	*by car*
	en avión	*by plane*
	en tren	*by train* (but see also **por**)
language	**en español**	*in Spanish*
duration	**lo haré en una semana**	*I'll do it in one week*
after certain adjectives	**es muy buena/mala en geografía**	*she is very good/bad at geography*
	fueron los primeros/ últimos/únicos en + infin	*they were the first/ last/only ones* + infin
after certain verbs	see p 66	

por

motion: *along, through, around*	**vaya por ese camino** **por el túnel** **pasear por el campo**	*go along that path* *through the tunnel* *to walk around the countryside*
vague location	**tiene que estar por aquí** **le busqué por todas partes**	*it's got to be somewhere around here* *I looked for him everywhere*
vague time	**por la tarde** **por aquellos días**	*in the afternoon* *in those days*
rate	**90 km por hora** **un cinco por ciento** **ganaron por 3 a 0**	*90 km per hour* *five per cent* *they won by 3 to 0*
agent of passive: *by*	**descubierto por unos niños** **odiado por sus enemigos**	*discovered by some children* *hated by his enemies*
by (means of)	**por barco** **por tren** **por correo aéreo** **llamar por teléfono**	*by boat* *by train (freight)* *by airmail* *to telephone*
cause, reason: *for, because*	**¿por qué?** **por todo eso** **por lo que he oído**	*why?, for what reason?* *because of all that* *judging by what I've heard*
+ infinitive: *to*	**libros por leer** **cuentas por pagar**	*books to be read* *bills to be paid*
equivalence	**¿me tienes por tonto?**	*do you think I'm stupid?*

+ adjective/ + adverb + **que**: *however*	**por buenos que sean**	*however good they are*
	por mucho que lo quieras	*however much you want it*
for	**¿cuanto me darán por este libro?**	*how much will they give me for this book?*
	te lo cambio por éste	*I'll swap you this one for it*
	no siento nada por ti	*I feel nothing for you*
	si no fuera por ti	*if it weren't for you*
	¡Por Dios!	*For God's sake!*
for the benefit of	**lo hago por ellos**	*I do it for their benefit*
on behalf of	**firma por mí**	*sign on my behalf*

por also combines with other prepositions to form double prepositions usually conveying the idea of movement. The commonest of these are:

over	**saltó por encima de la mesa**	*she jumped over the table*
under	**nadamos por debajo del puente**	*we swam under the bridge*
past	**pasaron por delante de Correos**	*they went past the post office*
behind	**por detrás de la puerta**	*behind the door*
through	**la luz entraba por entre las cortinas**	*light was coming in through the curtains*
+ donde	**¿por dónde has venido?**	*which way did you come?*

ante

faced with, before	**lo hicieron ante mis propios ojos**	*they did it before my very eyes*
	ante eso no se puede hacer nada	*one can't do anything when faced with that*
preference	**la salud ante todo**	*health above all things*

antes de

before (time)	**antes de las 5**	*before 5 o'clock*

bajo/debajo de

These are usually equivalent, although **bajo** is used more frequently in a figurative sense and with temperatures.

under	**bajo/debajo de la cama**	*under the bed*
	bajo el dominio romano	*under Roman rule*
below	**un grado bajo cero**	*one degree below zero*

con

with	**vino con su amigo**	*she came with her friend*
after certain adjectives	**enfadado con ellos**	*angry with them*
	magnánimo con sus súbditos	*magnanimous with his subjects*

contra

against	**no tengo nada contra ti**	*I've nothing against you*
	apoyado contra la pared	*leaning against the wall*

delante de

in front of	**iba delante de mí**	*she was walking in front of me*

desde

from	**desde aquí se puede ver**	*you can see it from here*
	llamaban desde España	*they were phoning from Spain*
	desde otro punto de vista	*from a different point of view*
	desde la 1 hasta las 6	*from 1 till 6*
	desde entonces	*from then onwards*
since	**desde que volvieron**	*since they returned*
for	**viven en esa casa desde hace 3 años**	*they've been living in that house for 3 years* ⚠ (NOTE TENSE)

detrás de

behind	**están detrás de la puerta**	*they are behind the door*

durante

during	**durante la guerra**	*during the war*
for	**anduvieron durante 3 días**	*they walked for 3 days*

entre

between	**entre 8 y 10**	*between 8 and 10*
among	**María y Elena, entre otras**	*Maria and Elena, among others*
reciprocal	**ayudarse entre sí**	*to help each other*

excepto

except (for)	**todos excepto tú**	*everybody except you*

hacia

towards	**van hacia ese edificio**	*they're going towards that building*
around (time)	**hacia las 3**	*at around 3 (o'clock)*
	hacia fines de enero	*around the end of January*

Hacia can also combine with some adverbs to convey a sense of motion in a particular direction:

hacia arriba	*upwards*
hacia abajo	*downwards*
hacia adelante	*forwards*
hacia atrás	*backwards*
hacia adentro	*inwards*
hacia afuera	*outwards*

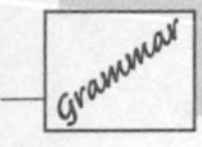

hasta

until	**hasta la noche**	*until night*
as far as	**viajaron hasta Sevilla**	*they travelled as far as Seville*
up to	**conté hasta 300 ovejas**	*I counted up to 300 lambs*
	hasta ahora no los había visto	*up to now I hadn't seen them*
even	**hasta un tonto lo entendería**	*even an imbecile would understand that*

para

for	**es para ti**	*it's for you*
	es para mañana	*it's for tomorrow*
	una habitación para dos noches	*a room for two nights*
	para ser un niño, lo hace muy bien	*for a child he is very good at it*
	salen para Cádiz	*they are leaving for Cádiz*
	se conserva muy bien para sus años	*he keeps very well for his age*
+ infin: *(in order) to*	**es demasiado torpe para comprenderlo**	*he's too stupid to understand*
+ **sí**: *to oneself*	**hablar para sí**	*to talk to oneself*
	reír para sí	*to laugh to oneself*
with time	**todavía tengo para 1 hora**	*I'll be another hour (at it) yet*

salvo

except (for)	**todos salvo él**	*all except him*
	salvo cuando llueve	*except when it's raining*
barring	**salvo imprevistos**	*barring the unexpected*
	salvo contraorden	*unless you hear to the contrary*

según

according to	**según su consejo**	*according to her advice*
	según lo que me dijiste	*according to what you told me*

sin

without	**sin agua/dinero**	*without water/money*
	sin mi marido	*without my husband*
+ infinitive	**sin contar a los otros**	*without counting the others*

sobre

on	**sobre la cama**	*on the bed*
	sobre el armario	*on (top of) the wardrobe*
on (to)	**póngalo sobre la mesa**	*put it on the table*
about, on	**un libro sobre Eva Perón**	*a book about Eva Perón*
above, over	**volábamos sobre el mar**	*we were flying over the sea*
	la nube sobre aquella montaña	*the cloud above that mountain*
approximately	**vendré sobre las 4**	*I'll come about 4 o'clock*
about	**Madrid tiene sobre 4 millones de habitantes**	*Madrid has about 4 million inhabitants*

tras

behind	**está tras el asiento**	*it's behind the seat*
after	**uno tras otro**	*one after another*
	día tras día	*day after day*
	corrieron tras el ladrón	*they ran after the thief*

❒ Conjunctions

There are conjunctions which introduce a main clause, such as **y** *and*, **pero** *but*, **si** *if*, **o** *or* etc, and those which introduce subordinate clauses like **porque** *because*, **mientras que** *while*, **después de que** *after* etc. They are used in much the same way as in English, but the following points are of note:

- Some conjunctions in Spanish require a following subjunctive, see pp 60 to 63.
- Some conjunctions are 'split' in Spanish like *both ... and, either ... or* in English:

tanto ... como	*both ... and*	→ 1
ni ... ni	*neither ... nor*	→ 2
o (bien) ... o (bien)	*either ... or (else)*	→ 3
sea ... sea	*either ... or, whether ... or*	→ 4

- **y**

  — Before words beginning with **i-** or **hi-** + consonant it becomes **e** → 5

- **o**

  — Before words beginning with **o-** or **ho-** it becomes **u** → 6
  — Between numerals it becomes **ó** → 7

- **que**

  — meaning *that* → 8
  — in comparisons, meaning *than* → 9
  — followed by the subjunctive, see p 58.

- **porque** (Not to be confused with **por qué** *why*)

  — **como** should be used instead at the beginning of a sentence → 10

- **pero, sino**

  — **pero** normally translates *but* → 11

  — **sino** is used when there is a direct contrast after a negative → 12

Examples

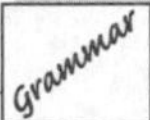

1 **Estas flores crecen tanto en verano como en invierno**
These flowers grow in both summer and winter

2 **Ni él ni ella vinieron**
Neither he nor she came
No tengo ni dinero ni comida
I have neither money nor food

3 **Debe de ser o ingenua o tonta**
She must be either naïve or stupid
O bien me huyen o bien no me reconocen
Either they're avoiding me or else they don't recognize me

4 **Sea en verano, sea en invierno, siempre me gusta andar**
I always like walking, whether in summer or in winter

5 **Diana e Isabel**
Diana and Isabel
madre e hija BUT: **árboles y hierba**
mother and daughter — trees and grass

6 **diez u once** — **minutos u horas**
ten or eleven — minutes or hours

7 **37 ó 38**
37 or 38

8 **Dicen que te han visto**
They say (that) they've seen you
¿Sabías que estábamos allí?
Did you know that we were there?

9 **Le gustan más que nunca**
He likes them more than ever
María es menos guapa que su hermana
Maria is less attractive than her sister

10 **Como estaba lloviendo no pudimos salir**
Because/As it was raining we couldn't go out
(Compare with: **No pudimos salir porque estaba lloviendo**)

11 **Me gustaría ir, pero estoy muy cansada**
I'd like to go, but I am very tired

12 **No es escocesa sino irlandesa**
She is not Scottish but Irish

❐ Augmentative, diminutive and pejorative suffixes

These can be used after nouns, adjectives and some adverbs. They are attached to the end of the word after any final vowel has been removed

e.g. **puerta → puertita**
doctor → doctorcito

⚠ NOTE: Further changes sometimes take place (see p 296).

Augmentatives

These are used mainly to imply largeness, but they can also suggest clumsiness, ugliness or grotesqueness. The commonest augmentatives are:

ón/ona → [1]
azo/a → [2]
ote/a → [3]

Diminutives

These are used mainly to suggest smallness or to express a feeling of affection. Occasionally they can be used to express ridicule or contempt. The commonest diminutives are:

ito/a → [4]
(e)cito/a → [5]
(ec)illo/a → [6]
(z)uelo/a → [7]

Pejoratives

These are used to convey the idea that something is unpleasant or to express contempt. The commonest suffixes are:

ucho/a → [8]
acho/a → [9]
uzo/a → [10]
uco/a → [11]
astro/a → [12]

	ORIGINAL WORD	DERIVED FORM
1	**un hombre** a man	**un hombrón** a big man
2	**bueno** good	**buenazo** (person) easily imposed on
	un perro a dog	**un perrazo** a really big dog
	gripe flu	**un gripazo** a really bad bout of flu
3	**grande** big	**grandote** huge
	palabra word	**palabrota** swear word
	amigo friend	**amigote** old pal
4	**una casa** a house	**una casita** a cottage
	un poco a little	**un poquito** a little bit
	un rato a while	**un ratito** a little while
	mi hija my daughter	**mi hijita** my dear sweet daughter
	despacio slowly	**despacito** nice and slowly
5	**un viejo** an old man	**un viejecito** a little old man
	un pueblo a village	**un pueblecito** a small village
	una voz a voice	**una vocecita** a sweet little voice
6	**una ventana** a window	**una ventanilla** a small window (car, train etc)
	un chico a boy	**un chiquillo** a small boy
	una campana a bell	**una campanilla** a small bell
	un palo a stick	**un palillo** a toothpick
	un médico a doctor	**un mediquillo** a quack (doctor)
7	**los pollos** the chickens	**los polluelos** the little chicks
	hoyos hollows	**hoyuelos** dimples
	un ladrón a thief	**un ladronzuelo** a petty thief
	una mujer a woman	**una mujerzuela** a whore
8	**un animal** an animal	**un animalucho** a wretched animal
	un cuarto a room	**un cuartucho** a poky little room
	una casa a house	**una casucha** a shack
9	**rico** rich	**ricacho** nouveau riche
10	**gente** people	**gentuza** scum
11	**una ventana** a window	**un ventanuco** a miserable little window
12	**un político** a politician	**un politicastro** a third-rate politician

❐ Word order

Word order in Spanish is much more flexible than in English. You can often find the subject placed after the verb or the object before the verb, either for emphasis or for stylistic reasons → [1]

There are some cases, however, where the order is always different from English. Most of these have already been dealt with under the appropriate part of speech, but are summarized here along with other instances not covered elsewhere.

- Object pronouns nearly always come before the verb → [2]
  For details, see pp 228 to 231.

- Qualifying adjectives nearly always come after the noun → [3]
  For details, see p 224.

- Following direct speech the subject always follows the verb → [4]

For word order in negative sentences, see p 272.

For word order in interrogative sentences, see p 276.

1 **Ese libro te lo di yo**
I gave you that book
No nos vio nadie
Nobody saw us

2 **Ya los veo**
I can see them now

Me lo dieron ayer
They gave it to me yesterday

3 **una ciudad española**
a Spanish town

vino tinto
red wine

4 **– Pienso que sí – dijo María**
'I think so,' said Maria
– No importa – replicó Daniel
'It doesn't matter,' Daniel replied

❐ Negatives

A sentence is made negative by adding **no** between the subject and the verb (and any preceding object pronouns) → [1]

There are, however, some points to note:

— in phrases like *not her, not now,* etc the Spanish **no** usually comes after the word it qualifies → [2]

— with verbs of saying, hoping, thinking etc *not* is translated by **que no** → [3]

Double negatives

no ... nada	*nothing*	*(not ... anything)*
no ... nadie	*nobody*	*(not ... anybody)*
no ... más	*no longer*	*(not ... any more)*
no ... nunca	*never*	*(not ... ever)*
no ... jamás	*never* (stronger)	*(not ... ever)*
no ... más que	*only*	*(not ... more than)*
no ... ningún(o)(a)	*no*	*(not any)*
no ... tampoco	*not ... either*	
no ... ni ... ni	*neither ... nor*	
no ... ni siquiera	*not even*	

Word order

- **No** precedes the verb (and any object pronouns) in both simple and compound tenses, and the second element follows the verb → [4]

- Sometimes the above negatives are placed before the verb (with the exception of **más** and **más que**), and **no** is then dropped → [5]

- For use of **nada, nadie** and **ninguno** as pronouns, see p 236.

Examples

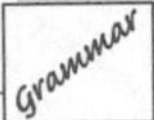

	AFFIRMATIVE		NEGATIVE
1	**El coche es suyo**	→	**El coche no es suyo**
	The car is his		The car is not his
	Yo me lo pondré	→	**Yo no me lo pondré**
	I will put it on		I will not put it on

2 **¿Quién lo ha hecho? – Ella no**
Who did it? – Not her
¿Quieres un cigarrillo? – Ahora no
Do you want a cigarette? – Not now
Dame ese libro, el que está a tu lado no, el otro
Give me that book, not the one near you, the other one

3 **Opino que no** — **Dijeron que no**
I think not — They said not

4 **No dicen nada**
They don't say anything
No han visto a nadie
They haven't seen anybody
No me veréis más
You won't see me any more
No te olvidaré nunca/jamás
I'll never forget you
No habían recorrido más que 40 kms cuando …
They hadn't travelled more than 40 kms when …
No se me ha ocurrido ninguna idea
I haven't had any ideas
No les estaban esperando ni mi hijo ni mi hija
Neither my son nor my daughter were waiting for them
No ha venido ni siquiera Juan
Even John hasn't come

5 **Nadie ha venido hoy**
Nobody came today
Nunca me han gustado
I've never liked them
Ni mi hermano ni mi hermana fuman
Neither my brother nor my sister smokes

❐ Negatives *(Continued)*

Negatives in short replies

- **No**, *no* is the usual negative response to a question → 1

⚠ NOTE: It is often translated as *not* → 2
(see also p 272).

- Nearly all the other negatives listed on p 272 may be used without a verb in a short reply → 3

Combinations of negatives

These are the most common combinations of negative particles:

no ... nunca más	→ 4
no ... nunca a nadie	→ 5
no ... nunca nada/nada nunca	→ 6
no ... nunca más que	→ 7
no ... ni ... nunca	→ 8

Examples

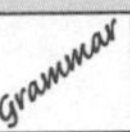

1 **¿Quieres venir con nosotros? – No**
Do you want to come with us? – No

2 **¿Vienes o no?**
Are you coming or not?

3 **¿Ha venido alguien? – ¡Nadie!**
Has anyone come? – Nobody!
¿Has ido al Japón alguna vez? – Nunca
Have you ever been to Japan? – Never

4 **No lo haré nunca más**
I'll never do it again

5 **No se ve nunca a nadie por allí**
You never see anybody around there

6 **No cambiaron nada nunca**
They never changed anything

7 **No he hablado nunca más que con su mujer**
I've only ever spoken to his wife

8 **No me ha escrito ni llamado por teléfono nunca**
He/she has never written to me or phoned me

❒ Question forms

Direct

There are two ways of forming direct questions in Spanish:

- by inverting the normal word order so that

  subject + verb → *verb + subject* → [1]

- by maintaining the word order *subject + verb,* but by using a rising intonation at the end of the sentence → [2]

⚠ NOTE: In compound tenses the auxiliary may never be separated from the past participle, as happens in English → [3]

Indirect

An indirect question is one that is 'reported', e.g. he asked me *what the time was,* tell me *which way to go.* Word order in indirect questions can adopt one of the two following patterns:

- interrogative word + subject + verb → [4]
- interrogative word + verb + subject → [5]

¿verdad?, ¿no?

These are used wherever English would use *isn't it?, don't they?, weren't we?, is it?* etc tagged on to the end of a sentence → [6]

sí

Sí is the word for *yes* in answer to a question put either in the affirmative or in the negative → [7]

Examples

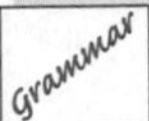

1 **¿Vendrá tu madre?**
Will your mother come?
¿Es posible eso?
Is it possible?
¿Lo trajo Vd?
Did you bring it?
¿Cuándo volverán Vds?
When will you come back?

2 **El gato, ¿se bebió toda la leche?**
Did the cat drink up all his milk?
Andrés, ¿va a venir?
Is Andrew coming?

3 **¿Lo ha terminado Vd?**
Have you finished it?
¿Había llegado tu amigo?
Had your friend arrived?

4 **Dime qué autobuses pasan por aquí**
Tell me which buses come this way
No sé cuántas personas vendrán
I don't know how many people will turn up

5 **Me preguntó dónde trabajaba mi hermano**
He asked me where my brother worked
No sabemos a qué hora empieza la película
We don't know what time the film starts

6 **Hace calor, ¿verdad?**
It's warm, isn't it?
No se olvidará Vd, ¿verdad?
You won't forget, will you?
Estaréis cansados, ¿no?
You will be tired, won't you?
Te lo dijo María, ¿no?
Maria told you, didn't she?

7 **¿Lo has hecho? – Sí**
Have you done it? – Yes (I have)
¿No lo has hecho? – Sí
Haven't you done it? – Yes (I have)

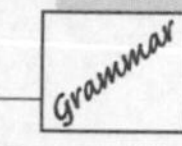

TRANSLATION PROBLEMS

Beware of translating word by word. While on occasions this is quite possible, quite often it is not. The need for caution is illustrated by the following:

- English phrasal verbs (i.e. verbs followed by a preposition), e.g. *to run away, to fall down*, are often translated by one word in Spanish → 1
- English verbal constructions often contain a preposition where none exists in Spanish, or vice versa → 2
- Two or more prepositions in English may have a single rendering in Spanish → 3
- A word which is singular in English may be plural in Spanish, or vice versa → 4
- Spanish has no equivalent of the possessive construction denoted by ...'s/...s' → 5

❐ Specific problems

-ing

This is translated in a variety of ways in Spanish:

- *to be ... -ing* can sometimes be translated by a simple tense (see also pp 54 to 56) → 6

  But, when a physical position is denoted, a past participle is used → 7
- in the construction *to see/hear sb ... -ing*, use an infinitive → 8

  -ing can also be translated by:

  — an infinitive → 9
  (see p 46)

  — a perfect infinitive → 10
  (see p 50)

  — a gerund → 11
  (see p 52)

  — a noun → 12

1	**huir** to run away	**caerse** to fall down	**ceder** to give in
2	**pagar** to pay for **encontrarse con** to meet	**mirar** to look at **fijarse en** to notice	**escuchar** to listen to **servirse de** to use
3	**extrañarse de** to be surprised at **soñar con** to dream of	**harto de** fed up with **contar con** to count on	
4	**unas vacaciones** a holiday **la gente** people	**sus cabellos** his/her hair **mi pantalón** my trousers	
5	**el coche de mi hermano** my brother's car *(literally: … of my brother)*	**el cuarto de las niñas** the children's bedroom *(literally: … of the children)*	
6	**Se va mañana** He/she is leaving tomorrow	**¿Qué haces?** What are you doing?	
7	**Está sentado ahí** He is sitting over there	**Estaba tendida en el suelo** She was lying on the ground	
8	**Les veo venir** I can see them coming	**La he oído cantar** I've heard her singing	
9	**Me gusta ir al cine** I like going to the cinema **En vez de contestar** Instead of answering	**¡Deja de hablar!** Stop talking! **Antes de salir** Before leaving	
10	**Después de haber abierto la caja, María …** After opening the box, Maria …		
11	**Pasamos la tarde fumando y charlando** We spent the afternoon smoking and chatting		
12	**El esquí me mantiene en forma** Skiing keeps me fit		

to be

(See also **Verbal Idioms**, pp 74 to 76)

- In set expressions, describing physical and emotional conditions, **tener** is used:

tener calor/frío	*to be warm/cold*
tener hambre/sed	*to be hungry/thirsty*
tener miedo	*to be afraid*
tener razón	*to be right*

- Describing the weather, e.g. *what's the weather like?, it's windy/ sunny,* use **hacer** → 1
- For ages, e.g. *he is 6,* use **tener** (see also p 306) → 2

there is/there are

- Both are translated by **hay** → 3

can, be able

- Physical ability is expressed by **poder** → 4
- If the meaning is *to know how to,* use **saber** → 5
- *Can* + a 'verb of hearing or seeing etc' in English is not translated in Spanish → 6

to

- Generally translated by **a** → 7
- In time expressions, e.g. *10 to 6,* use **menos** → 8
- When the meaning is *in order to,* use **para** → 9
- Following a verb, as in *to try to do, to like to do,* see pp 46 and 48.
- *easy/difficult/impossible* etc *to do* are translated by **fácil/difícil/ imposible** etc **de hacer** → 10

Examples

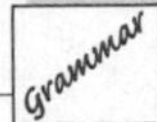

1 **¿Qué tiempo hace?**
What's the weather like?

Hace bueno/malo/viento
It's lovely/miserable/windy

2 **¿Cuántos años tienes?**
How old are you?

Tengo quince (años)
I'm fifteen

3 **Hay un señor en la puerta**
There's a gentleman at the door
Hay cinco libros en la mesa
There are five books on the table

4 **No puedo salir contigo**
I can't go out with you

5 **¿Sabes nadar?**
Can you swim?

6 **No veo nada**
I can't see anything

¿Es que no me oyes?
Can't you hear me?

7 **Dale el libro a Isabel**
Give the book to Isabel

8 **las diez menos cinco**
five to ten

a las siete menos cuarto
at a quarter to seven

9 **Lo hice para ayudaros**
I did it to help you
Se inclinó para atarse el cordón de zapato
He bent down to tie his shoelace

10 **Este libro es fácil/difícil de leer**
This book is easy/difficult to read

must

- When *must* expresses an assumption, **deber de** is often used → [1]

  ⚠ NOTE: This meaning is also often expressed by **deber** directly followed by the infinitive → [2]

- When it expresses obligation, there are three possible translations:

  — **tener que** → [3]
  — **deber** → [4]
  — **hay que** (impersonal) → [5]

may

- If *may* expresses possibility, it can be translated by:

  — **poder**
  — **puede (ser) que** + subjunctive } → [6]

- To express permission, use **poder** → [7]

will

- If *will* expresses willingness or desire rather than the future, the present tense of **querer** is used → [8]

would

- If *would* expresses willingness, use the preterite or imperfect of **querer** → [9]
- When a repeated or habitual action in the past is referred to, use

  — the imperfect → [10]

  — the imperfect of **soler** + infinitive → [11]

Examples

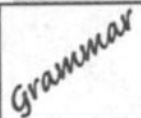

1 **Ha debido de mentir**
He must have lied
Debe de gustarle
She must like it

2 **Debe estar por aquí cerca**
It must be near here
Debo haberlo dejado en el tren
I must have left it on the train

3 **Tenemos que salir temprano mañana**
We must leave early tomorrow
Tengo que irme
I must go

4 **Debo visitarles**
I must visit them
Debéis escuchar lo que se os dice
You must listen to what is said to you

5 **Hay que entrar por ese lado**
One (We *etc*) must get in that way

6 **Todavía puede cambiar de opinión**
He may still change his mind
Creo que puede llover esta tarde
I think it may rain this afternoon
Puede (ser) que no lo sepa
She may not know

7 **¿Puedo irme?**
May I go?
Puede sentarse
You may sit down

8 **Quiere Vd esperar un momento, por favor?**
Will you wait a moment, please?
No quiere ayudarme
He won't help me

9 **No quisieron venir**
They wouldn't come

10 **Las miraba hora tras hora**
She would watch them for hours on end

11 **Últimamente solía comer muy poco**
Latterly he would eat very little

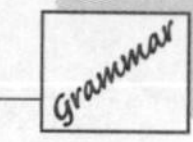

PRONUNCIATION

❐ Pronunciation of Vowels

Spanish vowels are always clearly pronounced and not relaxed in unstressed syllables as happens in English.

	EXAMPLES	HINTS ON PRONUNCIATION
[a]	casa	Between English *a* as in *hat* and *u* as in *hut*
[e]	pensar	Similar to English *e* in *pet*
[i]	filo	Between English *i* as in *pin* and *ee* as in *been*
[o]	loco	Similar to English *o* in *hot*
[u]	luna	Between English *ew* as in *few* and *u* as in *put*

❐ Pronunciation of Diphthongs

All these diphthongs are shorter than similar English diphthongs.

[ai]	b**ai**le, h**ay**	Like *i* in *side*
[au]	c**au**sa	Like *ou* in *sound*
[ei]	p**ei**ne, r**ey**	Like *ey* in *grey*
[eu]	d**eu**da	Like the vowel sounds in English *may you*, but without the sound of the *y*
[oi]	b**oi**na, v**oy**	Like *oy* in *boy*

❐ Semi-consonants

[j]	hac**i**a, **y**a t**i**ene, **y**eso lab**i**o, **y**o	**i** following a consonant and preceding a vowel, and **y** preceding a vowel are pronounced as *y* in English *yet*
[w]	ag**u**a, b**u**eno ard**u**o, r**u**ido	**u** following a consonant and preceding a vowel is pronounced as *w* in English *walk*

⚠ EXCEPTIONS: **gue, gui** (see p 286)

❐ Pronunciation of Consonants

Some consonants are pronounced almost exactly as in English: [l, m, n, f, k, and in some cases g].

Others, listed below, are similar to English, but differences should be noted.

	EXAMPLES	
[p]	**p**adre	They are not aspirated, unlike English *p*ot, *c*ook and *t*en.
[k]	**c**o**c**o	
[t]	**t**an	
[t]	**t**odo, **t**ú	Pronounced with the tip of the tongue touching the upper front teeth and not the roof of the mouth as in English.
[d]	**d**oy, bal**d**e	

The following consonants are not heard in English:

	EXAMPLES	
[β]	la**b**io	This is pronounced between upper and lower lips, which do not touch, unlike English *b* as in *b*end.
[ɣ]	ha**g**a	Similar to English *g* as in *g*ate, but tongue does not touch the soft palate.
[ɲ]	a**ñ**o	Similar to *ni* in o*ni*on
[x]	**j**ota	Like the guttural *ch* in lo*ch*
[r]	pe**r**a	A single trill with the tip of the tongue against the teeth ridge.
[rr]	**r**ojo, pe**rr**o	A multiple trill with the tip of the tongue against the teeth ridge.

❒ From spelling to sounds

Note the pronunciation of the following (groups of) letters.

LETTER	PRONOUNCED	
b, v	[b]	These letters have the same value. At the start of a breath group, and after written **m** and **n**, the sound is similar to English *b*oy → [1]
	[β]	in all other positions, the sound is unknown in English (see p 285) → [2]
c	[k]	Before **a, o, u** or a consonant, like English *k*eep, but not aspirated → [3]
	[θ/s]	Before **e, i** like English *th*in, or, in Latin America and parts of Spain, like English *s*ame → [4]
ch	[tʃ]	Like English *ch*urch → [5]
d	[d]	At the start of the breath group and after **l** or **n**, it is pronounced similar to English *d*eep (see p 285) → [6]
	[ð]	Between vowels and after consonants (except **l** or **n**), it is pronounced very like English *th*ough → [7]
	[(ð)]	At the end of words, and in the verb ending **-ado**, it is often not pronounced → [8]
g	[x]	Before **e, i,** pronounced gutturally, similar to English lo*ch* → [9]
	[g]	At the start of the breath group and after **n,** it is pronounced like English *g*et → [10]
	[ɣ]	In other positions the sound is unknown in English → [11]
gue	[ge/ɣe]	The **u** is silent → [12]
gui	[gi/ɣi]	
güe	[gwe/ɣwe]	The **u** is pronounced like English *w*alk → [13]
güi	[gwi/ɣwi]	

Examples

1	**bomba** ['bomba]	**voy** [boi]	**vicio** ['biθjo]
2	**hubo** ['uβo]	**de veras** [de 'βeras]	**lavar** [la'βar]
3	**casa** ['kasa]	**coco** ['koko]	**cumbre** ['kumbre]
4	**cero** ['θero/'sero]	**cinco** ['θiŋko/'siŋko]	
5	**mucho** ['mutʃo]	**chuchería** [tʃutʃe'ria]	
6	**doy** [doi]	**balde** ['balde]	**bondad** [bon'dað]
7	**modo** ['moðo]	**ideal** [iðe'al]	
8	**Madrid** [ma'ðri(ð)]	**comprado** [kom'pra(ð)o]	
9	**gente** ['xente]	**giro** ['xiro]	**general** [xene'ral]
10	**ganar** [ga'nar]	**pongo** ['poŋgo]	
11	**agua** ['aɣwa]	**agrícola** [a'ɣrikola]	
12	**guija** ['gixa]	**guerra** ['gerra]	**pague** ['paɣe]
13	**agüero** [a'ɣwero]	**argüir** [ar'ɣwir]	

❐ From spelling to sounds *(Continued)*

h	[-]	This is always silent → 1
j	[x]	Like the guttural sound in English lo*ch*, but often aspirated at the end of a word → 2
ll	[ʎ]	Similar to English *-lli-* in mi*lli*on → 3
	[j/ʒ]	In some parts of Spain and in Latin America, like English *y*et or plea*s*ure → 4
-nv-	[mb]	This combination of letters is pronounced as in English *imb*ibe → 5
ñ	[ɲ]	As in English o*ni*on → 6
q	[k]	Always followed by silent letter **u**, and pronounced as in English *k*eep, but not aspirated → 7
s	[s]	Except where mentioned below, like English *s*ing → 8
	[z]	When followed by **b, d, g, l, m, n** like English *z*oo → 9
w	[w]	Like English *v*, *w* → 10
x	[ks]	Between vowels, often like English e*x*it → 11
	[s]	Before a consonant, and, increasingly, even between vowels, like English *s*end → 12
y	[j]	Like English *y*es → 13
	[ʒ]	In some parts of Latin America, like English lei*s*ure → 14
z	[θ]	Like English *th*in → 15
	[s]	In some parts of Spain and in Latin America, like English *s*end → 16

1	**hombre** ['ombre]	**hoja** ['oxa]	**ahorrar** [ao'rrar]
2	**jota** ['xota]	**tejer** [te'xer]	**reloj** [re'lo(h)]
3	**calle** ['kaʎe]	**llamar** [ʎa'mar]	
4	**pillar** [pi'jar/pi'ʒar]	**olla** ['oja/'oʒa]	
5	**enviar** [em'bjar]	**sin valor** ['sim ba'lor]	
6	**uña** ['uɲa]	**bañar** [ba'ɲar]	
7	**aquel** [a'kel]	**querer** [ke'rer]	
8	**está** [es'ta]	**serio** ['serjo]	
9	**desde** ['dezðe]	**mismo** ['mizmo]	**asno** ['azno]
10	**wáter** ['bater]	**Walkman®** [wak'man]	
11	**éxito** ['eksito]	**máximo** ['maksimo]	
12	**extra** ['estra]	**sexto** ['sesto]	
13	**yo** [jo]	**yedra** ['jeðra]	
14	**yeso** ['ʒeso]	**yerno** ['ʒerno]	
15	**zapato** [θa'pato]	**zona** ['θona]	**luz** [luθ]
16	**zaguán** [sa'ɣwan]	**zueco** ['sweko]	**pez** [pes]

❐ Normal Word Stress

There are simple rules to establish which syllable in a Spanish word is stressed. When an exception to these rules occurs an acute accent (stress-mark) is needed (see p 292). These rules are as follows:

— words ending in a vowel or combination of vowels, or with the consonants **-s** or **-n** are stressed on the next to last syllable. The great majority of Spanish words fall into this category → [1]

— words ending in a consonant other than **-s** or **-n** bear the stress on the last syllable → [2]

— a minority of words bear the stress on the second to last syllable, and these always need an accent → [3]

— some nouns change their stress from singular to plural → [4]

❐ Stress in diphthongs

In the case of diphthongs there are rules to establish which of the vowels is stressed (see p 284 for pronunciation). These rules are as follows:

— diphthongs formed by the combination of a 'weak' vowel (**i**, **u**) and a 'strong' vowel (**a**, **e** or **o**) bear the stress on the strong vowel → [5]

— diphthongs formed by the combination of two 'weak' vowels bear the stress on the second vowel → [6]

⚠ NOTE: Two 'strong' vowels don't form a diphthong but are pronounced as two separate vowels. In these cases stress follows the normal rules → [7]

1	**ca***sa*	**ca***sas*
	house	houses
	co*rre*	**co***rren*
	he runs	they run
	*pa***la***bra*	*pa***la***bras*
	word	words
	cri*sis*	**cri***sis*
	crisis	crises
2	*re***loj**	
	watch	
	*ver***dad**	
	truth	
	*bati***dor**	
	beater	
3	*mur***cié***lago*	
	bat	
	pá*jaro*	
	bird	
4	*ca***rác***ter*	*carac***te***res*
	character	characters
	ré*gimen*	*re***gí***menes*
	regime	regimes
5	**ba***ile*	
	dance	
	bo*ina*	**pe***ine*
	beret	comb
	ca*usa*	**re***ina*
	cause	queen
6	*fui*	*vi***u***do*
	I went	widower
7	*me ma***re***o*	*ca***er**
	I feel dizzy	to fall
	ca*os*	*co***rre***a*
	chaos	leash

❐ The acute accent (´)

This is used in writing to show that a word is stressed contrary to the normal rules for stress (see p 290) → [1]

The following points should be noted:

- The same syllable is stressed in the plural form of adjectives and nouns as in the singular. To show this, it is necessary to
  - — add an accent in the case of unaccented nouns and adjectives ending in **-n** → [2]
  - — drop the accent from nouns and adjectives ending in **-n** or **-s** which have an accent on the last syllable → [3]
- The feminine form of accented nouns or adjectives does not have an accent → [4]
- When object pronouns are added to certain verb forms an accent is required to show that the syllable stressed in the verb form does not change. These verb forms are:
  - — the gerund → [5]
  - — the infinitive, when followed by two pronouns → [6]
  - — imperative forms, except for the 2nd person plural → [7]
- The absolute superlative forms of adjectives are always accented → [8]
- Accents on adjectives are not affected by the addition of the adverbial suffix **-mente** → [9]

Examples

1	**autobús** bus		**revolución** revolution
	relámpago lightning		**árboles** trees
2	**orden** order	→	**órdenes** orders
	examen examination	→	**exámenes** examinations
	joven young	→	**jóvenes** young
3	**revolución** revolution	→	**revoluciones** revolutions
	autobús bus	→	**autobuses** buses
	parlanchín chatty	→	**parlanchines** chatty
4	**marqués** marquis	→	**marquesa** marchioness
	francés French *(masc)*	→	**francesa** French *(fem)*
5	**comprando** buying	→	**comprándo(se)lo** buying it (for him/her/them)
6	**vender** to sell	→	**vendérselas** to sell them to him/her/them
7	**compra** buy	→	**cómpralo** buy it
	hagan do	→	**háganselo** do it for him/her/them
8	**viejo** old	→	**viejísimo** ancient
	caro expensive	→	**carísimo** very expensive
9	**fácil** easy	→	**fácilmente** easily

❒ The acute accent *(Continued)*

It is also used to distinguish between the written forms of words which are pronounced the same but have a different meaning or function. These are as follows:

- Possessive adjectives/personal pronouns → [1]
- Demonstrative adjectives/demonstrative pronouns → [2]
- Interrogative and exclamatory forms of adverbs, pronouns and adjectives → [3]

⚠ NOTE: The accent is used in indirect as well as direct questions and exclamations → [4]

- The pronoun **él** and the article **el** → [5]
- A small group of words which could otherwise be confused. These are:

de	of, from	**dé**	give (pres subj)
mas	but	**más**	more
si	if	**sí**	yes; himself etc → [6]
solo/a	alone	**sólo**	only → [7]
te	you	**té**	tea

❒ The dieresis (¨)

This is used only in the combinations **güi** or **güe** to show that the **u** is pronounced as a semi-consonant (see p 284) → [8]

Examples

1 **Han robado mi coche**
They've stolen my car
¿Te gusta tu trabajo?
Do you like your job?
A mí no me vio
He didn't see me
Tú, ¿que opinas?
What do you think?

2 **Me gusta esta casa**
I like this house
¿Ves aquellos edificios?
Can you see those buildings?
Me quedo con ésta
I'll take this one
Aquéllos son más bonitos
Those are prettier

3 **El chico con quien viajé**
The boy I travelled with
Donde quieras
Wherever you want
¿Con quién viajaste?
Who did you travel with?
¿Dónde encontraste eso?
Where did you find that?

4 **¿Cómo se abre?**
How does it open?
No sé cómo se abre
I don't know how it opens

5 **El puerto queda cerca**
The harbour's nearby
Él no quiso hacerlo
HE refused to do it

6 **si no viene**
if he doesn't come
Sí que lo sabe
Yes he DOES know

7 **Vino solo**
He came by himself
Sólo lo sabe él
Only he knows

8 **¡Qué vergüenza!**
How shocking!
En seguida averigüé dónde estaba
I found out straight away where it was

❐ Regular spelling changes

The consonants **c, g** and **z** are modified by the addition of certain verb or plural endings and by some suffixes. Most of the cases where this occurs have already been dealt with under the appropriate part of speech, but are summarized here along with other instances not covered elsewhere.

Verbs

The changes set out below occur so that the consonant of the verb stem is always pronounced the same as in the infinitive. For verbs affected by these changes see the list of verbs on p 81.

INFINITIVE	CHANGE			TENSES AFFECTED
-car	**c + e**	→	**-que**	Present subj, pret → [1]
-cer, -cir	**c + a, o**	→	**-za, -zo**	Present, pres subj → [2]
-gar	**g + e, i**	→	**-gue, -gui**	Present subj, pret → [3]
-guar	**gu + e**	→	**-güe**	Present subj, pret → [4]
-ger, -gir	**g + a, o**	→	**-ja, -jo**	Present, pres subj → [5]
-guir	**gu + a, o**	→	**-ga, -go**	Present, pres subj → [6]
-zar	**z + e**	→	**-ce**	Present subj, pret → [7]

Noun and adjective plurals

SINGULAR		PLURAL
vowel + z	→	**-ces** → [8]

Nouns and adjectives + suffixes

ENDING	SUFFIX	NEW ENDING
vowel + z +	**-cito**	**-cecito** → [9]
-go, -ga +	**-ito, -illo**	**-guito/a, -guillo/a** → [10]
-co, -ca +	**-ito, -illo**	**-quito/a, -quillo/a** → [11]

Adjective absolute superlatives

ENDING	SUPERLATIVE
-co	**-quísimo** → [12]
-go	**-guísimo** → [13]
vowel + z	**-císimo** → [14]

1 **Es inútil que lo busques aquí**
It's no good looking for it here
Saqué dos entradas
I got two tickets

2 **Hace falta que venzas tu miedo**
You must overcome your fear

3 **No creo que lleguemos antes**
I don't think we'll be there any sooner
Ya le pagué
I've already paid her

4 **Averigüé dónde estaba la casa**
I found out where the house was

5 **Cojo el autobús, es más barato**
I take the bus, it's cheaper

6 **¿Sigo?**
Shall I go on?

7 **No permiten que se cruce la frontera**
They don't allow people to cross the border
Nunca simpaticé mucho con él
I never got on very well with him

8 **voz** → **voces** | **luz** → **luces**
voice — voices | light — lights
veloz → **veloces** | **capaz** → **capaces**
quick | capable

9 **luz** → **lucecita**
light — little light

10 **amigo** → **amiguito**
friend — chum

11 **chico** → **chiquillo**
boy — little boy

12 **rico** → **riquísimo**
rich — extremely rich

13 **largo** → **larguísimo**
long — very, very long

14 **feroz** → **ferocísimo**
fierce — extremely fierce

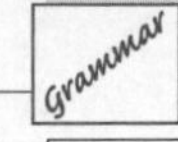

THE ALPHABET

A, a	[a]	**J, j**	['xota]	**R, r**	['erre]
B, b	[be]	**K, k**	[ka]	**S, s**	['ese]
C, c	[θe]	**L, l**	['ele]	**T, t**	[te]
Ch, ch	[tʃe]	**Ll, ll**	['eʎe]	**U, u**	[u]
D, d	[de]	**M, m**	['eme]	**V, v**	['uβe]
E, e	[e]	**N, n**	['ene]	**W, w**	['uβe'doble]
F, f	['efe]	**Ñ, ñ**	['eɲe]	**X, x**	['ekis]
G, g	[xe]	**O, o**	[o]	**Y, y**	[i'ɣrjeɣa]
H, h	['atʃe]	**P, p**	[pe]	**Z, z**	['θeta]
I, i	[i]	**Q, q**	[ku]		

- The letters are feminine and you therefore talk of **una a**, or **la a**.
- Capital letters are used as in English except for the following:

— adjectives of nationality:

e.g. **una ciudad alemana** — a German town; **un autor español** — a Spanish author

— languages:

e.g. **¿Habla Vd inglés?** — Do you speak English?; **Hablan español e italiano** — They speak Spanish and Italian

— days of the week:

lunes	Monday
martes	Tuesday
miércoles	Wednesday
jueves	Thursday
viernes	Friday
sábado	Saturday
domingo	Sunday

— months of the year:

enero	January	**julio**	July
febrero	February	**agosto**	August
marzo	March	**se(p)tiembre**	September
abril	April	**octubre**	October
mayo	May	**noviembre**	November
junio	June	**diciembre**	December

PUNCTUATION

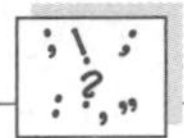

Spanish punctuation differs from English in the following ways:

Question marks

There are inverted question marks and exclamation marks at the beginning of a question or exclamation, as well as upright ones at the end.

Indications of dialogue

Dashes are used to indicate dialogue, and are equivalent to the English inverted commas:

– **¿Vendrás conmigo? – le preguntó María**
'Will you come with me?' Maria asked him

⚠ NOTE: When no expression of saying, replying etc follows, only one dash is used at the beginning:

– **Sí**. 'Yes.'

Letter headings

At the beginning of a letter, a colon is used instead of the English comma:

Querida Cristina: Dear Cristina, **Muy Sr. mío**: Dear Sir,

Punctuation terms in Spanish

.	punto	!	se cierra admiración
,	coma	" "	comillas (used as '...')
;	punto y coma	"	se abren comillas
:	dos puntos	"	se cierran comillas
...	puntos suspensivos	( )	paréntesis
¿ ?	interrogación	(	se abre paréntesis
¿	se abre interrogación	)	se cierra paréntesis
?	se cierra interrogación	–	guión
¡ !	admiración		
¡	se abre admiración	punto y aparte	new paragraph
		punto final	last full stop

Cardinal numbers (*one, two, three etc*)

cero	0	**setenta**	70
uno (un, una)	1	**ochenta**	80
dos	2	**noventa**	90
tres	3	**cien (ciento)**	100
cuatro	4	**ciento uno(una)**	101
cinco	5	**ciento dos**	102
seis	6	**ciento diez**	110
siete	7	**ciento cuarenta y dos**	142
ocho	8	**doscientos(as)**	200
nueve	9	**doscientos(as) uno(una)**	201
diez	10	**doscientos(as) dos**	202
once	11	**trescientos(as)**	300
doce	12	**cuatrocientos(as)**	400
trece	13	**quinientos(as)**	500
catorce	14	**seiscientos(as)**	600
quince	15	**setecientos(as)**	700
dieciséis	16	**ochocientos(as)**	800
diecisiete	17	**novecientos(as)**	900
dieciocho	18	**mil**	1.000
diecinueve	19	**mil uno(una)**	1.001
veinte	20	**mil dos**	1.002
veintiuno	21	**mil doscientos veinte**	1.220
veintidós	22	**dos mil**	2.000
treinta	30	**cien mil**	100.000
treinta y uno	31	**doscientos(as) mil**	200.000
cuarenta	40	**un millón**	1.000.000
cincuenta	50	**dos millones**	2.000.000
sesenta	60	**un billón**	1.000.000.000.000

Fractions

un medio; medio(a)	½
un tercio	⅓
dos tercios	⅔
un cuarto	¼
tres cuartos	¾
un quinto	⅕
cinco y tres cuartos	5¾

Others

cero coma cinco	0,5
uno coma tres	1,3
(el, un) diez por ciento	10%
dos más/y dos	2 + 2
dos menos dos	2 – 2
dos por dos	2 x 2
dos dividido por dos	2 ÷ 2

4 6 2
8 1 5
9 3 1

❒ Points to note on cardinals

- **uno** drops the **o** before masculine nouns, and the same applies when in compound numerals:

  un libro *1 book,* **treinta y un niños** *31 children*

- 1, 21, 31 etc and 200, 300, 400 etc have feminine forms:

  cuarenta y una pesetas *41 pesetas,* **quinientas libras** *£500*

- **ciento** is used before numbers smaller than 100, otherwise **cien** is used:

  ciento cuatro *104 but* **cien pesetas** *100 pesetas,* **cien mil** *100,000* (see also p 206)

- **millón** takes **de** before a noun:

  un millón de personas *1,000,000 people*

- **mil** is only found in the plural when meaning *thousands of:*

  miles de solicitantes *thousands of applicants*

- cardinals normally precede ordinals:

  los tres primeros pisos *the first three floors*

⚠ NOTE: The full stop is used with numbers over one thousand and the comma with decimals i.e. the opposite of English usage.

❒ Ordinal numbers *(first, second, third etc)*

primero (primer, primera)	1°,1ª	**undécimo(a)**	11°,11ª
segundo(a)	2°,2ª	**duodécimo(a)**	12°,12ª
tercero (tercer, tercera)	3°,3ª	**decimotercer(o)(a)**	13°,13ª
cuarto(a)	4°,4ª	**decimocuarto(a)**	14°,14ª
quinto(a)	5°,5ª	**decimoquinto(a)**	15°,15ª
sexto(a)	6°,6ª	**decimosexto(a)**	16°,16ª
séptimo(a)	7°,7ª	**decimoséptimo(a)**	17°,17ª
octavo(a)	8°,8ª	**decimoctavo(a)**	18°,18ª
noveno(a)	9°,9ª	**decimonoveno(a)**	19°,19ª
décimo(a)	10°,10ª	**vigésimo(a)**	20°,20ª

Points to note on ordinals

- They agree in gender and in number with the noun, which they normally precede, except with royal titles:

  la primera vez — the first time
  Felipe segundo — Philip II

- **primero** and **tercero** drop the **o** before a masculine singular noun:

  el primer premio — the first prize
  el tercer día — the third day

- Beyond **décimo** ordinal numbers are rarely used, and they are replaced by the cardinal number placed immediately after the noun:

  el siglo diecisiete — the seventeenth century
  Alfonso doce — Alfonso XII
  en el piso trece — on the 13th floor

  ⚠ BUT: **vigésimo(a)** 20th
  (but not with royal titles or centuries)
  centésimo(a) 100th
  milésimo(a) 1,000th
  millonésimo(a) 1,000,000th

❐ Numbers: Other Uses

- collective numbers:

un par	2, a couple
una decena (de personas)	about 10 (people)
una docena (de niños)	(about) a dozen (children)
una quincena (de hombres)	about fifteen (men)
una veintena* (de coches)	about twenty (cars)
un centenar, una centena (de casas)	about a hundred (houses)
cientos/centenares de personas	hundreds of people
un millar (de soldados)	about a thousand (soldiers)
miles/millares de moscas	thousands of flies

* 30, 40, 50 can also be converted in the same way.

- measurements:

veinte metros cuadrados	20 square metres
veinte metros cúbicos	20 cubic metres
un puente de cuarenta metros de largo/longitud	a bridge 40 metres long

- distance:

De aquí a Madrid hay 400 km	Madrid is 400 km away
a siete km de aquí	7 km from here

❐ Telephone Numbers

Póngame con Madrid, el cuatro, cincuenta y ocho, veintidós, noventa y tres
I would like Madrid 458 22 93
Me da Valencia, el veinte, cincuenta y uno, setenta y tres
Could you get me Valencia 20 51 73
Extensión tres, tres, cinco/trescientos treinta y cinco
Extension number 335

⚠ NOTE: In Spanish telephone numbers may be read out individually, but more frequently they are broken down into groups of two. They are written in groups of two or three numbers (never four).

❐ The Time

¿Qué hora es? *What time is it?*
Es … *(1 o'clock, midnight, noon)* } *It's …*
Son las … *(other times)*
Es la una y cuarto *It's 1.15*
Son las diez menos cinco *It's 9.55*

00.00	**medianoche; las doce (de la noche)** *midnight, twelve o'clock*
00.10	**las doce y diez (de la noche)**
00.15	**las doce y cuarto**
00.30	**las doce y media**
00.45	**la una menos cuarto**
01.00	**la una (de la madrugada)** *one a.m., one o'clock in the morning*
01.10	**la una y diez (de la madrugada)**
02.45	**las tres menos cuarto**
07.00	**las siete (de la mañana)**
07.50	**las ocho menos diez**
12.00	**mediodía; las doce (de la mañana)** *noon, twelve o'clock*
13.00	**la una (de la tarde)** *one p.m., one o'clock in the afternoon*
19.00	**las siete (de la tarde)** *seven p.m., seven o'clock in the evening*
21.00	**las nueve (de la noche)** *nine p.m., nine o'clock at night*

⚠ NOTE: When referring to a timetable, the 24 hour clock is used:

las dieciséis cuarenta y cinco 16.45
las veintiuna quince 21.15

Examples

¿A qué hora vas a venir? – A las siete
What time are you coming? – At seven o'clock
Las oficinas cierran de dos a cuatro
The offices are closed from two until four
Vendré a eso de/hacia las siete y media
I'll come at around 7.30
a las seis y pico
just after 6 o'clock
a las cinco en punto
at 5 o'clock sharp
entre las ocho y las nueve
between 8 and 9 o'clock
Son más de las tres y media
It's after half past three
Hay que estar allí lo más tarde a las diez
You have to be there by ten o'clock at the latest
Tiene para media hora
He'll be half an hour (at it)
Estuvo sin conocimiento durante un cuarto de hora
She was unconscious for a quarter of an hour
Les estoy esperando desde hace una hora/desde las dos
I've been waiting for them for an hour/since two o'clock
Se fueron hace unos minutos
They left a few minutes ago
Lo hice en veinte minutos
I did it in twenty minutes
El tren llega dentro de una hora
The train arrives in an hour('s time)
¿Cuánto (tiempo) dura la película?
How long does the film last?
por la mañana/tarde/noche
in the morning/afternoon *or* evening/at night

mañana por la mañana
tomorrow morning

ayer por la tarde
yesterday afternoon *or* evening

anoche
last night

anteayer
the day before yesterday

pasado mañana
the day after tomorrow

❐ Dates

¿Qué día es hoy? **¿A qué día estamos?**	What's the date today?
Es (el) ... **Estamos a ...**	It's the ...
uno/primero de mayo	lst of May
dos de mayo	2nd of May
veintiocho de mayo	28th of May
lunes tres de octubre	Monday the 3rd of October
Vienen el siete de marzo	They're coming on the 7th of March

⚠ NOTE: Use cardinal numbers for dates. Only for the first of the month can the ordinal number sometimes be used.

❐ Years

Nací en 1970
I was born in 1970
el veinte de enero de mil novecientos setenta
(on) 20th January 1970

❐ Other expressions

en los años cincuenta	during the fifties
en el siglo veinte	in the twentieth century
en mayo	in May
lunes (quince)	Monday (the 15th)
el quince de marzo	on March the 15th
el/los lunes	on Monday/Mondays
dentro de diez días	in 10 days' time
hace diez días	10 days ago

❐ Age

¿Qué edad tiene? **¿Cuántos años tiene?**	How old is he/she?
Tiene 23 (años)	He/She is 23
Tiene unos 40 años	He/She is around 40
A los 21 años	At the age of 21

INDEX

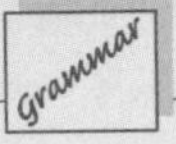

The following index lists comprehensively both grammatical terms and key words in English and Spanish.

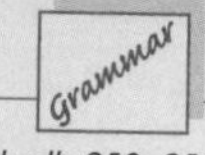

Grammar

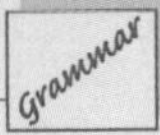
Grammar

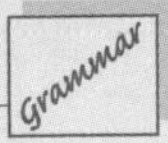
Grammar

Grammar

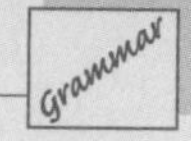